# The Edge of the World

## *How the North Sea Made Us Who We Are*

MICHAEL PYE

VIKING
*an imprint of*
PENGUIN BOOKS

VIKING

Published by the Penguin Group
Penguin Books Ltd, 80 Strand, London WC2R 0RL, England
Penguin Group (USA) Inc., 375 Hudson Street, New York, New York 10014, USA
Penguin Group (Canada), 90 Eglinton Avenue East, Suite 700, Toronto, Ontario, Canada M4P 2Y3
(a division of Pearson Penguin Canada Inc.)
Penguin Ireland, 25 St Stephen's Green, Dublin 2, Ireland (a division of Penguin Books Ltd)
Penguin Group (Australia), 707 Collins Street, Melbourne, Victoria 3008, Australia
(a division of Pearson Australia Group Pty Ltd)
Penguin Books India Pvt Ltd, 11 Community Centre,
Panchsheel Park, New Delhi – 110 017, India
Penguin Group (NZ), 67 Apollo Drive, Rosedale, Auckland 0632, New Zealand
(a division of Pearson New Zealand Ltd)
Penguin Books (South Africa) (Pty) Ltd, Block D, Rosebank Office Park,
181 Jan Smuts Avenue, Parktown North, Gauteng 2193, South Africa

Penguin Books Ltd, Registered Offices: 80 Strand, London WC2R 0RL, England

www.penguin.com



Typeset in 12/ [illegible] k, Stirlingshire

A CIP catalogue record for this book is available from the British Library

ISBN: 978-0-670-92232-1

www.greenpenguin.co.uk

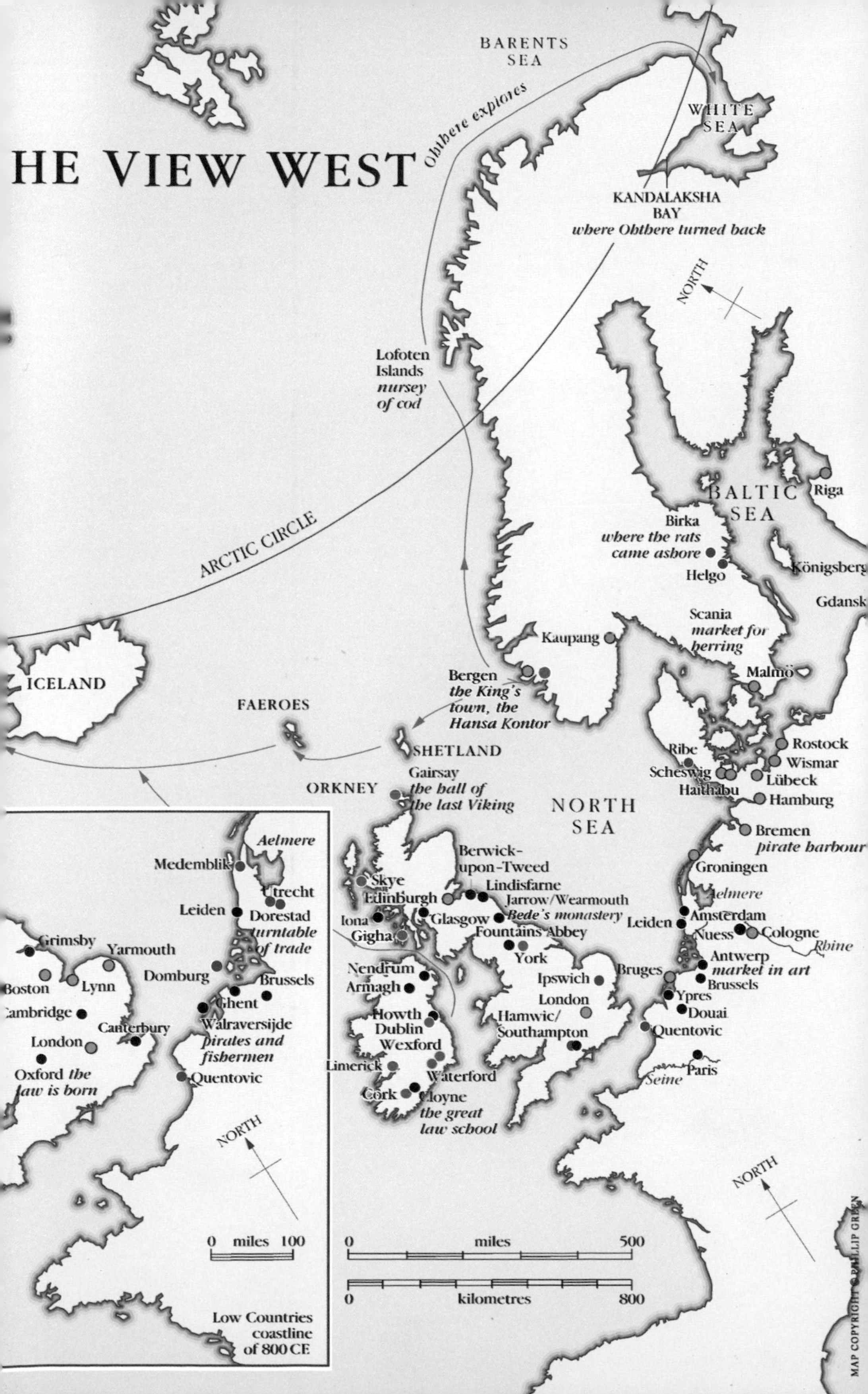
HE VIEW WEST
BARENTS SEA
Ohthere explores
WHITE SEA
KANDALAKSHA BAY
where Ohthere turned back
NORTH
Lofoten Islands
nursey of cod
ARCTIC CIRCLE
BALTIC SEA
Riga
Birka
where the rats came ashore
Helgo
Königsberg
Gdansk
Scania
market for herring
Kaupang
Malmö
ICELAND
FAEROES
Bergen
the King's town, the Hansa Kontor
SHETLAND
ORKNEY
Gairsay
the hall of the last Viking
NORTH SEA
Ribe
Scheswig
Haithabu
Rostock
Wismar
Lübeck
Hamburg
Bremen
pirate harbour
Groningen
Aelmere
Berwick-upon-Tweed
Lindisfarne
Jarrow/Wearmouth
Bede's monastery
Skye
Edinburgh
Iona
Glasgow
Gigha
Fountains Abbey
York
Leiden
Amsterdam
Nuess
Cologne
Rhine
Antwerp
market in art
Brussels
Bruges
Ypres
Douai
Quentovic
Paris
Seine
Nendrum
Armagh
Howth
Dublin
Wexford
Limerick
Waterford
Cork
Cloyne
the great law school
Ipswich
London
Hamwic/ Southampton
Aelmere
Medemblik
Utrecht
Leiden
Dorestad
turntable of trade
Grimsby
Yarmouth
Domburg
Boston
Lynn
Brussels
Cambridge
Ghent
Canterbury
Walraversijde
pirates and fishermen
London
Oxford the law is born
Quentovic
NORTH
0 miles 100
Low Countries coastline of 800 CE
0 miles 500
0 kilometres 800
NORTH
MAP COPYRIGHT © PHILLIP GREEN

# The Edge of the World

'An utterly beguiling journey into the dark ages of the North Sea. A complete revelation . . . Pye writes like a dream. More evocative than Braudel's *Mediterranean*, and more original than Schama's *Embarrassment of Riches*, *The Edge of the World* deserves a prize for services to the north. Magnificent'

Jerry Brotton, author of *A History of the World in Twelve Maps*

'For more than a millennium, the North Sea was our trading floor, our Crossrail and our internet. It was what connected these islands with the world. With elegant writing and extraordinary scholarship, Michael Pye focuses not on lands but on the waters that unite them'

Hugh Aldersey-Williams, author of *Periodic Tales*

'Rich and astonishing. There's a fascinating anecdote, an original slant on history, a forgotten intellectual giant on every page'

Neal Ascherson, author of *Black Sea*

'Splendid. A heady mix of social, economic and intellectual history, written in an engaging style. It offers a counterpoint to the many studies of the Mediterranean, arguing for the importance of the North Sea. Exciting, fun and informative'

Michael Prestwich, Durham University

*By the same author*

Maximum City: the Biography of New York

The Drowning Room

Taking Lives

The Pieces from Berlin

# Contents

# Introduction

Cecil Warburton went to the seaside in the summer of 1700: two weeks at Scarborough on the east coast of England, north of Hull and south of Newcastle. He was not at all impressed.

He was a northern gentleman, son of a Cheshire baronet, and he did what gentlemen do at a spa: he drank down five pints of the famous waters almost every day, waters that smelled of ink and tasted of acid, and his system was duly flushed. He refused the full cure his companions took, which was four quarts a day. He wrote to his brother-in-law: 'I was in hopes I might here have met with something would have made my letter diverting to you, but I find myself disappointed for I yet can see nothing but coarse hooks and drying fish which is all the furniture of both in and out side of their streets and houses.' The streets were littered with 'garbage of fish and Cods Heads . . . I wish you find no ungreatful smell inclosed, for I think it impossible any thing can go hence free from it.'[1]

He'd chosen the town where the idea of seaside was starting, where the first changing huts were about to appear on the beach, where people came to flirt and be seen; he did not want reminders of all the uses of the working sea. People, 'Nobility, Quality and Gentry' according to the guide for 1733, were flocking to Scarborough: earls and baronets, misses and marchionesses. They drank and ate and drank, knowing the waters would wash them out and keep them well. They went swimming in the cold sea and horse racing on the long, wide sands and dancing in the evening.[2]

They chose to see the spa and not the working town, not the castle that had fired on enemy ships only fifty years earlier when the Dutch and English were at war, not the fishing fleet of maybe three hundred boats or the harbour, the only practical refuge in foul weather between the River Tyne to the north and the River Humber to the south. The town was a reminder of the web of connections over the water: food, trade, war and all kinds of arrivals and invasions, including the invasions of ideas.

Cecil Warburton, like millions after him, had no interest in all that. He had more immediate worries; as he complained in a letter to his sister: 'am still as fat as ever . . .'[3]

This new idea of seaside came between us and the story of the sea.[4] The seaside was becoming a destination, not a harbour on the way to somewhere else over the water; and it was a playground, not a place of work and war. It was hard to imagine that there had once been a world that centred on the sea itself. Over the years even the coastline was fixed in place as it never used to be when high winds could make a storm out of the sand, and high tides could break deep into the land. Stone and then concrete made sea walls, promenades, esplanades, a definite squared-off boundary between man and sea. Behind them, seafront hotels and villas could stare out with perfect indifference at the sea, which had made them so desirable in the first place.

That was just beginning in Warburton's time. In Scarborough, a whole catalogue of grand persons paid their five shillings and signed the book to use the two rooms built on the beach for drinks and company and dressing and undressing. They came north from London by the York coach, or else by way of Cambridge for the sights, but only if they could tolerate the country inns. Otherwise they paid a guinea for passage from the docks at Billingsgate to Scarborough on one of the coal boats going back empty from London to the Tyne.

The women bathed discreetly with the help of guides. A local poet complained that 'A spreading Vest the nymph secures / And every prying glance defies'. The men could either 'retire and undress at some distance from the company, or . . . push a little off the beach in boats' and then 'jump in naked directly'. The sea was considered safe enough for brisk exercise or medicinal baths. Indeed, the anonymous author of *A Journey from London to Scarborough* insisted: 'What Virtues our Physicians ascribe to Cold Baths in general are much more effectual by the additional Weight of Salt in Sea water, an Advantage which no Spaw in England can boast of but Scarborough.'

Seawater, like spa water, was meant to cure sickness. Doctors were immediately and deeply worried; water was a rival to the chemical medicines they prescribed. There was an obvious need for 'more careful analysis of spa water', as Dr Simpson wrote in 1669, a 'chymical anatomy' to show what chemical medicines it happened to contain; only then could the sea be approved and annexed by the medical men. When the analysis was done, in the 1730s, it became a matter of civic pride and general interest, something important about the friendly trivia of the seaside: Scarborough, tourists and residents, all went to public lectures about exactly what they were drinking.[5]

Now waters had once been a matter of another kind of faith: holy waters, holy springs and wells, found by saints and other amateur hopefuls. Scarborough's spring was first found, or so a Dr Wittie wrote in 1667, by a Mrs Farrow, who was walking on the beach in the 1620s and noticed that stones had been turned russet by a noisy, bubbling spring at the foot of 'an exceedingly high cliffe'. She liked the taste of the waters. She thought they would do people good.

Word spread.

Dr Wittie wrote a little book to make sure that it was doctors who prescribed them. He already believed in bathing because that was what the English did at spas: they drank the waters, but they also bathed in them, unlike the Europeans, who thought drinking was quite enough. He told men with a taste for port wine to go swimming in the sea because that was how he had cured his own gout, 'frequent bathing in the Sea-water cold, in Summer time . . . after which I take a Sweat in a warm bed'. The summer months were the best; Dr Wittie was quite shocked that 'in German spas, they drink in winter'.

He knew that 'many go to the spaws not for necessity but for pleasure, to withdraw themselves a while from their serious imployments and solace with their friends'. But pleasure, too, was going to be the business of doctors: a modern profession staking claims on as much of life as possible. Swimming itself was no longer simple exercise. Dr Robert White wrote on the 'Use and Abuse of Sea Water' in 1775 to warn that 'they who are in full health and strength should not sport with such recreations so freely'. They could perhaps bathe early in the day, but the more nervous cases should wait until 'a little before noon'; 'nobody should continue above a minute in the water'. Seawater might be less of a shock than the stone cold of spring water, but even so Dr White felt obliged to warn of the 'Fatal Effects of Bathing in Healthy Persons'. He told how 'a man, about 40 years of age, who had lived a sober and temperate life, was induced to bathe in the sea'. The man didn't think of himself as a patient so he went into the water without being bled and without being purged, and without a doctor's say-so; the consequence, so Dr White says, was 'violent pain which shot through his head, great dizziness and a fatal Apoplectic fit'.

The sea was 'useful' against leprosy, he thought, 'of great use' against epilepsy, and able to take away jaundice. The sea could also cure gonorrhoea, which might be a comforting thought for randy gentlemen but no consolation at all for the next person they bedded. Even so, he reckoned people were not careful enough with 'so general and popular a Medicine' because 'the Stomach and Bowels are kept in constant agitation' by it. He recorded 'the propensity which people of all ranks have discovered towards Sea Bathing'.

It was not only the English. The Dutch went walking on the beach in the seventeenth century, the boys throwing the girls in the sea at Scheveningen every spring, everyone drinking. Their prince-like *stadhouder* had a sand yacht with sails and wheels to bowl along the strand. The spas brought people to the seaside, but the seaside took on a life of its own: there were beaches that did not need a doctor's licence, a new kind of resort like Norderney on the German North Sea coast, like Ostend and Boulogne, like Doberan on the Baltic, places you went simply for pleasure. Anyone could flirt with the water, visit and go home when they wanted. They turned the waves and currents into a backdrop for very urban ideas of how to be well, stay fit, look good and be amused. The old business of the sea was hidden away and the new business was holiday. The harbour at Visby, on the Swedish island of Gotland, had been famous and hustling for a thousand years, but in the nineteenth century the town faced only stagnation and oblivion unless it installed a bathing station, a place for bathers to change clothes and take a drink; or so the promoters of the bathing station claimed.[6]

Reality was screened off behind the bathing huts and seafront attractions and later the piers and donkey rides and fish and chip shops, behind archery stalls and bowling greens (as at Blackpool) and music halls and bright electric lights. The secret was secure. By the late nineteenth century Mr Baedeker's *Handbooks for Travellers*, usually so meticulous on artworks and the cost of transport, did not seem to notice what was missing. His guide to the Netherlands gets after a while to Middelburg in the coastal region of Zeeland, and all the excursions possible from there.[7] He noted the omnibus which ran twice daily to a 'small bathing place' called Domburg, 'frequented by Germans, Dutchmen and Belgians'; he mentioned 'pleasant walks in the neighbourhood'. He tells you the price of a two-horse carriage to get there, and full board at the Bad-Hôtel.

He does not mention what happened at Domburg, even though people still alive remembered. It was at that 'small bathing place', on a lovely beach, that the sea gave back its secret: its history.

High winds tore up the dunes and made the sea wild in the first days of January 1647. The sand was forced out of the way to show something in the subsoil that should never have been there: stone. There is no stone at all on the coast near Domburg; there is only sand, peat, clay. So someone must have brought the blocks on the foreshore from far away – from seven hundred kilometres away in the quarries of northern France as we now know – and moving it must have been serious business; one stone weighed two tons and no machine in 1647 could shift it. An excited letter to Amsterdam, which went into print as a newsletter, reported: 'About a fortnight ago some great stones of white limestone appeared on the beach near the sea.'[8]

There was also what looked like 'a little house with the base of columns'. There were half-erased images on the stones, prayers to a goddess called Nehalennia, thanking her for success, for the welfare of a son, for the safe passage of goods across the sea. That made it likely that the 'little house' was some kind of temple. The remains of trees, petrified and salted, suggested the kind of grove that was often planted around temples. The newsletter was sure that what the sea uncovered was 'a monument of greatest antiquity'.

Among the stones were altars to known gods – Neptune, of course, for the sea and sailors, and Hercules – but Nehalennia with her twenty-six altars had been unknown for more than a millennium. On the altars she sits under a shell-shaped canopy, which makes her a goddess of Heaven like Venus or Juno or Minerva, or she stands on the prow of a ship on an unquiet sea; she sometimes has a throne, often there is a basket of apples around, and there is always a fine-faced dog gazing up at her. Ships were not always just a means of transport; they have a curiously deep connection with fertility in people's minds, especially Northerners', so it seems she was the local goddess of good harvests, good luck at sea, even good connections like carts and roads.[9] She had once been everything to the people around Domburg, and she had been entirely forgotten.

There was huge excitement across learnèd Europe: something unknown had come out of the sea. Now the past began to come back and wash away and come back again as though history itself were a sea in motion. Peter de Buk, an old man from Domburg, remembered that in 1684, 'during the very cold winter, when the ice piled up very high on the beach', the immovable stone started to loosen and then shift and then 'gradually it moved to the sea'. The ball-players who had used the stone for years, so the local Minister said, had to find somewhere else to play.

Three years later there was a storm so violent that in the morning there were bodies on the beach: ancient bodies, each in a coffin of wood a couple of centimetres thick. The skulls all faced west. The coffins were full of sand. There were slim, ornate chains around the necks with coins hanging on them; one skeleton had a goblet stacked on its chest, another had a silver dagger at its side. Christians were not supposed to bury goods with the dead, so the graves must have been made before the coast started to turn Christian round 700 – or after Christians had been beaten inland a century and a half later by Viking raiders. For a few days the past was as solid as a coffin, unexplained like a ghost; and then the waters swept back and hid the dead before anyone could find out who they were.

In 1715 a very low tide stretched the land out so far that there were the remains of wells to be seen, and the foundations of buildings. One more statue appeared: a great headless Victory, in the middle of what was certainly a temple of some sort, paved with round and square stones. Victory stayed stranded for years until she was carted bodily inland and parked in the local church. She survived, turning green now that she was out of the salt water and in the rains, but she was ruined when lightning brought down the church in 1848. The remains of this ancient Domburg were reduced to a few damaged pieces and two cubic metres of rubble dumped in the garden of the town clerk.

The dead did not stay away. The cemetery was uncovered again in 1749 and in 1817: twenty rough and worm-eaten coffins held together with wooden pegs, no nails, and locked down in the sand by the sheer weight of the old dunes. There were round brooches on the right shoulder of each body, sometimes on the chest, which looked like money for a sea goddess to buy safety, maybe treasure for a new life. One corpse was buried with a sword. But the locals knew about buried things by now and what they might be worth, and they went through the coffins secretly and wouldn't say exactly where they found what. They were busy selling to the Amsterdam collectors.

The shoreline kept changing with the winds and tides, so when the low tide pulled back in 1832 it opened a quite different site, one that would be seen again and for the last time in 1866: the scattered outlines of houses, and a burial ground with the coffins laid out like a star on the sand. There were now three different stories under the rough water. There was a Roman temple to an unknown goddess which stood at the point where ships went out into the open sea and looked as though it was abandoned very suddenly. There were the remains of a settlement along the shore, a single road laid out east to west with wooden huts for storing and sorting goods and enough coins to prove it was a place of serious business. And there were graves that had to be un-Christian because they were rich with pretty bronzes decorated with animal masks, and a square-cut silver collar. These looked like Viking things.[10]

The written record shows only faint traces of all the life that the money and altars and grave goods suggest. Nobody mentioned Domburg or anything like it in surviving Roman writings, but then Romans were deeply provincial at the heart of their empire and quite usually ignored their own rich provinces. When the scholar Alcuin came to write the life of St Willibrord, he told of the saint evangelizing on the island of Walcheren around 690 CE in a town 'where an idol of the old errors still stood'; this is the site of Domburg, which was an island before man started reorganizing the coastline. Willibrord smashed the statue in front of its guardian, who in a fit of mad anger struck the saint on his head with a sword. 'But,' as Alcuin writes, 'God looked after his servant.' Magnanimously, the saint saved the pagan from those who wanted to punish him, and from the demon occupying his soul, but the man died anyway three days later, as persons who have been seized by angry crowds tend to do.[11]

In the annals, the histories that monks kept for their own use, there are references to a brutal Viking raid in 837 on Domburg – '*in insula quae Walacra dicitur*', on the island called Walcheren – in which many were killed, many women taken off, and 'countless money of various kinds' was shipped out, and the Norsemen were left with the power to organize regular payments of tribute. That single hidden street on one great dune was evidently a rich little place, worth pillaging.

We read about raids and struggles, but the ground itself tells a rather different story. When modern archaeologists investigated sites around the beach, they found nothing much to suggest war, nothing burned or smashed or piled up: none of the bloody events that make up the usual kind of history, the events that people record. There were just centuries of life, and its slow, sad retreat as the sand blew inland, with nothing much of value left behind: except of course the dead.

All that vigour got itself buried on a sandy bit of shore, where the bathers played and still play to this day.

This book is about rediscovering that lost world, and what it means to us: the life around the North Sea in times when water was the easiest way to travel, when the sea connected and carried peoples, belief and ideas, as well as pots and wine and coal. This is not the usual story of muddled battles and various kings and the spread of Christianity. It is the story of how the constant exchanges over water, the half-knowledge that things could be done differently, began to change people's minds profoundly. This cold, grey sea in an obscure time made the modern world possible.

Consider what had to change after the end of the Roman Empire in order to take us to the start of the cities, states and habits that we now know: our law, our idea of love, our way of business and our need for an enemy in order to define ourselves. Traders brought coins and money, and with them an abstract idea of value that made mathematics and modern science possible. Viking raids built as many towns as they ruined, and towns free from bishops and lords could start a new kind of trade. That created a community of people who did business, strong enough and self-conscious enough to go to war with royal and political powers: our world of tension between money and every other power.

Humans changed the landscape and, in the course of learning to manage the damage to the natural world, they also spread the idea of being free and having rights. Travel around the sea made fashion possible, and visible, and desirable; we have not yet escaped. Women's choices, including celibacy or pregnancy on their own terms or else marriage, changed the economic life of the North Sea in quite unexpected ways.

Law changed from the local customs everybody knew to a language and a set of texts that needed lawyers: professions were born, first priests, who had to stay out of the secular world, then lawyers, who made law into a kind of religion, then doctors and all the rest. Without that, we would have no idea of a middle class: people whose power came from being experts. Plague began to separate the poor into the worthy and the unworthy, to allow authorities to regulate the intimate stuff of life – how to raise children and where to live – and eventually to put up barriers between cities and nations; all of which was, of course, for our own good, just like airport security or constant surveillance. Co-operating to save the land from flooding, to send out a ship with many cargoes or insure it, to organize cash when taking fish to the Baltic and grain back to Amsterdam: on this we built, eventually, capitalism. And all this time facts and information were becoming one more commodity, just as they are today.

All this happened in the times that most of us don't really know:

the millennium and more between what we all think we know of imperial Rome – armies, straight roads, villas, temples, central heating and snails for dinner – and what we think we know of Amsterdam in all its seventeenth-century imperial glory – fleets, herring, gold, gin, paintings, gables and clean, swept streets. Between these two visions, between roughly 700 and 1700 CE, lie times that we still unthinkingly call the 'Dark Ages' and then the 'Middle Ages', which, as we all know, consist entirely of castles, damsels, knights and lovely illuminated manuscripts. It is as though we imagine human invention and perversity and will were suspended for centuries, as though life turned into decor.

Documents do get lost or burned or rotted, of course; the written record is bound to be imperfect. Documents keep best when some long-lived institution needs them in a building like the cathedrals which can survive a thousand years or so. A letter about planting crops or buying shirts may disappear along with love letters and old court records; but a charter for land belonging to the Church is very likely to survive. Only bits of life are written down and kept, and they are recorded for very particular reasons and only from some special viewpoint – judge or bishop or king or abbot. They leave out what everyone knew at the time, what nobody wanted mentioned at the time. Even written histories with great authority, based on all the written histories before them, are best treated only as clues to the past.

We have great good luck, though. We now have a whole new kind of evidence to fill some of the gaps, and watch as our view of history changes almost beyond recognition. Archaeology uncovers and reveals, just like the sea at Domburg; but unlike the sea, it does so systematically, providing evidence to set alongside the written record. The picture is suddenly wider; we see life and connections. Sometimes what's dug up will be a flat contradiction of familiar texts and the archives we would like to trust because they are what we have. Sometimes, it will be hard to interpret because each pile of objects grubbed out of the ground makes sense only when it is put into context, and deciding on the context means we have to rely on what we think we already know from other finds in other places.

Bring the words and the objects together, though, and the new story is much more convincingly human. Life no longer stops dead when Rome falls and the empire collapses and the tradition of classical Latin writing comes to an end, not even when the Saxons and Vandals and Goths and Huns make their various pushes to the west. Human beings didn't lose their ability to connect, trade, fight wars and generally move about to change their lives just because there are so few surviving documents; indeed, they didn't lose their ability to write and read those documents. Life goes on; we just need different tools to find and describe it.

Roman towns sometimes survived, but they changed. Roman roads still worked, as did the old Roman system of posthouses where you could rest on a long journey, change horses and ride on. Useful ploughs and workshop tools didn't disappear from the land because historians decreed a change of era; indeed, some rather advanced devices like horizontal watermills were built centuries before we can trace them in documents. The technology of travel – from the hogging trusses that ran the length of a boat to make it seaworthy by tightening bow and stern, to the sun compasses which allowed navigation out of sight of the shore – was always developing; people wanted to move and were thinking hard about how to do it. The very shape of the world and its limits were shifting in people's minds.

Take away the idea of dark times and ruin and you begin to hear other voices. Women were not always silent, or without the power to make choices – we may just have been listening in the wrong places; the erudite and holy Hildegard of Bingen lived out most of the twelfth century as a nun, had visions, was a mystic, wrote music appropriate for her convent life, but she also wrote letters all round Europe at the heart of a learnèd conversation. She knew how to make contraception work, and she wrote about that, too.

To find this story means burrowing through libraries and staring at ploughed fields, both. It means close attention to what people recorded of the stones on the beach at Domburg and then imagining all the connections that the story contains: human beings in movement, along with anything they can make, think or believe. Nothing is ever quite new, or settled, or empty. Frontiers shift. Languages change.

Peoples migrate. The Romans built a temple to send their merchant ships out to the sea, then merchants made a trading town whose name we've lost, then the Vikings who were famous for raiding and pillaging settled down here; this one beach holds the story of a world always changing, always on the move. There are also the weapons that invading Frankish soldiers left behind around 800 CE. Armies travelled and power shifted; but sometimes the biggest changes came when peoples travelled, and not always when and why the schoolbooks told us. Identity became a matter of where you were and where you last came from, not some abstract notion of race; peoples were not separated sharply as they were by nineteenth-century frontiers, venturing out only to conquer or be conquered. Indeed, quite often they ventured out to change sides.

Instead of the dark mistakes about pure blood, racial identity, homogeneous nations with their own soul and spirit and distinct nature, we have something far more exciting: the story of people making choices, not always freely, sometimes under fearsome pressure, but still choosing and inventing and making lives for themselves.

The idea of 'darkness' is our mistake. What our forefathers lived could better be called the 'long morning' of our world.

To be clear: none of this is at all modern, because it belongs to a time of quite different thinking and behaviour. Distance wasn't the same, the maps of the world were not the same, the institutions may have similar names but they were quite different from the ones we know. The necessary conditions of the world we know could have grown into a quite different world. But if we can tease out what happened, and why, then we can begin to see how our modern ways and times became possible – from the calendar to a futures market, from the first publishers of holy manuscripts to experimental science.

There is one more complication in this story: how we tell it, usually. We see the glories of our past through the screen of the Southern Renaissance, when civilization was rediscovered, they say, on the shores of the Mediterranean in pages that had been written a thousand years earlier around the same sea. The law that started to order societies in a way we find more familiar is called Roman law. The Church across Northern Europe was organized from Rome. It seems downright obvious that the North was just waiting to be civilized from the South; after all, Christianity came from there. As early as 723 a bishop called Daniel was telling a saint called Boniface that his best argument against Northern pagans was to point out that the world was becoming Christian and their gods were doing nothing at all about it; 'the Christians possess lands rich in oil and wine and abounding in other resources, they have left to the pagans lands stiff with cold where their gods, driven out of the world, are falsely supposed to rule'.[12]

When we talk of 'Dark Ages' we emphasize war, invasion, raids and conquests, even genocide; but we have all that at home, in our own time, and we still live our lives. Until quite recently it was possible to write of 'mass exterminations' when the Anglo-Saxons crossed the North Sea to take power over Britons and Britain, a wiping away of one people by another, even though the evidence suggests a far longer, gentler and more friendly process.[13] We were in danger of forgetting what really happened around the sea, in its zone of trade and faith, which stretched at least from Dublin to Gdansk, from Bergen to Dover. Around the Mediterranean we take for granted links and influences, back and forth: the biblical stories, the epic voyages in Homer and Hesiod, the trade routes from east to west and back again. The North Sea had most of those things, and the consequences were remarkable.

I mean to tell that story as best I can find it in the sources and in the work of scholars round the sea. This is not a chauvinist exercise; the South is no less important because we remember what happened in the North. This is an attempt to paint a fuller, more colourful and more precise picture of where we come from.

The seaside mob never went very far beyond the comforts of the shore. We're going out further, even if it means going out of our depth.

There was a time when nobody could imagine going further: the northern sea was the very edge of the world. In 16 CE the Roman Drusus Germanicus tried to take his fleet north and was beaten back by storms; the poet Albinovanus Pedo was with him and wrote that the gods were calling them back to stop them seeing the very end of everything. Pedo wondered why their ships were violating these foreign seas and stirring up the quiet homes of the gods. For the northern sea was not just, as the Arab geographer Al Idrisi wrote, 'the sea of perpetual gloom',[14] it was the place where the oceans clashed, where the tides were made as the waters rushed in and out of bottomless caves and the waters fell away into 'primordial and first matter, that was in the beginning of the world . . . called the "abyss"'.[15]

The seventh-century Isidore of Seville thought the known earth 'was called *orbis* because it was like a wheel with the ocean flowing all around it'. This ocean had to be much smaller than the dry land, because the apocryphal Book of Esdras told God so: 'on the third day, You ordered the waters to collect in a seventh part of the earth; the other six parts You made dry land.' But it was also a formidable obstacle, a barricade around the continents; perhaps too wild, but more likely too shallow, too muddy, too full of weeds to be crossed. It might just be possible to pass through the hot and torrid zones to the south, but the frozen north was the very end of the world.[16]

The barrier was not just physical. The sea was a place of evil, where lived the biblical Leviathan, monster of the deep. The Antichrist, the 'man of pride', rode backwards on the head of a sea dragon just as the Vikings rode on ships with snakes' heads for prows.[17] Genesis and the Book of Job confirmed what the geographers agreed: that the sea was unruly, that the dragon who lived there was the dragon of chaos, that the abyss lay in wait. When the Book of Revelations promised that the sea would be no more, it was understood to mean the end of evil itself.[18]

This was a sea that was hardly known, waiting to be explored: a zone between Heaven and Earth, between the familiar coastline and whatever lay out in the waters. The Irish told extraordinary holy tales about sea voyages, called *immrama*,[19] which means 'rowing about'; they told how hermits took to the sea because they wanted to settle somewhere far away and entirely peaceful. Saints sailed off to find the promised land to the west, the islands of the blessed.

These are fables full of wonders, but also very practical advice. In the eighth-century *Voyage of St Brendan*, a holy saga about going to

Heaven and the gates of Hell, there are also instructions on how to make a boat for such a voyage, a coracle built of oxhide and oak bark on a wooden frame and then greased with animal fat. We are told that the saint and his fellow voyagers took along spare skins and extra fat.[20] The sea was there to be used, even if it took a saint to make the attempt, and although some of the marvels are doubtful – like being stranded for months each year on the back of a highly complaisant whale – some of the ones that seem most fanciful are teasingly likely.

The sailors see a high mountain rising out of the sea behind sheer black cliffs, its peak hidden in what looks like cloud but turns out to be smoke. The mountain vomits flames sky-high and then seems to suck them back. The rocks, right down to the sea, glow red like fire. Here Brendan and his crew find Judas Iscariot crouching on a bare rock, waves crashing over his head, which he says is a grateful respite; at night he goes back to the mountain, the home of the great Leviathan, where demons torture him for his sin and he burns 'like a lump of molten lead in a crucible, day and night'.[21]

The sinners and demons, the notion that the mountain welcomes damned souls with a joyful blast of flames, do not make a historical record, although they make a very powerful lesson for the faithful. But we're told that when Brendan turns away from the mountain island he is heading south; that implies the island must lie far to the north. Far north of Ireland, where the *Voyage* was written, is volcanic Iceland, and seas where small islands do indeed suddenly come smoking up out of the water along one of the major fault lines of the Earth. Brendan's voyage is a voyage to known places after all.

The monk Dicuil wrote about all the islands to the north of Ireland: 'Among these, I have lived in some, and have visited others; some I have only glimpsed while others I have read about.'[22] Most likely he never got further than the Hebrides or maybe the Orkneys, but others went much further: as far as Thule, the half-mythical island to the very north of everything. Dicuil quotes classical writers who knew about an island which in summer 'shines both by day and by night under the rays of the sun' and in winter has no day at all. He also writes that 'clerics, who had lived on the island from the first of February to the first of August, told me that [around the days of the summer solstice] the setting sun hides itself as though behind a small hill in such a way that there was no darkness in that very small space of time'. He says a man had enough light to pick the lice out of his shirt at night.

This Thule sounds very much like Iceland.

More, the early-twelfth-century *Book of the Icelanders* says that when the Norsemen first began to settle Iceland around 870, they found priests already living there, but the priests refused to live with heathens and they went away, leaving 'Irish books and bells and croziers from which one could know that they were Irishmen'.[23] So for all Dicuil's other stories of men born with horse's feet, others with ears large enough to cover their whole bodies, and elks whose upper lip hangs down so much they can eat only if they walk backwards, not to mention the difficulty of trapping unicorns because they make so much noise, there is fact here: the fact of constant, eager movement on the sea.

The sea was not yet criss-crossed with long established trade routes and war routes like the Mediterranean; in the North, the sea was still full of legend, so when men went sailing they knew they were testing the edge of the world. Around 1075 the bishop Adam of Bremen wrote his dubious history of the previous archbishops of the northern German town of Bremen. He was writing from a seaport where he could listen to what sailors thought they knew about the sea. He reckoned the way north went through the seas around Orkney, water so thick with salt a ship needed strong winds to pass, and led on to Iceland with its black ice so old it would burn. 'Beyond Norway, which is the farthermost northern country, you will find no human habitation, nothing but ocean, terrible to look upon and limitless, encircling the whole world.' Black mist would come down here, the seas would go wild, and you would come to the point where all the tides of the sea are sucked into the deeps and then vomited back. If you still kept sailing, sailing, as King Harald Hardrada did, you would come to the 'darksome bounds of a failing world'; 'by retracing his step he barely escaped in safety the vast pit of the abyss'.[24]

Men wanted to cross that abyss, to find what lay beyond. Some time around the turn of the thirteenth century, the anonymous author of the *History of Norway* thought he knew all about the dangers and the wonders of the north. He knew there were whirlpools and frozen headlands which send huge icebergs headlong into the sea; and sea monsters that swallow down sailors, horse-whales with spreading manes and giants without head or tail.[25] He says that in living memory the sea came to boil and the earth gave out fire and a great mountain came up out of the waters; but he is a sophisticated man, and he doubts that this is any kind of evil omen. He says only that God understands it; and we don't.

What interests him now is not the terror of the sea, but what you find when you get across it. Adam of Bremen filled the north with men who never walked, only hopped on one foot, and those who ate human flesh ('as they are shunned, so may they also rightfully be passed over in silence'). There were Goths and blue men, worshippers of dragons and Prussians who seemed 'a most humane people'. There were dogheaded men and men with one eye in the middle of their foreheads; and when the Amazons gave birth, which they did after seducing passing merchants, or forcing their male captives, or perhaps just by sipping water, the boys that resulted had their heads on their chests and the girls became beautiful women who drove away any man who even came close. The edge of the world was also the edge of reason.[26]

Between the time the story of Brendan was first composed and the writing of the *History of Norway* many ships had been sailing out north and out west, carrying people and cargoes and using the sea that once had been a source of pure, holy terror. The change is profound, but not at all complete: there was still a great unknown beyond the ice in the north, a place to be filled up with stories. Yet the mystics of Germany and the Netherlands, who once used the sea as a symbol of hostile, purifying space, now start to use the desert as their metaphor instead. The sea is too busy, too practical; the desert is still pure and utterly strange. The sea was beginning to be known. When the mystic Hadewijch writes about water in the thirteenth century, she does not see it as the terrifying prospect it once was; the abyss is no longer a threat to life or the end of the world, for her it is a way to think about the tempestuous nature of God himself and the way you can be lost in love. Leviathan has, for the moment, gone away.[27]

There were other monsters still present and they travelled. Polar bears and their pelts hardly ever turn up in customs records, but the ferocious live beasts were brought to Norway as bribes, and successful ones: they even turn up, but not often, at the French and English courts.[28] The edgy North had become like Africa and Asia: a distant place, a strange place, but a source of wonders that could be known, traded and used.

Take the medieval tale of Audun: a man with almost nothing, who had to work and live with relatives in the Westfjords of Iceland and had a mother dependent on him. He did have luck, though, and it got him a bear. In Iceland almost everything was sold on credit, because people had to be able to eat in spring even if the wool and the cloth that they traded for food would not be ready until summer. They depended for supplies on sea captains from Norway, who had a pressing interest in knowing who was truly creditworthy. Audun helped one captain so well that he was offered passage to Greenland. He sold off his sheep to support his mother, because by law he had to provide her with enough to take her through six seasons – three winters, three summers – and he sailed out.[29]

On Greenland he met a hunter with a polar bear that was 'exceptionally beautiful with red cheeks'. He offered the man all the money he had to buy the bear; the man told him that wasn't wise, and Audun said he didn't care. He wanted to make his mark on the world by giving the bear away to a king: a gift as exotic, as rare, as any rhinoceros given to a Pope in later centuries.

Shipping a polar bear for days out at sea in a small boat is wild, but not implausible. A bishop on his way from Iceland to the mainland to be consecrated took with him 'a white bear from Greenland and the animal was the greatest of treasures'; the beast ended up in the Emperor's menagerie. When Greenlanders wanted a bishop of their own in 1125 they sent a bear to the King of Norway to encourage him, and the ploy worked.[30] Bears went much further, in fact. King Håkon of Norway sealed his deal with King Henry III of England with gifts of falcons, furs, whale tusks, a live elk and a live polar bear.[31] The monsters of the North start to seem almost domestic; the law in Iceland, where any polar bear at all was a rare sight on the floating ice, laid down that 'if a man has a tame white bear then he is to handle it in the same way as a dog'.

Audun found himself penniless, in the middle of a warzone, with a starving bear who could be forgiven for considering his minder as lunch; his journey south took so long that even if the bear was a cub in Greenland it must have been big and hungry now. The King of Norway offered to buy the beast, but Audun refused and kept moving. He made it across to Denmark, but now he had quite literally nothing except a bear that was starving to death; a courtier offered both of them food, on condition he could own half the bear. Audun had no choice.

This is a story, so naturally the Danish king saves Audun and his bear. He pays for Audun to go to Rome and back again, and even the King of Norway acknowledges that Audun probably did the right thing when he refused to sell him the bear. Norwegian kings gave ships, food and time like Danish kings, but not silver; by holding on to the bear until he reached Denmark, Audun made a solid fortune in money which he could use for anything. A man no longer skirts the abyss in the far north and lives in fear of monsters; instead, he does business with them for cash.

The story is the folktale of a man and a bear, but it also signals a moment when the world becomes recognizable, if not downright modern: money, travel, trade, ambition. But of course we choose what we want to recognize.

That is why the reality of this hidden past matters so much. It involves whole peoples' ideas about who they are, how they think, where they come from and why they rule: all the things they choose to recognize.

'Forgetting history or even getting it wrong is one of the major elements in building a nation,' Ernest Renan wrote, and he said history was a danger to nationalism; Eric Hobsbawm added: 'I regard it as the primary duty of modern historians to be such a danger.'[32]

For national history has a way of being radically incomplete. The Irish were and are deeply attached to the notion of an island of saints and scholars, which is not wrong at all, except that it leaves out the raiders, slavers and traders. Some Dutchmen used to have a deep mistrust of anything medieval on the grounds that it was bound to be Catholic and therefore unpatriotic and wrong, but it's tough to get right a history that has to be a perfect blank before the Protestant sixteenth century; and it can be silly. When the Rijksmuseum in Amsterdam first opened in its pseudo-medieval glory, all Gothick spikes and towers, King William III in 1885 announced: 'I shall never set foot in that monastery.' Norwegian attitudes are even more complicated, since the Middle Ages were the time when Norway was independent and powerful, before Danes and Swedes took over and started to write the national story; so instead of leaving out the medieval, Norwegians chose to leave out the next four centuries, the 'four-hundred-year night'. When the first Norwegian national assembly, a thoroughly democratic body, opened in 1814 the President perversely declared: 'Now is re-erected the Norwegian royal throne.'[33]

There is worse. The peoples around the North Sea have a remarkable story, the one I mean to tell, but it all too easily degenerates into a claim on Northern superiority: one in which the Southern lands where the lemon trees blossom, and the people have time to sit under them, are meant to learn from their betters, and long, thin blond people are meant to rule short, stocky, dark people. As a short, stocky dark person from the North, I am unhappy with this; the fact that Nordic saga-writers made all their thralls and slaves look like me is infuriating.

And particular evils rest on the Northern legend: the story of connections is twisted to justify separations of the bloodiest kind. German nationalism was always fascinated by its Scandinavian connections; think of Wagner tweaking dragon-slaying superhero stories from the *Nibelungenlied* and the gods of old Iceland into the *Ring* cycle, think of Fritz Lang tweaking Wagner in the movie version of *Die Nibelungen*, setting out to make a perfectly medieval epic about 'Germany searching for an ideal in her past' and having to put up with praise from Goebbels for 'an epic film that is not of our time, yet is so modern, so contemporary and so topical'.[34]

The rediscovery of the great Saxon poem *Heliand*, the Gospels retold in the ninth century in the manner of some North Sea epic, produced a number of fits of fantasy: in the nineteenth century August Vilmar took it to show 'all that is great and beautiful, with all that the German nation, its heart and life, were able to provide'. It celebrated all sorts of things he reckoned to be especially German, like 'the lively joy of the Germans in moveable wealth'. He somehow deduced that the Christian conversion of all German lands was proof that Germany was a single nation, 'clean and resolute, its inner unity and its unity to itself transferred by the poet . . . onto the persons with his holy story'.[35] The Saxon detail and thinking of *Heliand* became a pan-German myth: Jesus lining up with Bismarck. Vilmar was delighted by the rude remarks throughout the text about the 'sluggish' people of the South, who were mostly Jews, and the obvious superiority of the 'Germanic' disciples. His ideas persisted. At the time of the First World War the Gospels, told in Saxon verse, had somehow become 'a pithy story of German manhood'.[36]

In the 1930s, the history of the Hanseatic League – trading towns working together so they could effectively subvert national powers – somehow turned into a claim for German national dominance. It was as though the fact that the Hansa had happened once could wipe away all those hundreds of years when it didn't happen at all; and there are papers in the essential French journal *Annales* from the 1930s which are now unreadable because they claim all kinds of 'powerful spiritual and intellectual forces' behind a merchants' union, make metaphysics out of the account books.[37] That is not the worst. In pursuit of a criminal idea of race, the SS was to become a perfect, almost mystical bunch of Nordic thugs, not only identified by type and shape of head but also bound into a carefully chosen past. With absolutely no irony at all there were posters in wartime Norway which showed a Viking standing most approvingly behind an SS man, freelance freebooters and a foreign state police oddly united against Nazism's mirror, Bolshevism.[38]

History helps kill, if you're not careful, so let me make one thing clear. I am celebrating the North's contribution to the culture of Europe, but that does not mean forgetting the glories of the South; this is a story of connections. I want to isolate one part of the whole story only in order to get it clear, because it is the part that is so often missed.

German nationalism went wrong, that is obvious, and in a particularly ugly way. By contrast an Englishman can read some of the English and British nineteenth-century versions of the past – just as determined to sing anthems and wave flags – and try to find them simply absurd.

That would be a mistake. They still have extraordinary power.

The English have a story every schoolchild knows, how Anglo-Saxons stormed the coast of Britain some time in the fifth century and pushed out or even exterminated the British and Celtic natives and changed the island for ever; we became Germanic, and we started to speak a kind of English. We became Christians in a world still pagan. We qualified to be a separate nation, six centuries before that meant much, and we had what every nation needs: a story about its origins.

We've good authority for this. Bede's *Church History of the English People*[39] is the work of a great scholar who had access to a very decent library in his monastery at Jarrow. It was finished around 731 CE, which is as close as we can get to the invasion he describes, but not very close. Bede does say how he did his research, which was impressive: he had a Canterbury abbot to tell him what happened at Canterbury, who in turn drew on the memory of older men as well as what was written down. Meanwhile, a future Archbishop of Canterbury went to Rome to work through the Vatican book chests with the Pope's permission and bring back letters of Pope Gregory for Bede. When he writes in his history about St Cuthbert and his island life on Lindisfarne, he says he wrote or talked to any credible witness he could find.

But is Bede himself credible? He wrote about the times that mattered most to him: the times of Christian missions and their success. When he writes about earlier times, he says he followed older writers, which is natural enough since he believed in such authorities.[40] His book was not scientific, and not historical in a modern sense. He didn't question his sources so much as paste them together on the page, a brilliantly considered scrapbook. His book is naturally a Saxon account of Saxon triumphs, a Christian treatise. A Saxon monk was never likely to write anything else.

This is where the trouble starts. Bede says that long before the Saxon missionaries landed, a king in Britain called Vortigern had invited Saxon mercenaries to come across the North Sea and help beat back the enemies of the Britons. He and his allies had asked for Roman help before, but the Romans were otherwise occupied, and the Picts and the Irish were still marauding. Three longships came in 449 CE, Bede says, carrying men who were expected to defend the country as friends but really meant to conquer it like enemies; Gildas, his sixth-century source, writes more colourfully that 'a pack of cubs burst forth from the lair of the barbarian lioness, coming in three keels'.[41] They found the country rich, they thought the Britons cowardly and they summoned from home a much larger navy with many more fighting men. Jutes, Saxons and Angles arrived, with Hengist and Horsa as commanders, and they were followed by mobs of settlers, so many that the native Britons became nervous. They were right: the Saxons were about to turn their weapons on their allies. They ravaged almost all the island – the 'dying' island, Bede calls it. Houses fell, Christian priests were slaughtered at the altar, there was nobody prepared to bury the dead bishops and when the Britons took to the hills they were murdered in heaps. Some were starved into surrender, some quit the country altogether, some were exiled to the forests and mountains to scrape together what living they could. The Britons went away and England was Saxon.[42]

This is loaded stuff, and a little confusing. For a start, Bede was not just on the Saxon side; he seems to be on the pagan side against Christians. He had to believe that Christianity had somehow gone wrong in Britain, that the Britons deserved everything they got for being sinful, drunk and arrogant, including the plague he says was so sudden and violent there was nobody alive to bury the dead. The Saxons were God's next means of punishment 'that evil might fall on the reprobates'. He was particularly angry that the Britons, clergy and lay alike, threw off 'the light yoke of Christ'; he says later that the Britons were rotten with heresy, corrupted by the comforting notion that man is not stained with original sin at all but is free to choose good or evil for himself. Bede gives a brief account of a British victory at Mount Badon which seems to contradict his notion that all the surviving Britons had died or run away, and then he gets to his real story: the coming of Saxon missionaries and their very rapid success. These are Saxons preaching to Saxons: what could go wrong? After all, the British – still around, it seems – collapsed into civil strife when they found they had no foreign wars to fight.[43]

Bede's version is very powerful. It gives England a clean start and Christian faith. It turns history into a Saxon story. It has been used to explain how English was formed, why the English are somehow a racial group. But what if there never was an invasion? What if the real story was one of connections, of Saxons invited in over the years to help out in battles, of 'Belgic' peoples on the east side of England who spoke a Germanic language, as Tacitus said, even before the Romans arrived in 43 CE? The Romans certainly had Germanic mercenaries, then small mobile field armies with Germanic soldiers who were billeted on civilians with plenty of opportunity to fraternize and put about their genes. Saxon mercenaries did indeed come to Britain to help the Britons, but it would take a prodigious number of ships to bring enough people to repopulate a whole island; did the Saxons also improvise, with the help of the British women? The best estimate is that there were two million natives at the time, and at the most a very few hundred thousand newcomers, and more likely tens of thousands.[44]

If the Britons were driven out, why is it that archaeologists look at the human remains through this period and find so little change?[45] Of course, the survival of bodies to check is an arbitrary business, and it is almost always easier to study the remains of someone rich and powerful, the kind of person who can afford a visible tomb full of famous riches. But even so: check the enamel on teeth, and the isotopes will tell where the deceased grew up, and it doesn't seem to have been in Saxon territory; measure skulls and they start to get bigger only after the Norman Conquest; the DNA is such a muddle that the main movements of human beings must have taken place long before.

If bodies didn't change, did language? Such a rush of new people, all speaking Germanic languages, might explain why Anglo-Saxon became the base and root of English; but it seems there were Germanic-speaking peoples in England already, the Belgae. During Roman rule, there was a 'Count of the Saxon Shore' in Britain, as there probably was across the Channel in Gaul, with nine shore forts to defend the coastline,[46] but was it the 'Saxon' shore because it had to be defended against Saxons or because the Saxons were already there? The *Gallic Chronicles* mention a Saxon territory in England in 423, two decades before Bede says Kent had its first Saxon king. If you choose to trust Bede's careful collection of other people's stories, these questions don't matter; but if you start to have doubts, they begin to seem important enough to change history.

Bede insists on a new world in England – Saxon, Christian, with the old pagan Britons swept aside. The trouble is, the record of physical remains shows that not even the place, let alone the people, was reinvented. Roman sites were used again, new buildings sometimes raised over baths and basilicas. Sometimes the buildings themselves remained in use, which we know from the late Anglo-Saxon coin found on the steps of a Roman basilica in Caerwent. The Romans left resources, after all. Stone buildings do seem to have come down, replaced by wooden structures or nothing at all, but that may have been the aftermath of sixth-century plague and war, and their dire economic consequences. Old Roman towns – Dorchester, for example – were used as churches and monasteries. The sunken buildings that look like novelties in the landscape, and were still being used in medieval times, can sometimes be dated all the way back to the second century AD. The evidence for sudden change is very hard to find. And yet Bede gave the English a story we seem to have needed: the English as the new Israelites, crossing the North Sea instead of the Red Sea into freedom of a kind.

Our very separate identity turns out to be an error, even a lie.

Mind you, all the connections across Europe, the links that crossed religious and official and language frontiers, can also be celebrated in very dubious ways. The Vikings are hailed as the first Europeans, at least by some French scholars, breaking cultural divisions as well as breaking heads,[47] and made into a foundation myth for our flabby, neo-liberal Europe. In this version of history Charlemagne, autocratic, imperial, a tycoon of the slave trade and aggressively brutal to his neighbours, becomes the patron saint of a fairly quiet customs union because at least he tried to rule both North and South. I do not think he would be flattered. The easy flow of ideas between individuals, the shared culture of Europeans, is turned by the magic of grant-giving into a kind of infrastructure for particular central institutions whose main characteristic is that they seem to take no notice at all of the easy flow of ideas that already exists between individuals who disagree with them.

That is why we need to try to tell this story straight. It is a way of thinking again about who we really are.

We have to get away from the raucous seaside, the holiday place that Cecil Warburton knew; the North Sea is much more than the water between a thousand beaches. It seems minor, it seems grey, but it has a furious and brilliant history. We can start with the stones on the beach at Domburg and ask: who brought them there and why, and what did they think they were doing?

1.

# The invention of money

The Roman army on manoeuvres: first century CE, on the North Sea coast, roughly where Belgium now stops and the Netherlands starts. Plinius Secundus was one of the commanders, and when he came to write his famous natural histories, he remembered what he had seen.

There were wide salt marshes and he saw no trees at all. He could not make up his mind if he was on the land or on the sea. There were houses built on hillocks and he thought they looked like ships in the water, or maybe more like shipwrecks; he reckoned the houses must be built that way to escape the worst daily surges of the tides. He sounds almost nervous in this strange marsh landscape, being an inland Roman and used to having the ground stay firm under his boots; now he was looking out at a landscape of shifting clay, all cut up with creeks and gullies where the tides pushed salt water in and out. He might as well have left the empire altogether because this coast was cut off from the mainland by lagoons and brackish peat, as good a frontier as the forests that kept whole peoples apart, better than any river. To reach the marshes, and the water people who lived there, you had to know the marshes. You also had to be welcome, because you would be seen.

Pliny considered the water people and he decided they were not worth the bother of conquering. Fish, he wrote, was all they had.[1]

Seven centuries later opinions had not much changed. Radbodo, Bishop of Utrecht, was most uncharitable about the Frisians, the people of these marshes: he wrote that they lived in water like fish and they rarely went anywhere except by boat. They were also crude, barbarous and remote: sodden provincials.[2] And yet between the writing of those two accounts the Frisians reinvented all the links and ties across the North Sea, as far as Jutland at the northern tip of Denmark and even beyond. They founded a new kind of town on the coast that thrived as the old Roman towns were in decline. They made themselves a capital on the left bank of the Rhine at Dorestad, just where the river divides to run down to its delta, which became the turntable of all Northern trade. And they ruled the North Sea, dominating all the trade that went by water, so for a time its name was changed: the Frisian Sea.

They did something else which helped to shape our world: they reinvented money. They took coins with them on their trading voyages, money for buying and selling and doing business. Other territories had run out of cash, or lived off gifts and barter, or stopped using money for anything except tax and politics, but the Frisians carried the idea of using money wherever they went. It was not at all a trivial idea. With it came ideas of the value of things and how to calculate that abstract value on paper – the value that objects in the real world share, a pot with a pile of grain with a fish with a plank with a place in a boat going up the Rhine, even when it seems obvious they have nothing else in common at all. The idea of value had to work wherever the Frisians came ashore. Trading meant taking that value and working with it, even experimenting with it: seeing the world in mathematical terms.

Money was going to change people's minds.

That story is easy to miss, but then it is extraordinary how much Pliny missed and he was there. He saw ramshackle shipwrecks on the little hills, most likely fishermen's shacks, and missed the solid houses with their sod walls a full metre thick. He didn't notice the real business of the marshes.

He says nothing about the two temples facing each other across the water at the start of the open sea, on the very last point of the land: Roman temples dedicated to Nehalennia, a goddess of death and trade and fertility, almost everything that matters. On her altars, salt merchants gave thanks for voyages she had made successful, and so did men who dealt in potter's clay and fish sauce, wine, cloth and pottery and anything that was going out to England across the sea; sometimes the same merchant thanked her on both sides of the river.[3] At the temple in Colijnsplaat, to the north, the goddess was all business; the one to the south, at Domburg, where the stones later came back from under the sea, makes clear her darker side. Here she has a hound sitting by her, as she stands by a set of curtains that screen away a passage to the next world; she is watching over the dead as they go out to sea, sailing west to the isles of the blessed.[4] Practical cargoes and magical journeys, life and death, were all going over the beach at Domburg.

A hundred years later there would have been nothing much for Pliny to miss. Domburg was abandoned. Pirates moved in, some of them local and Frisian, some of them from the Frankish kingdoms to the south.[5] Rome began to lose control. Then the water took over by force: the sea rushed in and drowned the temples around the end of the second century. The dunes moved, the channels for boats changed, and the site became impossiblc. All that was left was a fragile stretch of sand which a single wind storm could skirl into a new landscape, a coastline where a surging sea could wash away all the business that had made so many merchants give thanks to the goddess. There was no sign of life or business there for almost four centuries until the story began over again.

But in the marshes there were heavy barges which had come down the Rhine from the middle of Europe, boats thirty metres long and three metres across, steering oars forward and steering oars aft: solid, flat-bottomed craft made out of thick slabs of oak. They were rowed and hauled down the river, carrying loads of slate and stone, or wine or pots, and when they reached the marshes, they moved their cargo onto sea-going ships.[6] From the marshes, the goods could go north or south by sea in the lee of the islands along the coast, down to where Calais now stands to cross to England or directly across the sea to markets where York and London and even Southampton stand now, or up to the start of the Danish peninsula, where they could cross by land and river into the Baltic and reach up to Birka and Helgö in Sweden. The marshes held the trade of half a continent.

All this is unfamiliar in part because there is so little written evidence. We wouldn't know that 'Frisian' meant 'merchant' in seventh-century London, except that Bede mentions in his *History* that some young aristo from Northumberland ended up in Mercian hands, and was sold in the market to 'a Frisian'. This Frisian couldn't manage to keep the kid safely tied up, and so allowed him to go off and ransom himself.[7] Bede says he checked the story with particular care, so we can assume that Frisians were practical merchants who did not deal in bothersome merchandise. We would find it hard to prove that there was a Frisian colony in eighth-century York, except that Altfrid wrote the life of a saint called Liudger and mentions the time a Frisian merchant happened to brawl with the young son of a local duke and the boy ended up dead; at which point all the Frisians, Liudger included, got out quickly for fear of the anger of the young man's family. Frisians stuck together, like any expatriate community.[8] We owe the idea that Frisians had a distinctive kind of ship, nothing like the Viking ships, to the *Anglo-Saxon Chronicle*, which mentions in the entry for 896 that King Alfred ordered fast, steady longships to be built with more oarsmen than ever before, and 'they were neither of Frisian design nor of Danish'.[9]

The abbey at Saint-Denis, close to Paris, has a royal document which guarantees that its monks will keep all the revenue from selling wine at their annual fair and also extract a kind of commission from the merchants 'Saxon or Frisian or people of other indeterminate nations'.[10] So the Frisians were important in the wine trade. It is likely that the Bishop of Liège in modern Belgium had to send to Domburg for his German and his Alsatian wine.

The stories of saints, meanwhile, bear traces of how the Frisians worked up and down the Rhine. St Goar was a hermit left in a cell by the Rhine not far from the alarming Lorelei rocks, where the river was twenty-seven metres deep and the surface was a roil of violent currents; passing travellers might well be in need of miracles. One Frisian merchant was carried downstream onto the rocks, asked the saint for help and was saved; he had on board a garment of silk splendid enough to be his offering of thanks, so he must have been a middleman shipping exotic and valuable goods since Frisia produced wool, not silk. Another was being hauled upriver by porters, alone in his boat with one servant, and refused to stop to pray to St Goar. He couldn't steer on his own, the current dragged him over to the dangerous side, all the porters managed to drop the rope except for one. The boat smashed on the opposite shore, and the body of the last porter was found, drowned, at the end of the rope. The merchant now thought that a prayer might be in order. The drowned man revived, stood up, coughed some blood and went back to leading the porters who were hauling the barge. The grateful merchant left a full pound weight of silver to thank the saint, which must mean he was carrying much more than a full pound weight of silver coins; business was good.[11]

This sparse patchwork of clues can now be combined with the physical record, the evidence that has been dug out of the earth or washed up on the beaches. Together they tell a story that was almost lost, as the story of losers tends to be. The old Frisians were enthusiastic pagans, so when they stopped smashing the skulls of passing saints and accepted Christianity, they were not supposed to honour their pagan past. They were subjects inside the Frankish empire that Charlemagne was building, whose pride in their separate identity and their past had been known to send them on murderous raids up the Rhine against the imperial powers; defeated, they were supposed to adopt the empire's history. Worse, they did not have a land fit for monuments. They lived in a water world where high tides and sandstorms could cover or ruin their past: 'a pagan people divided by the intervening waters into many farming hamlets, with all kinds of names but belonging to just one people'.[12] Even in the years when they owned the sea lanes, the sea could ruin them. The water swept back over the land at full moon in 834, flooding the land strongly; and again in 838 when the earth shook, the sun burned the earth, there were dragons in the air and around Christmas high winds broke the usual pattern of the tides and whipped the sea inland, wrecking houses along the coast and levelling the high dunes; more people died than it was possible to count, although there were curiously precise reports that 2,437 people died.[13] Being out at sea, with all kinds of choices to make, was sometimes more secure than staying on land with none at all. Again in February 868, when a comet passed overhead, the winds got up and a vast flood killed many who were not prepared for it. That year, the famine was so terrible that men ate human flesh to survive.[14]

Yet the Frisians lived well on these difficult margins. They had a long record of being separate, and being independent.

They left their first traces on the east shores of the Aelmere, a sealed freshwater lake that was later flooded from the sea and became, for a time, the salt Zuiderzee and is now the freshwater IJsselmeer. They moved as the other peoples of Northern Europe began to move: some pushed, some ambitious, some displaced. They went east up to the River Weser, and west to the delta of the Rhine, the Meuse and the Scheldt. As political boundaries shifted, as the Franks wanted a name for their neighbours, Frisia grew. The islands and marshes of Zeeland, where the temple at Domburg once stood, became the nearer part of Frisia.

As they were settling, the Germanic peoples across the Rhine, famous for their seamanship, were also on the move. Many shipped out to England: Angles, Saxons, Jutes. Some went overland into Gaul. Some of them chose to stay in the new Frisian territory, which made them Frisian; before there were passports and papers and notions of national identity, or even national history, you identified with where you happened to be, not where your mother and father were born. Your identity was lived in the present tense.

Since these Frisians spoke a language much like Saxon they never had to lose touch with their countrymen and cousins now in England. So these water people had connections in place over land and over the sea: south to Gaul, east to Saxony, as well as north and west to Jutland and to England.

It took one other tidal move of human beings to give the Frisians their living. Tribes who poured into Eastern Europe in the sixth century blocked the old trading links between Scandinavia and Byzantium, the river routes that tracked across what is now Russia. Any goods that Scandinavians wanted had to come by some other route and from some other source, and so they came up from Frisia; in the two centuries before the Viking times began around 800 CE, everything that we know reached Scandinavia came by way of Frisian traders.[15] They had a monopoly without the need to create it.

Along the coast the Frisians made slipways so they could build their flat-bottomed boats, the kind that moved easily in the shallow waters between the dunes and the coast. These boats could be beached on any stretch of sand and their bows and stern came up sharply so the incoming tide could get underneath to float them. Since the easiest trade routes were over water, the beaches were the obvious places for markets. The markets led to year-round settlements, and those settlements became quick, small and independent towns: 'mushroom' towns.

Inland towns depended on royal favour, or a local lord who required taxes, or on the presence of a church or a monastery; these economies were about supporting their masters. Monasteries were factories and farms and workshops, turning out all kinds of goods: shoes for holy feet, saddles for holy riders, swords and shields when needed, leather and cloth and gold. They had builders, blacksmiths, glass-makers; but all this was so the monastery itself could be self-sufficient. They did not make to sell or trade; and when they took goods from the towns around them, they took them as tribute, not as business.[16]

On the coast, individuals did business for themselves. Frisians opened up the trade routes that had been dormant since Rome fell, and added some: they sold pots, wine, human slaves. They shipped and sold whatever people wanted. The name of Frisian came to mean merchant, overseas trader, the perfect example of the long-distance seaman. The sea was truly 'the Frisian sea'.

The water people chose their place in the world. It had once been possible to build directly on the surface of their salt marshes, but that was five hundred years before Pliny passed by. When the sea rose again and broke into the land, human beings were faced with a choice. The obvious tactic was to run away, which is what happened almost everywhere else; water people could move like so many other peoples who were moving across the face of Europe. Instead, the Frisians chose to stay and keep their place on the edge of things.

For that, they had to build their own land. They heaped up hillocks on the marshes, built on them, and the hillocks became permanent settlements all the year round: the *terpen*. They owned the land outright as peasants never could in the feudal systems around them, and they were settled and at home; you can tell because houses were rebuilt again and again, twice or more in a century, but always on exactly the same site.[17] They also had to co-operate, house to house, *terp* to *terp*, if only because finding sweet water was never easy, not even when wells replaced the old clay-lined reservoirs for collecting rainwater; the supply of water to drink depended on the discipline of the community.[18] Co-operation, not always within the law, was a Frisian habit.

As the farms on *terpen* disposed of their rubbish, the *terpen* grew taller. Each hillock started as a single farm, but as they expanded they merged one into another to form villages on higher ground: communities of houses built round an open space at the top of the *terp*, the back doors for the cattle and sheep to wander out onto the salt pastures, the front doors facing each other across the common space.

Anyone who lived there had to be a boatman, or they were trapped; they were peasants raising beasts because the salt land would not support most grains. Their situation gave them the advantage over inland farmers who ploughed and sowed and tended and reaped and were generally busy all year round. As cattlemen and sheep herders they weren't tied to the land day by day, always working to make the next crop happen. Ram and ewe, bull and cow, would do that for them. They were left with the luxury of time.

Their kind of farming had other advantages. The rest of Europe around them lived on cereals, on bread and beer and gruel, and a pot kept permanently bubbling on the fire with anything sweet or savoury or fleshy that would help the gruel down. A poor harvest meant starvation, and crop yields were low at the best of times, just enough to keep people alive. The Frisians were rich by comparison. They had grazing for their animals, mostly cattle; so they had milk and meat as well as fish and game, a diet that was nourishing twelve months a year. For a while, the marshes that Pliny dismissed were more densely populated than anywhere else in Western Europe except for the Seine around Paris and the Rhine around Cologne.[19]

The marshes weren't barren, of course. There were sedges and rushes, and enough grass to make haystacks; obstinate pagans went out to cut hay on a fine, still Sunday when the saintly Anskar was preaching and missioning, and saw their disrespectful work go up in spontaneous fire as punishment.[20] The hides from their cattle became leather and, conveniently, sea lavender grew on the marsh, its root used for tanning. The salt peat made sod for the walls of houses. There was common grasswrack, the sea grass whose ashes produce a salt to preserve meat and whose stems, up to a metre and a half long, had a dozen uses: stuffing mattresses, making the seats for chairs, thatching houses, lining ditches, even as a kind of woven fence that would keep back the drifting sands. It made excellent litter for the animals in the byre and, dug into the ground of the *terpen* afterwards, it fertilized the gardens. Turnips grew there alongside broad beans and oilseed rape, barley and a few oats.[21]

The people on the *terpen* couldn't produce everything they wanted, not even everything they needed. They couldn't make wine and they couldn't produce much grain, but they wanted both; they were prepared to ship out down the rivers to Alsace for wine and as far as Strasbourg for grain. They also needed timber for the roof frames of their sod houses. So they had to do business to get necessities: to send out anything they could produce from animals – parchment and bone, leather and wool, cloth woven from the wool – in order to buy what they couldn't grow. They already knew all about adding value to their basic products, starting a kind of Frisian brand; one farm close to modern Wilhelmshaven kept two different breeds of sheep for two different kinds of wool so as to make all kinds of fine cloth.[22]

The *terpen* must have worked a little like islands, holding people's fierce local loyalties. They seem isolated but they are often full of sailors who have been away to everywhere. Frisians became famous for travelling, and for their women who waited behind and their constancy. There is a ninth-century poem in *The Exeter Book* that turns Frisian marriage on the *terpen* into a moral example, and perhaps a report of a loving ritual. 'He's so very welcome, so dear to his Frisian wife when his boat is back,' the poem says. 'He's the one who provides for her, and she welcomes him, washes his clothes dirtied by the sea and gives him clean ones. She gives him on dry ground all that his love could wish: the wife will be faithful to her husband.'

The poet's realistic; he knows some women are constant, and some want novelty, the available stranger when the husband is away; indeed the laws of Frisia that Charlemagne codified suggest a tolerance for brisk infanticide to dispose of the evidence of indiscretion.[23] But he remembers the sailor, too. 'He's at sea a long time, always thinking of the one he loves, patiently waiting out the journey he can't hurry. When his luck turns again he comes back home – unless he is sick, or the sea holds him back or the ocean has him in its power.'[24]

The sea could kill, and yet it was the easy route: the connection, not the barrier. The network of Roman roads survived, but they were broken and rutted and hard work for a loaded waggon in many months of the year. The Roman system of posthouses was in place so you could change horses on a long ride, but it was a cumbersome business compared with going by sea or river; and it was slower, and often less safe than the water. It is true there were pirates, but the reason pirates went on working the North Sea from Roman times to the seventeenth century was that they knew civilians were always willing to risk being raided for the ease of a sea crossing. There were also storms, but there were prayers and saints to calm them: the lives of saints tell so many stories of miracles at sea that they tend to prove the general terror of foul weather. Believers clung to the Church as sailors cling to a ship, and ships came to be signs of faith.

Even saints knew that no voyage was ever quite certain. Willibrord was a missionary, the first Bishop of Utrecht, and he had thirty convert boys to ship down from Denmark to Frisia. He made sure to baptize them all before setting out, because of the 'dangers of such a long sailing and the attacks of the ferocious natives of those parts' and the awful possibility that they might drown and be eternally damned despite all his good work.[25] The prefect Grippo, returning from a diplomatic mission to some kings in England, faced the violence of the storm and learned it was best to let the ship drift until there was calm. He suffered a night of furious wind and crashing waves, shipping water, and he had to wait for the sun to rise before he could see the old-fashioned lighthouse up ahead, probably the Roman tower at Boulogne that Charlemagne had rebuilt. Only then did he hoist again the sail that must have been lowered hours before.[26]

All this was a gloriously alarming muddle of the practical and the fearful. On one hand fresh water was supposed to be Godly and good, renewing and refreshing life itself, while salt water was a desert, a cliff off which ships could fall; it was an abyss where Leviathan lived with other terrible creatures, 'a king over all the children of pride', according to the Book of Job, 'made without fear' and able to make 'the deep boil like a pot', with terrible teeth, breath to kindle coals and the power to lay a trail of phosphorescent light behind him on the water.[27] On the other hand, you could always hunt the smaller terrible creatures and eat them; St Bridget of Kildare fed her guests fresh seal, the same St Cuthbert who was famously kind to ducks sometimes existed on the flesh of beached dolphins, and St Columba prophesied the coming of a gigantic whale off the island of Iona but said God would protect his fellow monks from its terrible teeth. He did nothing to save the whale.[28]

For Christians, as you can see in the vivid pages of some Psalters designed on Frisian territory, the land was almost Heaven and the sea was Hell, full of beasts and tortures and also temptations to sin; the coastline was a kind of battleground between the two, and inland was where good people could get on with their industrious and virtuous lives.[29] Sea was where holy men might go and put away the rudder and trust to God, knowing they were at risk. The sea, after all, was where pagan heroes went, where unfamiliar and unholy things abounded. But it was also the Frisians' workplace, and they saw no reason to rush conversion to Christian attitudes. They were used to working together on their boats so they held to the old view that shipping out implied all sorts of virtues: loyalty, trust and competence.

They used anchors on their boats, as the Romans did, with heavy chains to pull them up and let them down in shallow water or on the sands. Once the anchor was raised, their flat-bottomed boats might still be settled in the sand, so they carried a gaff in the shape of a metal

V at the end of a wooden pole to push themselves clear.[30] The main power was muscle power, rowers sitting on sea chests, which was the kind of power a captain could control; but there were also sails to help out the oarsmen, and since nobody could yet tack into a headwind, each journey had to wait for the right wind to blow the ship forwards. Boniface shipped out from England on his mission to convert the Frisians in 716, clambered up the side of a quick ship with the sailors bustling about and had to wait for the great sail to be puffed out with the right winds;[31] or so Willibald says in his life of the saint. Willibald refers to the sail as '*carbasa*' in the Latin, which more usually is a word for linens, even though we know most sails were sewn from lengths of woven wool. When Boniface's body was shipped over the Aelmere on a more ordinary ship with 'swelling sails', the word used this time was '*vela*', the more common word.[32] Did fast ships need a different kind of sail?

Since the sea was not a barrier like the land, the world had a different shape. We would find it hard to recognize.

Suppose you crossed from Domburg to the trading port at Ipswich on the east coast of England, newly opened in the seventh century; your cargo might be pots from the Rhineland or glass or the hefty lava quernstones used for grinding grain in mills.[33] Stand on the banks of the River Orwell and look out at the world. If you think in terms of the time it takes to get to places, then Bergen in Norway is closer than York in England, even if your boat to Bergen depends on the muscle power of rowers; but York is only 340 km away by road on modern maps while Bergen is 510 km by sea. The coast of Jutland is closer, and better connected, than an English Midlands city like Worcester. You could be over the water and in the port of Quentovic, on the border between modern France and modern Belgium, in half the time it took to get to London overland; and if you had a faster ship, under sail, you could be in Jutland sooner than London. Travel by land had none of the sea's advantages, such as the prevailing summer winds that virtually blow a Norseman home from around Calais; and at sea, despite the habit of clinging to the shore for the sake of navigation and being able to sleep on dry land at night, it was actually safer out in the open, away from the shoals and currents of the English coast.[34]

It was easy for Scandinavians to be in York, Frisians in Ipswich, Saxons in London, and the fact was so unremarkable that it is hardly recorded. You didn't need a harbour to land because you could beach a flat-bottomed boat on any stretch of sand; so the great customs ports like Quentovic were tucked into estuaries or else, like Dorestad, upstream on the Rhine. More, going off to sea did not always mean building a huge ship and recruiting a large crew, although having more men who could fight off raiders was often a good idea; there was no need, on the coastal runs, to share the costs and risks because they were not that high; an individual could do it for himself.

A sea change, if you like, was coming.

All through the seventh and even the eighth centuries, much of the business across the sea looked like ceremony, a way of moving around all those luxurious goods that a king, chief or emperor needed to ensure alliances, make friends and keep his men loyal. Traders were more escorts than dealers, transporting bribes and rewards, moving goods so someone else could give them away. Again, the Frisians were different. They had their own tastes and they moved goods to satisfy themselves. From the sixth century, they were buying pots for their own use from the Frankish kingdom to their south, simply because they liked them.[35] They bought jewellery from England and Scandinavia, and they got their weaving battens made out of whale-bone from Norway. They may even have kept souvenirs: among their stashes of useful coins are pretty cowrie shells from the Red Sea.[36]

Their kind of business required money: not a heap of gold and silver wealth that would go well in your grave, but live money, coins to use in trade. All through Gaul the only point of coins was an easy way to ship gold about. In England it took two hundred years after the Romans left before coins were used as money again. There were no mints at all east of the Rhine until Regensburg, and that mint produced very little.[37] It was the Frisians who reinvented useful money, and taught their ideas to the Franks under Charlemagne.

For gold had always been about power, ceremony, buying support and paying taxes: the currency of politics. Romans used it that way, the great landowners paying into the state and a bit of subsidy flowing back (as usual) to the people who needed it least, the great landowners. In the sixth century, gold still flooded into state coffers – the ones belonging to the Frankish kings and no longer the Roman emperors – but it hardly even dribbled back out; it was money that did not circulate, fit only to be kept, counted, buried and, quite usually, stolen.[38] Gold was often a gift, not always entirely voluntary, which showed how and where you fitted: who were your allies, who were your masters. You did not necessarily get anything in return: you couldn't give gold to a church and expect a measure of salvation. You certainly didn't get a load of grain or a shipful of amber or a posse of slaves for your gold; the return was wonderfully abstract, an idea of yourself. In early medieval epics, its commonest form is not even coins: it is small gold rings, against which the poets measured any other gifts in circulation, however substantial, and ultimately the value and standing of the people who got them and gave them.[39]

When the big Roman estates folded and the diminished cities were no longer the focus of life, all of a sudden something smaller, less valuable, more flexible than gold was required: a currency of trade. It was not just the long-haul international trades which needed a token of value that made sense at both ends of the voyage and everywhere in between. Peasant farmers taking their goods into local markets needed some way to buy and sell with coins;[40] they couldn't simply go home with more of the same kind of grain or cabbage or beans they'd taken to market, even if that was what their neighbours had to sell; they needed a way to buy cloth or pots, things produced in other places and by other kinds of people, and in any case there was a limit to the beans or cabbage or grain that the cloth and pot merchants wanted.

Silver worked: small, thick silver coins that were often minted locally. The Frisians minted them with the old god Wotan on one side, with spiked hair, a drooping moustache and eyes that stare out like goggles; and on the other side a serpentine kind of monster with clawed feet and a high tail. The Anglo-Saxons in England imitated the Frisians, and put a creature like a porcupine on their silver, or sometimes a king.[41]

These silver *deniers* were scarce in all the wide Frankish territory until the Franks grabbed Frisia and its mints in the 730s. After that, mints were most common along the Frankish route into Frisia; even from around 700 CE there are *deniers* scattered about the stops on that trade run. The most commonly found ones were struck in Frisia, although it is not always easy to tell them from the Anglo-Saxon kind made across the water. The record buried in the ground suggests that Frisia was the centre if not the home of practical cash.[42] But it wasn't the countryside, the inland territory, which had money; it was the trading ports. The sands at Domburg gave up almost a thousand of the early pennies, the *sceattas*,[43] and from there the coins went where merchants went: to the Frisians' cousins and their trading partners in England, but also all the way up the run of the Rhine as well as south to Marseilles and the Mediterranean. In Aquitaine Frisian coins were much preferred to the debased money coming from what is now France.

The silver had to come from somewhere else since there were no mines in Frisia. To be able to manufacture this money, the Frisians had to make money in the first place and they got it by selling to the Franks, who wanted slaves and furs and fish and Frisian cloth, especially cloth of many colours. The white, grey, red and blue kinds were expensive and much appreciated in the East – so Charlemagne thought when he gave some to the Caliph of Baghdad, along with fierce and agile dogs for catching lions and tigers.[44] Frisian cloaks were mostly for the mass market, given away by the Emperor Louis the Pious to the lower orders in his court at Easter, while nobles got belts and silks, and the grooms, cooks and scullions got linen, wool and knives.[45]

The Frisians were notorious for cashing in on style; in Gaul, when shorter tunics were in fashion, the Frisians sold them but at the price of the longer, old-fashioned kind, and the Emperor had to intervene.[46] On the Rhine and round the Baltic they distributed tiny bronze 'keys to Paradise' with a round handle and a cross cut out of the metal, a Christian talisman; the Frisians may have resisted conversion manfully, but they worked out how to profit from it.[47] With all the cash they raised, they could buy what the Franks had to offer, which was corn, wine, metal, pottery and glass; and the rest of the silver, whatever form it took, could be turned into their own coins. It was not just that trade gave coins a use; the Frisians would not have had the metal to make them in the first place without trade.

In turn, the Franks had to get their silver from somewhere, and they found it in the East: the Middle East, in Byzantium and beyond. At the start of the eighth century, even the monks at Corbie in Picardy expected an allowance of exotic Eastern goods from the Frankish royal warehouses: pepper, cumin, cloves and cinnamon, dates and figs, rice and papyrus. Northern Europe liked drugs from the East, camphor in particular, to sort out various ailments that their local medicine did not seem to touch. The Franks had to trade to pay for that kind of luxury. They had little that the Middle East needed except bodies to labour, so they sold slaves, and they took back the silver *dirhams* from the caliphate in the East. Coins from Aleppo turn up all round the North Sea.

For a long time, silver wasn't mined; it was circulated, passed hand to hand. Only in the 960s were veins of silver discovered in Saxony, and suddenly there were new riches in Germany, enough to buy furs from Scandinavia and make money worth something again in England.[48] By then, silver coins had gone from being a convenient way to carry a valuable metal to a symbol in their own right. Coins were value you could carry about, which other people recognized the same way you did. They didn't need to be sheltered and fed like cattle, or ploughed and reaped like fields, and best of all they didn't die; their value persisted. They could be buried in times of trouble and dug up to spend later. The laws of the Franks show, equivalent by equivalent, how gold and goods gave way to silver and this idea of value. For example, a murderer was obliged to pay off the heirs and survivors of the man he had killed, and the rate of the blood money, *wergeld*, was fixed. At first it was set in gold *solidi*, with an equivalent in goods and perishables: a cow for 3 *solidi*, a horse for 12 and a sword and sheath for 7. Once silver money was in use, the exchange rate was about coins, not solid goods: 12 silver *deniers* to the *solidus*.[49] The value of money was a theory that everyone accepted, and it was anchored in the real world in the most surprising ways. Life itself had a price:

roughly 1,664 grains of fine silver in the form of coins. To make that kind of equation you have to have the habit of paying off every kind of debt with silver money.[50]

It's hard to overstate just how radical this idea was going to be. It wasn't just that money made two quite different things into equivalents: a barge full of timber equal to a barge full of salt, say, at least in value. You could take that abstraction, put it down on a small bit of parchment or a tally stick and work with it: calculate, estimate, add, divide and subtract, and, if you were lucky, multiply. Buyer and seller had to have the same idea about what money means: a measure and a concept of value more than a thing of value in itself. Merchants found that out later under Charlemagne when coins were clipped and adulterated and were still supposed to be worth the same.

There had to be a way to say how one thing was equal to something quite different and then make calculations: so buying a fish or a glass meant using a kind of equation. A new way of thinking became possible.

The men who sailed out were professional merchants and mariners now, not farmers with boats who sometimes went away on business. They were a class of persons to be watched. Charlemagne approved of true pilgrims, he said in a letter to the Saxon king, Offa of Mercia, who carried with them all the things they needed for their journey; but 'we have found there are some men who mix fraudulently with the pilgrims for the sake of business, chasing profit and not serving religion'.[51]

The merchants made an inland headquarters at Dorestad, some two hundred kilometres upstream on the Rhine where the river splits in two. They had a natural beach at first, perfect for landing their boats, but the river was beginning to meander and it formed a wet, slippery shoal between the water and the land; so they built causeways into the river, one jetty to each house, jetties which grew longer over the years as the bed of the river dodged to the east. Roadways of wooden planks ran over the causeways so goods could be loaded and unloaded. Those goods were rich: elegant glass and expensive weapons, pots of the style that buyers wanted wherever it was made, and not the rough local stuff. Even the wood barrels that lined their wells were imported: from Mainz up the river. The houses were long and boat-shaped, wider inland and narrower on the waterfront where they stood at right angles to the water, each claiming a private, personal access to the business of the river.[52]

Dorestad was so important to making money that it had the second most-active mint in the empire after the one in Charlemagne's own court.[53] In Charlemagne's time so much business passed through that the town became one of the main customs posts for the empire; most likely, it was along its harbour that cargo was shifted from sea-going boats to river-going boats, which would make it much easier to check value and take the Emperor's share. The town was a turntable for travellers, too, on the long haul from the upper Rhine to the sea, which implies some sort of schedule for services and a fair amount of traffic, and maybe somewhere to stay while you waited. Not all travellers found the welcome they expected. The scholar Alcuin of York told his friends in a poem to raise their sails and get out of Dorestad quickly because it was very likely a merchant called Hrotberct wouldn't open his house to them, just because 'this greedy merchant doesn't like your poems'. Alcuin clearly expected merchants to do their duty and offer a bed to distinguished strangers, so '*niger Hrotberct*', 'wretched Hrotberct', let everyone down.[54] In doing so, mind you, he got a minor kind of immortality; his very Frankish name is the only name we have for a merchant in Dorestad.

Look a little closer, and the port is much odder: a port that only men from the *terpen* could have imagined. The houses by the Rhine were packed closely but each made itself into an island: there was a wood palisade to mark its boundaries and a gallery that ran round the outside of the building to look out towards the neighbours, all the connection and the isolation of the *terpen*. There was not just one well to provide water, but two: one for humans, one for animals. In the north of the town there were substantial farms, linked by wooden plank roadways, and they raised more meat than the town could possibly eat. Each merchant house made things on a small scale, tanned leather or carved amber or did basic blacksmithing, produced ropes and baskets and maybe also cloth. The warehouses were storing goods, but also producing more goods than the town could use.[55] Dorestad was a port and a market town which kept the habits of the *terpen:* raise animals, make anything you can, go into business with what you have and then go as far as you can with the business.

All this required organization. Frisians sailed in convoys, which means they had to time and plan their voyages and share the information; we know this because the priest Ragenbert was sent north to what is now Sweden by way of Schleswig, 'where there were ships and merchants who were to make the journey with him' (and it was just bad luck that he was set upon by robbers and never made it alive).[56] Later they definitely had guilds, sworn brotherhoods; but perhaps they always had associations capable of keeping their members informed of and organizing the convoys and also defending their interests. In the Baltic in the eleventh century the Frisian guild at Sigtuna put up stones to the memory of members who had distinctly un-Frisian names, as though by the eleventh century 'Frisian' meant simply merchant and 'guild' meant something very close to Chamber of Commerce.[57]

They were also settled in Jutland, in the port called Haithabu, or else Schleswig, where there were many Christians 'who had been baptised at Dorestad';[58] or else at Hamburg, where the Frisians came and went. When the city of Worms on the upper Rhine burned down in 886 the chronicler at Fulda reports the burning of the best part of town, 'where the Frisian merchants live';[59] they also had the best quarters of Cologne and Mayence on the Rhine. They were settled enough to be buried abroad, although it was always possible to take the bones back home after a decent time; funerals in Yorkshire looked remarkably like Frisian funerals. They also left traces around the Humber and in Northumberland, which may help explain why Northumbrian missionaries found it quite easy, martyrdoms aside, to bring Christianity to their brothers in Frisia itself.

They went to live even at the outer limits of their trading world. There was a Frisian house in Kaupang at the mouth of the Oslo fjord in south Norway, on the way from the North Sea to the Baltic through the Kattegat, where the trade of the two seas criss-crossed in sheltered waters. The glass beakers found there are like the ones used by the Franks and the Frisians, which means Southern drinking habits, and there are double-ended dress hooks, which would have been useless on local clothes but which any Frisian woman would have needed; there were copper brooches, which were pretty, but nothing worth trading and certainly not worth stealing, so they were for use then and there; there were loom weights, which might mean cloth was woven in the house, but on a small scale. People were making a whole life onshore, women and men, sociable drinkers who liked the styles familiar from home. The house is unusual because it has two side aisles for sleeping, which take up much more space than in other houses around, as though crews were coming in and going out with cargo and needed somewhere to stay together: foreigners.

The house wasn't used for very long, just from the 800s to around 840, the time when Kaupang went from being a seasonal base to a settlement where people lived all year round. Those are also the years when the Frisians' tight control of trade on the southern North Sea was at its height and the time when it was starting to fray. The business of the house was basic goods, raw materials, the perfect opposite of all those crafted, gaudy bits and pieces once shipped about for the benefit of kings and grand persons. The Frisians dealt in ingots of copper alloy, most likely for the craftsmen in Kaupang; and they left behind such a trail of iron fragments that they may have been exporting iron. From Kaupang there were long valley routes by water and then land, up onto the vast mountain plateau of Hardangervidda, a treeless waste which produced remarkable ore; it made iron that was much less brittle than other sources, which made better steel and famously better axes. It was worth shipping out. They may have brought in amber, which commonly washed up on the Frisian coast; they left behind a very little waste from cutting and carving amber. They introduced hacksilver to Kaupang, silver goods chopped up to make them useable as money; and they certainly brought north their great idea: money itself.[60] The quantity of hacksilver, mind you, implies that coins were still too strange for daily deals.

*

Don't think for one moment that trade meant peace, not for the Frisians. The Franks to their south wanted their territory, their connections and their business, and took all of them by force. Radbod, the last independent king of Frisia before the Franks took over, sailed up the Rhine as far as Cologne, vengefully ruining and wrecking most thoroughly as he went;[61] a few years later a chronicler called the Frisians '*gens dirissima maritima*' – the hard men from the sea, ill-omened and terrible.[62]

The Vikings came raiding in 837 CE and found Frankish soldiers in Domburg to kill.[63] They also took away many women as captives and countless money of all kinds, and went up the Rhine to overrun Dorestad, a victory which cost them many dead;[64] they were stealing the Frisians' business, and the Frisians were murderously good at fighting back. When there was a Danish ruler later in Frisia, the Frisians shipped out with the Viking raiders when it suited them, even though the Vikings were taking over their bases, their ports and their business; they adapted, but their dominance was over because, in a way, they had taught their methods all too well.

They ending up doing their business on the very edge of the law. In Tiel, between Utrecht and Arnhem, the merchants complained that the Frisians were hard men with no respect for the law, working with robbers in the woods so that it was no longer possible to sail safely out to England or to have the English come with goods. The monk Alpert also noticed that, apart from being drunk in the morning and being unnecessarily tolerant of adultery (as long as the wife kept quiet) and running off at their filthy mouths, the Frisians were unusually tight-knit. He noticed they were sworn to support each other's stories even if it meant lying. They co-operated; they pooled their money at their drinking bouts, to pay for wine but also to share the profits of business. They kept their *terpen* principles even when the imperial army finally drove them out of their woods and their trade runs, and faced them down among the ditches and moats close to modern Rotterdam: the battle was the last, great Frisian victory, 29 July 1018.[65]

But the Frisian Sea: that already had new owners.

2.

# The book trade

There was nobody else alive, nobody who could read or preach or sing the service, except the abbot, Ceolfrith, and one bright boy: who was local, well-connected and about sixteen, and whose name was unusual. He was called Bede, and he wasn't called 'saint' or 'venerable', not yet.

In 686, the sun went dark behind the moon. When the eclipse ended the plague came suddenly from the sea. It broke into the monasteries like this double house at Jarrow and Wearmouth in Northumbria and all the little ports along the coast. It killed quickly. The old abbot, Eosterwine, was sick and dying and he called all the monks to him. 'With the compassion that was second nature to him, he gave them each the kiss of peace,' Bede remembered.[1] Nobody worried then about touching the sick; sickness was known to come in an impersonal miasma, a kind of mist; so the abbot's kindness killed almost all of them.

The deaths left a quiet in the stone church that was as bad as the sight of walls stripped of pictures or a library without books: the house was reminded that it had lost its glory. Music was not yet written down; it lived only in men's minds and could be learned only by ear; if it was not sung, it was lost. The monks had been taught 'at first hand' by the chief cantor of St Peter's in Rome,[2] and plainsong was one of great riches of the house; they were the first to sing Gregorian chant in Britain. But now the familiar antiphons, the sacred conversation of voices answering each other back and forth across the choir, were gone.

Ceolfrith was miserable, even tearful, and he stood the quiet for only a week. He needed to begin the familiar services again. He began by singing on his own, and then the boy Bede joined in: two voices instead of a dozen taking the parts. It was a thin sound in the small stone chancel, but they did what had to be done: they kept the music alive.[3]

The plague went away almost as suddenly as it had come, and Bede lived to see the monastery thriving again. A whole new generation of novices arrived. There were new political crises, especially a tyrant king called Osred, which made the monasteries into a most welcome refuge. When Ceolfrith decided to go to Rome in 716 he left 'behind him in his monasteries brethren to the number of around six hundred'.[4]

And this was all the world that Bede ever knew. He'd been taken to the monastery at the age of seven, and dedicated to the Church by parents who may have been quite grand and certainly lived close by. He hardly ever left, except for study in another monastery;[5] he never went on pilgrimage; he never travelled the fixed route from his home in the north-east of England to Ireland, which other men used in order to study or to escape the world or go out missioning. He could have gone overland from one church guest house to another, taking the usual three days and nights in each; he could have met up with the professional sailors who worked in the monastery on the island of Iona off the west coast of Scotland; he could have followed the tracks of his colleagues and predecessors to the Firth of Forth and then to the Firth of Clyde and then across to Derry. Those were regular routes even after the strong connection between the Christian communities at Lindisfarne and Iona was broken.[6] Instead, Bede lived almost always inside his new, closed family. He shared all its high emotions.

Before Ceolfrith there had been two abbots for the two monasteries, one at Jarrow and one at Wearmouth: Benedict Biscop and Sigfrith. The two men were deathly sick at the same time and Bede remembered how Sigfrith had to be carried on a pallet to see his friend, and set down to lie side by side on the same pillow. Their two faces were close, but the men did not even have the strength to kiss;

the monks had to reach down to turn their heads towards each other. Bede found it, he wrote, 'a sight to move you to tears'. When Benedict decided that the two houses should be run by one man, and that man should be Ceolfrith, Bede tells how their virtues bound the two men together 'more closely than any family relationship'.[7] This Ceolfrith was central to Bede's life, the father who never sent him away, and when Ceolfrith decided he would go again to Rome, this time to die, Bede had the one moment of crisis he acknowledges in all his life. In the preface to one of his biblical commentaries he writes of the consternation he felt, the 'sudden anguish of mind'.[8]

Being shut in by the monastery walls, the only way Bede could know the world outside was to read, study and ask; he had to build his whole world with books. The library Bede knew, some two hundred manuscripts, had been assembled by men who thought books for reading were just as important as pictures or relics or music. Benedict Biscop, the founder of the house, brought back 'a large number of books on all branches of sacred knowledge' from his third trip to Rome, 'some bought at a favourable price, others the gifts of well-wishers'.[9] The book trade was flourishing and it was complicated: Bede could read at Jarrow a codex of the Acts of the Apostles, Greek and Latin versions, which had been in Sardinia until the seventh century and ended up later in Germany.[10] On Biscop's next trip, he brought back 'spiritual treasures of all kinds' but 'in the first place he returned with a great mass of books of every sort'. Everything else – relics of the saints, holy pictures, music in the Roman manner and even a promise of perpetual independence from any outside interference – comes further down the list in Bede's account. His friend and mentor Ceolfrith, the third abbot, 'doubled the number of books in the libraries of both monasteries', he says, 'with an ardour equal to that which Benedict had shown in founding them'.[11]

These books were Bede's work. From the time he became a priest at the age of thirty 'until the age of 59' he says he spent his time studying Scripture, collecting and annotating the works of the Church fathers and making extracts from them, adding his own explanations, even putting right one rotten translation from the Greek.[12] He was under orders from his bishop to gather and make a digest of the books around him because they were so many and so long that only the very rich could own them and so deep that only the very learnèd could understand them.[13] He was to take the riches of the Jarrow and Wearmouth library, manuscripts of all ages and origins, and publish them to all those houses which did not have a decent library at all.[14] Books were not fine possessions to be stored away, precious but not for use; they were a practical way to distribute ideas and information, ship them out and share them.

Bede knew the whole process of making books from imagining and dictating the words to being the clerk who took them down, in the medieval version of the Roman shorthand called 'Tironian notes', a puzzle of dots, bows and teardrops, curved, wavy and straight lines all tilted five different ways and taking their meaning from where they were placed on the page. The code was an important part of literacy; it was schoolroom stuff.[15] He also knew about being the scribe, the one who made fair or even lovely copies of the final result; he worked on one glorious coloured and decorated Bible, the *Codex Amiatinus*, which was given to the Pope.[16]

So he worked in the *scriptorium*, the writing place, a narrow world inside the monastery. Everyone wrote exactly the same way: a neat, uniform and impersonal hand. In Jarrow, the writing was an uncial script, which is round like your first schooldays writing, but all in capital letters. Getting it right was very important because uncial script was Roman, and Jarrow was very much a monastery which looked to Rome. The Irish monks on Iona used an island script, and they had full heads of hair; at Jarrow the monks had the tonsure and they wrote in the Roman way because to do anything else would have bordered on heresy. Rome and the Celtic Church in the North were still arguing over issues such as how to date Easter, and writing was a way to choose sides. The scribes could sometimes play and make something personal in the decoration of the page, even glory in the beauty of what they could make, but it would be centuries before scribes could have reputations as artists. The act of writing was anonymous and a matter of monastic discipline.[17]

They wrote with black ink made of oak galls and iron salts, using goose feather quills. They wrote on parchment: sheepskin or the hide of a calf, shaved, polished and cut until it had the texture of a kind of suede and a colour close to ivory, between white and yellow. When they wanted colours, gold was gold leaf, silver was silver leaf, fixed to the page. Black in the painted patterns and images was usually carbon, white was chalk or crushed shells; blue was woad before the much more costly lapis lazuli was easily available, purple came from lichen, yellow from a salt of arsenic, oranges and reds from toasted lead, and for green the scribes used verdigris, made by holding copper over vinegar for a while. A scribe making a book as lovely as the bible made at Jarrow for the Pope, or the Gospels made at Lindisfarne, was chemist and artist all at the same time, especially in the making of subtler colours like the surprising, polished pinks.[18]

Writing hours were daylight hours because that was the best possible light, three hours at a time and usually two shifts in a day; 'it is hard to bend the neck and furrow parchment for twice three hours,' a scribe writes on one manuscript, and another, on an eighth-century manuscript, says, 'He who does not know how to write thinks it is no labour. Yet although the scribe writes with three fingers, his whole body toils.' Irish scribes had a way of gossiping and complaining in the margins: 'I am very cold' or 'That's a hard page and a weary work to read it' or 'Oh that a glass of good old wine were at my side.' Their notes may have been for people working alongside them, because sometimes a team of four or more would work together on a single manuscript;[19] but some were entirely personal, as when a scribe writes out the scene of Judas Iscariot betraying Christ with a kiss and adds in the margin: 'Wretch!'

Then after the evening service of Compline there was time for cutting, polishing and ruling the skins for parchment. The ruling, done with the sharp point of a stylus or an awl, was vital if the text was to line up; pages were written separately and they had to face each other squarely in the finished book. There was also the business of discreetly correcting the pages already written. Correcting meant adjusting the letters and making sure they were the proper ones, but also putting in punctuation, which was often done after the words and letters had been written out.[20] Punctuation was points, and the longer the pause the more there were and the higher they appeared above each line.

Everything about Bede's life makes it seem that he was regulated and confined – everything except the books he wrote. His monastery was not strictly Benedictine but he closely obeyed the Benedictine rule of stability: to stay put. He chose never to be a pilgrim like the abbots of his house, even though he knew very well that the Irish thought you could hardly be Christian without travel to Rome, to shrines, to other places of learning. Most of his writing is careful, thoughtful accounts of the Bible, book by book, the kind of work that is best done in a closed, quiet room; and he was also, as he says, very familiar with the brisk, meticulous business of being in a *scriptorium*. So what liberated his mind to puzzle over where he was in time, and how the moon affected the sea and what might explain the plague even better than God's anger?

For a start, monasteries were not at all cut off from the general world. Plague proved that. In the months after the sickness 'of great villages and estates once crowded with inhabitants only a tiny scattered remnant remained, and sometimes not even that,' Bede wrote.[21] The monasteries shared their fate because they were often on the coast, which was where plague landed; plague travelled fastest by sea. They were also connected to all those great villages and estates, for monasteries were markets, hubs for trade in commodities like salt; people were always arriving and leaving. Villagers came in to worship, and monks went out to minister to the villages. Even on the more remote monastery island of Lindisfarne, sickness persisted for a year and almost every man died; even Lindisfarne was in the world.

The most surprising scraps of knowledge filtered into the *scriptorium*. In the bible that Jarrow made for the Pope there are curious marks on the golden halo round the head of Ezra the Scribe: they may just be *tefillin*, the tiny leather boxes holding fragments of the Torah that some Jews wear. Ezra also wears the headdress and breastplate of a proper Jewish high priest.[22] It is true that Christians later had to be stopped from wearing St John's Gospel as a cure for headache, which is a mutation of the same idea, but someone knew actual Jewish customs. The elegant designs on the page that look like the most subtle carpets owe much to Coptic art, and to the kind of prayer mats that were used in the Middle East and only later in Northumbria. When the monks came to bind up St Cuthbert's own bible, buried with him as a kind of Book of Life, they sewed the binding in a distinctly Coptic style.

These elaborate decorations meant experiments with new techniques and new tools. Eadfrith of Lindisfarne, in the very early eighth century, started to use lead to draw out his designs on the back of the page; then he set the sketches on a frame of transparent horn or glass and put a strong light behind them so he could consult his design as he painted the page itself. He worked alone so his inventions went no further at the time, they were as hidden as he was, but they were remarkable: he made the first lightbox and the first lead pencil.[23]

Bede did much more than make scrapbooks out of the texts he knew. He checked and changed, left things out and added to the old ideas; he thought again. He chose which old books to believe when he wrote history and he reshaped history by fitting the particular history of England into the grand and biblical story of the whole world.[24] He was trying something extraordinary: to see where he stood in time.

He puzzled over things that others took for granted, like the plague and how it could be God's will when these were the happiest times for the English and their Church,[25] the age when they had Christian kings to rule them and priests to teach them and the whole of England was learning to sing holy songs. If disease was God's judgement on sinners, 'the avenger of evil deeds'[26] as it was supposed to be in pagan times, then why was He punishing His people now for doing the right thing?

When he came to write his schoolbook about nature, *De rerum natura*, Bede looked beyond the Bible and the usual written authorities; he used experience. He connected plague with the thunderstorms that break up summer and start the autumn, to the corruption of the air due to excessive dryness or heat or rain. He had no grand theory, but he looked and asked questions. He was right about the season for plague, although he never knew the reason. The sickness was spread by fleas that lived on the bodies of rats, which fed on the corn transported by ships, which sailed in the summer.[27]

He saw the moon riding higher in the sky than the sun and asked how that was possible when everyone knew the moon was closer to the Earth. His explanation was an elegant experiment in thought: he asked his readers to imagine they were walking at night into an immense church, all brightly lit for some saint's day and with two particularly brilliant lamps: one hanging high at the far end, one hanging lower but closer. As you walked into the church the lamp that's closer would seem to be hanging higher than the lamp in the distance and as you walked forward it would seem to move higher and higher still until you were directly under it and the truth was obvious: it seemed higher precisely because it was closer.[28]

He casually suggested that it would be easier to work out the age of the moon if you knew your fifty-nine-times table, which suggests that he did; he used mathematics even though it was hard to manage any complicated sum using the inflexible Roman numerals. His near contemporary Aldhelm used to complain that remembering the numbers to carry over when adding or dividing or multiplying or subtracting was so difficult that he could manage only when 'sustained by heavenly grace'.[29] Bede's method was to do sums on his hands, not on paper, with a system of straight and bent fingers in different combinations that could reach 9,999; after that, he says without explaining, you need other parts of the body. The system had other attractions for a boy in the quiet monastery, a scribe in the silence of the *scriptorium*. Just agree a simple code, settle on a number for each of the twenty-three letters of the Roman alphabet, and the system allowed silent talk across a room.[30]

Bede fixed the story of how the Anglo-Saxons came to Britain and how they brought true Christianity; he wrote commentaries on Scripture that were in demand across Europe; but more than those, he was the hero of *computus*. It may have been his most remarkable achievement at the time, but even the word is unfamiliar now, let alone the thinking: a blend of maths, astronomy and ideas about how the universe is shaped, all combined to establish a true and proper calendar. Anything to do with number had an element of holy mystery since as one Irish text has it 'take number away and everything lapses into ruin'. The calendar also had everything to do with medicine, since diagnosis and treatment were linked to astronomical time, but *computus* had one main use: to calculate the date of Easter.

The whole Christian year was shaped by the date of Easter; but the Church's own rules for fixing it meant Easter fell on a different Sunday each year, a floating feast. It was not just the most important festival, the day for remembering the event that gave Christianity meaning; it was also one of only two feast days on which anyone could be baptized into the Church, unless they were in imminent danger of dying unsaved. The other was Whitsun,[31] and that always fell seven Sundays later. Without a settled date for Easter, nobody would know when to begin the long forty-day fast of Lent, which ends on Easter Day. So the date had to be set well in advance; it was not like the Islamic Ramadan which can be fixed by observation, watching for a full moon and the equinox. Fixing Easter required a kind of calculus.

It involved bringing two different calendars into line: the thirteen months of the Jewish calendar and the twelve months of the Roman calendar. The Gospels say Christ died during the Jewish feast of Passover, and Passover is fixed on the first full moon of 'the first month' in the Jewish lunar calendar. That would seem clear enough, except that the early Church fathers decided that it really meant the first full moon after the spring equinox, and that is where the trouble started. The date of the equinox was fixed according to the very different Roman calendar, which follows the sun. And since the solar year isn't a round number of days, the actual equinox tends to come adrift from its official date, which complicates things even more.

This was a political issue. The Church was one Church, united, so it could not celebrate Easter on different days in different places. The Church was ruled from Rome, whatever the Irish Church thought, so the date had to be the one set in Rome. But the Irish insisted that news did not always travel reliably from Rome, so they devised their own way of fixing the date, and those ways did not agree with Roman ways. Bede was a true Roman, and he set out to find a universal answer to the problem.

He had to be radical. He was not being a historian now; he was looking to future dates and saying what would happen. He had to find names for years that were still in the future, something which neither Germans nor Romans did; they both named years after the king, emperor or consul in power at the time, so that Bede's own monastery was begun in the twenty-ninth year of the reign of King Ecgfrith rather than what we know as 674 CE.[32] He used thought and facts to solve an immediate problem, which was something the ancients hardly ever did in writing; their science was the recording of facts for their own sake. He needed a practical result from numbers, with (and despite) all their holy and mystical significance. He then had to deal with the Irish, and find a formula that Rome could happily endorse.

He showed how the moon years and sun years came together in cycles of nineteen Roman years. Writers before him had worked out the cycle, but he was the writer who gave them authority and spread the idea; he published it. For that, he had to understand the movements of sun and moon. He began with the written authorities in the library, who had ideas on how the moon works in the world: the bishops who said oysters grow fatter as the moon grows fuller, that wood cut after the full moon will never rot, that the more moonlight there is, the more dew. Then Bede observed for himself the phases of the moon and their real effect in the world.

He took what the Irish already understood, the connection between the stages of the moon and the force and height of the tides, and he brought that to everyone's attention. He also refined it. He understood that the moon rising later each day was linked to the tide rising later each day, a pattern he could never have recognized without knowing that the Earth was round.[33] From this he built a theory: the tides were not water gushing out of some northern abyss, nor water somehow created by the moon, but the moon tugging at the sea ('as if the ocean were dragged forward against its will'). He measured the tides against the phases of the moon, and he measured them exactly, to the minute. For his history he had correspondents in many other monasteries along the coast from Iona in the west to the Isle of Wight in the south, and he may have asked the monks in each place to make observations for him, too.[34] However he did it, he certainly knew that the time of the tides could be different in different places ('we who live at various places along the coastline of the British Sea know that when the tide begins to run at one place, it will start to ebb at another'). He found that both moonrise and high tide were a little later each day, later by exactly 47½ minutes.

For centuries his work was mined for astronomical information. When it was finally printed and published eight centuries later – in Basle in 1529 and then in Cologne in 1537 – it was not out of antiquarian interest. It still had immediate, practical value,[35] despite the need for notes to explain all the difficult bits. Indeed, his work has often survived better than his reasons for doing it. We still date events from the 'year of Our Lord', *Annus Domini*, the year of Christ's birth; that was Bede's invention – part of his solution to the problem of the calendar. Christianity was only just growing out of its eschatological phase, when the world was expected to end any day, and Bede wanted to rewrite world history and its ages to prove that the world still had a long time to live. He wanted to place himself in time, past and future, and in doing so he built the Western calendar as we know it.

He found himself arguing on occasions with the living and the dead, which could be dangerous in a Church that valued authority so much, and Bede had reason to know that. He once heard that he had been accused of heresy by someone who was having dinner with a bishop. He was aghast, he told his friend Plegwin, he went white. He said the talk was from 'drunk peasants', that it was 'abusive talk of the foolish'; but it was disconcerting to be denounced, and denounced for a detail. His offence was that when calculating the seven ages of the world, he implied that each age need not be exactly one thousand years, which was the usual version; he wrote of 'the unstable ages of this world'.[36] He was arguing with everybody else's assumptions, which would later seem his great and even heroic virtue.

Twenty years later, writing a new book, he was still furious.

Christians and missionaries bought books, shared books, copied books. Having their doctrine on the page gave it a particular authority; they were, after all, the People of the Book. Since all information had to be shipped about, on the page or in someone's head, it can seem that they must have carried reading and writing itself into the North, that we owe them literacy and not just in Latin. But the story is more complicated than that. The habit of writing and reading had reached Ireland before St Patrick came over on his mission; and what brought it was the trade that went back and forth across the sea.

For Ireland wasn't isolated before the missionaries arrived. Tacitus says the approaches to its ports were well known to traders in the first century CE. Words crossed from Latin into Irish even if Irish made them hard to pronounce; so the Latin *purpura* for fine cloth turned into *corcur*; the Irish *long*, a ship, is from the Latin for a longship, *navis longa*; and the Irish *ingor* comes from the Latin *ancora*, for an anchor. These are sea words, about sailing and about the goods that ships were carrying, and the words made the crossing before the fifth century. Military words also crossed, words the Christian missionaries did not need: words for a legion, a soldier, weapons and weekday names that are tributes to Roman gods such as *Mercúir* for Wednesday (and Mercury) and *Saturn* for Saturday.

The Irish were outside the empire, so they did not have to play by Roman rules. They did not need reading and writing in order to rise in the imperial bureaucracy. They settled questions about who owned which piece of land by hearing witnesses and swearing oaths and paying attention to the memory of a community. When they first carved words onto stone, using the Irish *ogam* script, they were making simple memorials to the names of the dead, markers that were solid enough to stand as boundary markers and more reliable than memory. But the Irish were also trading with the Romans, and that required either memory or records that the Romans would understand; in their voyages to Gaul or to Wales, the Irish quickly learned that the Romans' language was different, and was written a different way. At the same time they were working out their own way of writing down their Irish language. The *ogam* alphabet grew out of the marks made on wooden tally sticks to count sheep and cattle, but its other purpose may have been to mystify the Roman functionaries and merchants, who knew only their own letters.

This meant that when Patrick arrived to convert Ireland in the fifth century, he had a head start. He was preaching the faith of the Book, carrying with him books of the law and the Gospels, and the Irish had their own habit of writing and reading already. They knew something about the technology. There are clues in the Irish law tracts written later, in the seventh century, which lay down that a contract can be proved by, among other things, 'a godly old writing', and witnesses can make a dead man's agreement stand but only if they are not contradicted by relevant texts cut onto stones. Writing settles deep into Irish law.[37] Much more remarkably, in his life of Patrick, the seventh-century monk Muirchú tells how the missionary found himself in a contest of magic with King Lóeguire's druid. The king told the two to pitch their books into the water, and they'd see which god was worth adoring. The druid said he'd rather not because he knew about baptism and Patrick's God was obviously a water god. It's true that Muirchú was writing two hundred years later, and maybe he took for granted that the Irish had always had books because he had them himself, but the more likely story is literal: druids had some form of book, perhaps metal leaves, perhaps wood or stone, which could rival the Book. Patrick taught some men their alphabet to make them priests and bishops, but not all men needed the lessons.[38]

This fact that the Irish wrote down Irish very early still matters very much: it made books useful.

Books could always be lovely things, used like jewels: sealed into shrines or put on an altar where nobody could possibly read them or sent to Rome as splendid presents for the Pope.

Boniface wrote to the Abbess Eadburga on his mission to convert Frisia, asking her for a truly showy book, 'a copy written in gold' of the Epistles of Peter so as 'to impress honour and reverence for the Sacred Scriptures visibly upon the carnally minded to whom I preach'.[39] His other need, with age, was for clarity. He asked the Bishop of Winchester for a particular copy of the Prophets that he knew was written out clearly, because 'with my fading sight, I cannot read well writing which is small and filled with abbreviations'.[40]

His books were written in an unbroken caterpillar of letters, nothing to separate the words, and they were meant to be read out loud, which required a reader who could make words and sense out of the string of letters on the page, and an audience used to hearing Latin. Many other peoples in Western Europe spoke a version of Latin, and they could understand the real old thing, but the Irish spoke a very different language; when a text was read out loud it was entirely different from daily talk and it gave them no clues to its meaning. They wanted words for the eye, not the ear. They wanted to see the form of the words clearly so they could translate their meaning, and therefore they began to put spaces between the words. Then they introduced their most brilliant invention: punctuation. Not only were the words distinct on the page: it was also clear where an idea stopped or paused or started.[41]

Silent, individual reading now became much easier. It had always been a way to meditate on the meaning of a book, and understand it better, right back to the fourth-century St Ambrose, who was notorious for reading silently even when he had visitors. Now the habit could spread. New monastic rules punished anyone who read aloud, but just under their breath so as not to seem old-fashioned; they spoiled the quiet reading for everyone else.[42]

Books for reading could be written out quickly and plainly: they were books for use. The Irish scribes trained Anglo-Saxon scribes. The first Christian missionaries to England had had to send for their books from Gaul or Rome, but in Bede's time their libraries were being sent to Gaul to be copied. Bede, Boniface and the less famous Tatwine were all copied in northern France, in the monastery at Corbie.[43] The most careful and solid text of Jerome's Vulgate Bible was written out at Jarrow and Wearmouth and Lindisfarne, based on a manuscript from Naples; it rapidly became the standard version in all Northern Europe.[44] By the seventh century there were already significant libraries in England. The Anglo-Saxons went out to found schools across the Germanic lands, and they became missionaries for words: the scholar Alcuin learned the new writing techniques in York and then took them over the sea to Charlemagne's court in the 780s. He promoted a new idea: 'the close study of letters'.[45]

Anglo-Saxon scribes, too, were on the move, and not just with the various missions. They taught the court of Charlemagne the new idea of a library which should be well stocked with books and well organized for study.[46] Charlemagne's held historical books and 'the doings of the ancients', which were read aloud in the king's presence, along with Charlemagne's favourite, the works of St Augustine. When Alcuin was away from the court and wanted a copy of Pliny's *Historia naturalis*, he asked to have it sent to him. On another occasion he wrote simply to ask someone to look something up in the bookchests of the court for him. This taste for books and the production of manuscripts caught on.[47] Well into the ninth century, Anglo-Saxons were still crossing the sea to write in German monasteries, long after the first waves of missionary work.[48] Some of the books they wrote were lovely and even spectacular, but most were portable information. With separate words and clear marks of where ideas began and ended, anyone could read in her own time for her own reasons.[49]

People wanted to read Bede. Anglo-Saxons overseas wanted his account of Saxon triumphs. The growth of the English Church inspired a wide audience as English missionaries worked to convert the Frisians and the Germans. By the ninth century, the books reached St Gallen on what is now the Swiss border, where the monk Walahfrid Strabo put together a collection of key quotes for teaching and included Bede. They were in Reichenau, the island monastery in Lake Constance, and the cathedral library at Würzburg in Bavaria. They turn up in central France as deep as Tours. Bede from the edge of the world was being published over the sea to the known world.

It was a world of gifts, a routine of absolutely unavoidable exchanges: gifts up and down the social ladder, from kings to knights to keep them loyal, from knights to kings to keep them giving, from bishops to cardinals and from cardinals to priests; from Ireland to Northumbria to Frisia to Rome and beyond. Gifts bound people together in their proper ranks and obligations. Gifts were about power, and making it visible. When in Germany, the missionary Boniface sent silver to Rome and got back incense, and on one occasion a face towel and a bath towel; he sometimes sent unspectacular things like 'four knives made by us in our fashion' or 'a bundle of reed pens' because gifts were messages and statements much more than requests for something in return, and the act of giving was the whole point. At times his gifts were as diplomatic as state gifts to royalty today, but a bit more pointed. Boniface sent a hawk and two falcons to the King of Mercia to get him to listen to a message that he was not going to like at all, a dressing-down for his appalling sexual habits, especially in convents.

Of all the gifts that he received, Boniface tells the Abbess Eadburga, he most appreciated 'the solace of books and the comfort of the garments'.[50] Giving and sharing books became a system for putting ideas out into the world.

The glorious bible that Bede and others made at Jarrow was a gift for the Pope. Books were also buried with the saintly dead as gifts to keep them company. The book as gift, then, was sometimes quite different from the book to be read, a difference which later became almost ridiculous. One famous English calligrapher called Earnwine gave a fine book of psalms to King Canute and Queen Emma, who promptly sent it off to Cologne as a gift. When the Bishop of Worcester was in Cologne on the king's business, he was naturally given a present, which happened to be Earnwine's psalter. He brought it back to England, where it began.[51] Nobody ever had to read a book like that.

Books were also sent about so they could be copied and copied again; the text itself was the gift. Boniface, like Bede, wanted that kind of book. He sometimes knew exactly which one he was after, and at other times he fished about for titles. He asked a former student for 'whatever you may find in your church library which you think would be useful to me and which I may not be aware of or may not have in written form'.[52] Just knowing which books existed and which you wanted was not at all easy; which is why Bede added a list of all his works at the end of the *Historia ecclesiastica*, including the biblical books he studied, the heroic verse he wrote, the terrible translation of a Greek text that he edited and corrected, his books on time and the nature of things, his hymns, his epigrams and his book on spelling.[53] It reads a little like the back matter of a modern paperback. A librarian at Murbach in the ninth century was drawing up lists of books the monastery needed from the catalogues of other libraries and references in the manuscripts that he could examine; he was still using Bede's list.[54] He made notes alongside the names of some authors: 'we are seeking his remaining books' and 'we want to find many others'.[55]

This world of books was not a locked room full of chained volumes, the picture of later monastery libraries. Books moved. The territories that did not have Bede's *History* directly from Jarrow sometimes took copies of a copy made from the copy in Charlemagne's court library, and distributed by his orders.[56] Boniface had to tell Abbess Bugga that he couldn't send the writings she wanted 'for I have been prevented by pressure of work and by my continual travels from completing the book you ask for. When I have finished it, I shall see that it is sent to you.'[57] The notion of a busy missionary archbishop copying whole books for someone else may be less surprising if copying was also a way of studying. A bishop tells an abbot he's not returning a book because 'Bishop Gutbert has not yet returned it.'[58] Gutbert was Archbishop of Canterbury at the time. A young abbot can't send back a book because, he says, the very important Abbot of Fulda wants time to make himself a copy.[59]

The books that circulated this way were not just books about the Bible and the Church. Later, holy libraries consisted mostly of the Church fathers, the founders of the story of the Church, although even then one monk wanted Suetonius and those good dirty stories about the Caesars.[60] But in Bede's time, and for centuries afterwards, monasteries and cathedrals also cared for the pagan leftovers of Rome. Long before the official Renaissance brought back classical culture and Latin texts, which would not have been possible if nobody had bothered to preserve them in the first place, the Irish were fussing with Virgil; when a seventh-century schoolmaster says he's just had some valuable copies from 'the Romans' he might just possibly mean the ones in Rome, but more likely he means the Irish scholars influenced by Rome.[61] In the mid eighth century a nun called Burginda made a copy of a commentary on the Song of Songs and added a careful, wordy letter to the 'distinguished young man' who received it; her Latin misfires a bit, and she makes a mess of the subjunctive, but she knows how to quote Virgil so she must have found Virgil in her convent library alongside assorted holy works. Ecburg, Abbess of Gloucester, used Virgil too in a letter to explain in proper, flowery terms her pain at being separate from her sister: 'everywhere cruel sorrow, everywhere fear and all the images of death', almost a direct quotation.[62]

And yet a pagan poet was a problem: essential, but dangerous. The scholar Alcuin read Virgil as a boy, imitated him in his own poems, but when he became an abbot he forbade his novices to read the man at all.[63] In Carolingian schools Virgil might have been the very first heathen author the children read, mostly as an example of how to make verse scan,[64] but he was firmly labelled heathen. Monasteries filed the heathen books among the schoolbooks and grammar because they were to be read in gobbets only, for their style and not their meaning, and under careful supervision. Nobody was supposed to pay attention to all the love, sensuality and battles.

If you had the right connections, you could borrow books from these holy libraries. One affluent noble, Eccard of Macon, had to write into his will instructions to send back the books he had from the monastery at Fleury, a chestful of them that he obviously had never meant to return in a hurry. The cathedral librarian at Cologne wrote loans down carefully at the end of his book list, but he had to leave whole pages blank in case Ermbaldus, a most enthusiastic borrower, decided to borrow yet more books 'for the exercise of his ministry'.[65]

To know laws and charters, to rule and know what you were ruling, it was very useful to read if not essential. Laymen owned books about law, about God, about farming and about war: the knowledge a noble needed. We know because they left them to their children in their wills, each title given to a particular child, so the books were something valued and considered. They often included history books, the history of the popes, the doings of the Franks. We can guess that the long poems in Latin and the historical stories at Charlemagne's court were meant for a lay audience, and a rather grand lay audience at that. But the mighty were not exactly encouraged to take this literacy business too far. One eighth-century boy called Gerald was told to stop reading when he had worked through the Psalms and it was time for him to study more serious matters like archery, riding to hounds, and flying hawks and falcons. He did go back to books, but only because 'For a long time he was so covered in small spots that it was thought he could not be cured. So his mother and father decided he should be put more closely to the study of letters.' In Gerald's case, remarkably, 'even when he became strong, he continued to study'.

Books could be heirlooms, and they could also be assets. In Bede's time Benedict Biscop bought a lovely book of cosmographies while he was in Rome, an account of the whole known world. Back in England the very literate, even bibliophile, King Aldfrith offered to give the monastery land in return for the book, enough riverside land to support eight families.[66] The deal meant books were a very important part of a monastery's useful wealth. When the Emperor Charlemagne died, he left his library to be sold 'for an appropriate price' and the money given to the poor.[67] He knew there would be a market.

What's more, books were stolen. The Baltic pirates who caught Anskar, 'the Apostle of the North', sailing to Sweden and made him walk the rest of the way were not at all averse to the forty books he was carrying with him.[68] The Benedictine Loup de Ferrières in the ninth century worried about sending a work of Bede's to an archbishop because the book was too big to hide on anyone's person or even in a bag, and even if it could be hidden 'one would have to fear an attack of robbers who would certainly be attracted by the beauty of the book'. More tellingly, a monastery in the Ardennes lost a psalter written in gold and decorated with pearls, which turned up intact and was bought in good faith by a pious woman; so it was the book that had value, not its incidental jewels.[69]

Laymen could always hire a scribe out of the *scriptorium* to do their copying, although they need not expect any holy indifference to the price; as the scribe says in Ælfric Bata's eleventh-century instructional text, 'Nothing is more dear to me than that you give me cash, since whoever has cash can acquire anything he wants.' Some laymen chose to write books out for themselves. Someone on a mission with the army, most likely a lay soldier, spent his time copying a collection of saints' lives. Someone else, called Ragambertus, wrote out the letters of Seneca and put a note on the manuscript in ornate capital letters: 'Ragambertus, just a no-account layman with a beard, wrote this text.'[70]

Other people wrote books out of love, and terror. The noblewoman Dhuoda was apprehensive when her oldest son, William, went away to battle at the age of sixteen, and she wrote him a little book to take with him. 'I want you,' she wrote, 'when you are weighed down by lots of worldly and temporal activity, to read this little book I have sent you.' She wrote of the joy other women had in living with their children, and how anxious she was about being separated from William and how eager she was to be useful. She had read widely, even if what she read may mostly have been books of extracts from homilies and the lives of saints and the works of the Church fathers. She knew the Bible and she had read and thought about a poet like Ovid, and she culled what she thought would help her son while he was away. Her pain is vivid even now, a loving woman whose child was suddenly wrenched away into an adult and murderous world; she writes of her 'heart burning within'. She wants her son to go on reading as a kind of moral shield against the life he was going to live at court and the wars he was going to fight; 'I urge you, William, my handsome, lovable son, amid the worldly preoccupations of your life, not to be slow in acquiring many books.'[71]

Books took effort, time, skill. Books required dead calves, polished skins, the making of ink and colours and pens, the ruling of guidelines. They had to be written out by hand, carefully, and corrected and punctuated and decorated; they had to be sewn together so they would stay in their proper order. They required craft. They also required words, either a book to copy or else someone to invent and dictate. They mattered for their content, of course: Bede helped change people's minds about the proper date of Easter, the way to date our lives in the history of the world, what happened in Britain when it became both Christian and Anglo-Saxon. But books also began to matter for themselves, even when they were practical books for reading and not jewelled, painted lovelies.

Books were becoming independent of the way they were meant to be read. It came to this: books were worth burning.

Gottschalk found this out. He was a monk, a poet, a bit of a wanderer who never wanted to settle in one house, and he had unconventional ideas: he was, roughly, a Calvinist seven hundred years before Calvin. He had come to think that all men were predestined either to Hell or to Heaven; that was God's will, and no amount of good deeds or even bad ones could undo it.

This was not the view of the Church, so he was ordered to appear, in 849, before the synod of the clergy in Quierzy, which is a town in Picardy, to answer for his opinions. He went along thinking he would be allowed to argue his case, so he carried with him the Bible texts he had used, and the writings of the Church fathers, the papers he needed to make his points: evidence, if you like. He expected discussion, but he was too optimistic. He found himself accused of heresy, flogged until he was on the point of death and told to keep silence for the rest of his life. Later, he'd be told he could be buried in holy ground only if he declared that he had changed his mind. He refused.

The priests insisted on something else: they burned his books. They took Bible passages and Church fathers, books available in many places and entirely proper, and burned them publicly as though they could purge and cauterize all of Gottschalk's thoughts about them in one fire. They were determined that nobody should read those books as Gottschalk read them, that his view of them and his opinions should be silenced as his mouth was: they were killing the ideas. The ashes from the fire are brutal proof that they now knew reading could change the use and meaning of a book. Nothing about a book was safe any more.[72]

# 3.

# Making enemies

Their ships were on the move from around 700 CE. The Vikings didn't burst out of the north like some flight of arrows; they had been trad ing, sailing about widely enough to know where there were riches, and better yet where the riches were portable and close to the coast. They came south to find a regular connection with anyone in Western Europe who wanted skins and furs and walrus ivory. They brought luxuries out of the eastern Baltic and the rivers of Russia,[1] the goods so expensive they were worth carrying in small quantities in a small ship: like amber, which was lovely and almost as obscenely valuable as diamonds now. They were the mercenaries of Byzantium, the traders of Kiev and capable of coming ashore at will in the Black Sea, the Mediterranean, the Atlantic coast of Spain and finally North America. Their connections to the trade routes gave them the local knowledge they needed to decide where it was worth going out as pirates, and also where they could dispose of the loot; because a man can't eat a gilded reliquary or a few hundred metres of fine cloth.

They were also less predictable than other pirates and the imperial raiders, because they knew how to tack into the wind, so they did not have to let the wind decide their course, or wait for it. A startled cosmographer from Andalucia reported that they had 'big ships with square sails and could sail either forwards or backwards'.[2] Owning a great ship that was moved solely by manpower was a sign of high social standing, but they did not depend on oars and muscle; their ships had single sails, some of them huge affairs of woven wool sewn[3] together, as much as a hundred square metres for the grandest. A ship was an investment of money, time and life. It took thirty weeks to weave a sail sixteen metres square, and half a kilometre of planks to make the hull, not to mention timber for mast and spars and the iron that had to be smelted and formed for nails and rivets to hold the ship together.[4] A ship didn't just show how rich or powerful or grand a man might be; it was his being.

Their armies leaving port would run up the sails but then use manpower to row the ships out to sea, into the strongest waves; and row on even when the sails were set higher. Rowing was good for manoeuvring a warship or the heavier freighters that came later, but sails gave ships stamina and speed. Saxons may have used them before the Vikings came, and there may have been others on the North Sea,[5] but it was Viking boats with sails that became such extraordinary machines. They could cross the widest part of the North Sea, more or less six hundred kilometres, in four or five days and without any of the usual need to cling to the shore and spend the nights on dry land.

So the world of the Norsemen was not the same as other people's worlds, not even the world that the Frisians knew. The Old Norse texts make it clear that the centre of their world was in the North, not in Jerusalem as it was on the usual world maps further south, and their headquarters were not in Rome as the Church imagined; Vikings did not see themselves on the edge of things. They could already operate through a world much wider than the world of Romans or Saxons or Britons. They knew there was land across the ocean to the west, but they did not know its shape or exactly where it lay. They defied a strain of Christian orthodoxy just by thinking that people could live south of the Earth's hot zones, where it is summer when the north has winter. Most likely, too, their time at sea, navigating with the help of wide horizons, had taught them that the Earth itself was a sphere and not a pancake on top of a ball as learnèd men were supposed to think. They knew how to sail out to sea so the curve of the earth would hide them from the land. They knew they could trick an enemy, as King Olaf tricked Erling in the sagas, by lowering their sails gradually so they seemed to be sailing over the horizon.[6] They used every advantage that a round Earth could provide.[7]

And they knew where they were going. The magnetic compass arrived in the North some time in the thirteenth century, but the Vikings already had a brilliantly simple sun compass. It worked as a sundial works, by tracking the tip of the shadows thrown by a stick at different times of day; where the shadow is shortest and the sun is highest, the shadow points north and south. It was useless in rain or snow or fog, but in the sailing season, which was the summer of endless light, it was a huge advantage. Such a compass belonged among Norsemen because the North had winter; people who were used to travelling over blank snowscapes, where the landmarks are buried and the detail is all smoothed away, needed to make such a device.[8] Once they had it, they could also sail a featureless ocean as far as America.

As for who they were, what they were, that was easy: they were enemy. They were the others, the ones not like the rest, and their brilliance at sea brought them far too close for comfort. Their sense that voyaging was something worth recording and praising and honouring[9] did not make them sympathetic, as it would in later years. Their great stories had not yet been written down, not even told aloud, so their habits and their history were unknown. Since what they did – raid, plunder, slave – was all too close to what everybody else did, given the chance, there had to be some other dimension to make them a proper enemy: they had to be demons. Nobody expects to understand what demons do.

There were clues, though. For a start, the Danes were unsettled by the steady spread north of the Frankish empire. In 734, Charles the Hammer took Frisia for the Franks and was all too close to the Danes' southern borders. Within three years the Danes were working on their defences, building a strong oak palisade, two metres high, to cross their southern frontier, and putting a barrage across the bay at the south of Jutland. They could never have built such a barrier without the kind of powerful king who makes local nobles anxious enough to obey his commands. Somebody had to organize and commandeer a quick and large operation, not to mention the naval support it needed. That somebody had the power to be just oppressive enough to persuade local Danish lords, used to their own independent power, that they might as well take their chances on the sea.[10]

Further north there was less kingship. Harald Finehair was still struggling to create a Norway he could rule, even if some men were already calling themselves 'Norwegian'. There was less of a state, but the same squabble of nobles. So little of Norway could be ploughed and planted that even the kindness of the climate in the last centuries of the first millennium could not make the land truly valuable; it was swamp, lakes, mountain and the kind of conifer forests that ruin the soil.[11] Riches had to come from somewhere else, which meant the sea; nobles who felt just marginal were willing to ship out.

The idea of going away, being curious about the world, began before the Viking age. In a village with a couple of families running large farms, at Helgö, not far from Stockholm on Lake Mälar, someone buried objects from the sixth and seventh centuries: a Coptic bronze ladle from Egypt, which might have been used in baptisms; a whole series of love scenes cut into gold foil; and, quite astonishingly, a Buddha. His caste mark on his forehead is gold, his eyebrows and lips are painted, his cloak is finely embroidered and he sits on an intricate lotus blossom throne; he is a true rarity even in Kashmir, where he was probably made. No Scandinavian is known to have travelled as far as India, which is a huge distance over land as well as sea. There was the whole Muslim world in between and it is highly unlikely any Arab trader would risk the contamination of such a heathen and infidel object, even if he thought he could find a buyer in the West. The Buddha was known in Byzantium – he's a character in a popular epic called *Barlaam and Josaphat* – and perhaps the Jewish traders working throughout Asia and Europe might have brought the statue as a curiosity and sold it on. But then why would a farmer on the edge of a Swedish lake have wanted it?[12] It had no religious significance for him, it had no magic, although it has great beauty. Did it satisfy curiosity about a wider world, perhaps?

Around the middle of the eighth century, Scandinavians began to make their way from the Baltic down the great river systems of what is now Russia. This, too, seems strange. It is one thing to raid rich and easy targets on the coasts of the North Sea or the Irish Sea, sailing off with lovely treasure. Helgö lies a good distance from the North Sea, but the farm with the Buddha also owned a bronze from Ireland: an eighth-century crook from some priest's crozier in the shape of a dragon, with blue and silver eyes and enamelled jaws, circled round a human head with a wolf and a bird in attendance. Such things could be had quite easily. But the same sort of men were making an extraordinary effort to work their way overland through swamp and forest into Russia, daring an unfriendly menagerie of creeping, stinging and biting beasts, having to push or abandon boats when they came to the cataracts that roared on the rivers and made them even more vulnerable to bandits. The famous predators had to keep armed guards onshore so as not to become prey. They did all this in territory that was miserably poor, where there were few people and no friends; there is evidence of only one town in all of north-western Russia in the eighth century. The Scandinavians – the ones whose brothers owned bronze and gold and even a Buddha – were the richest targets around.[13]

There is one likely reason for their determination to break through Russia: silver. Neither Russia nor Scandinavia had sources of silver, but silver coins travelled north from the Arab caliphates in the form of the famous *dirham*. Opening a trade route for furs, for amber and for slaves and bringing back silver could be hugely valuable. Besides, if a man had nothing to sell he could always sell his services, as the 'friendly' troops of Swedish and Russian kingdoms in the East, as the palace guard of Byzantine emperors, as mercenaries for the Khazars beyond Byzantium between the Black and Caspian seas. By the eighth century, a voyage down the Volga was commonplace; within a single generation, the first decades of the ninth century, Vikings worked out how to use the great rivers to travel regularly as far as Constantinople. They opened up vast territory by daring to go through the badlands. Everyone around the Baltic would have known of silver coming north, could have met with the merchants on the routes into Asia, but only the Vikings chose to go hunting the source of that wealth.

There is a cultural difference here, a willingness to be unsettled: men trapped by long winters, barely scratching a living out of narrow lands, found the sea their obvious escape. They had no great riches to defend at home, no neighbour enemies. They had every reason to move on and on.

Ohthere knew that. He was 'among the foremost men in that land', or so he said when he met King Alfred in southern England some time in the late ninth century. The king was always eager to meet strangers who knew strange corners of the world. Ohthere brought him walrus ivory, perhaps as a sample of things to trade, perhaps to pay for protection, or simply as a gift: a formal courtesy. He was certainly a trader of some kind because on his journeys he called at trading places like the seasonal settlement Kaupang in the south of Norway.[14]

He answered questions before Alfred, he explained himself and his country, and his answers were written down and slipped into the translation Alfred was preparing of the historian and geographer Orosius, his *Histories against the Pagans*. So we know that Ohthere had more wild than domestic animals: six hundred reindeer 'unsold' in his herds, for the meat and the hides, and six of the beasts who led the moving herd and acted as decoys when there were wild reindeer to catch. 'However, he did not have more than twenty head of cattle and twenty sheep and twenty pigs, and the little that he ploughed he ploughed with horses.' Southerners were surprised; they ploughed with oxen.

He said he 'lived furthest north of all the Norsemen' beside the Western Sea, far north on the coast we know as Hålogaland; and although he does not mention it, perhaps because it seemed so obvious to him, he was living close to the winter spawning grounds for codfish, which will have fed him in the bleak months. Those long winter nights were lit with whale oil from blubber pits along the shore, maybe worked by the hunting and herding Sami peoples on the coast.[15] His wealth depended mostly on those same nomads: he was worth what he owned in skins and bone and feathers (which means eiderdown), tunics of marten and otter (which sold at three times the price of sable in the South), and ship's ropes made from walrus hide. As for farming as Southerners knew it, up north on the very edge of the zone where cereals can ripen, he said that the land 'that may be grazed or ploughed, that lies along the sea . . . is nevertheless very rocky in some places, and wild moors lie to the East and above, running parallel to the inhabited land'.[16]

This is a man who lived in a poor place on the very edge of the world, close to the great ocean which was supposed to encircle the world. He could travel only between April and September, when the winds were not too violent, the cold was bearable in open ships and there was light;[17] and when he travelled, he kept moving through the short nights because the winds were famously unreliable and might change at any moment. On his journey south he noted Ireland, the Orkneys and the Shetlands, but he also knew his contemporaries were on Iceland (and looking west from there). He knew 'the land extends a very long way north from' his northerly home, although he had heard that it was 'all waste, except that in a few places here and there Finnas camp, engaged in hunting in winter and in summer in fishing by the sea'. He told Alfred he decided to go north in part because he reckoned he might find a supply of walrus for their tusks and for the hides. But he also wanted to 'investigate how far the land extended in a northerly direction, or whether anyone lived north of the wilderness'.

He was exploring.

He sailed north, which to him meant a particular quadrant of the sky rather than an exact compass point, keeping open sea to his port side. Going south, he always had seamarks to show where he was and knowledge of where best to beach and rest overnight; the further north he went, the less he knew and the more he was watching and chancing.

He watched a wilderness gliding past him, rocky and frigid; but he kept sailing. 'Then he was as far north as the furthest the whale hunters go,' the limits of the usual world for men like him; he had been there before, once killed sixty whales (or it may have been walrus) in two days, or so he said. 'Then he travelled further north, as far as he could sail in the next three days.'

When he found that the land turned east, he waited for a wind to take him eastwards; and when he came to the mouth of the White

Sea he waited for a northerly wind to take him south. He was beyond the help of maps, which showed only a maze of islands in the north and behind them a world of legends he must have heard: the land where griffins lived and the land of the Amazons and the savage peoples locked away behind a great wall by Alexander the Great.[18] He met only a few fishermen and hunters camping out on the barrens, heard their more fantastic stories and was properly sceptical; he trusted only what he could see and test for himself.

There were no settlements on the land until he came to a wide river mouth on the coast of the White Sea. He did not cross, because he could see the land was settled on the other side and he already knew the settlers were not friendly. He was ready to go out in the unknown ocean, but not to risk ship and crew against this more usual human kind of obstacle. At last he decided to turn back.

All this is something new. Ohthere in the White Sea, far beyond the point where his countrymen sailed after whales, is a man aware of a world waiting to be found, not confined to the usual, regular routes like some sailor on the easier straits between, let's say, Dunkirk and Dover. His voyage is extraordinary in itself, but you can see why a man might think this way. If his contemporaries had riches, they were mostly bits of animal that only Southerners valued very high; so Northmen were obliged to travel to turn their goods into money. Slaves were worth nothing where they were captured; they had to be shipped to the market. Travelling was honourable in itself but finding something new, perhaps a ship carrying valuables, perhaps a monastery full of gold and money, perhaps somewhere to settle: that was a much better prospect. Sons of a fine title went away with their followers to make both a living and a life.

Others had the same mindset: Christian missionaries, for example. When the self-aggrandizing bishop Adam of Bremen wrote the story of missions in the Northlands, he included a book of geography that shows his own passion to know 'how far the land extended'. His story isn't first-hand, it is pockmarked with legends and forgeries, and he does mention dog-headed and one-eyed cannibals blocking the way to the lands that Ohthere had managed to visit,[19] but he is still read for his other information. He thought the Northerners were excellent fighters because they did not eat fruit, that they 'more often attack others than others trouble them' but, even so, that 'poverty has forced them thus to go all over the world'.[20] Perhaps there were too many of them at home and they had to travel to live.

That is much too simple. Vikings weren't just forced onto the seas. They chose to move, for profit, for occupation, to get away from the authority of kings (in the case of lords) and sometimes to escape the power of lords (if they were commoners). And yet the growing population, small as the rise seems to modern eyes, did matter very much: human beings were merchandise. They could be caught and then held for fat ransoms if anyone was available to pay. They could be kept as necessities as the Norsemen travelled, farmhands and wives and cooks. When the Norsemen began to settle the empty, ashy spaces of Iceland around 870 they took slaves from all around the Irish Sea and more than half the women on the island were Gaelic. When they reached out to the Americas and their small, fragile colony in Vinland, they took along a German slave called Tyrkir for special chores.[21]

Better still, slaves could be sold on a huge scale. Paul the Deacon, writing in the eighth century, says the North is such a healthy place that the people breed and breed; Germania got its name from all that 'germination'. He says: 'That is why countless troops of slaves are so often driven away from this populous Germania and sold to the southern people.' All that Arab silver in Northern hands, lost on the Isle of Skye, buried in hoards, had to be earned; all the silk that came north and the various dried spices that were needed to practise the new Arab medicine had to be paid for.

Human beings paid.

The Arab world was suddenly desperate for people to work. Plague had wasted the population, and labour was in short supply. A time of peace didn't help; war had been the usual way to bring in prisoners. Their slave labourers from Africa were alarmingly restive and then rebellious. They were forced to go to the slave markets – as far north and west as Utrecht as well as busy Venice – and they were ready to pay very well; so a slave was worth two or three times the Northern price when she or he had crossed the Mediterranean going east.[22] The numbers were enough for the church council at Meaux in 845 to take notice of the merchants of Charlemagne's empire moving columns of human property through so many cities of the faithful 'into the hands of the faithless and our most brutal enemies'. The issue was not just the miserable life the slaves faced; 'they are swelling the vast numbers of enemies of the kingdom' the council complained, and 'increasing the enemy strength'. The council wanted to make sure men were sold inside Christendom, which they said was for the sake of their immortal souls.[23]

The trade was lucrative, wide and growing; the trader Vikings wanted their share. They were opening their own reliable trade route to the east, through the Baltic, by way of Novgorod in western Russia and then south to the Caspian, the Black Sea and beyond. They had fur, ivory, amber, honey, beeswax and good swords to sell to the Arabs and to the middlemen along the way, Bulghars, Khazars, Russians. Slaves were one more line of business, and a good one.[24] They were quite breathtakingly ambitious. Amlaíb, chief and king of the Norsemen at Dublin, went to war across the Irish Sea and came back in 871 with two hundred shiploads of captive 'Angles and Britons and Picts'. He brought them back for sale in Ireland, at least six thousand of them, because there was simply no market for that many slaves in Scotland or Wales.[25]

So when trouble starts, expect the Vikings to loot, to pillage, but more than anything else: to kidnap. For as long as the Eastern markets needed labour, the Norsemen were shipping out human cargo. In doing so, they helped break up all the frontiers, genetic and cultural and political, of the North.

Hardly anybody had yet seen the Norsemen up close by 800 CE, but they could be beautiful, they could be terrifying and quite often they were simply repellent. They had the habits of men cramped together on long voyages with little water, little shelter and absolutely no idea of privacy; they knew what it was to be bored through long idle winters so they drank; they had the perpetual traveller's passion for the rituals away from home that make him feel he might still have a home. They carried absolutely all of their culture with them. And curiously, at least in Hedeby on Danish soil, they all wore some kind of indelible cosmetic, which may have been a tattoo, to draw attention to their eyes: men and women alike.[26] They wanted people to be afraid of their gaze.

The Arab merchant Ibn Fadlān said he met them in a Bulghar encampment on the Volga, far east of Kiev. He was there on a mission: to make proper, settled Muslims of a people with shamans, horses and a tendency to wander about the place. He was startled and impressed when the Rūs, the Vikings living in the East, arrived to do business. 'I have never seen bodies more perfect than theirs. They were like palm trees,' he wrote. They were tattooed all over with intricate designs in dark green. They were dirty, they hardly washed except in filthy communal bowls, they were 'like wandering asses'; they had companionable sex with their slave girls in full view of all their companions, and if a buyer arrived at such an inconvenient moment, 'the man does not get up off her until he has satisfied himself'. Naturally, they drank; and what they drank was probably mead, although it may have been fermented mare's milk. They knew very well 'the heron of forgetfulness that hovers over ale-gatherings and steals the wits of men'.[27] In time they developed a taste for good wine. When the Danish king, Godfrid, was asked by the Emperor to take control of Frisia in 882 and keep it safe against raiders, including his own Danes, he accepted; but he was back inside three years with a new demand. He couldn't stay in any land where the wine did not flow freely – 'this wine which is in such mean supply in Frisia'.[28]

If one of the Vikings fell sick, he was put out in a tent far away from the others and left alone; he was welcome back, if he happened to survive. If he died, and he was poor, the Rūs built him a boat and burned him in it; if he was rich, they made sure he was known to be rich and a Viking in their own way, which meant a ceremony of fire, sex and murder.

They found a volunteer among the dead man's slave girls (or slave boys) to die with him. The slave drank and sang, drank and sang, in a perfect show of joy. The man's boat was dragged onshore, and onto a wooden frame. His body was dug up and uncovered when everything was ready, smelling good but turned quite black,[29] and put into the boat along with a dog cut in two and horses which had been run to exhaustion and butchered. The slave girl had sex with the master of each of the pavilions built around the boat, and the men all said: 'Tell your master I only did this for your love of him.' Since the girl, according to Ibn Fadlān, could just as well have been a boy, it seems the Vikings followed the rules of the sea: the best sex is available sex. They certainly had the half-joshing insults to go with the habit: the great god Thor was dressed up in women's clothes to steal back a magic hammer, of all things, and terribly afraid he'd be thought a 'cock-craver'; a rude ogress in the song of Helgi Hjörvardson tells the princeling Atli that 'though you have a stallion's voice' his heart is in his arse.[30]

Evening came. There was a frame like a doorway, and the girl was hoisted up to look over it as though it was the door to Paradise: to see first her parents waiting for her, then all her relatives waiting for her, and then the third time her master calling to her. She drank until she did not know what she was doing. On the boat, six men raped her, and then two men caught her with ropes tight around her neck. An old crone came forward, the Angel of Death, and stabbed her until she died. The men kept banging furiously on their shields so nobody could hear the girl's cries, especially not any girls (or boys) who might one day think of dying with their masters.

The man's closest male relative now stripped naked and walked backwards towards the boat, covering his arse with one hand, holding a piece of flaming wood in the other. He threw the wood onto the boat and he was followed by the crowd, each with a piece of burning wood. The boat caught, the tents caught, the bodies burned in a violent wind.[31]

Ibn Fadlān got some things right; we know from the uncovered remains of a Viking grave at Ballateare on the Isle of Man. There is the body of a middle-aged man wrapped in a cloak. Higher up in the same grave, a woman, quite young with her arms over her head and her skull broken.[32] She had to die so he could be buried.

Such things startled a devout Muslim. Christians were not just startled; they were contradicted. The Church was busy preaching the unfamiliar doctrine of the family unit, not a tribe or a pack but parents with their own children, and here were loyalties that went in all directions, loyalty shown by slaves as well as daughters, crew as well as sons; it was a quite different way to organize life. The Church was also busy trying to cram sexuality back into the frame of monogamous marriage, and here was a kind of open, public, sacramental sex. As the Danes moved into more polite or at least more Southern society, they even changed the official meaning of marriage. Frankish law in Christian territory allowed first- and second-class wives, not to mention 'wives of your youth', an expedient until a man settled on a serious contractual and property-owning marriage, and even concubines; the ninth-century list of penances prepared by Halitgaire of Cambrai condemns a married man who keeps a mistress but accepts a man who has a mistress instead of a wife. This kind of living was called marriage '*more danico*' – in the Danish, meaning in the Viking, way.[33]

Viking women were even more extraordinary: famous for sex, ruthlessness and such military skill that their own lovers did not recognize them in armour. They could make up their own minds, and act accordingly, even when it came to staying married. In the port town of Schleswig, the merchant Ibrāhīm ibn Ya'qūb reported in 965 that 'women take the initiative in divorce proceedings. They can separate from their husbands whenever they choose.'[34] It sounds as though divorce was not much more than a formal declaration in front of witnesses. Naturally, independence in women made men think women must be wonderfully loose. 'None of their women,' an optimist said, 'would refuse herself to a man.'

They might also be considered fighters, at least in legend and story. In various poems Gudrun avenges her dead brothers, not least because, as she says, 'we were three brothers and a sister, we seemed to be unconquerable . . . we hastened our ships on, each of us captained one, we roamed where our fate led us.'[35] Women might dress to look like men and train as soldiers; they 'aimed at conflicts instead of kisses' according to Saxo Grammaticus in his twelfth-century *History of the Danes*.[36] 'They devoted hands to the lance which they should rather have applied to the loom,' he wrote, censoriously. He told the alarming story of Alvid, who really did not want to marry a man called Alf, turned pirate to get away, and was elected captain when she happened upon a pirate crew mourning their dead leader and in need of a new one; she 'enrolled in her service many maidens who were of the same mind'. When she met Alf in battle, it was only when her helmet was knocked off that he realized 'he must fight with kisses and not with arms'. Saxo, a very conventional cleric, reports that Alf later laid hands on her more lovingly and they had a daughter.[37]

A woman's choice might, just sometimes, even affect the all-important business of family, inheritance and honour. A daughter could choose to count as a son, and act as a son, if her father had no sons to compete with her. In Icelandic tradition, Hervör grows up playing well with weapons, robbing people while dressed as a man, and captaining an otherwise male band of Vikings. All this begins because of a slight to her honour: a slave who dared to say her father was a slave. She wants to fight with the family sword, and she argues with her father's ghost for the right to use it. The sagas say her father agreed, and wished her very well: 'I wish you twelve men's lives.' Storytellers, guardians of tradition, saw nothing very wrong at all with what Hervör wanted. She was unusual enough for a story, but what she did was thinkable.[38]

In 789 a royal official called Beaduherd, who happened to be in Dorchester at the time, heard that three foreign ships had come into the harbour at Portland in the English Channel. The law said anyone landing had to come to town at once and declare how many men were with him, so Beaduherd galloped down to meet them, 'thinking that they were merchants rather than enemies' as Æthelweard's *Chronicle* says; merchants were nothing new close to the great trading emporium at Hamwic, which stood where Southampton now stands.

But Beaduherd was wrong. As the *Chronicle* says: 'He was slain on the spot by them.'[39]

There is another version in the *Anglo-Saxon Chronicle*, which insists he had no idea who was waiting for him, nor what they were, which is why he wanted them to come as quickly as possible to the king's town of Dorchester to identify themselves; but the chronicles all agree on the killing. 'These were the first ships of the Danish men which sought out the land of the English race.'[40]

Three years later, the skies opened over Northumbria, 'there were immense flashes of lightning and fiery dragons were seen flying in the air and there immediately followed a great famine'. [41] A Viking fleet out of Norway assembled at its summertime bases in the Orkneys, freebooters with no official orders. Most of them were planning to sail round Cape Wrath and down to the Hebrides, but a splinter group went down the east coast of Scotland, looking for soft targets.[42] They came ashore at the monastery of Lindisfarne, with its rich shrines and its treasury of gifts from the devout. 'The raiding of heathen men,' the *Chronicle* says, 'miserably devastated God's church in Lindisfarne island by looting and slaughter.'[43]

The Vikings – and their reputation – had arrived.

Alcuin of York knew what this meant: his whole history, the Saxon people coming to England and the triumph of his Christian faith, was rapidly going to fall apart. Alcuin was settled in the very heart of the court of Charlemagne, which was the very heart of power in Europe; he was scholar and cleric and adviser, 'the most learned man anywhere to be found', according to Einhard's *Life of Charlemagne*. When Alcuin heard the news from Lindisfarne, he wrote to Ethelred, King of Northumbria: 'it is three hundred and fifty years now that we and our fathers have settled in this lovely land, and never was such terror seen before in Britain, such suffering at the hands of the heathen.' He mourned 'the church of St Cuthbert splattered with blood, treasures pillaged, the heathen despoiling the most holy place in Britain'.[44] To Higbaldus, the Bishop of Lindisfarne, Alcuin wrote again of his horror that 'the heathen defiled God's holy places, and spilled the blood of saints all around the altar, destroyed the house of our hopes. They trod on the bodies of the saints in God's temple like they were treading on shit in the open street.'[45]

A few years earlier, he'd casually asked an Anglo-Saxon friend 'what hope there is of the conversion of the Danes?'[46] Now he was looking at the Danes and the Norsemen as the unconverted, undoubted enemy. The Danes clearly meant to change the world, and if they did, it must be because they were heathen. They burned and killed, ruined monasteries and churches, just because they could do nothing else to stop the advance of Christ.

The logic is very particular. Alcuin tried to console Higbaldus that 'the more God punishes you, the more he loves you', that even Jerusalem had fallen once and so had Rome; so the attacks meant that Higbaldus was right. Alcuin thought other people's sins had caused the problem in the first place, he worried about incest and adultery and fornication flooding the land,[47] but more than anything he worried about the Church, how the Church in Britain was 'to keep its self-esteem when St Cuthbert and such a number of saints do not defend it'. He tried to enthuse Higbaldus: 'Be manly, fight strongly, defend the places where God has settled.' To missionaries, after all, God is also a migrant, moving to new territory and liable to challenge from even more recent newcomers like the Vikings.

He was also very concerned about manliness, about modesty, about propriety. In his next letter to Higbaldus he denounces excess and display and he insists that 'vanity in dress is not fitting for men'.[48] He wants a plain kind of virility, able to fight to keep the successes of the past centuries, able to be moderately Viking in face of the Viking menace. But this virility cannot simply be a military matter. Alcuin also wrote to a priest from Lindisfarne who had been captured by the Northmen and then ransomed, and told him he should move away from the 'din of arms' and practise solitary prayer.[49] Piety was a weapon.

The next year Offa, King of Mercia, gave the churches of Kent all the privileges they could want, including their old freedom from taxes, an exemption that went back at least as far as the laws of Wihtred, King of Kent, in 695, whose first ruling was that 'The church is to be free from taxation.'[50] This time, though, the Church had to pay up in one situation that was very serious and very pressing: 'expeditions within Kent against the seafaring heathen, the fleet that moves from place to place'. This 'moving' is not plain travel by sea; it is 'migration', and it means heathen who mean to settle.[51] Fighting those heathen was written into grants of land for the next two hundred years; it was the reason for granting the Abbess Selethryth land in Canterbury as a refuge, and a duty mentioned even when a king was giving land to an archbishop in return for a gold ring.[52] The state was a state of war.

The Orkney fleet went through the Hebrides: 'the devastation of all the islands of Britain by gentiles', as the *Annals of Ulster* put it. They did not have everything their own way. In 796 a small fleet put in to the estuary of the Tyne and went against the monastery at Jarrow but this time the monks were ready for them. The Viking leaders were killed, the crews fled on board their ships only to be forced ashore at Tynemouth and slaughtered.

For forty years, there were no more attacks on England, but the enemy was not forgotten. There had to be a designated enemy that could be judged and condemned, an opponent who could justify the righteous armies and the Godly monarchs who had, as it happens, more or less the same habits and tactics. A man could no more forget the Vikings than his own bloody image in a mirror.

The Church proposed a proper enemy, daemonic, unconverted and bloody, the kind anyone could be proud to defeat or at least unashamed to suffer, since being a martyr was most respectable. In the *Annals*, the Vikings become just such an enemy, no longer a rival out after the same plunder and advantage. Those records are known because they were kept in institutions which survived century after century, monasteries or cathedrals, which had an interest in recording who they were, what they did and what they owned; and which were so deeply entwined with kings and states that at times they performed as a kind of bureaucracy when a ruler had no way of organizing, let alone paying, his own. Official, useful to people's reputations and carefully conserved, their story blocks out all the other stories.

But consider what Charlemagne, enemy of the Vikings, did, and his imperial successors. His armies had to be supported out of whatever they could steal and whatever tribute they could demand; their loyalty was bought with regular gifts of horses, silver, gold or arms. When there was a true emergency like the Viking raids, the great Emperor found himself bidding and dealing with the men who would fight for him and taking what he could get: cutting back on his demands for military service from those who did not have much property, allowing minor landowners to nominate just one of their number to fight for them all. Such men, when they turned up, had to be rewarded. In order to move fast they had no baggage train, which meant they were so poorly supplied with basic goods that they ruined the lands they crossed in order to keep eating; famously in 860, when three of the Emperor's underlings met at Koblenz, their armies were left to hang around for a while, and laid waste to a large zone of perfectly friendly countryside. And like the Vikings, these armies loved easy gold, and were ready to wreck other people's holy places. They took gold and silver from the great Saxon tree temple, the Irminsul, before burning it to the ground. Once or twice they even managed to raid the Vikings back; in 885 a Frisian army beat off a Viking band and found 'such a mass of treasure in gold and silver and other movables that all from the greatest to the least were made wealthy'.[53]

Consider Charlemagne's habits and you see the Vikings not as an assault but as another set of players in the same very violent game. Norsemen demanded tribute; Charlemagne demanded not just tribute but also tithes for the Church that was so closely allied with his power. Charlemagne raided across borders just as Vikings did, plundered if he couldn't stay long enough to demand the regular payment of tribute, accepted tribute if he didn't want to settle and occupy the land. The difference lay in the way the Vikings ruled and used the sea.

Their raids began just as Charlemagne had broken his most irritating neighbours, the Saxons: who made a habit (so his courtiers said) of murder, robbery and arson; who were obstinately pagan and didn't think like Christians and were therefore unpredictable. They were a constant threat to the Frankish need to control the Rhine and the trade which went up and down it. They seemed to be on excessively good terms with various other peoples that the Franks were determined to subdue, especially the Frisians. They also managed to organize their lives without kings, and were rather proud of the fact; earlier Bede reported that they cast lots when war was imminent to choose one lord whom everybody would obey for the duration, but when war ended 'the lords revert to equality of status'. That was an affront to a man like Charlemagne who was very willing to be obeyed, and a practical problem for a king who wanted to rule them.

By 800, Charlemagne had won so well he could even be a little magnanimous about recognizing Saxon laws, but he also knew that he had to be more than a king to keep them in line.[54] On Christmas Day in Rome he went into pray before the tomb of St Peter and the Pope put a crown on his head and the crowd wished him 'life and victory' in his new rank with his new name: Augustus, Emperor of the Romans. Charlemagne said (or at least his biographer Einhard said he said) he would never have gone to church if he had known what was going to happen.

The new emperor didn't preach; he attacked. He didn't try to persuade the Saxons to become Christians, he made new law. A man was killed if he persisted in pagan ceremonies, killed if he hid away and refused to be baptized, and punished harshly if he did not take on all the obligations of the observant. The fines for failing to have a child baptized were the equivalent of thirty head of cattle, even for a man who wasn't free or noble, and much more for the more visible classes. Even the dead were required to conform. There were to be no more mound graves, only cemeteries, and no more cremation; the penalty for being accessory to a cremation was death. The missionaries waited decorously on the side until the laws were in force, and then they came in preaching to intimidated people who did not dare say they were not already converted.

Legends of conversion are shining things, full of brave martyrs, furiously convincing preachers, truth triumphing. The actual business of conversion was exceedingly muddy: sometimes brutal, sometimes shallow, sometimes expensive and it never had much to do with hearts and minds. The missionary Anskar went north to save the souls of Scandinavia in the 820s and even his biographer Rimbert acknowledges he 'distributed much money in the northern districts in order that he might win the souls of the people'. His first monks were bought in a slave market as boys: 'he began also to buy Danish and Slav boys so that he might train them for God's service.' To Anskar's fury, the boys ended up as servants to a grandee who got control of their monastery; they were never free. And when Rimbert himself went north to the Swedes Anskar gave him and his colleagues 'whatever they needed to give away in order to secure friends'.[55]

Laypersons did much the same. Louis the German paid all kinds of pagans for their help against his father. In return his rival Charles the Bald paid bribes to the Bulghars to encourage them to attack Louis the German. Conversion looks very much like politics by the usual means.[56]

Not every soul had to be bought, though. Sometimes calming a terrible storm at sea or inexplicably staying dry in the rain was useful. It showed what the Christian god could do spontaneously without all the magical apparatus that a god like Thor would need. Mind you, Christian crosses quite often still had Thor's great hammer on the back, just to be sure. Sometimes converting a king or a court was enough, and the Emperor was happy to help with the conversion by impressing any monarch with the scale of his imperial power, his usefulness and resources; Louis the Pious did that when King Harald of Denmark was driven out of his kingdom, not so much for the sake of spreading the true faith but because in future 'a Christian people would more readily come to his aid'.[57]

Some time in the early ninth century, an anonymous poet was even more ambitious; he retold the stories of the four Gospels to convince at least the Saxons, and perhaps the Frisians, too, about the history of Christ. He wrote, on a grand scale, verses to be sung out loud at banquets, just as poets did for the history of human kings. Since he was writing for a listening audience, a mead-hall mob, and since monks and priests should not have needed such convincing, it's likely he was addressing nobles and grandees. His language is Saxon but with bits of vocabulary from all along the North Sea coast. Finding his name sounds a hopeless quest, but we do know of one bard who sang at banquets, with a repertoire of songs like the great epic of *Beowulf*; who sang about Frisian kings with relatives from Denmark and Jutland; who had reason for Christian enthusiasm because he had been cured of blindness by the missionary Liudger himself. His name was Bernlef, and it is possible that *Heliand* is his work.[58]

The Gospel according to *Heliand*,[59] which means 'Saviour', is all four Gospels moved away from the Mediterranean to a Northern, colder world, where years are measured in winters, where there are deep forests and concealing woods rather than open deserts, where the disciples of Jesus are like the band of men a chieftain might assemble in the expectation of their personal loyalty. 'That is what a thane chooses,' Thomas tells the other disciples in a crisis: 'to stand fast together with his lord to die with him at the moment of doom.'[60] Old man Zacharias, astonished at the angel's notion that he might still have a child at his advanced age, is not at all surprised by what later Christians might find astonishing: that the angel tells Zacharias to bring up the future John the Baptist in the virtue of absolute loyalty, *treuwa*, so he can be a 'warrior-companion' for Christ.[61]

The poem is clearly not made for ordinary persons, and ordinary persons hardly feature. Mary becomes a 'woman of the nobility', Joseph is a nobleman and the herald angels ignore the shepherds and talk to his grooms and sentries at the stables. The baby Jesus wears not swaddling clothes but jewels. When he grows up and begins to bring together the disciples, they reckon him a generous man, free with the gold and gifts, and also with the drink, or at least the mead; he does as Saxon nobles do, as Anskar learned to do among the pagans he wanted to convert. For Jesus, the disciples become in turn 'a powerful force of men from many peoples, a holy army'.[62]

The Gospel story and the Saxon world begin to merge. Jesus is baptized, and the dove that represents the Holy Ghost comes down; but the dove doesn't stay above his halo'd head, it settles on his shoulder, just as Wotan's sacred bird, the raven, settles on his shoulder. The disciples wait for him on the shores of a lake that is really a sea, with sands and dunes, and they sail out in 'well-nailed' boats made from overlapping planks ostentatiously nailed in place, 'high-horned' ships with prows like Viking vessels. They sail like veterans of such North Sea ships, turning into the wind to stop the waves catching the flanks of their ship.[63]

Lazarus is raised from the dead, but not from a cave as he is in the Gospel; he rises from a grave mound with a stone on top in the old Saxon tradition. When Christ rises, he also bursts out of such a grave. High priest and Pharisees meet much like some Saxon assembly, the kind that Charlemagne had carefully forbidden. Where the New

Testament goes back to books of law 'as it is written', the *Heliand* has law-speakers, the men who had memorized the oral traditions of Saxon law. Salt is not for flavouring the world but for medicine, as it was for the Saxons. The disciples ask to be taught the sacred runes, and they are given the Lord's Prayer: a magic access to God. And when the wife of Pontius Pilate has nightmares about the consequences of Jesus' death, the *Heliand* says the dreams were the work of the serpent devil, invisible under that staple of Germanic legend, the magic helmet.[64]

Sometimes the poet has to take a very deep breath and discuss Scripture thoroughly. Nobles were used to proving their innocence in court by swearing oaths, so it was hard to tell them that Jesus forbade swearing any oaths at all. They should answer only 'Yes' or 'No'. After all, the poet argues, if everyone swears and not everyone is telling the truth, what would be the value of an oath? Who could believe it? At other times he keeps an action but changes its meaning. When the biblical Christ in the garden accepts that the cup will not pass from him, that his fate is sealed, he drinks it down to show his acceptance. The poet has him drinking the wine to the honour of God. Acceptance would be too mild; instead he salutes his chieftain. Christ clears the moneychangers out of the Temple, but in *Heliand* the moneychangers are usurers and they are all of course Jews. Jews in *Heliand* are 'a different kind of people', and Christ tells them: 'You Jewish people never show any respect for the house of God.' The constant sense of Northern virtue, of the slinking, untrustworthy nature of Southerners, and Jews as people of the South, flickers into life all through the poem: the Jews who oppose Christ become 'arrogant men' and an 'evil clan'. Christ is no longer a Jew, nor are his disciples; they are Northerners. Some abominable thoughts are being born.[65]

Cultures muddle, even if they fail to fuse, and the Gospel changes subtly to accommodate the newcomers. It's not just that no chieftain could ride into Jerusalem on a donkey, so Jesus doesn't, and no chieftain would ever wash his followers' feet so a whole new explanation is required. Even the stories left out – no prodigal son, no good Samaritan so no family conflict or social difference – are not as striking as what happens to the lessons that are left. The Saxon disciples are told to be humble, to be gentle, which is almost biblical language from the familiar Beatitudes, but then the blessed who mourn become the blessed who cry over their own evil deeds; the ones who 'hunger and thirst after justice' become 'fighting men who wanted to judge fairly' because an audience of nobles would expect to be the ones who judged; the merciful are told to be kind but inside 'a hero's chest'; and the 'peacemakers', whose blessing must have seemed odd to a warrior caste, are limited to men who 'do not want to start any fights or court cases by their own actions'. As for the men who are 'persecuted for justice's sake', they are present in the poem; they are perhaps the rebellious Saxons now suffering from the attentions of Charlemagne and his lords.[66] It would be hard for Charlemagne's missioners to preach against the defeated being patient in the circumstances; *Heliand* thinks it tactful to leave out Christ's promise to 'bring not peace but a sword'.

This is political alchemy. Kings and emperors already knew that a literate clergy could make very useful bureaucrats, writing, checking and disputing documents, and the structure of a church, parish by parish, brought a kind of tax-gathering and administration into every part of a kingdom. Churches and monasteries often looked like forts, carefully guarded, and sometimes violent in their own defence; their interest in trading routes, in connections for vats of wine as well as pictures, books and relics, gave them secular importance. What remained was to bring the warrior class into the system, to anchor them with ideals and Christian messages, to allow for the regular business of war in what was supposed to be a religion that taught peace. When warrior lords decided to follow Christ, they needed what *Heliand* provided: a sense that their warlike occupations could be Godly, that war made sense to a carpenter and his fisherman followers.

Once that was established, a new and virtuous and considered kind of military style could blossom. There would be bloody battle, of course, but there could also in time be chivalry: war in the form of jousts, war with rules, war as a matter of honour as well as necessity, with the prospect of Heaven (as well as more money, more land or a better class of wife here on Earth). And since Northerners were so obviously Christ's people, they had every right to go after Southerners of any kind, the infidel in particular: they had every right to go crusading. The show and colours of chivalry, the brutal enterprise of the Crusades: both depend on this early marriage of God and warriors' manners.

The Vikings were not interested in all this. They struck where they wanted and took what they wanted.

They had already ruined some islands off Aquitaine in 799, although they did not find it easy; they lost some ships and more than a hundred men. They could not be countered with land armies, so Charlemagne ordered the building and manning of a fleet, and ordered more new ships in 802, 808 and 810; by which time he had fleets on all navigable rivers.[67] It was still not enough. The Danish king, Godfrid, was supposed to meet Charlemagne in 804, close to their frontiers at the port of Schleswig, but he never turned up; he was advised by his own court to keep his distance. He decided, four years later, to reinforce the border from the Baltic to 'the Western Sea', which we call the North Sea, and physically to move the merchants who were doing business out of a lost port called Reric into Schleswig; he must have known that Charlemagne had a habit of raiding. And then, just as the new emperor was considering a serious expedition against Godfrid, there was shocking news: a fleet of Norse ships, two hundred strong, had come down the shallow seas to the islands off the coast of Frisia and wrecked them, after which they had come ashore and fought the Frisians in three fixed battles and taken back home to King Godfrid one hundred pounds of silver as tribute.[68] A minor king was ruining the weak frontiers of Charlemagne's empire.

That was when war went to sea: when battles were fought on the water between fleets that had equal ambitions if not equal hulls. A year after the ruin of Frisia, Charlemagne was inspecting his fleets at Ghent and at Boulogne, restoring the old Roman lighthouse at Boulogne so the fleet could come home safely, starting a chain of warning beacons for when the Vikings came again and ordering his lords to get ready for fighting at sea.[69] A new enemy had changed the boundaries of power, made a coastline seem like a weakness.

Yet that same year Charlemagne was also making peace with another Danish king, Godfrid's successor, called Hemming; twelve nobles from each side met to swear oaths 'according to the custom of their people'.[70] You could be savagely attacked and yet respect the laws and customs of the enemy, it seemed, and even trust him a little in some circumstances. The Vikings and the Emperor could see that they were in the same game.

It was the Christians who wailed about this in unison, and carried on wailing. It was as the Prophets had predicted, they said: 'A scourge from the North will extend over all who dwell in the land.' The shrine and abbey at Iona had been raided in 795, and again in 802 and again in 806 when sixty-eight of the monks were murdered; in 807 a fourth raid made the monastery move its men to the comparative safety of Kells in inland Ireland. Jerusalem had fallen once again; Rome had been sacked by the heathen; their shrine, their place, their culture had been made to run away, and the worst was yet to come.

'The innumerable multitude of the Northmen grows incessantly,' wrote Ermentar, the chronicler of Saint-Philibert de Noirmoutier, around 855. 'On every side Christians succumb to massacres, acts of pillage, devastations, burnings whose manifest traces will remain as long as the world endures.'[71] Three centuries later the *Liber Eliensis* (Book of Ely) was still overexcited by the thought of how in 870 a 'mob of evil ones' reached 'the monastery of virgins' – the convent and shrine at Ely on the edge of the English fens; 'The sword of rabid men is held out over milkwhite, consecrated necks.' These things may not actually have happened, but the rhetoric is real and once again the Vikings were very useful; their inconvenient ravaging distracted the holy and was the reason monks and monasteries were imperfect, or so later monks would claim.[72]

From across Europe, from an island in Lake Constance, the monk Walahfrid Strabo ('the squinter') denounced the murder of Blathmac, a monk with very serious connections ('of a kingly line').[73] Blathmac had chosen to go to Iona, knowing very well that the 'heathen mob of Danes used to call there, armed with all the fury of their evil'; he was a man who wanted the stigmata, and even martyrdom, so the danger was the whole point, and the Danes were his best chance of finding armed and murderous men to oblige. Strabo's poem about the 'martyr of Iona' has him standing with God on his side, as you would expect, and saying Mass in a golden dawn when the furious gang of the damned burst in. Blathmac, unarmed, defies them; he says he has no idea where the bones of Cuthbert are buried in their shrine of precious metals. 'If Christ told me, I would never let it reach your ears.' He tells the Danes to take their swords, and they do exactly as he says. They hack off his limbs and tear wounds in his cold body so he has stigmata and martyrdom, both.[74]

His triumph, his sainthood, depended on a victimhood he arranged for himself; without his terrible death, he was just one more socially presentable holy man. He needed enemies in his binary world: us and them, the right and the wrong, Godly and devilish. The Roman world was very aware of barbarians at its limits, but it did not depend on being opposed to be sure of itself; Christians insisted on a sense that they were being opposed and displaced, even as Christianity moved into more and more territories, changed people's minds, changed the organization of their lives in alliance with kings and lords.

The Irish monk Dicuil wrote in around 825 that hermits from Ireland had been living in holy isolation for almost a hundred years on islands north of Britain: the Faroes, probably. 'But,' he complained in his geographical treatise *Liber de mensura orbis terrae*, 'just as those islands were deserted from the beginning of the world, so now because of the Norseman bandits they lie quite empty of hermits, but full of countless sheep and far too many seabirds.'[75]

That is the familiar story: the destructive power of the raiding Norsemen, their campaigns against isolated hermits and also against all the new brilliant towns that were growing around the coasts of the southern North Sea. Those towns were based around churches, monasteries, convents or else feudal powers; they were new foundations serving an old kind of power. Attack them, and the Norse attacked the fragile institutions of the North Sea world. But the perpetual travellers and pillagers from the North were not just wrecking and burning. They were also, almost accidentally, creating a new kind of town that did not depend for its life on king, lord or church: our kind of town.

We can see that in Ireland, which is where it all began.

# 4.

# Settling

'If a hundred iron heads could grow on a single neck, if each head had one hundred tongues of well-tempered and indestructible metal and if each tongue shouted ceaselessly with a powerful and unstoppable voice, it would never be enough to list all the pain the people of Ireland – men and women, laymen and clerics, young and old – have suffered at the hands of these pitiless pagan warriors.'[1] So a twelfth-century chronicler told the world. It is true the Vikings came to Ireland with the overture you expect in legends: drought, monstrous thunderstorms, famine, floods, murrain, dysentery and smallpox. All this, along with a nasty outbreak of rabies and the constant problem of bloody flux, filled fifteen years towards the end of the eighth century with proper, apocalyptic thinking.[2]

Then the real troubles began. St Patrick's Island was burned, the monastery at Inishmurray went up in flames, Iona was attacked and attacked again in a murderous kind of reconnaissance. Local lords fought back, and so did local clergy, who were often the relatives of local lords. Sometimes there would be no raids for years, but after an eight-year pause Howth was plundered in 821 and the *Annals of Ulster* report that the heathens 'carried off a great number of women into captivity'.[3] The women most likely went for slaves, although sailors also needed lovers, wives and expedients.

The monastery at Clonmore was burned to the ground on Christmas Eve and again 'many captives were taken'.[4] The holy places at Armagh were overcome and 'great numbers . . . were taken captive'.

Perhaps the pauses and sudden restarts in the slaving business had something to do with demand in Arab markets.

By 837 there were sixty Viking ships in the River Boyne, and sixty on the Liffey, and each fleet carried at least fifteen hundred men: a very organized expedition, perhaps with royal backing, but still mostly adventurers come down from the Norse bases in Scotland. They battled through the kingdoms of east-coast Ireland, 'a countless slaughter', the *Annals* say. Irish exiles reckoned Ireland was overrun, that 'the Vikings have taken all the islands around without opposition and have settled them'. Yet nobody could be quite sure what Vikings wanted: plunder or territory or both. Nobody could even be sure to what authority they answered, if any. They worked up the rivers and into the lakes, they took to spending the whole winter on Lough Neagh: settlers, almost. They may have used the islands in the Lough as holding camps for their prisoners, because from there they went raiding for slaves into County Louth and took away 'bishops, priests and scholars, and put others to death'.[5]

The Irish provincial kings were made to notice that the invaders were not simply landing, pillaging, ravaging and plundering; they were turning into neighbours, which was just as alarming. The Irish briefly stopped warring among themselves and defined the Vikings as the enemy; they won battles against the Norsemen, and for a moment it seemed they might even drive them out of the country. The victories were obviously splendid because victories always are but they were also useful in the long term because they formed the basis for a story about a glorious past – how the great kings disposed of a great enemy – a propaganda that would live for centuries.

But then in 849, as the *Annals* say, 'A sea-going expedition of 140 ships of the King of the Foreigners came to exercise authority over the Foreigners who were in Ireland before them, and they upset all Ireland afterwards.'[6]

Instead of a single Viking enemy, worth uniting to fight, the Irish discovered that foreigners came in at least two varieties. They had long known the raiders and settlers from Norway who shipped out from bases in the islands north and west of Scotland: the *Finngaill*, the 'white' foreigners. Now there were also the fleets that belonged to the settled Danish kings carrying the *Dubgaill*, the 'black' foreigners, who sailed out from bases in England and Scotland.[7] The two factions seemed to be at war, but they'd been known to work together, so they could be allies, rivals or enemies and they could always change their minds. They weren't some single force of evil; they had politics, like the Irish.

There was a brief time when the Norsemen had to scrap among themselves to settle who would rule. The Danes took over for a time, then the Norwegians fought back – at first in 852 with 160 ships, which was not quite enough, and then in 853 with enough men and sails to take back power. Once control of Dublin was settled, at least among the Northerners, a remarkable exchange could begin. The lovely worked metals of Ireland went north; walrus ivory and amber and furs came south. The Irish were sometimes obliged to pay tribute, but the Vikings on their side gave hostages. Marrying a Viking became thinkable for the upper-class Irish: the King of Leinster's daughter married the Viking King of York, who was later the King of Viking Dublin, and after that she married the King of Ireland, who was not Viking at all, so her first husband evidently did no harm to her social standing. The King of Munster, meanwhile, was married to the daughter of the Viking ruler of Waterford. They must all have had some kind of language in common.[8]

Co-existence began.

The Irish had their own settled sense of all being Irish, something beyond the local loyalty they felt to a chief or a place or a king; they had songs and laws in common, stories about how things started and family trees for saints and kings, a particular style of religion. Northerners seemed to be the same; they understood what each other said, shared laws and gods and stories.

The two sides had other, disconcerting things in common, which was convenient. The Vikings had their *berserkrs*, who went about in pairs or groups of twelve, who went into battle 'without mailcoats and were frantic as bears or boars; they slew men but neither fire nor iron could hurt them'. Their frenzy in battle was famous and it could be used.[9] The Irish had their own wild men: the *fían*,[10] lawless fraternities called the 'sons of death', who went about ravaging 'in the manner of pagans'. Pagan here does not mean being like the Vikings; it means like Irishmen before the Christian missionaries arrived. *Fían* were men without a fixed standing in society, unsettled because they had been exiled as outlaws or they were young or they were waiting to come into their own. They were alarming all the time, and not least when they planted themselves in settled communities during hard winters. They were wilderness people out on the moors, sure they had a right to plunder, warriors who went howling into battle like wolves and who were said to have the power to change their shape at will (which may have been a question of dog-like hairstyles). The sons of kings and nobles got their military training in the *fían*; which meant they might change completely in a day if the right person died, from outsider to ruler, from landless to magnate.

Like *berserkrs*, such men were also a useful resource for kings and nobles, who used them as mercenary soldiers, just as Viking warriors made excellent mercenaries and useful allies for any Irish king whose power was otherwise all too equal to his rivals. War was more an occupation than an event, after all, and paid help was required.

The Vikings went on raiding, though, and Christians were persistently, officially outraged. The priests were shocked that the Vikings dared to go 'as far as the door of the church', that they violated the temples of God and went into the zone of holiness and sanctuary at the heart of monasteries. They were especially shocked that when people crowded into a church for safety, they were not just unprotected; they might as well have helped the slavers by rounding themselves up.[11] Their objection was not so much to the sin itself, which was common to both sides, but to who was doing the sinning. It is true there are lovely brooches with Celtic patterns and workmanship found in Norway, which prove the Vikings did pillage churches: those brooches began as mountings, which were ripped from shrines or holy books and conveniently had pins already on the back.[12] But the Irish king, the King of Cashel himself, famous as a scribe and as an anchorite, or hermit, felt free to burn his first monastery in 822, including its oratory, and in 832 burned another 'to the door of the church'.[13]

Being raided, even ruined, was a matter of routine for the holy places. This may seem curious in such a Christian society (and even the Vikings were beginning to convert), but holiness was not the first thing anyone noticed about a monastery. Much more visible were their close resemblances to towns, forts, strongrooms.

Monks were meant to live in a walled world, according to the rule laid down by St Benedict, with gardens, water, mills and crafts all within an enclosure so that they 'may not be compelled to wander outside it, for that is not at all expedient for their souls'. At its very heart would be the holiest places, churches and relics; outside that, a ring of kilns and crafts and houses for settlers and helpers, and outside that a kind of estate farmyard. The holy shape was remarkably like the secular shape of a ringfort.[14] Monasteries were often set on rises in the land, with solid walls and banks of earth with palisades on them, and ditches that worked as moats. They often had round towers, which held their bells but also their treasury of relics and valuable objects: a conspicuous safe place.

Communities grew around churches. The southern district of the settlement at Armagh was a holy community, built around a basilica housing relics, including a linen cloth soaked in the blood of Christ himself, and a church for the clergy. The community had monks, clergy, nuns, but it also had a married lay population and a separate church, in the north, for laypersons. It included the sick, the disabled and children unwanted by their families. Monasteries grew into holy villages, even a kind of town.

These communities had remarkable engineers. The monastery at Clonmacnoise in the very heart of Ireland made kilometres of road through bog which led to a bridge across the Shannon some 160 metres long and five metres wide, wide enough for carts and animals as well as walkers and riders; and all this was for monks and pilgrims.[15] At Nendrum on Strangford Lough, they built millponds on the foreshore, held in place by embankments of stone and holly branches, which filled with the high tide; and they built solid stone channels to carry the rush of water down to the waterwheel which worked the millstone above. The first of their tidal mills was built around 620; the tree rings in the timber prove the trees were felled then, and the sapwood is in such good condition the timber must have been used soon after felling. No earlier tidal mills are known anywhere.[16]

Kings had the right to billet their troops on the population of a church, which says something about how much free space they had, and the right to pasture animals on the monastic estates, which says something about how well the space was protected. Monasteries were often tightly controlled by the family of the founder, so they were dynastic. They were also belligerent: monasteries fought not just the good fight but also each other. Long after clerics had all been exempted from military service, in 845, two neighbouring abbots were both killed by the Danes in a single battle, both in charge of small armies, conscripts but holy.

So far, so secular; but what made the monasteries truly vulnerable was the safety they offered to other people. Their land was sanctuary land: a fugitive could feel safe there. Offering sanctuary could be a dangerous virtue; if enemies caught up, there was no great difference between burning down a man's house and burning down the church where he was taking shelter. Churches were still mostly wooden – stone roofs were a kind of insurance that was first taken out in the twelfth century – so the fire spread fast.

When kings were brawling or bandits were about, the rule of sanctuary could make strongrooms out of the monasteries. Locals could store their valuables, which also meant their herds; in 995 more than two thousand cows were taken from a single monastery, which is more than any simple and holy community of cheese-eaters could possibly need. There was often food stored inside the church; so times of famine brought on plundering. All this was especially true of island monasteries, which were hard to attack unless the water was frozen in a vicious winter: attack an island, either swimming or on rafts, and you were always vulnerable to counter-attack from the islanders, who knew exactly what they were doing.

There were Viking pirates who came ashore at monasteries because they were supposed to be easy, and full of gilded shrines and lovely jewels: like the raiders who killed St Blathmac. Their raids even had a kindly effect on the local economy since the treasure went into circulation instead of staying near the altars, and the church patrons had to replace what was stolen so their church would still have glory. But much more often, the raiders were cattle rustlers or else slavers, looking for the same loot the Irish wanted from their enemies; which is why the Irish, for all their talk of shock and blasphemy, went on raiding just as often as Vikings, and the Vikings saw no reason to stop just because they had converted to Christianity. The two sides even staged joint operations.[17] Whatever Alcuin thought, faith was not the issue.

The Vikings were settling, in their way, which did not prevent them taking over the territory of Picts across the water in Scotland, then coming home to beat back an Irish attack, then going after the kingdom of Strathclyde in south-west Scotland and coming back with magnificent plunder and almost too many slaves for the market. They raided more monasteries. They feuded among themselves. Some started settlements which had flocks and herds worth stealing, so naturally they were stolen.

At the centre of all this was Dublin and the claim of Dublin's king to be the overlord of all the new settlements and trading depots, like Waterford, and in time the overlord of all the Vikings in the British Isles, even when his hold on Dublin itself was none too certain. The smaller centres learned to resent this claim. Dublin was not much more than a waterfront row of houses and storerooms, set carefully behind a palisaded embankment, but it was beginning to look like a new kind of town: not an accident of a holy place, not built to hold a chieftain and his people, but deciding and serving its own ends. It was a base for trading, it was distinct from the territory around it. The first craftsmen and merchants were moving in. The burial grounds held more and more women who had lived and died there. You could make an urban business and an urban life. The needs of Norsemen, from a place that hardly had towns at all, were helping to invent the town in Ireland.

They had post and wattle fences to mark the boundaries between plots; which means that someone had the authority to divide up the land. Around Dublin thickets of hazel trees were planted and tended in order to supply the flexible branches that were woven to make the walls of houses – simple buildings, one storey tall, the roofs thatched. To get to them, you walked streets of small stones and gravel, which mostly followed some natural contour like the crest of a hill. The houses stood end-on to the street, which is a pattern familiar from the warehouses along the water at Northern ports;[18] so when you found the entrance to the plot you wanted, you had to walk straight through the first house on the plot if you were looking for someone in a house that lay behind it. There must have been a careful etiquette for asking for access, which means some sort of civility. There were still ports without towns, just harbours 'where more than one ship might come at once',[19] but in places like Waterford there would very soon be a recognizable town cramped on the shore.

Once settled, Dublin became a turntable for the various Viking trades: goods coming in, goods going out, but also the booty from raids which could be turned into cash to finance more-respectable business.[20] Money may explain why Norsemen ate their beef from cattle that were noticeably smaller than the Irish herds, whether they raised the cows themselves or bought them from the Irish; cattle were a practical source of food now, and no longer the obvious way to keep your wealth. Silver, which the Vikings had in generous amounts, began to matter much more. Coins were easier to tend than cows, easier to steal but far easier to hide, and useful wherever you went.[21]

Once Dublin was settled and secure in the middle of the ninth century, the Vikings could start their settlements in Scotland. On the offshore islands, the Norsemen found plenty of land compared to the narrow Norwegian coast, and no armies to oppose them; there was even enough wood inland to build ships, if ever they wanted to do that, and flocks to grow the wool that could be exported on their ships. Women, men and children landed and stayed: ordinary persons. To the Scottish islands, the newcomers brought money, weights and measures,[22] so there are Arab coins found on the Isle of Skye, merchant scales on the tiny island of Gigha.[23] Farmers, raiders, pirates were all being drawn into the same world: the coastal world of sailors.

Even fear began to change. Running from the Vikings was still seen as reasonable in Ireland; it was one of the few acceptable excuses for breaking the Sabbath. The new and greater fear, though, was of somehow not being able to tell the Norsemen from the Irish any more. The Irish were anxious about the prospect of 'an abbot from among them over every church; / one from among them will assume / the kingship of Ireland.' By 850 two kings already had suspiciously Norse names, and claiming to be an Irish king was a very fluid business, after all, full of legend and counterclaims. Norsemen even seemed to be acquiring Irish habits; Amlaíb, chief of Dublin, was in the business of commissioning poems from the Irish poets ('I bore off from him as the price of my song,' one wrote, 'a horse of the horses of Achall') and he was said to pay up rather more reliably than some of his Norse colleagues.[24]

And yet the Vikings were never secure in Ireland; their kingdom, even their empire, was always elsewhere or on the seas. Their towns looked outwards. In 866 their 'great heathen army' broke into England and took Eoforwic, which was a tiny town with a school, an archbishop and a port of sorts: the religious centre for the kingdom of Northumbria. When they left, the town was Jorvik, which became York: grown in less than a century to a thriving, stinking city,[25] all cesspits and middens and waste, where the hot-metal industries were alive and thriving as they had not been since Roman times, smelting iron, silver and gold, turning lead into glass. There were craftsmen making combs from bone or antler, shoemakers and saddlers, jewellers working in amber and black jet. The scatter of houses on open spaces had been organized into streets and plots, a new plan which owed nothing to the Roman city on the same spot. The city also got its parish churches in Viking times, or most of them, for Norsemen and archbishops alike wanted independence from the English kingdoms, and power of their own, so they worked together. The Archbishop of York was once besieged alongside the Norse king, Olaf, who was on a murderous but profitable raid into England at the time; and this was when Olaf was still a pagan, not yet baptized under English influence.[26] The city had such a separate character, a mix of Anglo and Scandinavian, that it was furiously resistant later to the Norman invasion of England: Norsemen's descendants against Norsemen's descendants.

King Alfred, the ninth-century English hero, recognized other kings who were properly English but entirely subservient to the Danes; 'puppets', you could say. He tried to make a working relationship with the Norse kingdom of East Anglia: each side acknowledging that the other had the power to impose his own law, but both sides agreeing rules for the business of buying horses, cattle or slaves. Churches did deals with the Danes over land, although sometimes the deals were very circumstantial: the Abbot of Carlisle claimed he'd been visited in a dream by St Cuthbert himself, told to buy a Danish slave called Guthred and make him king, and then to ask King Guthred for the land that had once belonged to the communities at Monkwearmouth and Jarrow and other monasteries which had been extinguished. Even when the Anglo-Saxons took back the Danish lands, the Northerners sometimes stayed put and had their tenure confirmed.[27]

For the moment the Vikings needed York as a military base, but 'they were ploughing', according to the *Anglo-Saxon Chronicle* for 876, 'and were providing for themselves'.[28] Just as Dublin was pulling in craftsmen and merchants, laying out streets and defining zones for industry, so in York the Viking influence made a city from a settlement.

A city means a choice of pleasures, some for the belly. There were seeds of dill, celery, opium poppy and coriander: all kinds of spices. There were puffball mushrooms to eat, a luxury out of the woods. There were bees for honey, chickens scratching in yards, oysters in quantity and sometimes mussels, cockles, winkles and whelks. There was herring and eel for everyday eating but there was also cod and haddock from the seas, sturgeon and salmon; and the state of the bones suggests that Vikings knew not to overcook fish.[29] Wine came from the Rhine, soapstone vessels from Scotland, even brooches made by Pictish craftsmen who somehow escaped the various Viking slaughters of their countrymen. Through Denmark came the world: the silver coins of Samarkand, the silks of Byzantium, the cowrie shell currency of the Red Sea.

The base coins of Northumbrian times became pennies rich in silver, coins which manage to muddle together the Viking sword, the hammer of the god Thor and some inspirational Christian messages. 'The city is crammed beyond expression,' the *Life of St Oswald* says, 'and enriched with the treasures of merchants who come from all parts, but above all from the Danish people.'[30]

There was also a point on the riverbank at York called Divelinestaynes, or 'Dublin stones', which suggests a landing place for ships from Dublin, still the closest thing the Vikings had to a capital city. It remained so. Even when the Norsemen were beaten out of England after the battle of Brunanburh, the *Anglo-Saxon Chronicle* breaks into verse to show them 'disgraced in spirit' leaving 'to seek out Dublin and their own land again'.[31] The trouble with 'their own land', which is to say Ireland, was that it had belonged to others in living memory, and those others wanted it back; the Norsemen had to fight. After the battle at Limerick in 968 it was the Irish who 'carried away their soft, youthful, bright matchless girls; their blossoming silk-clad young women; and their active, large and well-formed boys'.[32] Such an appetizing list suggests a very settled and civilized place, the kind that Vikings used to raid. Dublin now became subject to fire setting, to raids and slaughter, but this time from the Irish. Finally its Norse king, Amlaíb Cuarán, went out against all the Irish kings; and he lost. The 'red slaughter' at the battle of Tara in 980 ended the military power of the Vikings in Ireland.

In every other way, though, they remained. They had come as raiders, half-hearted settlers, merchants and slavers and fighters, and in setting up their business they also created towns: Dublin, Wexford, Limerick, Waterford and Cork. Those towns had a life that any Irish king would want to encourage, and of course tax; they were not going to be dismantled just because they were connected to the failing Vikings. In fact, Irish poets came to quite approve of the old enemy's ways, 'sailing ships skilfully over the sea, the greed and business of the Vikings'. Ireland went on buying English Christian slaves until well after the Normans took England, not least because William the Conqueror was in no hurry to change things; 'he enjoyed a share of the profits from this trade,' William of Malmesbury reports.[33]

The Vikings had adjusted reality all round the North Sea. They ran up the Canche River and took out Quentovic, the port for British pilgrims on their way to Rome, the emporium for trade back and forth to England. They stormed the new fort on the island of Walcheren off Zeeland; they are a part of the hidden history of Domburg that the sea once briefly revealed. Their ships forced their way up the Rhine and the IJssel, reached inland ports like Dorestad and Deventer and left traces everywhere: a whalebone batten for a weaving loom left in Frisia, a whalebone T-staff engraved with Anglo-Frisian runes left in one of the raised living mounds along the coast, Arabic coins and coins with Scandinavian images.[34] Charlemagne's empire lost so much silver to the Vikings, in raids and tributes, that tight control of coinage had to be loosened and nobody bothered any more with standardizing weights and types of coin. A fair amount of silver also went underground, buried to protect it from civil unrest, or maybe as a kind of tax avoidance when the Vikings came to demand tribute.[35]

They also left behind their genes. Vikings were not famous for being continent. Dudo in his *History of the Normans,* which was written at the end of the tenth century, wrote that 'by mingling in illicit couplings they generate innumerable children'. Saxo Grammaticus complained: 'they seem to have outlawed chastity and driven it to the brothel'.[36]

More, they broke the limits of the usual world. They went on pirate raids, sometimes as far as the frontiers of the Chinese empire on the Caspian Sea; in the ninth and tenth centuries the Chinese outriders were surprised to meet men who were tall, red-haired and blue-eyed. They connected the Norwegian coast with the Russian badlands all the way south to Constantinople. In Constantinople itself, Vikings became Varangians, the guards who did odd jobs for the Emperor, jobs as odd as collecting his taxes and castrating his enemies. They were the muscle round the throne, big men because the emperors had grave doubts about the usefulness of small men; they were paid off with plunder and trusted, up to a point, because they stood outside the politics of the court. Their privileges could be curious, like the right to steal the palace decorations on Palm Sunday, not just the expensive hangings but also the palm fronds which carried a blessing worth money. They were riotous drinkers, a fact so famous there were satires written about it, where Varangians are the jury in the trial of the Grape, who naturally is convicted, sentenced to be cut down, trampled and have his blood drunk by men until they lose their senses. They also had a stern sense of justice, perhaps surprising for men famous for their violence. If a man tried to kill another, he died. When a Varangian tried to rape a woman he fancied, she grabbed at his sword and stuck him through the heart; and his Varangian colleagues applauded her. They awarded her all the man's property, and threw their friend's body away without burial. He was, they said, a suicide.

Many men went south to Byzantium, so many that the old Swedish law codes had to write special rules on inheritance for those who were living 'in Greece'.[37] Some of them had exceptional stories, both before and after their mercenary careers: Harold Hardrada, for example.

Harold Hardrada ruled Norway for a time, and he led an army into the north of England in 1066 in high hopes of being king there, too. He had also been, for a time, a Varangian. When his half-brother Olaf was forced off the Norwegian throne, Harold waited for his wounds to heal and then prudently went into exile. He became a commander for the prince of Kiev, a mercenary who didn't expect his master to interfere with his wars or his profits. After a while, according to the text called *Advice to the Emperor*, he took five hundred men in armoured ships and made his way to Byzantium; the sagas say he was blown to port by a cool wind, watching the shine of the metal roofs of the city. Onshore, he didn't boast about his rank, because the Byzantine court had every reason to fret about royal and noble plotting, and he didn't claim a great title; instead he again signed up with the mercenaries. He went out with the patrols tackling pirates in the Aegean, because Viking seamanship was a valuable commodity. He went to fight in Sicily and later in Bulgaria. He is said to have fought in Africa, which must mean North Africa. He was a specialist, sent off to take small forts, small cities with a small force of skilled men; eighty towns in Arabia alone. In one of his own poems he says: 'I reddened swords far from my fosterland. The sword sang in the town of the Arabs but that was long ago.'

His world went at least as far east as Jerusalem. The sagas say he 'made the whole way to Jerusalem peaceable, slaying robbers and other wicked folk', that 'all cities and castles were opened for him', that in Jerusalem he made offerings at the shrines of 'so much money in gold and jewels that it is hard to compute the amount'. Most likely he went with the masons who were to rebuild the Church of the Holy Sepulchre, commanding the guards who protected them; and since he was a Varangian, an imperial bodyguard, it's likely he was also guarding members of the imperial family, maybe the exceedingly pious sisters of the Empress. There were robbers on the way – there always were – and he dealt with them. There was really no reason for castles or cities to stay closed to him: he was not crusading; he went in a time of peace, when the Caliph himself was the son of a Byzantine mother and quite happy to have Christians on his territory.

He knew when it was time for him to go home, though, as Vikings so often did. He wanted to be king in Norway alongside the new King Magnus; he wanted to be recognized in the place which had sent him away. His problem was that the Byzantine Emperor was fighting off a general who was set on a coup, and also preparing to fight off the threatening Russians. Harold was much too useful to be allowed to leave.

There were iron chains strung across the harbour at Byzantium to stop anyone moving along the Bosphorus, but he had to go through the Bosphorus to get to the Black Sea and then to the rivers that would take him home. His solution was simple. He took two ships and sailed them right up to the chains in the water. He ordered men to take the oars, and anyone who was not needed to row was to take all his goods and bedding and cram everything together at the stern of the ships. The prows rose and caught on the chains; the ships stopped dead. Then Harold ordered the men to run suddenly forward into the bows and the ships tilted down. One of them stuck fast and broke open; many men died. The other tilted and slid down into the water.

Harold Hardrada was free to go home.

He turned out to be a generous king, remembered for helping out the Icelanders in time of famine and for his princely gifts. He was 'famous and excellent for [his] long and successful travels'. He was also ambitious; Norway was not enough. In 1066 there was no obvious heir to the throne of England and Harold went after the crown. His invading army ran into the defending Anglo-Saxons at a village called Stamford Bridge. Carnage followed, and Harold was among the dead.

'He went out as a Viking to gain fame and wealth,' the saga says, 'and then took rule over all people he could conquer. Therefore he fell on another king's soil.'

All this was happening in the warm years when the seas were open and the Northern lands looked green, before the returning cold began to jam the Northern seas with ice. The Norsemen made the most of the opportunity. They were used to brutal, lightless winters, and they did not have high expectations of summer, but they did know about the seasons for travelling. They knew when to move.

They did what almost no other people has done in the Common Era: they settled truly empty lands. They came to the Faroe Islands around 825 and panicked a few hermits into leaving, which accounts for the grievance of the monk Dicuil. They noticed the birds going north each year, and they guessed at land even further out. Around 860 they began cautiously exploring the coasts of Iceland. They found traces that Irish hermits had left behind after they, too, had been frightened away by the Norsemen's reputation for being bloody and persistent. The fact that hermits had survived at all in such a remote place may have encouraged the newcomers. They saw the fish, birds and seals, the scrubwood everywhere and the driftwood, and above all open spaces in a climate that was still mild. They were herdsmen looking at empty pastures.[38]

The result was a small empire without enemies for a while, an almost innocent kind of pioneering. After all, there was no law at all in either Iceland or the Faroes before the Norse, no customs and rules, no assemblies to make decisions and judge the guilty; no farms to divide up land and produce food, no trade and no burial places to keep a common memory alive. The new Iceland maintained for centuries a curious kind of democracy, rather more democratic in our modern sense than anything in ancient Greece. There was no king. Many women and men had independent farms with no landlord, and no feudal overlord. When they met in assemblies, the *Alþingi*, each could vote to choose which of the local chieftains he would follow.

They had no towns, and none of the pecking order that goes with a settled town; their social order was too new for that. Authority rested not on title or name, but on what people knew or thought they knew about each other. Farmers took to writing in their own Icelandic version of Old Norse, or at least to having the priests write for them in Icelandic, because they needed a solid form of memory to tell them what laws they had made, who owned what, where boundaries ran, how they had come to Iceland in the first place and from what family. They constructed a past for themselves, which was a practical thing to do because it set the rules and decided who owned what, and then they recorded it. They also wrote down a past that was heroic and even glorious if you have a good stomach for gore: the past of the sagas. The process was costly, so it must have been very important: to write down one saga you first had to kill between fifty and a hundred calves to get the skins for vellum.[39]

In time, the farms merged into great estates. The Church took over half the land. Norway's king and then Denmark's ruled over Iceland and introduced the very alien notion of tax. But around 1000 CE, the island itself told a story: how you could live out beyond the waters that had once been taken for the very edge of the world, how you could satisfy the hunger for land and space, and how a whole society could invent itself.

The temptation was always to go further. The world had not yet turned colder and the waters were as open as they ever would be. Land that would in time be snowed under and iced in was still alive and fertile. And there were always people with good reason to move on. Erik the Red left Norway for frontier Iceland 'on account of some killings' and after a while he had to leave Iceland on account of some more killings; he needed a fresh start after his first fresh start. He had to find a new frontier.

He heard stories about islands lying off a great land mass to the west, the skerries off the coast of Greenland: Gunnbjarnarsker, notorious for their brutishness to visitors and settled by a man who himself was running away from the consequences of doing murder. Erik sensibly went beyond the skerries. He came into land under the white ice of a glacier, and he tacked south along the coast looking for somewhere to settle; for three winters he went up and down the coast, claiming site after site by giving them names, choosing between the possibilities. He saw pasture for sheep and maybe some cattle, rich fishing, walrus to hunt for their tusks and the hide that made such good ropes. He also saw the emptiness of the land, just like Iceland, just like the Faroes. It would be two more centuries before the Inuit moved south into Greenland as the seas began to freeze, and began their challenge to the Europeans: a Norse sheep turned out to be much easier to hunt than a wild walrus, even with the Inuits' special skills.

Erik had found a place where a man could invent himself and be what he said he was, not the sum total of what other people thought. He named the land 'Greenland' because, as he said, 'men would be keen to go there since the land had a good name'. And he thrived. He had room, he had land and he had life on his own terms.[40] He was no outlaw any more; 'He was held in the highest esteem and everyone deferred to his authority,' the *Saga of the Greenlanders* says.[41]

Nothing forced the Greenlanders to look further west; they did so by accident. The sagas start to disagree at this point about who first went further. It might have been a trader called Bjarni who got lost in north winds and thick fog until he didn't know where he was but thought he was probably not off Greenland any more. It may have been Leif, son of Erik the Red, who makes a weightier story. He was commissioned, one saga says, to bring Christianity to Greenland. He had low expectations; he did not expect his message to be welcome. The Norse were turning Christian almost everywhere, but in Greenland, in the hard winters when hunters didn't always return from the hunt and those who came back caught very little, it was still quite usual to invite a 'little prophetess' to tell the future and try magic to improve it. She'd come in black, jewels down her front, with white gloves of catskin. She sat on a high chair stuffed with chicken feathers, she fed on a diet of hearts and she listened to the magic songs which even good Christians knew from their childhood. She took her time until she could hear, she said, the spirits summoned by the songs.

On his voyage out from Norway to Greenland, Leif was blown off course, tossed about at sea for many days. When navigation depended on a clear view of the sun and stars it was easy to be entirely lost, terrifyingly alone on the blank ocean. Leif found himself running along the shoreline of a land that should not have been there, territory beyond the waters at the edge of the world: a land with forest, with something like self-sown wheat, probably wild rye, and grapevines. When he eventually made it to Greenland, he was eager to return to this unknown place. His father, Erik the Red, meant to go with him as the official leader of the band, but he fell off his horse on the way to the boat, hurt his shoulder and broke his ribs. He was lucky. Leif's ships went wildly off course again, saw Ireland, saw Iceland and tacked back and forth all summer. They barely made it back home before winter began.

On the next voyage three ships set out, with 140 men, the saga says, and most of them from Greenland. This time, the Greenlanders landed on the unknown coast. They found a land of ice, flat like a stone, which did not seem hopeful, so they sailed south, where a forest rose gently up from white beaches. After a few more days at sea there was an island, which sheltered an inlet. There were shallows, there were salmon larger than they had ever seen, the winters were so mild that cattle could feed outside on the grass, which was never frosted and never withered, and there were butternuts, a kind of walnut the Norsemen could not have known before. The crews dug trenches in the sand and, in the morning, found them full of flounders. There were so many deer that the hill where they slept looked like a dunghill. There was more. The German slave Tyrkir, who had been like a foster-father to Leif, went missing one evening, and Leif was concerned; he took twelve men and went out to look for him. They met Tyrkir coming back and looking distinctly pleased. Leif asked why he was so late; Tyrkir said he'd gone only a little further than the others, but he had found something: grapevines and grapes. Leif asked if he could be sure, and Tyrkir said he was certain; 'where I was born there was no lack of grapevines and grapes'.

The sagas sometimes tell the same story with different characters, or tell the same story twice, or contradict each other: if listeners and readers want a history, they have to put it together for themselves. In another version, a matched pair of Scottish slaves, a man called Haki and a woman called Hekja, faster than any deer, were sent to run south down the shore and come back within three days; which they did, with the grapes they had found and a kind of wheat. The wheat was important, since Greenlanders had to bring grain from Norway, but the great constant in this story is the wild vines that climbed through the trees. Grapes meant wine, and wine was a treasure that was harder to find than gold. Wine didn't last well, was not yet a refined and crafted drink, but it was the drink of chieftains; the Viking chief of Frisia, you remember, was resentful at being left in charge of a land without wine. If Leif Eriksson had wine, he could build prestige and even power in Greenland by sharing it. Naturally, he called the new land after the vines: Vinland. He was in America.

This is where the saga story turns stranger. There are no dragons, but there is a one-legged monster with a fat belly. A woman, dark like the local people, appears suddenly to a Norse woman called Gudrid and says her name is the same: Gudrid. There is trouble, and she vanishes just like a spirit. There is even a proper, murderous villainess: schemer, cheat and axe murderer, and we shall come to her. Stranger than all this, though, is a sense that the Norse somehow tipped forward in time. They lived through the same threats and tensions that would wreck the first English colony in Virginia six hundred years later, or make life hard for the Dutch in New Amsterdam. They had to manage the edgy, sometimes bloody connections with the peoples living where the Europeans might want to live; the calculations of what they would risk in order to stay; and the internal rivalries that broke up expeditions which seemed to have such clear purpose at the start. There was also, as usual, sex.

These stories need a grounding in reality, if we are to understand them, and there is one. At L'Anse aux Meadows on the north edge of Newfoundland there are the physical remains of a camp that could hold a hundred people: a gateway[42] to Vinland and a careful foothold on the land. It lies close to the ocean, which is where the Norse always felt most easy, and it guards a broad inlet that leads south to the wheat and the grapes on the St Lawrence River. The building required long and hard work: eighty-six trees cut and shaped for the three halls alone, and fifteen hundred cubic metres of sod for the walls. The style of those halls dates the camp to the turn of the eleventh century, just as the sagas do, and the style is exactly what you would expect from Icelanders, exactly what they built at first in Greenland, with no stone foundations, with sod walls inside the stone walls, fireplaces and sunken huts. The buildings had proper roofs, so they were meant to go through winter; and in fact the sailing season from Greenland to the coast of America was so short that trying to get there and back in a single summer would leave hardly enough time for a serious look at the land. The stores are unusually large, as though the Norse expected to bring everything they needed or else ship out rich quantities of goods. The fact that there are three halls suggests the camp may have been organized for the crews of three ships, just as the saga says; and whoever lived there must have made serious journeys south because we know they ate butternuts, which are unknown in Newfoundland but grow where the wild grapes grow further south. So Greenlanders did come in large numbers to Vinland to test out the ground, and they had a long habit of going west. Given the numbers of human beings on Greenland at the time – no more than five hundred – a camp with room to sleep a hundred women and men was a work that implies a big decision: a plan to open a new world.

And yet the Greenlanders were scouting, not settling, because they had no byres or pens to protect their animals as breeding stock for the future; they brought only what they needed for milk and meat. They would expect to spend years exploring before settling; their fathers had examined Iceland for years before making homes there, and Erik the Red spent three winters exploring Greenland before he settled. The sagas tell the story of the Norsemen in Vinland over three years, too, and the physical remains confirm that they stayed no more than ten years. They had with them what they needed to maintain ships, catch fish and keep warm in winter. They had a simple iron smelter, and supplies of iron ore nearby, to make nails to mend their ships; they worked wood, and the remains are still in the ground; they kept fist-sized stones to sink fishing nets; their halls had fireplaces. When they left, it was an orderly planned retreat; they left behind mostly broken things.

So why did this America prove to be too far? Probably the first explorers always meant to return to Greenland from this voyage, but the whole point of their expedition was to think about settling later in Vinland, which did not happen. L'Anse aux Meadows itself was a site exposed to the brute Atlantic in winter, a site much like Greenland or even Iceland, with fish and forests full of softwood and not much else; but the pull of the place was the Vinland of stories, with grapes and wheat and the forests full of useful hardwoods. The trouble was that to get those good things meant going south and confronting two enemies: the local people and themselves.

The locals came visiting, short men, dark with tangled hair and broad cheeks and features that the Norse found threatening, huge eyes to scan the newcomers; and when they'd looked they went away in their hide-covered canoes. The next time, they came in such numbers that the water looked as though it was scattered with coals. They wanted to trade skins and furs for red cloth and swords and spears, but the Norse had no weapons to spare; and the locals' bargaining style was unexpected. When the red cloth was running out, they just accepted less and less for each skin, as though the point was to make an exchange not insist on a value. They took milk as well.

In the middle of the trading, the one bull the Norsemen owned came charging out of the woods, bellowing and snorting, and the locals took to their boats in panic and stayed away for three weeks. This time, they came back like an army: a steady stream of boats full of men who brandished poles and shrieked alarmingly. The Norsemen assumed they were at war and went out fighting until a large black object, the size of a sheep's gut, landed noisily on the beach among them: a stone, most likely, from a catapult. If weapons were going to rain down, the Norse wanted to move upriver and fight in just one direction, with a cliff to protect their backs. They began a very quick retreat.

A woman called Freydis came out of the camp and told the men they ought to be able to kill off the natives like sheep. She said she'd fight better than any of them if she only had a weapon, and she wanted to go upriver with them even though she was pregnant. She was moving so slowly that the natives caught up with her by the corpse of a Norseman called Thorbrand. Surrounded, Freydis took up the dead man's sword, slapped her bare breast against it and the locals ran away in terror, or so the saga says; she must have seemed like a spirit, violent, pregnant and appalling. The Norsemen came back and congratulated her on, of all things, her luck.

Something changed during this battle: an end to any sense of ease, the realization that 'despite everything the land had to offer there, they would be under constant threat of attack from its inhabitants,' the saga says. The locals moved in such curious ways, sometimes a whole flotilla of canoes going south or going north on puzzling migrations, sometimes bursting out of the dense forest. They didn't make sense. They could kill, but they did not understand iron, it seemed, because when they picked up an axe they tested it on wood, and then on stone, and then threw it away because it broke on stone and must be useless. They were an unsettling presence for would-be settlers, especially women and men who had been used to moving into empty places for a century and a half. After the fighting, the saga says, the Norse 'made ready to depart for their own country'.[43]

Freydis in *Erik the Red's Saga* is a kind of heroine. In the *Saga of the Greenlanders* she is someone quite different: a horror. She's a bully of a woman, married to a no-account man and strictly for his money; but she was the bastard daughter of Erik the Red, which made her half-sister to Leif Eriksson. She planned her own voyage to this western land called Vinland, and she went to ask Erik for his old houses there; he wouldn't give them to her but said that she could use them. She found two brothers with a ship and offered a deal: they would all sail out to Vinland and they'd divide whatever they made and whatever they found. From the very start she and her husband meant to cheat: they took extra fighting men. When she landed, just a little after the brothers, she found them already settled in the houses and she asked them what they were doing. They said they thought she'd meant to keep her word about sharing things. Freydis told them Erik had offered the houses to her, not them.

Her partners went off and built themselves a new longhouse. When winter came, the two parties tried to waste their time with chess and other board games, with any kind of amusement to get through the dead days, but their mutual distrust and dislike stopped all that. One morning Freydis went down to the brothers' hall and stood silent for a while in the doorway. The brothers asked what she was doing there. They said they liked the land well enough but they didn't understand why there had to be such tension between them for no reason at all. She asked if they would exchange ships with her because she wanted to leave, and the brothers agreed, anything for a more quiet life. She then went back to her husband, climbed into bed and her wet, cold feet woke him up. She told him the brothers had refused her offer, had even struck and hurt her; it was his duty to protect his woman against the single men.[44] She said he was a coward and she was far from home and if he didn't avenge her, she would divorce him.

The no-account husband called up his men and went down to the brothers' longhouse while they were still asleep. His men bound the brothers and their crew and took them outside. Freydis gave the orders now: she ordered death. The brothers' women stood among the bodies and none of her husband's crew would kill them. 'Hand me an axe,' Freydis said. She told her own men that if they were lucky enough to get back to Greenland, they should say the brothers' crew had all decided to stay behind. She said if they told a different story, she would make sure they were killed.[45]

The stories can't be mashed together to make history, but they may help explain what happened in Vinland. For a start, there must have been some talk of settlement – of 'staying behind' in Vinland – or else Freydis could never have made the men tell such a lie. The sagas produce a dramatic explanation for why it did not happen. The simple fact that the Norsemen were unnerved by the local people would not do because heroes are never unnerved; but they were certainly disturbed to meet peoples they didn't understand and couldn't predict, so different they didn't know how to classify them. They rescued two local boys from a rock at one point, and thought they might be 'trolls'. They taught them to talk, or so they thought, after which they never lacked for fish; so the locals might count as animals with no language. They also had very strong magic: after Freydis came back from scaring off the natives, the men came to think that the whole hostile army Freydis scattered was an illusion. They found it very difficult to live with magic and illusion, the sense of being out of their own world.

The camp evidently broke into factions, ship by ship, crew by crew; this was not an expedition sure of what it wanted and what it ought to do. The fact that the sagas show the factions trying to work together means they started by feeling truly separate, little nations inside a small community; and in the end they failed to get together. The Norse, alarmed by an incomprehensible enemy outside, managed to find even more enemies inside.

The oddity is that a woman takes the blame for all this. It is odd because it is taken for granted at first that Freydis has the right background to commission ships and plan an expedition and even organize the use of a camp already built in Vinland. Other women had done that sort of thing before; *Erik the Red's Saga* mentions Aud the Deep-Minded, widow of a king of Dublin, who secretly built a ship in the forests of Caithness and sailed out by way of the Orkneys to Iceland with twenty free-born men and many bondsmen who had been taken prisoner by the Vikings. Aud owned the ship, organized the crew, and led her free men even into Christianity; she stands as mother and a godmother to Iceland. The saga writers respected what a woman could do.

Freydis might be wicked, she might have magic to see off the natives' magic, but more than anything she stands for the other great anxiety: the disruptive power of sex. Some women came to Vinland, as she did, with their husbands, but most men travelled without wives, and they were away three years. A woman like Freydis, men feared, could stir up her husband's jealousy and get men killed, could play off the married faction against the single men; that alone gave her a disconcerting power. Even if she turned out to be an axe murderer, and she did, the situation would always make her desirable and essential; and even without a strong woman like Freydis, the facts of the situation were disruptive. The saga says flatly: 'Many quarrels arose, as the men who had no wives sought to take those of the married men.'[46]

Disagreements, ill-feeling, living together closely for three long years without a break and without the comfort of going home – all kept the camp edgy. There were times of hunger when a man might go almost mad, as Thorhall did: found on the edge of a cliff, mumbling and staring and scratching and pinching himself, trying to make sure he had found the right way to pray to a god who would send them something to eat. Men asked him what he was doing. He said it made no difference and that he'd got along without their advice for most of his life. The Norse were used to organized shipping in the Greenland summers, to sizeable stores, and above all to a settled pattern of loyalty and duty that kept a person fed, warmed and more or less safe. They had never before met weird peoples who talked like beasts but could kill, who blocked their way to what the Norse really wanted from Vinland.

They began to think they might have gone too far.

Being a Viking was a failing trade. In twelfth-century Orkney, Svein Asleifarson[47] had family estates and eighty followers spending the winter in his huge hall; he was 'the greatest man the western world has ever seen in ancient or modern times', the *Orkneyinga Saga* says, 'apart from those of higher rank than himself'. Such greatness cost a great deal to maintain; followers want meat, drink and money. So when he had carefully supervised the springtime sowing, he went off plundering in the Hebrides or in Ireland, which he called his 'spring trip'. He came back just before mid-summer and stayed until the fields had been reaped and the grain was safely stored, and then he went off on his 'autumn trip' and stayed away as a marauder until the first month of winter was ended. He had his seasons as a farmer, his seasons as a Viking.

He took five big ships on a good trip, ships fitted out for rowing to make them reliable and manoeuvrable. They tackled the Hebrides first, but the trouble with being a seasonal raider is that people know in which season they ought to bury everything valuable. The islanders did just that, and the Isle of Man was not much better. Svein evidently did not worry that he was raiding the settlements of men like him: from Norway, generations back.

His luck turned on the open sea when he challenged two English freighters carrying loads of lavish broadcloth. He boarded both ships and left the crews with only food and the clothes they wore, and then he sailed for the Hebrides to share out the loot with his crew and boast to everyone else about his robbing. He also made awnings for his ships from the broadcloth so everyone could appreciate his haul. If he could be farmer and Viking, they could be both victims one moment and admirers the next: nothing need be settled. For the voyage home, he had the cloth stitched to the front of the sails so that his ships came into harbour under the power of their loot.

His return home was the excuse for a grandiose feast, but there was one man who did not praise Svein: the Earl Harald. Instead, he asked him to stop his raiding. He said it was better to be safe back home, that 'Most troublemakers are doomed to be killed unless they stop of their own free will.' Svein acknowledged he was getting older and less suited to the hardships of war. He said he wanted one more trip and then he would give up raiding. 'Hard to tell which comes first, old fellow,' the earl said. 'Death or glory.'

The raider went out one last time. Again, he had bad luck in the Hebrides, where everyone was ready for him, but he sailed on to Ireland, looting everywhere he could. He came to Dublin, to the town that was founded by Vikings like him, walked through the walls almost without resistance; the settled people, the traders busy with business, were not ready for him. He owned the city that day. He put in his own men to run it, named his price for leaving the city in peace, left the townspeople to choose hostages and went back to his ships in triumph.

But the fact of settlement was very strong, and the Dubliners were not prepared to give up what they'd built. They'd had enough of this old anachronism and his kind, even if only a few centuries back his kind had been the necessary condition of their way of life.

They thought of Svein and his men as dangerous, disruptive

animals, and hunted them the same way: digging pits in the ground, disguising them with straw and waiting to see if the Orkney men would fall into the trap.

They did. They say Svein was the last of them to die.[48]

# 5.

# Fashion

The night was dry and the fire blazed out in one of the long wooden warehouses on the waterfront at Bergen. This is 1248 on the coast of Norway. The king was in the town with his bodyguard, the town was full, but despite all the people fighting the fire they 'could get no hold on it'. The steeple of the great church of St Mary went up in flames, and 'the force of the fire was so great that it was tossed up into the castle and that began to blaze. Many men were burned inside before they could get out.'[1]

'The force of the sin-avenging flames,' the English chronicler Matthew Paris wrote with the great moral certainty of a man who was safely offshore, 'flew like a fire-breathing dragon, dragging its tail after it.' He diagnosed 'the severity of divine vengeance'.[2]

The king went out in a boat to the barges lying offshore, and 'got there great kettles. They were filled with sea-water, and so hauled up onto the wharves, after that the sea-water was poured onto the fire and so it was quenched.'[3] But his stone castle was 'for the most part reduced to ashes', Paris wrote, and all that remained of eleven parishes was four religious houses and the 'palace, chapel and lodgings of the lord King'.[4]

A few days later, Paris was celebrating Mass when lightning tore off the thatched roof of the loft that sheltered the king's son and then struck Matthew Paris's ship and 'dashed the mast asunder into such small chips that they could scarcely be seen anywhere. One bit of the mast did hurt to a man who had got on board the ship from the town to buy finery.'[5]

We're three days after a fire that ruined a town, in the middle of a storm that is tearing off roofs, and someone is busy buying 'finery': clothes, and fine, fashionable clothes at that. Fashion must have a longer, stranger history than we thought.

The great sagas from Iceland have everything you expect: heroes, killings, dragons, feuds, great voyages and great horrors. They also have something less likely: they have dandies.

Consider Kali in the *Orkneyinga Saga* who comes back from five weeks away from Norway at a large, muddy gathering in the port of Grimsby in northern England, where he's been meeting men from the Orkneys, the Hebrides and mainland Scotland. He starts a round of the taverns back in Bergen to show off what he's learned. 'Kali was something of a dandy and was stylishly dressed now that he was just back from England,' the saga says; he saw style abroad and brought it back. He wasn't alone. His new mate Jon, son of Peter Serksson, 'was a great one for clothes'.[6] Bergen, the saga says, was full of people from abroad and the men needed an audience for what they were wearing. Kali and Jon later started a blood feud, as you might expect, and were devoted to drunk and murderous brawling and campaigns of revenge; but they also had style.

In the *Saga of Olaf the Gentle*, the thirteenth-century storyteller Snorri Sturlson tells how rich men started to settle in Bergen when it was still a new town, a hundred years or so before; how clubs were started and drinking bouts were common; and 'at that time, new fashions in dress made their appearance'. Men wore tight breeches, gold rings at the ankle, gowns that trailed and were laced with ribbons and high shoes embroidered over with white silk and gold laces: wilfully impractical for sailors, traders and warriors in a port in a cold climate, which was the whole point. Bergen men were already wearing the long, draped robes that would soon be the mark of the aristocracy further south. They matched their fashions with new and pretentious manners: King Olaf had cup-bearers to pour the drink at dinner and a candle-bearer with lit tapers beside each one of his guests.[7] Within a hundred more years – in 1174, because for once the sagas give an exact year – it was possible for a man to be damned socially for wearing clothes that everyone knew were out of date. The dreary statesman Erling, according to the *Saga of the Sons of Harald*, 'wore old-fashioned clothing – kirtles [long overshirts] with long waists and long sleeves, and likewise shirts and doublets with long sleeves, French cloaks and shoes coming high up on the calves'. This was when he was a kind of regent and the saga disapproves of the way 'he had the king wear similar clothes when he was young'. The king grew up correctly, even so: 'When he became independent, he dressed with much finery.'[8]

Remarkably, the people of Bergen were doing much the same. The town was a port tucked into a fjord on the Norwegian coast, a mass of wood buildings that burned down often and left behind whole tracts for archaeologists to investigate. In the layers from the eleventh to the thirteenth centuries, there are shoes – shoes for women, men and children – and a startling number of them are decorated with embroidery in silk. Now, Lucca was beginning to produce silk in the twelfth century, and grumpy Paris clerics had begun to denounce the wearing of 'worm's excrement', but silk still seemed a luxury to Southerners, mostly imported from the Middle East. In later illuminated manuscripts embroidered shoes are worn by grand and powerful people to show rank and to show money. But the Bergen evidence does not come from the parts of town with castles or riches; it is everywhere.[9] There are so many shoes, even old grown-ups' shoes cut down for children, that it's clear that silk yarn was being brought in quantity to the Norwegian coast long before it was the mark of social-climbing persons in Paris, a full century before the Queen of France, Jeanne of Navarre, became so famously angry at the glamour of women in Bruges and in Ghent for their silks and jewels; 'I thought I was the only queen,' she snapped, 'and here I see queens by the hundred.'[10]

Trade was stirring up the world, making new things available to new kinds of people for a price. Silk belongs to that world in motion: carried up Russian rivers from the east and across the Baltic or in Venetian galleys to the Flemish coast. So does fashion itself: it belongs to people who know something different from their settled ways and can imagine taking on other people's customs, other people's style. It is not about uniforms, as a monk or a courtier might wear; it is about choosing to reinvent yourself and your status. It didn't start at great courts when there were artists to record the tilt of a bosom or the length of a skirt, and it was never a woman's matter; it was of interest to the men brawling in the mud of Grimsby.

It left traces on Greenland, far out on the wild sea beyond Norway, even as the ice began to creep onto the meadows and start the process which drove the settlers out in the late fifteenth century. Long before the earliest-known patterns for cutting out clothes, which come from Germany and Spain in the sixteenth century, the Greenland settlers knew enough to cut clothes in new styles and they cared about doing so;[11] yet their lives were as raw and careful as could be. They didn't waste a single sinew, bone or organ of their sheep; scrotums became small bags for storage, horns became eating implements, some bones turned into reels for storing spun yarn and the tibia sometimes became flutes. They didn't waste wool, either, since they depended on it for sails to travel and clothes to keep out the cold. They paid their priests in the cloth known as *vaðmál*, and that name means a 'cloth measure' because cloth often worked exactly like money: a way to pay bills.

So they learned rather early not to waste cloth and they knew the old ways could be wasteful, making a shirt the width of the cloth coming off the loom and not bothering with seams or careful cutting. Instead they shaped clothes to the body, cut very carefully, sewed together the elements to make a shirt or a shift; in an astonishingly short time, your farmer and your farmer's wife in the blind Arctic winters had tailored clothes. It was a matter of sense and economy. Clothes were mostly pulled on over the head, but they had buttonholes which were an innovation and even a scandal further south, they had distinct collars, they were flared out from the shoulders, they could be dyed with borders of madder red, which had to be imported. Everyone wore a hood. These were not choices born of necessity, like the fur of arctic hare woven into cloth for warmth in the harshest months of winter; the Greenlanders brought in cloth when they did not need to, a reddish diamond twill from England, a rough weave from Ireland, because they liked and valued them. They sent away their own cloth for sale in distinctive stripes and checks and patterns, so other people could make choices.

When the settlers had been frozen out, chased out and starved, one last ship worked along the Greenland coast, captained by a man called Jon the Greenlander. He was blown off course deep into one of the fjords and there he found a body lying face down among the remains of deserted settlements: the last of the colonists. 'On his head he had a well-sewn hood,' Jon noticed, 'his other clothes were partly of vaðmál, partly of sealskin.' Even at the miserable end of a colonial experiment as far west from Europe as Europeans had ever managed to settle, what he noticed and reported was a 'well-sewn' hood.[12]

Fashion, choosing how to dress and changing it at will, was not just on Paris streets or in the flamboyant court of Flanders, places where people had rank to show, money to spend and time to waste. It is much more than those lovingly painted robes in illuminated manuscripts from the fourteenth century, those ladies posing very carefully because it would clearly be difficult to move. The shoes in Bergen, the shirts on Greenland, mark it as one of the aspirations born of the rough business of trade.

Since trade was involved there was one consolation: the ships that brought the material also delivered someone to take the blame. It was usually the French. Robert I, King of Naples, blamed the French for the bumfreezer styles of the 1330s, even though he was himself from Anjou. In the middle of the fifteenth century, Florence banned deep V-shaped necklines on a woman's dress just on the suspicion of being French. And the English, like the priest Alexander Barclay in his *Ship of Fools* of 1509, reckoned fancy clothing all came from France, as he said, 'like the pox'.[13]

There had once been a time when parents could bequeath clothes to their children knowing they would be wearable long after their deaths and, even more important, they would still have the same significance. A couple of aristocrats drawing up their will in 863 – the Emperor's sister and an Italian count – made a point of leaving to their oldest and second-oldest sons their clothes that were woven and decorated with gold; they were handing on badges of rank that everybody could understand, and they were sure their sons would be able to go on wearing them.[14] The social order was fixed, after all, and everyone knew how to read the clothes on other people's backs.

The sober, simple clothes of a monk had enormous significance to laypeople. Wearing the same clothes as a holy man was a kind of magic: for two centuries people reckoned they ought to wear monastic clothes when dying so as to be in the right style for the Last Judgement, until the *Lay Folks' Catechism* of 1357 found it necessary to point out that a man can't be guaranteed a place in Heaven even 'though he had upon him in his death the clothes that Christ wore here on earth in His manhood'. Nicholas of Bruère, who paid ten marks for a chance to live in a monastery and wear 'at my latter end the habit of St Benedict', was entirely out of luck.[15]

It was different if you were the ones obliged to wear these plain and meaningful clothes; even holy men revolted. Monks on Lindisfarne, Bede says, had to be 'discouraged from wearing expensively dyed cloth and are expected to be content with natural wool'.[16] In one of Alcuin's letters to Higbaldus from the court of Charlemagne, he worries about the manliness, the modesty and propriety of the church, which had just been wrecked and burned by Vikings; Alcuin denounces excess and display and he insists that 'vanity in dress is not fitting for men'.[17] Church councils in the ninth century had to order nuns and monks to wear their habits; twelfth-century monks were told off for going to Mass 'indecently dressed – in lay garments – open in front and behind'; and in the thirteenth century the punishment for taking the habit off at all was excommunication. Monks were particularly forbidden to wear anything split, tight, short, pleated or, worst of all, with the new-fangled buttons. It was not easy to insist on this because if someone in holy orders had a sizeable income – two hundred marks a year or more, itself an affront to vows of poverty – he was entitled to wear the same splendour as 'knights of the same rent'. Money has a way of dissolving the rules.[18]

Noble and royal courts, meanwhile, required liveries to identify who was who and show their loyalties. By 1303 the French were making uniforms to define everyone entitled to attend the opening of the Parlement: fashion had its bureaucratic uses. Students and professors at Paris University could be picked out in a crowd by the way they dressed, which was soberly. The fur you wore became an exact marker of your standing: ermine for princely families, because white was such a rare colour, down to lambskin for the king's fool and the children's servants. Rules could change, though, as they did when lambskin, always natural and never dyed, was taken up by the elegant people after 1430.

At fourteenth-century tournaments, the women all wore the same colour, had the same devices embroidered on their sleeves, led the knights out to the jousting field with colour co-ordinated ribbons, as consciously designed for a deliberate effect as any chorus line in a modern theatre; at Saint-Denis in 1389 the frocks were a rich dark green, the left sleeves were embroidered in silver and gold with the king's device of a broom pod set in May foliage, and the ribbons were green silk splashed with gold. The ladies became a walking sign of solidarity, nothing individual about them, and a flattering background to the queen who chose to wear scarlet from head to toe.[19]

A man displayed his class walking down the street. A professional wore a long robe, but nobles could afford to flaunt their buttocks with a short doublet as they did in thirteenth-century Flanders. Ordinary people weren't meant to change styles at all or even have an idea of style; or so the privileged thought. In Flanders, most women wore the same for centuries, and the only change for most men in the fifteenth century was that they brought their belts up from buttock level to the waist.[20] The problem was that rules could fall into disuse. Long robes were once reserved for the literate, for lawyers and priests, but in 1467 Jacques du Clercq noticed 'there wasn't a journeyman, however minor, who didn't have a long robe down to his ankle'.

For if clothes had such clear meaning, they were dangerous: anyone could open the wrong wardrobe and put on a different status, a different class. In the thirteenth-century *Le Roman de la Rose* there is a character called Faker who says he's good at changing clothes, so he can be 'now a knight, now a monk, a bishop, a chaplain, now a clerk, now a priest, or a student or a master or the owner of a proper castle or just a man who works in the forests. In short, I can be a prince or I can be a page, whatever rank I like.'[21] Clothes defined him, and he chooses how he wants to be defined: which is the essence of fashion, which means changing the way you dress just because you want to; and also means having a shrewd idea of what your time and place require so you can be defiant.

In a more settled society that might just seem absurd, suggesting kids out clubbing or some carnival queen in her crown and robes. In a time when rank and status and money were all shifting, the easy changes of fashion were alarming. All around the North Sea the old kind of manor was disintegrating, which meant that noble lands were losing their old value. Cities were growing where once there had only been a market. Nobody had to stay in place any more; if you left the land you had a good chance of work in the new workshops and manufactures in those cities. Some men were making serious money, merchants or manufacturers, and they wanted the glory that goes with being rich. They dressed like nobles.

These issues were so tangled that the law was invoked to make things at least seem simple. If law laid down who could wear what, and who was forbidden what, then perhaps all the other issues would somehow resolve themselves. So when the law started to regulate how people dressed in the thirteenth and fourteenth centuries, and tried to put down excess, there was always a common heart to the message: go back in time, know your place and dress it. Power did not like rivals. The King of France in 1279 issued an ordinance that no noble could own more than four robes made of miniver, the fur of squirrels, and none at all of cloth that cost more than thirty *sous tournois* the Parisian yard; the king wanted to go on standing out as king.[22]

And yet the technology of clothes began to allow all kinds of choice; tailoring, at least the cutting of cloth to create fitted clothing, goes back in London to the early thirteenth century,[23] which is also when you start to find specialist cutters and sewers of clothing, the first tailors, in northern France and along the Rhine. Tailoring was usual at grand courts, so tailoring allowed anyone to imply that they were part of the court without saying so, and without breaking the law.

In Italian cities, these laws were aimed at women for the most convoluted reason: their clothes cost so much that men couldn't marry, which was leading to sodomy, so fashion was distracting everyone from the serious business of replenishing the population of cities like Florence.[24] In the North, the aims were rather different. The English were much more concerned with men's clothes than women's (which was a quite general rule in the North).[25] England wanted to maintain its solid system of class, of course, but also to protect English trades against foreign goods. All this was itself dressed up with a moral anxiousness, so the laws about fashion were meant to adjust people's souls as well as their pockets and their wardrobes, and make them better persons. They would obviously be better if they knew their place.

The laws kept coming to make sure the wrong people did not wear the right clothes. In England, no furs for anyone making less than £100 a year; in Hainault no ermine or silk for servants; in Scotland after 1430, no dyed clothes in bright colours for the working classes; in France in 1485, a means test for cloth of gold, which was restricted to nobles who lived nobly and had at least two thousand *livres tournois* a year to pay for it. These laws suggest that the wrong people had the cash, and they were looking much better than they were meant to be.[26]

Fashion became something to talk about when you couldn't quite discuss all the alarming social change that it made visible. It was becoming a moral issue.

Mockery was the start. The sainted Bernard of Clairvaux in the twelfth century already had his doubts about the new generation of knights ('not military but malicious') because their hair got in their eyes, they were tripped and tangled by the length of their shirts and they buried their hands in wide sleeves; but at least they didn't insist, like some aristos, on tunic sleeves so tight they had to be sewn into them every day.[27] Clothes didn't need to be practical, which was a statement in itself; men and women both needed handbags attached to the belt because they had no pockets.

Then there was the question of honesty, since fashion allowed you to change the shape of your body, usually within reason. The long points on shoes, actually a notion imported from Poland, were said to be the invention of an Anjou count with appalling bunions.[28] Women, right into the fifteenth century, allowed themselves to be tailored to show high, firm and perfectly round breasts, ample haunches but tiny feet and a belly so prominent that in the late thirteenth century the poet Jehan de Meun thought: 'You often can't tell if they're pregnant or not. They're large about the hips however thin they are.'[29] It became chic in his time to be blonde, saffron blonde, 'the most beautiful and commonplace colour, that pleases both women and men', according to the surgeon Henri de Mondeville; naturally there were dyes, as there were simple depilatories involving opium, vinegar and henbane or else the oil in which a hedgehog has been cooked, and a kind of primitive hair transplant. Looks were work. A woman might bind her bosom to avoid the 'disgrace' of breasts that were too large. An older woman might take off the top layer of her skin with a razor so new and younger skin would grow.[30]

Anyone subject to fits of morality would clearly have to disapprove. There is an anonymous poem written around 1400, *Richard the Redeless*, in which Wisdom in person wanders about a royal household dressed in old-fashioned 'wholesome' clothes, 'not overlong', and for that offence he is reproached, often rebuked, scorned, hooted at, sent packing and kept outside the doors, subject to the disapproval of 'the beardless boys' whose fashionably long sleeves become 'sleeves that slide upon the earth'.[31]

St Birgitta of Sweden went to extremes and announced that clothes were the cause of the plague, especially when fitted, cut, slashed and pieced together; as though the boats that brought ideas and styles had also brought disease, which would have been a more plausible argument. Multi-coloured cloth and stripes came to stand for such evil that on the walls of one Danish church the murderer Cain wears red stripy socks while his innocent victim, Abel, wears plain ones, and everyone knew which was which; and the pair in another church are obviously illicit lovers because they wear clothes in two colours. That would be clear even to anyone who does not understand the word 'luxuria' painted behind them.[32]

Jehan de Meun already worried that husbands would go to hell because the cost of dressing their wives would drive them to usury 'or worse'; and he was left piously hoping that 'women do all this with good intentions, to keep their husbands away from fornication'.[33] An English proclamation of 1562 worried about followers of fashion, 'such as be of the meaner sort, and be least able with their livings to maintain the same'. To make things worse, the whole process of change seemed to be speeding up. In the 1390s Christine de Pizan complained of the changes every day, making women's clothes and men's clothes always more elaborate and ruining many people; 'just as sheep follow each other, if people see anyone do some extravagant or inappropriate thing in the matter of dress, they immediately follow him and say that they must do what everybody else does.'[34] In 1577 William Harrison denounced 'the phantastical folly of our nation (even from the courtier to the carter) . . . such that no form of apparel liketh us longer than the first garment is in the wearing, if it continue so long'.[35]

Dress was politics because it showed the cracks and changes in society. It was a moral issue because it was a sign of pride, greed and waste. It was also an unstoppable economic issue because it involved the vast industry around wool and cloth as well as all the silk and dyestuffs that were traded over the seas. The Duke of Burgundy maintained among many others a team of shoemakers, tailors, cutters, furriers, embroiderers, and a tailor as head of his wardrobe who worked for nobody else. All the other craftsmen could supply anyone who aspired to look ducal or even regal, and had the money. The merchant drapers, unsurprisingly, were always the richest men in town; the goods they sold were the basis[36] of how people defined themselves in public.

The business could be accused of somehow unbalancing the nation: it was alien, war by other and silken means. Thomas Smith in his *Discourse of the Common Weal of this Realm of England* in 1549 objected to the sudden glut of haberdashers in London selling 'French or Milan caps, glasses, daggers, swords, girdles', all of them suddenly arrived in the past twenty years. He saw good English wool sent out of the country to be dyed and made into caps or broadcloths and then brought back to be sold. 'What grossness be we of that we see it and suffer such a continual spoil to be made of our goods and treasure by such means?'[37] London, meanwhile, was doing rather well out of exactly the same process. Every nation in Europe was perfectly capable of making stockings, but London made them of a very fine worsted that everyone wanted because it was in style; the stockings went to France, Holland, Germany. They weren't cheap; the perpetually furious Philip Stubbes wrote that 'the time had been when one might have clothed all his body well from top to toe for less than a pair of these netherstocks will cost'.[38]

The Pastons were a family of Norfolk squires who, like most of their kind, worried more about clothing themselves than following fashion. They did, however, travel.

John Paston went to Burgundy in the middle of the fifteenth century and was dazzled. 'I heard never of none like to it, save King Arthur's court,' he wrote home to his mother.[39] He was astonished by the rich gear at a jousting tournament, the 'gold, and silk and silver' and the 'gold, and pearl, and stones'. The complexity of the court impressed him, all the ranks and social distinctions, and the women. Seven years later his estate manager, John Pympe, said he'd heard that 'the *fraus* of Bruges, with their high caps, have given some of you great claps' and that the women went to war with their own tactics: 'they smite all at the mouth and at the great end of the thigh'.[40]

The Pastons, muddled in the English dynastic wars, lawyers whose lands were under legal siege and never rich, wrote each other letters full of practical worries: Margaret thinks her husband has sent caps too small for the children; young John says he needs a second gown for a Christmas in Wales because 'we must wear them every day for the more part, and one gown without change will soon be done' and he needs two pair of hose 'ready made for me at the hosiers with the crooked back' because 'I have not a whole hose for to don.' He also needs a hat to go riding; he wants the man delivering the hat to 'bring the hat upon his head for fear of misfashioning of it'.

Margaret, heavily pregnant, needs a new girdle 'for I am waxed so fetis' (which means neat and elegant; she is being ironic) 'that I may not be girt in no bar of no girdle that I have but of one'. She wants not a London gown but gowncloth from London to make a dress locally – cloth still matters to her more than cut – but see how the family looks to London for what they want, since, as Margaret complained, 'I have done all the drapers' shops in this town and here is right feeble choice.' Style, as much as a person could afford, came from somewhere else.

Occasionally a Paston asks for clothes to be decorated, a gown of 'puke' – which is the devil's colour of mourning black – to be 'furred with white lamb', but that is all; the family does not seem eager to imitate the grandees, even if they know all about what they have. John Paston makes a list of what his master, Sir John Howard, gave to his wife in the single month of January 1467. There was gold, in the form of rings and necklaces, chains and girdles, set with rubies, pearls, diamonds not to mention an emerald and a sapphire and an amethyst; there was Holland cloth, green velvet and black velvet when velvet was still hugely expensive, and damask and cloth of gold; and five silver spoons. There was fur, the expensive marten, the squirrel skins known as miniver, and gowns trimmed with ermine. There was a bed of crimson damask and assorted hangings, tapestry from Arras. The list goes on and on, but the Pastons seem to be largely indifferent when they're not at court; they have other worries in the country, how to keep their land, how to survive the wars.[41]

Town was different; in town you had to get things right. The old man lecturing his much younger wife in *Le Ménagier de Paris*, that wonderfully fussy manual on household management from 1393, won't tolerate sloppiness, and he points out that people who say they don't care about appearances or about themselves are all hypocrites; they care about themselves quite enough when it comes to demanding respect. He says his new wife must be 'honestly clad, without new devices and too much frippery, or too little'. So a wife could underdo things, and that would be as bad as being too showy; she must follow rules. The old man's concerns go right down to his wife's new-fangled underwear, even if it ought usually to be hidden: 'see you first that the collar of your shift and your blanchet, your robe or your surcoat do not straggle out one upon the other'.[42] The etiquette of knickers was a work in progress; the Dominican Jean de Baume said men who didn't go to confession were like bad children who slept in their dirty shirts, while good children changed their underthings 'at least once a fortnight'.[43]

In the sixteenth century the first printed books of fashion arrived, full of pictures of what people wore in other times or other places. They helped define the notion of fashion as a long desire to be someone or somewhere else.

They were a show of clothes but also of how people lived, an intelligence report in pretty colours; and a moral lesson, how to tell bad people and good people by their style. The very first is attributed to François Deserps and it was published in Paris by the court bookbinder in 1562 with a dedication to the eight-year-old future Henry IV of France. The boy may or may not have seen it. It tells about the enormous trousers worn by Scotsmen, the clean refinement of the Dutch, the way the women of Brabant wear their hair 'like starched linen' and the long skirts of Zeeland; and to keep the boy's interest, some sea monsters, a cyclops with a single gross eye and some upright standing apes all dressed in rattan.

The pictures are based on drawings by a captain who was a pioneer in French Canada, a military man who knows about foreigners, and 'a certain Portuguese who has visited many and various countries', someone in business.[44] This is serious information, guaranteed by a soldier and a merchant. The compiler does not quite approve of fashion, although he knows that the lack of it matters – in Lübeck, for example, the men are natural hunters, falcons on their wrists, and neither men nor women are 'much bothered by fashionable clothes'. The book explains that all this variety came about in part because of different religions, which was a natural concern in the middle of bloody religious wars; but also because of people's curiosity about other peoples and far-away countries.[45]

Cesare Vecellio, who once worked in the studio of his cousin Titian, produced his account of 'all the world' in Venice in 1589. As well as Englishwomen 'showing their magnificence' and the women of Antwerp 'of whatever adult age going out on their own, with a fine straw hat on their heads', he was fascinated by the Northern women who lit their way with burning sticks carried in the mouth ('for convenience, and maybe safety') and put out rotten bits of oak along the path so light from tiny funghi would show the way home. He notes that even the grandest Dutch women 'do business in trade'. Clothes seem like one more piece of ethnographic evidence, a fact about foreign places and people, except that he also complains that it is hard to be certain about the clothes foreigners wear 'for they are varied at will and the *capriccio* of others'.[46]

The sheer wilfulness of fashion was about to become a scandal.

Nobody was more alarmed than Philip Stubbes, a professional moralist who went in fear of the judgement of God on almost everyone for almost anything. He published in 1583 a whole *Anatomie of Abuses*, a fluent and remarkably observant warning to the English nation. He disapproved of: music as 'the pathway to all Bawdry and filthiness', actors as 'painted Sepulchres . . . double-dealing Ambodexters', lawyers and usury because they could take away a man's home, strong ale even when brewed by churches on feast days, football as a 'bloody and murdering practice' and dancing for all the 'smouching and slabbering one of another'. In general he reckoned 'there are three cankers which in process of time will eat up the whole Commonwealth of England, if speedy reformation be not had: namely dainty fare, gorgeous buildings, and sumptuous apparel'.

'The inhabitants of England go bravely in apparel changing fashions for every day for no cause so much as to delight the eyes of their whorish mates withall, and to inamour the minds of their fleshly paramours.' He singled out women who put flowers at their breasts 'whereby I doubt not but they get many a slabbering kiss, and peradventure more friendship besides, they know what I mean'. He sensed sensuality, 'an example of evil before our eyes and a provocation to sin'. He resented the dizzy changes. 'For were I never so expert an Arithmetician I were never able to recompt [count] the one half of them, the Devil broacheth so many new fashions every day.'

He mocked, of course. Those 'great and monstrous Ruffs' around Elizabethan necks were fine until the rain caught them; 'then their great ruffes set sail and down they fall like dishcloths fluttering in the wind, like windmill sails'. People's hats matched 'the fantasies of their wavering minds'. A man in slippers went 'slipping and sliding at every pace, ready to fall down . . . they go flip flop up and down in the dirt, casting mire to the knees of the wearer'. As for doublets, they were useless for work and useless for play because they were too stiff and too hot.

Stubbes didn't mean to be a satirist so much as a preacher. He was horrified by the sheer effort that went into all these absurdities: 'millions of suits of apparel lying rotting by them,' he wrote, not being a man to understate things, 'when as the poor members of Jesus Christ die at their doors for want of cloathing'. He hated the way women coloured their faces and frizzled and crisped their hair 'like grim and stern monsters rather than chaste Christian matrons'; he told stories about the Devil himself being caught starching ruffs and frizzling hair. He told other stories about the fashion for fair hair, quite alarming ones: 'if any children have fair hair, they will entice them into a secret place and for a penny or two they will cut off their hair.'

His alarms were about a world that he was sure was being shaken off its foundations: a world where everyone's daughters all want fine clothes 'notwithstanding that their parents owe a brace of hundred pounds more than they are worth'. He saw the sin of Pride in 'wearing . . . Apparel more gorgeous, sumptuous and precious than our state, calling or condition of life requireth'. He complained that it was 'very hard to know who is noble, who is worshipful, who is a Gentleman and who is not'.[47] The settled order of society was supposed to be reflected in dress, but it was wrecked when anyone could buy the look of privilege; and this was the time when even the mighty codpiece was sliding down the social scale, going from aristo crotches to the private parts of even quite unrich and ungrand men.[48] An outraged Stubbes insisted that 'all may not look to wear like apparel but everyone, according to his degree, as God has placed him'.

The other certainty dissolving around him, so he feared, was sex. It wasn't just the wearing of soft shirts that concerned him, although he reckoned they made men 'weak, tender and infirm'. He saw men in general becoming effeminate, by which he meant all too inclined to the company of women and the pleasures of bedding them; he thought women were dressing as whores; and even children looked like 'whores, strumpets, harlots and bawds'. He was horrified to see women walking out in public in the same way men did. More than anything, he feared the corruption of all the distinctions between the sexes, which he seemed to think depended largely on what people wore; and he was especially aggrieved at the sight of a woman in a doublet. Such women, he said, 'may not improperly be called Hermaphroditi'.[49]

He was, of course, quite right as well as being wrong. Clothes were no longer decreed by court or convent, except at court and in convents. Something had unsettled some perfectly acceptable social order that Stubbes was almost sure he once knew, and clothes showed that. Class, position, power and money could no longer be taken quite for granted.

In doing so, he helped set the agenda for a thousand moralistic outbursts, a thousand secular sermons against fashion and the breakdown of comforting, solid hierarchy and the unkind way the young sometimes confuse the old about their gender. He taught hacks and preachers that they could always howl against anyone wearing fresh, unfamiliar clothes, that there was virtue in wearing what your father wore. He made change and choice seem like sin.

# 6.

# Writing the law

He's been three days in the church, living on watercress and water and bread without yeast. It is Sunday now and time for Mass: the time of his ordeal.

He comes out shaved, barefoot, wearing only a wool shirt.[1] The men around help strip him and then they put new linen on him for the sake of decency. They truss him, hands behind his knees, and leave an end of the strong rope free, with a knot tied in it as far down as the man's longest hair would reach. They lower him very gently by the rope into a pool of holy water that has been blessed and blessed again.

The ceremony at the church door could be some rough prison version of a baptism, and the onlookers and the lawmakers saw the connection;[2] but this is about justice, not salvation. This man has sworn an oath that he is innocent of the crime with which he is charged. If the water accepts him, if he sinks at least to the length of his longest hair, he is innocent. If he floats, it must be because the holy water refuses to take him. His oath was false. His guilt is proved.[3]

The charge might be something desperate like sorcery or murder, or the perjury that made nonsense of trials when a man and his friends all swore on oath that he was innocent. He might be a man 'much-accused', whose reputation was so bad that nobody was prepared to swear to his innocence. He might be trying to clear his name, or prove he was not a liar, that he was telling the truth about a claim to land. In a world without the files and archives we take for granted, without a paper trail to check a story or establish a precedent, the ordeal could be a way to establish a fact and even stop scandal among the powerful.

Like court trials later, the ordeal is full of ritual and meant to look as sure as magic. The difference is what it claims, which is the direct participation of God, and what it lacks, which is an over-riding idea of human law and the state machinery to back it.

No judge and no jury sort out facts and decide who is right and who is wrong, there is no public process of testing evidence and challenging witnesses. Instead, ordeals demand that God show what He alone knows: who is telling the truth. The advantage is that God's verdict is unanswerable, so ordeals settled cases that nothing else could resolve: cases where the evidence wasn't quite good enough and a bad man was about to go free, cases *per notorium*, where otherwise a man would have been condemned just by the fact that everyone was absolutely sure that he was guilty. The problem was that ordeals treated God rather like a hostile witness; they demanded something that He hadn't volunteered.

Right up to the start of the thirteenth century, ordeals seemed to make perfect sense. Imagine a world without the kind of state that we know, the power that can police and judge and make war on its own account. Imagine, instead, a world of small communities, where people knew each other and each other's circumstances almost too well, where reputation was like life itself because you weren't going to move away and it was hard to settle disputes or reason out crimes when everyone was involved with everyone else. Family ties could be so close that the Church had to change the rules about 'degrees of consanguinity' in 1215, how close a relative you could marry, because there were villages across Europe where nobody could legally marry anybody else at all.[4]

In such a world writing was only starting to be all-important. There were few records and few lawbooks. The questions of guilt had to be quite simple, and the proof had to be immediate and dramatic. Ordeals were a custom that communities could accept, and nothing like the sophistications of the system of common, universal law that once ran the Roman Empire and was only just being rediscovered in the eleventh and twelfth centuries.

That kind of law needed an author and an authority, king or Church, to draft one law for everyone, and books to hold the law so it could be consulted anywhere and shipped and shared, as well as learnèd men to interpret it. Such a law inevitably jarred against old habits and certainties. The point of ordeals was the same everywhere even if the ritual changed from town to town, and everyone could see what was happening; the rediscovered Roman law was a kind of mystery, requiring lawyers who had studied at university, been initiated into a different way of thinking and cut away from the customs of the places where they started. The only professional at the ordeal was the priest, and he was not there to judge or decide; in local courts that ran on custom, nobody brought down a book of laws to make sure they were doing the right thing. There was no great abstract noun – the Crown or the Law or the Empire or the Nation, all the different names of power – to take the blame for bringing charges.

Lawyers' law meant a change of mind that may be even more profound than it seems. In a trial by evidence, the whole point is to judge; so what seems strangest of all is the Gospel passage that always had to be read before the ordeal among the Franks.

It is: 'Judge not that ye be not judged.'[5]

Lawyers' law was Roman law rediscovered by a Roman Church, but that is not the whole story. Lawyers' law begins in Ireland, and Wales, and in newly settled Iceland, all of them well outside the Roman Empire.

All three trained up lawyers; the monasteries of Cloyne, Cork and Slane had something like law schools, and not just for monks, priests and clerics. Even though most manuscripts get lost or ruined with time, there are still seventy-seven legal texts surviving from Ireland between the seventh century and the start of the eleventh, traces of a formidable legal scholarship and a devotion to writing things down. And lawyers were taken just as seriously as lawyers like. Minor court workers counted only as farmers in the social order, but the grandest 'advocates whom judgement encounters' were considered among the high nobility. In a time when crimes had to be compensated, and the price of a stolen pig had to be judged on age, weight and health, there was a sliding scale for killing a man depending on his value. Killing a judge was very expensive.

This law was about words on the page. There had always been records, charters and conveyances and histories, and literacy was much more general in the Middle Ages than we used to think from the pages that survive; but the ability to write, not just read, was still a matter of privilege, something you often paid someone else to do properly. Anything written had an almost magical quality; it became more right, more real and always more essential than anything a live witness could say. Royal governments, Church governments, began to surf on a great tide of parchment and paper; and lawyers managed the flow. By the time lawyers' law was fully established, every law case required a regimen of writing, a suite of formal documents: written complaint, formal denial, proof of resources to pay all the bills, then a written rejoinder and a written counter-reply before the case was defined enough to go to court, where the lawyers presented all manner of written position papers. Witnesses had to be listed along with the questions to be asked and the answers that were expected; and when the witnesses were finally allowed to speak, a notary wrote down everything they said so that the parties to the case, or usually their lawyers, could mark up their copies in red ink to show the points they reckoned helped their case, and those that hurt the other side.

So the first condition of lawyers' law is writing: its magic and its uses.

The power of writing is as old as the runes, the early alphabet of the North Sea, which are almost as old as the Common Era: marks easy to carve, roughly based on Roman and imperial writing, useful but also extraordinary because of the magic they could carry. They were cut into wood or stone, they were stained a reddish colour, they had to be interpreted with great care; 'few folk have mastery of runes', as the old poem said.[6] To know runes well was a matter of pride, one of Kali Kolsson's nine skills before he came to power in the Orkneys in the twelfth century, along with chess, skiing, music, shooting and sculling, reading and writing and verse ('runes I rarely spoil . . .' he sang[7]); he carved in stone his claim to be the greatest expert in runes in the Western Sea.[8]

There were victory runes cut on the blade or the hilt of a sword[9] and sea runes on a ship's prow and rudder to make sure of a safe voyage,[10] runes for giving birth and runes for being strong-minded and sensible when dealing with someone else's wife. Runes could be 'very great symbols, very strong symbols'.[11] They could curse an unwilling woman with unbridled lust and a three-headed ogre for a lover,[12] they could make a woman speak when she was struck dumb with grief.[13] A malicious man would spoil the runes a good wife carved to help her menfolk on a sea voyage,[14] and unknown runes could be downright alarming – one Viking poem tells of a sinister cup cut with the signs for entrails of animals, a snake and seaweeds, which contained a drink that had the power to blot away the past.[15] Just writing out the *futhark*, all sixteen Viking runes in order like an alphabet, was a good-luck charm: so alphabet sticks had to do with life, and risk, not the schoolroom.

Then there were runes cut into stones: to carry the memory of the dead, to honour great travellers or to claim their estates when they were gone. Runestones were an archive that stood along roads, at bridges or on causeways to say who built them, and in whose honour: at Dynna in Norway a woman honours her lost daughter by building a bridge and putting up a runestone covered with newfangled Christian images, since Christians disapproved of making actual graves look grand. This daughter, Astrid, was 'the most gifted with her hands', the stone says; she made tapestries in honour of the Christmas star, the Baby Jesus and the Wise Men on their way to the stable, and versions of her pictures are carved onto the stone.[16] Often runestones were stone prayers, a way of talking directly to God or the Virgin Mary, or even Thor, although in Norse tradition it could be considered dangerous to address a Norse god directly.[17]

On one stone at Hillersjö in Sweden, the runes are cut into the body of a twisting snake and they carry a whole family history, including who died too young and who inherited, with the single word 'interpret' carved in the snake's eye.[18] Travellers were honoured with runestones when they failed to return, which was a way of certifying their death; absentees did the same from far away, honouring the dead to make sure of their part of the inheritance.[19]

Runes carry fragments of stories, too, very personal stories of loss or anger or sometimes ambition. We can't know who the Hrossketil was who 'broke faith and deceived his sworn friend', but that treachery is his one mark on history because it was carved in stone.[20] We can only guess why Thorir carved the words 'death of a mother is the worst that can happen to a son',[21] or why a widow called Ragnelf asked God to help the soul of her only son 'better than he deserves'.[22] Something happened in the family of Mael Lochon on the Isle of Man so that he honoured his adoptive mother, Malmura, and added: 'Better it is to have a good foster son than a bad son.'[23]

The stones honour the dead, which means they have to lay out the story of lives. Some died in the course of raids, some on Viking expeditions, or in battles raging between the various kings; once, the stone says that its sponsor and its subject 'went out to meet the warriors of Frisia and split the booty of war'.[24] Some died as mercenaries out of Byzantium, fighting the Lombards; at least one, a man called Ragnvald, 'was in Greece the head of the armed troops', which means he was in charge of the mercenaries at Byzantium.[25] Some were glorified tax-farmers, like Ulf who three times sailed to England and raised the tribute the Danes reckoned was their due.[26] And many were traders, going out with partners on voyages which could prove as dangerous and end as badly as war. Sons honour a father who died on board his freighter; a wife has the runes carved to say that her husband 'drowned in the sea of Holm'. His *knørr*, his ship, 'went down and only three men were saved'.[27] And if sometimes there are stones which say they mark the place where a boat full of gold is buried, brought back from the land of giants in the far north, others mark tragedy. A trading ship went out perhaps to the worst side of Greenland: 'Gone far out to sea, sadly without food or dry clothes, they washed up on a great plain of ice blasted by cold winds, a desert where nothing could live. Happiness can be wrecked by an unhappy fate and then a man finds death all too early.'[28]

These are public statements out on the open road, which means readers were passing. In time readers learn to write, and the skill becomes more general. Runesticks were used for labels to show who owned which sack of goods in a warehouse, and then for much more. In Bergen some time around 1170 a lover scratched on a runestick: 'I love that man's wife so dearly that fire seems cold to me. And I am that woman's lover.' Someone else, perhaps, wrote: 'I love that man's wife.' And someone boasted: 'Ingebjörg loved me while I was in Stavanger.' A few years later someone carved out a plea: 'Love me, I love you Gunnhild. Kiss me. I know you well.' Maybe these are only graffiti, but they sometimes seem like messages; so maybe Gunnhild could read. It's true that the next century there are runesticks that read like bathroom walls – 'Smith lay with Vigdis' is just a boast, and 'The cunt is delightful, may the prick fill it up'[29] is a hope – but there are also curiously domestic messages. Some time in the first half of the thirteenth century, someone wrote on the back of a stick already used for a message: 'Gyda says you must come home' and added something else that nobody can now read. Someone thought the easiest way to send a message, maybe to a boozing husband in the pub, was to write it in the knowledge he could read.[30]

Of course, lawyers' law needed much more than the magic and usefulness of the written record. Lawyers' law had to be able to do what custom did: reflect the shape and nature of all the connections and powers in a community, account for who owned what and who was free and the ranks of society, so it would somehow seem natural and essential. The tussles between law and custom went on for centuries because custom, in its way, worked.

The ordeal survived the coming of the lawyers, even when the experts made it seem blasphemous or an empty superstition. The ordeal was theatre, after all; it expressed the conflict between accuser and accused and then the moment of decision, it made an audience wait for the verdict. It was decisive where law was all too often conditional. It was also very public, with the community looking on, with all its layers of privilege and standing, just like in life, while the law put justice away in a closed room, to be handled carefully by outsiders.

There were dozens of local rules for the rite. A free man, not subject to a feudal lord, usually had to pull a stone out of boiling water or else grab red-hot metal, often ploughshares, from a fire and carry the glowing metal at least nine paces ('measured nine feet by the feet of the man who undergoes the ordeal'; justice was tailored). The hot iron was cooked red in a fire that could not be stoked once the consecration started, and then it had to lie on the embers until the last prayer had been read.[31] The ploughshares were 'on fire to discover the truth'.[32]

The water had to boil, and it had to be checked by two men for the accused and two men for the accuser; everyone had to see the tests and know. The accused plunged his hand up to the wrist for a single offence, or up to the elbow for three charges;[33] and then his hands and arms were bound up and sealed with wax. The test was how he healed. In three days he ought to be almost mended, or else he was guilty; and again, everyone could see.

A man who was not free, who belonged to a feudal lord, was trussed up and thrown naked into cold water because bare skin stopped the possibility of trickery. The verdict was immediate, as though there was no point wasting three whole days on a man who wasn't free; he either sank or he floated. That wasn't torture, because the pain had nothing to do with the result, although it might well lead to a confession. Pain was reserved, enthusiastically, for punishment.

The higher your rank, the less you suffered. The Church rulings were various, but the Council of Tribur in 895 laid down that greater men just needed twelve men to vouch for them by swearing oaths; servants, on the other hand, could suffer either the ordeal by cold water or the ordeal by hot iron.[34] Priests were never tested with fire or water; monks and priests who were accused of crimes, maybe theft inside a monastery, were told to take the bread of the Mass in their mouths because a guilty man would choke on it. Knights were exempt from ordeals after 1119, unless they were accused of heresy, in which case they carried hot iron like everyone else. Nobility preferred duels in which God would make the better man win, a moral test that survived long after any other kind of ordeal; of course, nobles could always hire champions to do the actual dying for them. Social climbers wanted the same privileges as the grandees, and from the twelfth century the burghers of the newly flourishing towns were trying to insist on exemptions.

Women usually had to carry hot iron because the ordeal by water was not modest enough; there was criticism of 'priests who peer eagerly with shameless eyes at the women who have been stripped before they enter the water'.[35] Even so, women might choose ordeals to prove their virtue; a woman charged with adultery had no other way to establish her innocence. It might be hard to find two credible eyewitnesses to an affair and a carefully closed door or a muffling curtain could spoil the whole case, but that would not save a woman's honour. When the legendary Isolde was accused of adultery with Tristan, her husband, the king, made her prove her innocence with hot iron.[36] She carried the glowing metal, had her hands bound up and sealed with holy wax, and after three days the bandages were opened to see if the wound had healed the way an innocent person's should.[37] Gudrun in the story of Siegfried and Brunhilde proves she is not an adulterer with the 'sacred boiling pot', 'plunging her bright hand down to the bottom' and snatching at the precious stones lying there; the servant who falsely accused her also faced the ordeal and was scalded badly. She was taken off to be properly suppressed in a peatbog, alive for a while under a mesh of wattle.[38]

Virtue meant much more than an absence of sin. A cleric called Poppo, at the court of the Saxon king, Harold, around 963, kept arguing out loud at public banquets that there was only one God, and finally the king told him to prove it. The priest was arrested overnight and the next morning was shown the glowing piece of iron 'of huge weight' which he was to carry for the sake of the faith. He did so, without hesitation according to his biographers, 'and carried it for as long as the king himself determined. He showed his unharmed hand to all; he made the faith credible to everyone.'[39]

The ordeal also stopped trouble by making a decision Godly and therefore final; or so even emperors hoped. When Charlemagne divided up his kingdom in his will, he specified that 'if there is any dispute over the limits and boundaries of the kingdom that the testimony of men cannot clarify or resolve, then we want the question put to the judgement of the Cross'. That meant his rival heirs standing in church during Mass, arms stretched out like crucified men, until one collapsed and the other won. The Emperor was trying to keep the peace in territory with enemies all around; he wanted a verdict everyone could accept so that at least within the empire there should be 'no combat of any kind'.[40]

All this depended on a holy process that took its slow, deliberate time right up to the moment when the body hit the water or the hand closed on the hot iron. When the ordeal was just putting holy bread in a man's mouth to see if he choked, the bread had to be properly consecrated. When there was fire involved, there was time for the priest to warn any guilty man to stay away from the altar, to insist he remove every charm and talisman he might be carrying: to make sure he put away 'the workings of foul spirits, no hurtful sacrileges, no magic acts'.[41] The hand that was to be plunged into boiling water had to be washed carefully first, with soap.[42] The water itself was exorcized so it could 'judge the living, judge the dead, judge the human race'. The ground at the church entrance was sprinkled with holy water before the fire was lit; the men who lowered the accused into the water had to take the time to kiss the Gospel reverently;[43] the men who lined the church for an ordeal by fire had to go without food and sex, to be clean enough to taste holy water.[44]

There was none of the law's impersonal, almost mechanical process. The ordeal was full of time for accuser or accused to think again.

The Church could not approve. Ordeals were local and variable; the Church wanted universal and written laws. They could find no commandments in custom.

Besides, ordeals were Germanic and faintly pagan, and quite un-Roman, which caused great offence to those legal scholars who were putting together ancient Roman texts about law and trying to make them fit their very different modern world.[45] A sixth-century manuscript turned up in Pisa, a kind of legal scrapbook of the writings of the great Roman jurists: *Justinian's Digest*. Chapters and fragments of the same collection turned up in Bologna, where the law school fell upon them eagerly. By the last quarter of the eleventh century there was the start of a legal textbook, used first for Church and canonical law, but also for the lay courts.[46] Priests had Scripture, lawyers had Justinian, and the church courts had the *Decretum* of Gratian, a twelfth-century Bolognese teacher whose anthology included anything that could affect a decision in canon law, from papal letters to the writings of the Church fathers to scraps of actual Roman law; quite a number of the canons were even genuine. Gratian's book was copied again and again; it has been called 'one of the most widely read books in Western history'.[47]

Gratian defined custom as 'the kind of law established by usages and recognized as an ordinance when an ordinance is lacking'. Without a written ordinance, a case had to be judged by the law of the litigants' region, so even a papal judge delegate like Vacarius had to learn the customs in each place as he went from Canterbury to York to teaching law in Lincolnshire and finally ending as a prebendary in Yorkshire.[48] Law was still often a matter of local habit, of local knowledge.

Without strong states to enforce a universal law, it was likely to stay that way. The long struggle between popes and emperors was a problem, since the secular had no strong reason to help the spread of what was originally Church law. The Emperor knew his own power rested on custom, and on peoples who valued those customs and whose support he needed. Popes might lay down the law in Rome, the law school at Bologna might put the rules in order and teach them, but on the edge of the world the *ius commune*, the 'common law', had to argue its way, negotiate and compromise, take second place especially when Pope and Emperor were at loggerheads. Written rules were trimmed and qualified, sometimes until they were barely recognizable. Law was several rival works in progress for centuries, Church law, canon law, private law, public law, and the memory of what your grandfather always did.

Then, in 1215, the Fourth Lateran Council decided to condemn the settlement of disputes by duelling; priests should not be involved in a legal event which always ended with spilled blood. The Council also forbade priests to bless or consecrate any of the elements which went into a trial by fire or water. In 1222, Pope Honorius III went even further: he banned ordeals from secular law. The ordeal was stripped of its holiness and its logic went away, and law had the advantage. True, the Church had to keep on banning and banning because ordeals continued – witches were still being thrown into ponds in the seventeenth century – but anyone going to trial by ordeal had been warned that God was not coming with him.

This was an old argument. Popes from the ninth century denounced the very idea of ordeals; Agobard of Lyons said they were wrong because 'God's judgements are secret and impenetrable.'[49] God was not to be bullied into telling what He knew. Church lawyers from the start of the twelfth century, like Ivo of Chartres, approved of ordeals only when all normal means of proof had been exhausted; although he did for some reason approve of using the hot iron when a man was accused of bedding his mother-in-law. Snobbery crept into the arguments, a kind still familiar any time an English judge has to sentence a middle-class professional: since ordeals were supposed to deter the very worst crimes, so Stephen of Tournai argued, they should be used only on the lower classes, whose morals were less secure.[50] The middle classes never do think they need as much punishing.

Peter the Chanter, who taught theology at Paris and was the *cantor* at Notre-Dame, had a personal interest in the matter of ordeals.[51] He'd once been consulted by a man wrongly accused of murder who had been given a chance to clear himself through the ordeal of cold water. Peter talked all the right theology and told him it would be a sin to submit to the ordeal. The man refused, and he was hanged.

Peter still thought ordeals were sin, because they were a way to tempt God to intervene in human affairs. He wondered why, when the ordeal was a duel of champions, each side worked hard to find the best fighter he could; nobody seemed to trust God's judgement. He worried how holy a champion could be when his clear, sometimes paid intention was to kill another man. He was also suspicious of the way ordeals were conducted; a guilty man could learn to blow out all the air in his lungs and sink in cold water as though he was innocent, and when three men were made to carry the same hot iron, the last one had a clear, unfair advantage as it cooled.

He collected stories of ordeals that went wrong. A man was

accused of stealing from the Pope, failed the ordeal of hot iron and paid his dues; but then the stolen goods turned up in someone else's hands. Two pilgrims took the Jerusalem road, but one of them was late returning, and the other was accused of his murder. The man underwent the ordeal of cold water, proved too buoyant for his own good, and was hanged. Very soon after that, his 'victim' arrived home, having made a brief sidetrip to the shrine of St James of Compostela.

Even so, it was not injustice that turned the Church against ordeals; it was the notion that a priest was a special kind of man, apart from others. He was forbidden now to marry, and encouraged to be chaste. He had professed his faith; he was a professional. There were many other literate men to run the bureaucracy of the new kinds of state, so priests were not obliged to take on that duty. They could stay apart from the ordinary world. If they were going to keep that separation, they could hardly continue with the ordinary and secular business of the ordeal; and since ordeals depended on their blessing, their absence changed the ritual for ever.

The lawyers were ready. Around 1150 there were scholars of law teaching classes in a few places, and some of them worked the church courts, but there was nothing you could call a legal profession in most of Europe. There were men called *advocati*, but it was a slippery word, sometimes meaning just a witness, sometimes the patron of a church or the champion in a jousting duel, sometimes an adviser to a judge and just occasionally what we would mean: the one who argues someone's case in court.

That had all changed by 1230: a profession had formed. Lawyers were trained formally at the newly founded universities, which started with clusters of canon lawyers at Paris and at Oxford, a town one scholar monk said was filled with lawyers. They were making a living and quite often they were claiming the same kind of *professio*, the solemn statement of intention, that a monk or a priest would make. Judges would hear only proper, qualified lawyers, which meant that lawyers could close off their profession. They were reviving a Roman tradition, but carefully; they refused the tradition mocked by the poets Martial and Juvenal, which was the underpaying of advocates with, say, a sack of beans, a mouldy ham, old onions, ordinary wine or just a handful of spices.[52]

Sometimes these men were true scholars of the law; sometimes, 'after having heard barely half of one lawbook they arrogate to themselves the task of pleading publicly', as a thirteenth-century Archbishop of Canterbury complained. The awful standards of the worst ones made it even more important to restrict the courts to men who had studied seriously, three years at least. They were the aristocracy, they thought, of a business in which proctors did property deals, pulled strings and found things out, while notaries acted as though they were much more than simple scribes and charged accordingly. In the church courts lawyers reckoned they were much like priests. They also wanted at least the social standing of knights, although they much preferred to be considered noble.

This was not everyone's opinion. The woman-hating poet Matthieu of Boulogne very rarely puts women above men, but he said lawyers were even worse than whores, because whores sold only their arses while lawyers sold a nobler organ, the tongue.[53] They certainly wanted to be paid for their experience and their expertise, not just their time. In *Piers Plowman*, the author William Langland has a vision of barristers-at-law who 'wouldn't open their lips once for pure charity's sake. You'd have more chance of measuring the mist upon the Malvern Hills than of getting so much as a "Hmm-er" out of them, without first putting down cash for it.'[54] Priests in England had a list of questions to ask lawyers in the confessional, just in case they had forgotten any sins such as helping a client perjure himself, or using abusive language to cover ignorance, or overcharging a client; and they include a sin they considered just as grave: 'were you ever content with a paltry salary, say four or six pence, while acting . . . in a large case . . .?'[55]

Being professional proved a most powerful idea. It depended on the schools and the teachers that banded together in the newly founded universities, in Oxford and in Paris in the North, and the idea of a qualification: a degree. Judges would hear only the qualified. That invented a class of lawyers who were licensed to talk in courts as well as read the books, which invented the very idea of a professional class, which in turn became the basis of the idea of a middle class – people with power based on their expertise, neither knights nor peasants but able from the middle to tell both what to do.

Doctors of medicine watched the lawyers devise all this: the university training, the special knowledge, the honorific degree, the social climbing and the income. Doctors wanted to be professionals, too.

The textbook law of Gratian and the lawyers was new in the North, but it was needed: there was such dizzying change in the new merchant towns round the North Sea, such unsettling of classes and movement of persons and a constant flow of foreigners and foreign ideas that citizens needed some constant way to sort life out. Where riches used to belong to nobles or the Church, now they were shared by new classes of merchant and dealer doing business for themselves; the women and men who had once been firmly attached to someone else's land could come to the cities and make new lives.[56] All this change was here and now, so logically the place to find stability was in the distant past.

The law of the Roman Empire was a powerful memory in Italy, the mould for local customs. When it became the basis of the Church's laws, and the civil law that was modelled on them, it was a good fit. Contrariwise, north and west of Italy, over the Alps and down the Rhine and across the North Sea, this kind of law had travelled only erratically and piecemeal. Some territories had never known the old imperial rule of Rome and were not enthusiastic about the new kind. Some had preserved their own laws and customs even under an emperor as ambitious as Charlemagne. There was a long history either of resistance or of downright indifference to grandiose ideas of a common, universal law: the *ius commune*.

Inevitably, though, under pressure from the new men who wanted to buy their position in the world, the old customs had to change.

Towns and cities were filling with classes of newly rich people, who did not have any strong connection to some rural base. The reason they wanted land was the reason land was not so easily for sale:

property was a family's whole identity as well as their wealth, their name and history as well as future income in a most uncertain world and the prospect of money to buy care and attention in old age. Land stayed mostly in the family line; it could hardly ever be legally sold, transferred or given away.

Family quarrels were mostly about which heirs or relatives had the right to dispose of land, and if those disputes could not be resolved the way people liked, then they started wrangling about anything growing on land or stored in a house, down to the provisions left in the pantry and cellar. Anything that belonged to the house was passed on with the house: in England, that included the hounds of the house, along with the mangers, doves, ovens, shutters and anvils. If it was moveable, then it could be divided and sold off. There were court cases in Ghent over trees, since wood was scarce and valuable as fuel and building material, and forests were a noble asset; but apple trees were reckoned moveable and saleable because you pick the fruit, as were willow trees because you cut the new gold branches in spring to make ties and to weave seats and fences. Houses, too, were considered moveable, which makes some sense when you remember that any house owner might want to divide up or rebuild or let out her or his house without worrying about handing on to the heirs exactly the house he inherited; moveable really meant changeable. It also meant saleable. The new Roman laws allowed that, custom was in the way, and the two were at perpetual war over who got to inherit what, and how.[57]

The law was needed, too, in the risky business being done even by the holiest of men. Some abbots had a head for business, but not all. Cistercian monks came to the Yorkshire dales to run flocks of sheep on wasteland, and live from the sale of wool. They sometimes needed cash and borrowed it, and sometimes acted as middlemen between the small farmers and the cloth merchants, offering credit to both. They paid out cash to the farmers for wool to be supplied in the future, and since it would be immoral to charge interest, they set a delivery date that everyone knew was impossible; then when that date passed, they collected a 'fine' for the sheer inconvenience of having to make a second visit to collect the goods. They also advanced cash to landowners in trouble with moneylenders, and so their estates grew and grew. Bishops and royals left money with them, a kind of current account on which cheques, or at least mandates, could be drawn. The monasteries of their austere order accidentally became banks: strongrooms for kings, merchants and popes, sources of credit for farmers. What they lacked was capital; they were not thinking in those terms. If things went wrong, then the money they owed, the money they had at risk, could be a disaster, as it proved when the king shut down the Jewish moneylenders and became the monks' main creditor. Their resources were not exactly liquid; they were churches, cloisters, dormitories. Without the resources, the ideas or the cash to save themselves, the monks made mistakes and then they crashed. Eighteen of their houses, and Fountains Abbey itself, were mortgaged and foreclosed at one time or another.[58]

If simple shepherd monks could fall into this range of legal and financial trouble, imagine what could happen to the unholy. A man claims he has been let down – by a horse dealer, a doctor, an innkeeper with thieving servants or a courier who fails to deliver – and he goes to court. If he does not have a *specialty*, a document written under seal to prove his arrangement with the dealer, doctor, innkeeper or courier, then he can be answered by the 'wager of law', in which the defendant and eleven of his friends simply stand up in court and deny any liability on oath. An old custom trumped new-fangled law, unless you understood the magic of writing things down. Even judges could find this unreasonable; in 1374 Justice Cavendish ruled that such a case could proceed even without any document 'because for such a small matter a man cannot always have a clerk to make a *specialty*'.

Innkeepers all across Europe now had responsibilities 'so that no loss in any way shall befall [their] lodgers through the default of the innkeepers or their servants'. If anyone stole your goods during the night you could bring a writ of 'trespass'. In a case from 1369, a doctor who took a great part of a man's salary to cure a wounded finger was sued when the finger was lost; and in 1387 a horse dealer hid some infirmity of the horse he was selling, and ended up in court. Anything that went wrong, and cost money, might now end up in the paperchase of the law.

It was never a simple matter. A doctor made a promise in London to cure a man, but he treated him in Middlesex; so, since medieval law wanted juries who knew things first hand, to begin with there had to be hearings on where the hearings could happen (the court settled on London). The same wrong, like not paying a debt, could be either a breach of contract, in which case the debtor was safe from jail, or a tort, a legal damage, in which case he could be jailed until he paid. (Damages for a tort were meant to punish, but for a breach of contract they were simply compensation.) Never mind that the plaintiff just wanted his money; the lawyers had first to decide what kind of wrong had been done. The risks were not always to do with common sense, since judges could disagree as late as 1482 on whether a man could be liable for a debt without any fault of his own; Chief Justice Brian wrote alarmingly that 'if a man is bound to me on condition that the Pope will be here at Westminster tomorrow, in this case if the Pope does not come, although there is no fault in the defendant, still he has forfeited his bond'.[59]

The ordinary stuff of economic life required tangles of paper that did not always do their job. Ulman Stromer of Nuremberg discovered in the fourteenth century that hiring someone to work in a paper mill required written contracts to prevent your skilled workers from running off with their skills to another mill. Stromer needed a millwright on a lifetime contract, a paper expert on a ten-year contract and an Italian family with arcane skills who were sworn not to teach anybody else how to make paper or help any Italian who wanted to make paper in Germany; the Italians 'swore a holy oath' and 'the conditions of this contract are registered *sub publica manu*' (that is, on public record). They also wanted more Italians to come from Lombardy to help them work the mill, and they had a plan to make Stromer rent them the mill so they could operate it for themselves, and despite all the oaths and papers the mill never did run properly. Stromer found it necessary to arrest the lot of them and lock them in a small tower room. He had to wait a while but after four days in the tower his men agreed to sign a whole new contract, in which they agreed to obey the first contract and not go to law anywhere except Nuremberg. That didn't work, either. Within four years, an exasperated Stromer decided he had had enough, and leased the mill to someone else who would make him paper 'in order that I have nothing to do with that'.[60]

When cash was short, the law sometimes did provide ingenious answers. At the end of the fourteenth century English grocers had trouble finding enough coin to stay in the cloth business, especially since the Italians had floods of silver out of Serbia and Bosnia. They needed credit on a generous scale. To get it the grocer John Hall in 1396 made a deed of gift of all his goods and chattels to someone else, a deed which was used most often to avoid some threat of confiscation by the law or creditors; but Hall made his in return for a bond worth £500. He still had the goods in his house, he was even allowed to sue anyone who damaged them or tried to take them away – anyone except the holder of the bond, who could seize them if the money was not paid back. He also had cash to buy and sell. This new use of an old kind of paper was seen more and more from the 1440s, a way to compensate for the desperate shortage of bullion: it made credit work.[61]

The scale of trade across the seas created even more complications, and the law was not good at keeping up. Consider the ships carrying freight in Danish waters from the eleventh century onwards; their wrecks lie out in the open sea, which suggests they were working the long sea routes, and many are real sailing ships with no room for rowers on board, built large to carry as much cargo as possible, fifty to sixty tons. That means professional merchant seafarers, who almost always needed to do deals before they set sail: the ship and its cargo might belong to a list of shareholders, and before sailing there might be a crude kind of insurance to organize, in which the shipmaster put up some money which the owners of the cargo would keep if he failed to get their goods safely to their destination. Whatever rules and customs covered all this, however it was organized, the law itself was not codified until the thirteenth century, which is hundreds of years after the ships were out sailing, and sinking.[62]

Partnerships in a ship once lasted for just one voyage and they could be settled on the docks; but by the middle of the thirteenth century they were the basis for big trading companies in Italy whose shares could be bought and sold, with responsibility for loss and profit, sale and delivery shared among people who might simply be trading the paper on the shores of the North Sea and might not know each other. This idea of shareholding was not entirely new; there was a kind of limited company operating windmills on the Garonne in France from the twelfth century, with shares that could be dealt in the marketplace at prices that varied according to the strength of the river currents, the state of the harvest, the likelihood of floods.[63] But that was local knowledge; now an investor needed to know about storms, pirates, the price of goods in two or three markets and the value of money. The small-town medieval markets ran on credit with not much coin in circulation, depending instead on the stall-holders knowing by name, address and credit each customer for eggs or bread or cabbage; now credit was needed on both sides of seas, in different languages and in different moneys, for goods whose price and value were constantly changing.[64]

The world felt the need of law to manage all this: to file the proof when properties did change hands, to check the contracts, to deal with the aftershocks of contracts that went wrong, to handle mortgages and credit and risk; later, much later, they would also be needed to organize proper insurance for sea voyages. Lawyers made things run, including royal courts and growing towns that were now more important than any rural, feudal territory. The age of the single Frisian boat owner, plying up and down the coast and the Rhine with goods, was a distant memory, and there were distinct classes of stay-at-home merchants and financiers, the shipowners and shipmasters who moved the goods, and the agents in distant ports who did the buying and selling. They needed a crude kind of accountancy, reliable information and lawyers to make them a little safer.

Writing it all down was vital. Only then could the serious talking begin.

The very best proof of how much writing mattered was the forgeries. Forgery had been an ecclesiastical habit for centuries. St Anskar made rather a mess of his mission in the 840s to turn Scandinavians into Christians, and he needed political backing to carry on with his work; so he faked documents to support his useful fiction that he had Charlemagne's permission for a diocese in the North, Hamburg and Bremen combined. He also used false documents to prove he was an archbishop, which he did not need to do; he was indeed an archbishop at some point in his career. He still needed written proof, though, and he wrote it. His disciple Rimbert also wanted to be in charge of the diocese of Hamburg–Bremen, so he invented the story and the proofs all over again: as though forging documents was like writing a kind of revisionist, hopeful history.[65]

There was in the ninth century an enthusiasm for the monks at certain monasteries – Corbie in France, for instance – to help out history by writing down the decrees and orders they felt popes and councils had always, obviously, meant to issue. Two centuries later, faking had become a monastic speciality; the fine, distinguished houses at Westminster, Canterbury, Durham and later Glastonbury offered less grand houses a forgery service when they needed charters to prove their title to land. They were told again and again that fakery was a menace to authority, in the Church and in the kingdom; a false papal seal, as John of Salisbury wrote, 'is a peril to the universal church since by the marks of a single impress the mouths of all the pontiffs may be opened or closed'.

The monks persisted. They were the archivists, the keepers of records, and they were quite prepared to improve on history to keep the record straight. The monks of Crowland in Lincolnshire invented thriller detail for the story of how fire took down their monastery in 1091; they had a hero abbot dodging streams of boiling lead and molten brass to wake up sleeping monks and save them from the flames. The hero also, naturally, had already saved the vital charters so that junior monks could have a chance to learn Saxon script; those charters survived the fire, the fake history said, which was convenient since they proved fake title to valuable lands.

The more respect for the written word, the more fakes. Of all the official documents of William the Conqueror, roughly a third were written down in the twelfth century long after his death, and more than a third of those had absolutely no basis in anything earlier.

Sometimes the riskiest faking was for the grandest causes. Austria tried to bargain its independence from Emperor Charles IV in 1360 by producing proofs signed by Julius Caesar and Nero; but, unluckily for them, the Emperor knew the humanist Petrarch, and Petrarch had several letters of Julius Caesar in his library, so he could compare them. The fake Caesar used the plural in the wrong places, 'we Julius Caesar' in the royal 'we', which was not a Roman style. 'This ox,' Petrarch wrote, 'did not know this.'

Forgery was some men's habit. Over forty years in the fifteenth century the soldier John Hardyng produced at least twenty documents meant to prove that Scotland was subject to England, of which seventeen, at least, are forgeries. He has Scotland acknowledging the English king as liege lord in the eleventh century, he has treason charges dropped against Scots who claimed it was no treason to serve the King of England, and various Scottish kings swearing various oaths, all with carefully faked seals: documents whose falsity, nineteenth-century scholars said, 'was most apparent'. There is no evidence any English king used the documents, but Hardyng still thought them worth the work; he had been in the service of various northern English lords who had lost their lands in Scotland and remained ever hopeful. He was acting like an enthusiast for a cause who self-publishes a book of history, except that he had to fake the handwriting, the wax, the parchment.

There was also the matter of Cambridge University's forgeries: its claim on an ancient past. The dons in 1381 had been forced by a local mob to give up 'all kinds of privileges and franchises granted to them by all kings of England since the beginning of the world' and agree to be ruled by the local citizenry, who, for the sake of certainty, took a knife to the seals on the old charters and then burned them in the marketplace. In 1429 the university wanted to be free of interference from archbishops, bishops or archdeacons, or any of their many officials, but they had no charters left; so they took refuge in fantasy. The university actually began in the thirteenth century, a refuge from Oxford and from Paris when both schools were having brief but heartfelt crises; but Cambridge offered papal letters from the seventh century. They did not, unfortunately, have the originals, but they had very old copies, they said; and apart from anything else the letters showed that Pope Honorius himself had studied at Cambridge, about six hundred years before anybody else.

The deception worked. The university now produced a wonderfully mythomaniac history which involved Alcuin, Charlemagne and King Arthur, who was supposed to have guaranteed in 531 'the study of learning undisturbed' on the grounds that the King of Britain had been converted to Christianity 'by the preaching of the doctors of Cambridge'. The fantasy was meant to align Cambridge with the fantasies of other universities, with a dream of the vivid intellectual life of ancient Britain, with all kinds of comfortable thoughts about the primacy of the university whose start was now put back so far it might seem as remote and wonderful and even mysterious as the start of the world itself. Besides the ambitious self-inflation, the documents also had the very practical effect of getting the bishops out of the university's affairs.[66]

This faking was not a simple matter: not like forging a charter to make people 'troubled and vexed in their Possessions' and grab land, not like faking a bank draft when you need money, or making trouble during a civil war by inventing the charges earlier kings should have brought against the enemy. Faking was sometimes a way to make real things somehow more real, or to confirm an image that an institution wanted for itself, or to make a political point that was entirely sincere. A town might forge charters so it could run its own affairs, as Barnstaple did in the West Country of England; and Barnstaple did quite well.

What mattered was the physical sign: the writing.

When the ordeal was banned, or at least made un-Godly and unofficial, the Church still had a persistent problem with secret crimes. There were priests who weren't chaste or even celibate; there was the buying and selling of jobs and power in the Church. Solid evidence was hard to find, so the ordeal had been a most convenient way to resolve these cases.

Now there had to be a new procedure: prosecution, or *processus per inquisitionem*. This involved basic changes of mind. Pope Innocent III was sure crime should never go unpunished, not least because the wicked would only get worse; prosecution was for the public good, and it could no longer be a private action. In the old way, the accuser brought charges, paid the costs of bringing them, swore to the truth of them and paid damages if he couldn't prove his claim. Now an accuser, as in modern courts, was simply a witness. If the accused was found guilty what he paid was a penalty, not compensation.

The process begins to seem almost familiar. The accused had to swear to tell the truth, not just to swear his innocence. The test of truth was no longer just how many respectable persons would swear to it, but how well it stood up to questioning. There was to be no more easy resolution, no more asking God; instead, judges had to reason their way to a verdict, testing the facts. Suppose a priest was accused of some unpriestly relationship with a woman: a judge did not have to wait for two bedside witnesses; he could consider evidence that priest and woman seemed to be living together as man and wife.[67]

The campaign for a common law had always been a campaign against the power of local customs; Pope Gregory VII had to point out, rather tartly, that 'Christ did not say "I am custom", he said "I am truth."' Customs could be pagan, after all, or murderous or even worse. Lawyers' law was a way to control the customary past and stop it coming back. It was also a practical matter as rulers put in place a bureaucracy of written records and general rules, following the example of the Pope himself.

This involved a fair amount of bluff. In Arras, the citizens liked to wreck and burn the house of any obstreperous criminal, which was an old Germanic custom. Now the custom was called *lex* in the town charters – law, in other words. Even when counts of Flanders were writing whole new codes of criminal law, they let such customs stand – 'because the law of the town happens to provide this'. They changed the words with the years, and let reality change with them. First, the city charter simply wrote down the '*lex et consuetudo*', the law and customs, of the citizens of Arras; for Ghent, a bit later, the charter lays down 'the customary law which Count Philip ordered the citizens of Ghent to observe' so everyone knows who is giving the orders; and, later still, the charters simply list those orders 'which the Count ordained to be observed throughout the county'.

The citizens in the towns often thought they had the right to trim and invent their local rules, and they knew it was sensible to have that right written into their charters. In 1127 the men of Ghent laid siege to the castle at Bruges where Charles the Good, Count of Flanders, had been cut up and killed by upper-class revolutionaries. The burghers brought 'bold plunderers, murderers, thieves and anyone ready to take advantage of the evils of war'; they had a plan to steal the count's body from the rough tomb where it lay in the castle gallery, to have the monks hand it out through the castle windows and 'carry it off, done up in bags and sacks', so it could lie where it belonged, in the monastery at Ghent. Such ruthless scheming and such numbers make it unsurprising that ten days afterwards the newly elected count found it wise 'in order to make our citizens well disposed towards himself' to grant them 'the right freely to correct their customary laws from day to day and to change them for the better as circumstances of time and place demanded'.[68]

These concessions had a way of wearing thin with time. The counts could make some minor reform in the public law and then order it to be respected in the private law of deals and business, which was where custom used to rule. Philip of Alsace did just that for Ghent when he ordered that twice the usual double fines be paid by anyone who stood surety for a condemned person but failed to pay up and had then to be taken to court to get the money. Criminal matters were the count's business, but he added a sentence to the new rule: it was to apply to 'all transactions', to all business as well as all criminal matters. He was making private law.[69]

Custom was such a strong and desirable idea that legislation in one century could be assumed to be a matter of custom three centuries later. In Ypres a town ordinance in 1293 laid down that when two families made peace after a feud they had to include each other's bastard sons. The rule was rewritten into a list of customs in 1535, virtually unchanged; an old law had become a habit. A great many customs were written down and published and had their own official standing alongside the law from Rome. In fact, for most people in

Flanders, the high reaches of Roman law never touched their lives. It was the fifteenth century before a majority of the judges in Flanders were professional lawyers with their university degrees and their libraries of lawbooks.

Jan van den Berghe wrote his own definitive book on the legal system of Flanders in the early fifteenth century, and knew its workings from inside, but he reckoned the way to learn lawyering was like learning any other craft: 'old people are obliged by law to teach the young'. He thought 'the more one has seen, the better an expert one is'. He did not think books and texts were everything. When he was faced with a tricky case involving marriage, money and death he said he'd ask someone who knew the books of law, but only because 'whenever custom is not opposed to the written laws, one ought to give judgement according to the latter'. The rule of law was still conditional.[70]

When merchants needed to sort out a business quarrel, or clerics wanted to prove title to land and income, they wanted results and as soon as possible. They got into the habit of sidestepping the slow, expensive courts.[71]

Just as Roman law was being rediscovered in the twelfth century, with all its cumbersome machinery, so was arbitration – the ancient system meant to get disputes out of the courts and briskly settled. You handed the evidence to the arbitrators, gave them the widest possible powers so there would be no delays in getting a judgment and expected a compromise more than a verdict.

Law could now be international, not just national, not just local and customary. When the parties to the dispute were both foreigners, then the decision could be made in line with the law where they came from. Law travelled, as money once travelled, along with trade. In time, the big ports like Bruges had consular courts which sorted out their own nationals – issues like drunks, gamblers, damaged ships, lost cargoes, labour disputes or brawls between sailors, provided nobody was killed. Even local courts speeded up when merchants were involved, because disputes often broke out at fairs, which would be gone in a week with everyone out at sea or back on the road; in Bruges from 1190 the courts had to rule within three days, and they had to meet at least twice a week.

But if the merchants were settled in a city, then arbitration was the best solution and debts were often the issue. Nobody wanted to call in debts because that would wreck a man's creditworthiness and make endless trouble for his other creditors, and the dates for repaying a loan were never very exact in any case. Creditors felt obliged to be patient. You started with friendly letters. Hildebrandt Veckinchusen lost money in the cloth business and in shipping salt, could not get the Emperor Sigismund to pay back what he owed, and couldn't raise money anywhere he tried, not in Antwerp, not in Cologne, not in Lübeck. He owed money to Weits and Kupere, whose first reaction was studied and polite: 'Hildebrandt, dear friend, do realise that I am surprised you did not give us your money, because we can make good use of it and we need it.' Veckinchusen then met all his creditors round a table at an Antwerp hostel, talked them into waiting and reorganizing his debts, but the money never came. His Antwerp agent was mobbed by angry traders, and told Veckinchusen to come back to town, which he did, but he still did not have the money. Only after more months of waiting did a banker from Genoa lose patience and lock him in the debtors' prison of Bruges.[72]

In these cases, paper mattered less, talk more. Truth, as one twelfth-century pope decreed, should be pursued '*simpliciter et pure*', which means 'pure and simple', without the subtle turns of Roman law which, he seemed to think, might actually get in the way. Arbitrators noticeably liked to leave lawyers out of their proceedings, the 'time-wasters' denounced in one judgment of 1259. Justice was a private matter again, since arbitration could work only if both sides agreed to abide by the outcome; there was no prosecutor, no idea of public good. In fact, custom was back, speaking Latin. The proof of how much law had become a set of rites and procedures and experts was the number of cases deliberately settled without it: '*sine strepitu advocatorum*', without the rumbling and rustling of lawyers.

Once it had been communities who knew how people should behave, what was appropriate, what was right; they knew their own rules.

When people could not move away from each other, they were obliged to be tolerant. Now it was the law and the professional class of lawyers who had more and more to decide what behaviour meant, whether it was odd or mad or wrong.

The clerk Richard le Pessoner was sick in 1285. One night he woke up in the same room as his master, Brother Walter: he was 'frantic and mad . . . [then] by the instigation of the devil, [he] smote Walter on the head as he slept', first with a form, then with a trestle, with all the sparse furniture he could lift, 'so that the brains came out'. He went to tell his brethren what he had done, confessed: 'I have killed my dear Master', and he laughed and laughed.

The laughter was the shocking part, the legal proof of madness. Richard was still obviously mad in prison a month later, which was not a disadvantage in some ways; already in the thirteenth century the law said 'madmen committing crime in their madness ought not by law to undergo the extreme penalty nor to forfeit their goods or chattels', and most people who seemed mentally ill were pardoned even if they had killed.

Bizarre behaviour was only part of the diagnosis; for the law memory also mattered. The tests for memory were much like the tests for dementia nowadays: asking the days of the week, which town someone lives in, the value of a handful of coins.[73] Mind and memory were what you needed, in good working order, to make your last will and testament; they were the law's notion of what kept a human being entire. A landowner born sick would lose his income to the crown, but if he fell ill later in life, his income was put aside for him in case he recovered. The wretched Hugh of St Martin, vicar of All Saints Beyond the Bridge in the Lincolnshire market town of Stamford, went mad in the winter of 1298 and was left so poor he was reduced to pawning even his own clothes. He was maltreated and robbed, which we know because his bishop excommunicated all those who had 'lain violent hands' on Hugh, and later all those who stole from him while he was out of his mind; but he was also sent away for a while to recover, and seven months later he was back at work. He had promised to behave discreetly; other priests had promised to tell the bishop if Hugh went wrong again.[74] There was a generous expectation that a sick man could get well again, and the courts reckoned they could tell if that was happening or not.

Once the ordeal had settled the question of whether someone was lying or telling the truth, and therefore innocent or guilty; but now the law was no longer just about who did what. It was about why and in what state of mind and with what intent and how a person acted before and after and during and what he was likely to do next. The law was opening little windows into souls.

# 7.

# Overseeing nature

1 October 1250, a new moon rising huge and red: a sign of storms to come – or so Matthew Paris wrote. There was dense mist. There were violent winds tearing down leaves and branches. The sea rose far above its usual level, the tide swept in and swept in again, there was a terrible, unfamiliar roaring like nobody could remember. 'In the darkness of the night,' Paris wrote, 'the sea seemed to burn as if set on fire and waves joined with waves as if in battle.'

Strong ships foundered. Houses and churches were broken down by the violent rise of the sea. In Flanders and in England there was damage beyond repair in areas that were low-lying. Rivers were forced back from the sea and flooded the land so that meadows, mills, houses were destroyed and 'the corn not yet stored in the barns was swept away from the flooded fields'.[1]

This is the usual story: how nature makes life difficult for man. Sand drifts and smothers, water breaks into the land, shorelines where people live are washed and battered into new shapes and sudden storms like the night of the red moon take a whole harvest and leave hunger behind. Nature is arbitrary and man is her victim. It is also much less than half the story: the more important half is what man did to nature. Deliberately, carelessly, accidentally, catastrophically man began to remake whole landscapes and change the balance of half a continent. In doing so, he turned the effect of wind and tide into a disaster.

Of course, it did not seem that way at the time. New towns wanted food, and couldn't grow it for themselves: no room, no time. New towns and their new industries needed fuel, more and more of it. Those two appetites began chains of change with consequences from floods and ruin to the careful cleanliness of streets in Holland and the first model of how to organize a limited liability company. Man imposed himself on the world, sometimes without meaning to.

These are the chronicles of the war between man and the natural world.

There were new dunes forming along the shore of the Netherlands, great loaves of sand, and so there was less land to plough and plant. Human beings started to quit the coast in the tenth century, and they moved inland to the peat zone. The domes and cushions of peat, standing four metres proud of the bog itself, looked like the *terpen*, the kind of hillocks which they had used as refuges before. A century of drought made the bogs seem almost accessible, and if drought could do that, man could do better. All it took was ditches and canals to drain off the water from the high peat domes to the pools that pockmarked the low bog, and you can dig a ditch with the tools any peasant owns: no new technology required. Once drained, the land could be farmed. All the sodden peat in Waterland, which is just north of Amsterdam, became land for farming in this way.

The first problem was this: the new system for drainage worked too well.[2] Peat that is wet will hold plant stuff without letting it decay, it keeps in the carbon dioxide essential for photosynthesis and it keeps back the rush of storm water. Peat without water is a fluffy thing, and almost nothing, a tenth of its original volume. As the floor of the bog dried and shrank, it sank closer and closer to the water level underneath, going down by as much as two centimetres a year. A whole landscape was dropping dangerously close to the level of the sea beyond the dunes. It was also growing hostile; without water, the top layer oxidized, letting off the carbon it stored and also turning sour. The cattle brought in to work the dried peat pastures only trampled the land down further.

The town of Medemblik sat in Waterland on the side of the Almere lake. It was a transit town for freight coming from the Rhine and heading to the North Sea on its way to Scandinavia and England.

It seemed almost secure. The more the peat sank, the higher stood the ridge of sand where Medemblik was built. Storm surges brought in sandy clay to bind and cover the sand. The town was surrounded with cornfields, with oats and barley, which could stand the occasional flood of seawater, with salt marsh where cattle and goats, some sheep and the occasional pig could graze; from their remains we know the sheep died old, which means they were raised for wool, not mutton. There was always more peat to reclaim, so it seemed, when the old land became too sour and salt for corn.

Then the waters turned on the land.

At first an old ridge of peat kept the North Sea out of the Aelmere lake, but the peat was becoming sour and it was unsettled by the sinking land. Storms beat it right down. The sea broke into the lake, and turned it brackish and tidal: what used to be called the Zuider Zee. The sunken land flooded. The south bank of the Middenleek River, where the town stood, was partly washed away; the empty north bank simply disappeared in the wind and waves and tides.[3]

Men are obstinate: Medemblik was built again, plot by plot. The ground was raised with peat and clay, the embankments were made to slope steep on the water side, gentle on the land side so there would be a barrier against water seeping through. A line of houses stood unbroken on the ridge. But trade routes were shifting; now the townspeople had to go out to trade rather than simply wait for the trade to come to them. The reclaimed land was almost ruined. Salt-marsh plants took root in the old bog. Farming stopped; cattle and sheep took its place. Villages moved to higher ground, sometimes built higher ground for themselves, or else were washed away as Medemblik so nearly was.

There was a lesson in this: water had to be managed, not just drained.[4] There were ditches and canals to make the water flow where it was needed, or at least harmless, but there also had to be dikes and dams to keep the water out. Every detail of slope and gradient mattered. Between 1100 and 1300 most of the Zuider Zee was lined with dikes to stop the land washing away: dikes made of cut peat and clay, sometimes with mats of reeds, sometimes with seaweed. The land was not all sinking at the same rate: it made a patchwork landscape with indentations, like a floor with tiles missing. To stop flooding from one level to another, all the land had to be pumped dry and the drainage canals had to run on embankments higher than the fields so there was enough of a gradient for them to drain. The Rhee, the same kind of high, narrow canal, was built across Romney Marsh in England above land that had been reclaimed, just to get a run of water which could break and move the silt in the harbour at Romney.[5]

Sand, silt and sinking land were problems all around the North Sea. From now on, there could be no more unconsidered landscape; even doing nothing to the land was a strategy and a plan.

The Dutch already had a reputation for managing water, even before 1250. They were invited to North Germany in the twelfth century to drain the peat bogs, to start the 'golden ring' of dikes on the North Sea coast. Their expertise was not even especially in building dikes, since the first to go north were men from Leiden, where dikes had not yet been built on any scale; they were simply thought to understand how water worked. They were invited by local lords, once by the Bishop of Bremen and Hamburg, and they carried with them much more than their expertise; they were allowed to settle and maintain their own Dutch laws, were granted fen and undrained land, and were accepted as freemen for centuries. They disrupted feudal rules entirely, and they did so in territory where land drainage had often begun with the collective efforts of local farmers rather than orders from above. When Germans drained land, with or without Dutch help, they were often allowed the rights the Dutch claimed: 'free ground with free people'.[6]

They would go travelling later for land or for money, to Prussia and to what is now Poland, but the knowledge of how to manage water also became a passport for Anabaptists going east, and Catholics who were uncomfortable when the Netherlands became the United Provinces under Protestant rule in 1581. They seem to have inspired the later reclamation of land from the sea in Ostfriesland on the North Sea coast where modern Germany meets the modern Netherlands; again, it was a scheme organized by local farmers, which led to the 'farmers' republic' of Dithmarscha. The Dutch took a certain style of landscape with them: houses strung out along a road, for example, and lines of houses on a dike with reclaimed land behind, but their politics were even more important. The word 'free' started to matter where they had been.

At home, everyone knew that water had to be watched and controlled. Everyone co-operated. Everyone also knew, unfortunately, that the towns needed more and more peat. Holland was beginning to have breweries on an almost industrial scale, and they needed peat as fuel to keep their fires burning. There were the furnaces of brickworks, the heat needed to dye cloth and later there would be the sugar works in Amsterdam. Dutch peat was being sold as far south as Antwerp. Where there was still peat it was first mined dry from the edges of the bogs, but the demand kept growing. Hollanders had to learn from Norfolk in England, where the miners were already in the twelfth and thirteenth centuries going deep for the brushwood peat buried under a scant surface of turf. Around 1300, the peat pits had filled with water, and the ponds began to flood together; water began to block the mining. It was necessary to find ways to dredge peat out of standing water and ferry it to dry land using boats; 'the ferrying of fen'. A new landscape formed in the Norfolk Broads, streams between marshy islands in an unsettled wetland. It should have been a warning of what would happen when the Dutch ran out of the easy stuff and started to use the same techniques.[7]

Peat-mining was an industry, not a sideline for small farmers and peasants any more; it needed more and more hands. The old drains, the small dikes, dams, sluices and canals that kept the land clear and accessible, also needed constant work. The situation would have been difficult in any case, but it was compounded by the appalling mortality from the Black Death: there were not enough strong backs to keep the land safe.[8]

Already in Flanders there was a new kind of authority: the water board, whose job was to protect the land from flood and the surges of the sea. The boards in other places only inspected what landowners had done, approved or condemned, but along the Flemish coast they started to organize the work themselves from the second half of the thirteenth century. They hired labourers, often whole families, including women and children; they hired contractors; and they levied a water tax on every landowner according to the size of his lands.

All this is remarkable because it could not start without capital, often raised from rich abbeys but later from investors: essentially a private company for a public good. Bruges had a money market sophisticated enough to hand out malignly expensive short-term loans, which was a start, but the cost of the money was far too high and over time the control of water required more and more spending: on new ways to make dikes solid, on sluices made of brick and stone with double doors with copper fittings, on the mechanization of the sluices that let water out and back to the sea. Landowners invested in the water boards to protect only the land which could make them money, and they were hard-headed enough to abandon whole islands, even small towns like Biervliet that had once been famous for salt and herring but now was cut off from the shore and subject to tidal plagues of rats. Land became an investment for city people, not the basis for a man's whole identity and his place in the world. Water boards, too, were an investment, and the shareholders had liability limited to the amount of land they owned in the board's area.

What started with peasant families determined to stop floods from taking everything they owned became a device for merchant investors to make their money grow. These new gentry had a taste for flooded land that could be drained to their exact specifications. The high bureaucrats among them particularly liked creating estates, magnanimously building villages and churches, getting titles and moving ever upwards in the social world: being cut-price grand.[9]

Man made the land vulnerable in the first place, and then invented limited companies, people borrowing money to buy safety, to save the situation. It was a crude first draft of capitalism, not the real thing. Economics now determined which towns breathed and which towns drowned. Trade also created new kinds of town. In Waterland, dams were built to protect the fields from the invading salt and tides, but they also blocked the freight-carrying rivers from the freight-carrying sea; cargoes had to be hauled over from one ship to another. A town could make serious money out of that kind of business. At Monnickendam, the citizens built higher ground for themselves, and then a dam, and they were so infuriated by the prospect of a new dam at Nieuwendam that they fired cannon at the rival builders and formed an armed scrum to run at them; for that, one of their mayors was beheaded in The Hague.[10] The towns had ruined the ground with their appetite for fuel, and now the fact that the ground was spoiled led to the building of dams and the new towns around them: towns like Amsterdam.

The process was unstoppable and it got worse. The drying peat formed mires, shallows full of stagnant brown water that kept changing shape as plants grew and plants died. The peat miners drove their canals into the heart of the peat, sometimes right through dikes and embankments, and the mire water went into the peat domes along with the miners' boats; in a bad storm, whole fields of peat were torn away and for months they floated about as islands on the newly open water. Between 1506 and 1509 there were terrible storm surges, enough to break the soft, vulnerable edges of the mires and merge the waters into lakes. Just south of Amsterdam a new lake was born, the Haarlemermeer, which lasted four hundred years and grew to more than 40,000 acres: big enough for the sea winds from the north-west and south-west to rush the water as much as a metre up the shore. Gravity was no help any more in draining the lakes; what was needed now was wind in the right direction to power the windmills required to pump the fields dry. Land itself became a technical achievement.

There was some unexpected profit in this. The sluices for controlling the waters helped fishermen because they funnelled the travelling eels right into traps and nets. Between ten and twenty tons a year were taken at the sluices between the Haarlem lake and the IJ by Amsterdam, and shipped out to London by a new class of entrepreneur. What had once been a basic, domestic kind of fishing had turned into an international business.

As for Waterland, it was marginal land. It was not until the start of the seventeenth century that money from the towns paid for new dikes, new windmills, the draining of lakes to make new pasture, and the farms began to make cheese and send milk down to Amsterdam twice a day.

The cutting of peat went on but now it looked like clearing away the past, a physical kind of forgetting. The new landscapes, entirely artificial, have become modern nature reserves.

Ruined land became pasture over all those centuries and that started changes which had one unlikely consequence: the scrubbed stoops, the polished windows and the swept streets of Holland.

The neat cleanliness of the province of Holland was notorious among travellers who did not always speak so kindly of the Dutch themselves. In 1517, the Italian Antonio de Beatis went round the Low Countries as chaplain to a cardinal, and what he most noticed were the doorstep cloths for wiping your feet, the floors that were sanded. In 1567 the Florentine Ludovico Guiccardini noticed 'order and tidiness everywhere'. In the countryside foreigners reported that cattle and carts were not allowed on the streets. This passion for cleaning has connections with the moral pressures of Calvinism, but foreigners describe it even before Calvin was born, and when de Beatis went travelling Calvin was still only eight years old. When Guiccardini was in Holland, the territory belonged in theory to Flanders, and Amsterdam was a Catholic city, proud of its very own miracle which involved the saving of a consecrated Host from the fire. Calvinism gave cleaning significance, but it was not the cause.

The itch for scrubbing, brushing, washing started out in the fields of spoiled peat, and the fact that they turned to pasture. From the fourteenth century, after the Black Death killed so many, peasants could not make a living from growing grains for bread. On their tax returns, farmers pleaded poverty, but with unusual conviction: 'we can hardly get the hay properly off the fields once every three years' and 'yes, we do keep cattle but we can't make a living out of that'. A farm family was likely now to include the captain of a ship – half of the Dutch skippers in the Baltic trade came from Waterland – and craftspersons so skilled in spinning and sewing clothes that they made the neighbouring towns nervous.

They also, mostly, kept cows, and that changed everything. One or two milk cows could produce enough butter to send to market, and now that townspeople had the money to pay for it, business was good. New weigh houses appeared across the northern part of Holland from around 1375, and some were designed particularly for the weighing of butter and cheese. The accounts for Kampen, on the German North Sea coast, mention 400 tons of butter a year passing through the toll, and 425 tons of cheese; Holland cheese was sold at the fairs in Brabant in the late fifteenth century; it was on the market in Denmark by the start of the sixteenth century. Milk made a living for half the houses in Holland spread through three-quarters of the villages. Guiccardini reckoned all this dairy produce was worth as much each year as all the shiploads of exquisite spices that came from Portugal to the Low Countries.

Butter has to be made in immaculate conditions, or else it spoils; it is not as forgiving as cheese. In England, butter was usually made for local markets, which was easier, but Holland was sending it out of the province and even out of the country. Dairy rooms had to be kept perfectly clean, and since often a family had only a pair of cows, the dairy was domestic, an extension of the house. When small farms began to be swallowed by larger landowners, when women and men moved from the countryside into all the new towns that were thriving, they naturally brought the habit of careful cleanliness with them. The burghers of Amsterdam hired girls to clean their houses who already knew what it took to make butter that would keep.[11] Calvinism gave cleaning a spiritual dimension, but for Hollanders it was already a matter of faith.

A seemingly simple activity, the digging of peat, changed a culture, redefined how the world thought of a people, changed the way money makes things happen, remade a whole landscape and turned peasant farmers into men with international connections, at least in the eel and butter trades. There never was a truly simple change.

Take fishbones, for example: the bones found when archaeologists sift through middens and try to work out what people ate. Around 1000 CE in England there is a noticeable shift from eating freshwater fish to eating fish caught at sea. Herring went inland and upstream in quantity, not just the occasional bones found in earlier years in York and London and Ipswich. Anglo-Saxon did not even have a word for cod, but within a couple of decades of the millennium cod was being eaten across England. In what is now Belgium, the herring and cod arrive around the middle of the tenth century, in Poland herring is traded inland from the eleventh century, and in France sea fish is much more common from the thirteenth century. Fishing at sea was, for the first time, feeding the land.[12]

There was early evidence of a coming change, but it was not easy to read. In Scotland the Picts ate fish they could catch close to shore, rod and line, but when the Vikings came around 800 CE somebody's diet changed: there are suddenly bones of cod, fish that have to be caught in open water, not to mention seabirds like gannets, cormorants and shags, which nested on the further islands. The question is whether the Picts learned about deep-water fishing and changed their tastes in food, or if the Vikings arrived in such numbers after their long deep-sea voyages that they alone explain the difference. A whole history of migration and conquest rests on the reading of those bones: food as culture.[13]

Fishermen in the tenth century still took and sold mostly eels and pike, minnows and burbots, trout and lampreys, 'and whatever swims in the rushing stream'; or so the fisherman tells the teacher in Aelfric's *Colloquy*, which is a Latin primer of the time. Asked why he does not fish in the sea, he says: 'Sometimes I do, but rarely, because a large ship is necessary on the sea.'[14] Those larger ships start to appear around the millennium, growing from a maximum of twenty tons or so around 1000 CE to sixty tons or more by 1025 CE. If you sift the fishbones on archaeological sites, the link between the ships you have and the fish you eat begins to seem obvious. The new towns emerging around this time were hungry for food, which they did not grow, and so diet changed all across Northern Europe: the salted herring and the dried cod with their long, long life began to edge out fresh fish, which was trickier to ship and keep and could be foul in the wrong season. The fisheries that supplied this new appetite were long established. Herring was a catch you could hardly miss; the fish were plentiful, and they thrashed enough to make the shallows boil in the right season. We can be sure that Norwegians had been eating them at least since 600 CE all over the country; settlements with the most men seem to have eaten the most fish. They also ate a bit of cod, and assorted meats, which suggests they were farmers bringing supplies with them down the fjord so they could catch the herring when the fish came close into shore to spawn.[15]

As for stockfish, the cod that is dried to a board, it was being hung out to dry along the Norwegian coast from the Iron Age, and it was part of a very important trade-off: chieftains who gave their men stockfish to eat did not need to feed them on barley, which meant they had barley for making beer. Without drink, no feast was worth while and no chieftain could expect loyalty. Stockfish, indirectly, was a pillar of political power.[16] Business and power started their long, intricate dance. Norway acquired kings, and kings thought they had acquired Norway. Stockfish was a very useful way to get money, mostly from the Baltic merchants of the Hanseatic League, who were eager to ship and trade it. The kings needed cash to hold their kingdoms together; the Hansa knew that stockfish could be sold anywhere. What had been a matter of prestige became a matter of business.

The way the German merchants of the Hansa organized things, stockfish was mostly taken from Bergen after being landed there by fishermen from the North. It was a credit and cash transaction mostly in one port, arranged so the fishermen were never quite clear of their obligations to the merchants and could never sell elsewhere: a classic company store. Herring, on the other hand, was a free market in various places, most of them along the southern shore of Sweden, in Scania. It opened on 15 August, on the day of the Assumption of the Virgin, and ended, depending on how the season went, either on 9 October, which was St Denis's day, or on 11 November, which was Martinmas. It was a new kind of commerce: open, international, outside the usual rules.

Cod required ships, but anyone could go out to catch the seasonal rush of herring along the shore. A farmer could do the job after harvest, or a student or anyone with working muscles. The fishermen worked from the beach, from huts built of wood and rush mats where they could dry their nets. Each day, or each night, they set off in small open boats with crews of five to eight men who had formed a kind of ad hoc company: a *notlag*. They weren't allowed, by royal decree, to use drag nets along the bottom, which would have scooped up flatfish and young fish, but they otherwise could net the fish as they wanted. They were obliged to land the fish at one of a half-dozen beaches where royal officials would claim their tax, but these places were already much more than customs houses. Merchants waited for the fish in their more comfortable quarters behind the sea wall – at Skanör or Malmö, for example – because they were forbidden to row out to try to do deals or fix prices before the catch came ashore. They waited for the signal the moment the first boat landed, and they were off running to the sand to check the fish and make their bids. The auction was open and brisk.

This was only half the market. Each of these fish towns had a fixed settlement behind the sea wall, a sort of colony: streets, shops, bakers, brothels, drapers, churches, anything they had at home, all set out in wooden huts. The merchants were allowed by the king to buy just enough land to build the huts, and they made sure they had a great deal to offer in return for fish: fine cloth, fine wine, all kinds of luxuries to get a fisherman through the winter, and his family, too. The beaches became an exchange where the herring was like currency, but rather more reliable than most coins.

The fish were gutted by women just inland who packed a precise number into each barrel – between 830 and 840 – and covered them in brine. The barrels were inspected, sealed and stamped; whoever bought this fish, however far away, would know who took responsibility for their quality. The Scania fish was a known quantity, so much so that one fishmonger in Maastricht in 1395 had to put a palm frond in front of his door as a kind of confession that he was selling some other kind.[17]

A great commercial machine was moving fish through Europe, buying it fresh, processing it in a standard way, packing it so that anyone could recognize it, branding it and standing by its quality, and sending it by sea, by river, by road; and, because the fish shrank and the brine evaporated on the way, making arrangements to repack it when it landed close to its final destination. Fish was business now, not just a matter of survival for the fishermen, food for their family; the lines of supply cut across the frontiers of a continent. Chiefs who had relied on stockfish to help keep their men in beer and maintain their standing now saw the dry cod making taxes for the king; money values were edging out the old forms of prestige.

Hunger changed much more than the social order. Growing towns needed grain as well as fish, bread and beer and oats as well as assorted herbs and vegetables for making a good thick pottage over the fire. To eat, man had to change the landscape.

The countryside looked scrubby after the Romans left, woods filled in with underbrush, sometimes forests and sometimes thickets, the line of the rivers marked by the taller, grander trees and bushes that grew alongside the water: a system that man was not yet trying to reinvent. Water ran clear, because the woodlands drew up the rainwater and held the soil in place, and in the wetlands, there was enough plant growth to absorb the solid matter. Floods did not scour off the rich soil and send it downstream.

Then the trees were steadily cut, the forests cleared, the fields began to grow larger and there were crops growing where the riverside thickets had been. Grain was king, and to grow it the ploughs made dust out of topsoil. The farming system meant that a third of the cultivated ground lay fallow and exposed at any time. Rainstorms or snowmelt sent water sluicing over the bare ground, and took the soil with it, and the shape of the land began to change. Valleys in Saxony have heavy deposits of topsoil that go back to the eighth century; the process is most dramatic in the upper Thames basin just around the time the Normans arrived in the eleventh century, by when the mouth of the Oude Rijn in the Netherlands was silted shut and the run of the Rhine changed for ever. The bay between Gdansk and Elblag was filled as the delta of the Vistula expanded. In time, Bruges would lose its battle against the silting of the River Zwin.[18]

None of this was good for fish like salmon that depend on fast, clear streams, but there was another obstacle which made things even worse. To turn all that grain into food required mills, usually watermills. Each had a reservoir of still water made by damming a river or making a weir, so there was always enough water to release into the buckets at the top of the millwheel and make it turn. A one-metre dam and gate and raceway could back up two metres of silt and gravel; it did at one twelfth-century dam on the Derwent in the English Midlands. It also blocked those fish that need both sea and fresh water, which breed in one and mature in the other: sturgeon, salmon, trout and shad. Along with herring, these were the staples of royal feasts – Henry III of England had them all for Christmas in 1240 with a dish of lampreys as well – but their spawning habits and the cycle of their lives were being blocked by dams and heavy millwheels and still, deep pools.

The effects were obvious. The draining of the Rhine delta for farmland in the eleventh and twelfth centuries meant dikes in the way of flowing water, and the sturgeon population collapsed. The great fish came back only after violent storm tides broke the barriers around 1400. To save the salmon, the Scots made laws so that all dams would have an opening for the fish, and all barrier nets would be lifted on Saturday; the law, under the early-thirteenth-century King Alexander II, demanded that 'the stream of the water shall be in all parts so free that a swine of the age of three years, well fed, may turn himself within the stream, round about, so that his snout nor tail shall not touch the bank of the water'.

The hungry towns were a problem in themselves: Cologne dumping its cesspits into the Rhine just downstream of the city, the garbage of Paris making the Seine downstream 'infected and corrupted' by the early 1400s. The pollution was compounded by work: the process of rotting raw hemp and flax to get out the fibres, the slaughter of animals with the blood and guts tipped into the river. People noticed what was happening, but not what had happened before: the shortage of fish, but not the various causes. Instead they chose to blame fishermen. Philip IV of France made rules in 1289 for the size of nets, for the size of fish that could be caught and the months when fishing was legal and outside the spawning season. He complained that 'today each and every river and waterside of our realm, large and small, yields nothing due to the evil of the fishers and the devices of their contriving and because the fish are prevented by them from growing to their proper condition.'

Freshwater fish may have been more scarce, but until the world turned colder around 1300 sea fish also had their difficulties: neither herring nor cod like water to be too warm. Besides, people still ate freshwater fish, even if the balance was shifting towards a greater consumption of the salt-water kind. In Schleswig in the eleventh and twelfth centuries the bones left behind show a taste for perch, pike and bream as well as cod; for the next two centuries, the cod bones are heavily outnumbered. Around the Louvre in Paris, the richer gentry ate more sea fish after 1500; but before that they ate salmon, trout, whitefish and sturgeon until the supplies ran out.[19] Sea fish from far away was cheaper, and local fish from fresh water became a luxury; but a luxury makes a market.

It also creates a challenge. To keep fish when fish stocks were declining was to show that man could keep control of the world around him. To make the fishponds showy was a statement of power, and a kind of privilege: to be able to eat the fish that kings and bishops ate. The mundane business of raising fish that thrive in still water and the shelter of weeds became a noble ambition.

A great family could remake the ground all round their tower, house or castle, and then boast, as did the twelfth-century Gerald of Wales about his family castle at Manorbier, that they had the biggest, the deepest ponds of all. The more obviously artificial, the more difficult to make, the better. The first pond built after the Norman conquest of England, the 'King's Pool' at York, was a full assault on the town: it required the flooding of farmland, taking down mills, changing the run of roads. It was an imposition. Fishponds were proof you were separate from ordinary people, which is why they were so often built at the edge of an estate or just within the fences and walls. They were meant to be seen on either side of the causeway that swept up to the main gate at Rothwell in Yorkshire, a bonus of grandeur; they were little lakes with walkways round them at Hopton in Shropshire, a decorative indulgence. Nobody could think they were natural.

The voracious pike, a greedy carnivore capable of taking anything from a swan to a minnow, was kept in separate ponds; the Bishop of Lincoln had a sizeable pike pond on the side of his other fishponds at

Lyddington.[20] That sounds practical, just a way to stop the 'water-wolf' eating the other stock; but it also showed that the bishop owned a very special kind of fish, not only good eating but important for the marks on its head, which looked almost like the nails, whip, cross and thorns of Christ's Passion. He didn't just want to sit down to the great dishes of pike, like the *chaudumé* that Taillevent's famous cookbook suggested (pike pieces grilled with a sauce of saffron, ginger, white wine and sour verjuice all mixed with bread that has been soaked in the liquor from cooking peas[21]); gastronomy was not the point. He wanted to show he was great enough to eat the great fish.

The fish were like the fallow deer and rabbits, newly introduced into England, which were kept closed in hunting parks; they should never have been there. Deer had 'hovells' for shelter in the Bishop of Durham's park; fish had artificial ponds. Deer had forests planted for them, fish had willows along the banks of their ponds so they could shelter between the roots. Deer had nothing to do with feeding the household, but they were very carefully tended and managed; they were the designated prey in a dream of chivalric slaughter, an ersatz version of old forest legends.

Hunting had its own elaborate etiquette, fixed enough to make a metaphor in pictures and poems, so serious that the stag at bay could stand for Christ in extremis; it took place between the true wild and the perfectly civilized, between the woods and the castle. It required thought. A true hunt, *par force de chiens*, meant singling out the strongest deer for the hounds to chase all day, followed by hunt servants and the grand hunters on horseback, until the huntsman could kill the exhausted beast with a sword to the heart. That was not what happened in the parks; there was no room and, besides, fallow deer have poor stamina and they like to run in herds. The best the park could offer was a shadow of the show, the deer herded into nets or towards stands where archers were waiting for them.[22] The audience had to suspend disbelief, as in a theatre.

The walls and fences of the hunting parks were to keep the uninvited out as much as to keep the deer in; poaching raids, as at Somersham Park in 1301, both broke and burned the boundary fences before taking away deer and hares, as though the boundary was itself an affront. Inside it, hunting was a spectacle both very showy and quite private, proving the essence of a knight's skill and his social standing in front of his friends. The animals were players in a staged show, the woods planned carefully to allow a horse to ride fast and freely after game, the prey always available.

Outside the boundary, the prey counted as food. The peasant uprisings in England in 1381 were followed by a decade of bloody and violent raids on the show and the privilege of the parks.[23]

The ponds of great estates were not fished for sport; domestic fish were caught by draining their ponds, ideally every three years or so, a sluggish end for slow creatures. The sport lay in rivers and lakes, where fish were taken with hook and line and another small fish for bait; we know this from Chrétien de Troyes's *Perceval*, his great story of the Holy Grail, which was written around 1190, in which the knight Perceval sees on the river the Fisher King, wounded so badly in the thighs that he cannot ride to any other kind of hunting. Evidently Chrétien saw fishing as a proper, royal substitute for chasing deer or flying hawks, but only in extreme circumstances. According to the minstrel Blind Hary, long after the event, fishing was what the Scots hero William Wallace chose to do when 'on a tym he desyrit to play'. He went out with a small cone-shaped net to be dragged on the river bed and a long pole which 'the Wallace' found most useful for clubbing any Englishmen who strayed.[24]

The fishponds were not about food. The bishops of Winchester had four hundred acres of ponds but used barely a tenth of the fish they could produce. Their fish were for show, like their deer. English kings bought freshwater fish for their feasts despite all the fish they bought to stock their fishponds, as though the show of the feasts and the show of the new landscape were entirely different things. It seems the best return a great man expected from his fishponds was not to eat the fish or sell them but to give them away to a monastery in return for their prayers; this happened often enough for monks to have a quite unjustified reputation as pioneers of fish farming. The fishpond was part of an idea, not a budget.

In the Renaissance the revival of Roman gardens, with statues, meaning, gods and heroes, made it clear that men were imposing ideas and ambitions on the landscape. In earlier years, in the time of the fishponds, people meant to do the same thing but we may have a little difficulty in recognizing it. Put up a statue of Minerva in a garden and you have a classic goddess of wisdom, and at once there are obviously abstract ideas among the trees. Put a fence round a new woodland and fill it with deer, and the park seems practical, or even trivial, an afternoon amusement for the rich. Build a fishpond and you assume people wanted to eat fish, not think about them. And yet the park and the ponds made great claims: for the theatre of chivalry and all kinds of knightly ideals, for the social standing of the owner and most of all for the idea that man can control and design the world around him, or at least a few acres of park.

Fish were also business, which complicates matters: business somehow taints all those lovely metaphors in poems and those coloured ideas in pictures, in a way that mirrors the later English snobbery about 'trade'.

The Fens in the east of England were fished day and night in the twelfth century, all through the year, and still the waters produced fish to sell. In the early fourteenth century, rich peasants in the Forest of Arden in Warwickshire had fishponds and at least some of their fish were sold. The London waterfront at Southwark had 'stews', which meant fishponds before it meant brothels, from the 1360s; a merchant named John Tryg had a pond there for 'feeding and keeping fish' worth 13s 4d a year. The ponds were entirely for fattening fish for the market, as practical as a cowshed, but some of them were still wrecked in the 1381 uprisings because they looked very much like someone's privilege.[25]

The English were used to eating bream and pike, sometimes perch, often tench, roach, dace: bony, slow-growing, muddy-tasting fishes. The great commercial change arrived in barrels, probably off a boat from Flanders: live carp, an exotic which survived the Ice Age far down the Danube, now being brought to England as a new crop. The king's kitchens knew where to find them in the fourteenth century, and the Duke of Norfolk was certainly raising them by the 1460s.

They were ready to harvest in three years instead of the eight it took to raise bream; carp were bottom feeders who could be encouraged to grow by a diet of grain, blood and chicken guts. Above all, when fish was money, they were more difficult to steal than other kinds. The carp, Thomas Hale explained later, 'is so shy that it preserves itself from common enemies'. He writes that 'They will not readily bite at the hook when grown to a size in rich ponds . . . they plunge to the bottom upon the first notice of any disturbance in the water and strike their heads into the mud. The net draws over their tails, without laying hold of them.'[26]

The carp was the ruin of fishponds with meaning. By the fifteenth century, they were just larders for food, nothing like the vast shimmering expanse they had once been: not the kind of lake a gentleman would want and no proof at all of riches. Tastes changed. Parks began to look far too wild and uncontrolled because now there was peace; a house could have a garden that was formal and complicated and deliberate in the expectation that it would never have to be defended against attack and there would always be enough labour to maintain it. The owners of great houses wanted straight and knotted lines, boxes of plants between neat hedges: diagrams and maps, not wilderness. The artificial ponds and canals and parterres were there merely to fill the gaps between the lines.

Gardens and parks no longer made some vast general claim about man's ability to dominate and remake the world around him. They made smaller, local statements about their owners, with an inordinate amount of heraldry in the shaping of stones and beds to proclaim names, ancestry, rank and connections. They were like the detail of a clever machine.

On the shoreline life was tough and it was conditional; however much the sea was used and known, it was still wilderness. Fishermen, pirates, seamen knew about the arbitrary force of winds and storms at sea, they lived on coasts which could be blown over with sand or washed away or broken up by surges of tide and waves; so they did not expect permanence. They did a great deal of praying, and a fair amount of pilgrimage, because when a great storm or tidal surge did come, the effects were devastating. In their wake, though, they left another kind of force to change people's lives: new kinds of economic reality. The people of the shoreline could never feel in control of either.

The sea gave the village of Walraversijde a living. The towns of Ghent and Bruges wanted herring and had rules to make sure it was always fresh; the counts of Flanders wanted new kinds of business from the people on their lands; the new floating nets made it possible to catch herring close to the shore and even in deep waters. Walraversijde obliged. From the eleventh century there were 'herring fishermen', *piscatori de harenga*, along the Flanders coast. They needed settlements where they could beach their boats and make a life. They lived on the shore because fishing was a constant process of going away, again and again, even if it did not involve being far out at sea.

The fishermen were just across the dunes from great sheep farms, which had once been more than enough to support a family; but the farmers were brought down by taxes they paid for works to keep the water off their land, and the division of land into smaller farms to raise food for the towns. Their homes were now, in tax returns, just 'the places where they live', no more than shelters. Such men needed work: fishing, digging peat, burning peat to get out the salt to preserve the fish. They were lucky that in the twelfth century the tug of the tides had shifted the sandflats and exposed the peat below and given Walraversijde something to mine.

That was, however, where their luck ended. By 1394 they were living in the wreckage of a civil war, they could see that war and overuse had weakened the sand dunes so that sand was drifting, and they had every reason to be afraid of flood and storm. On St Vincent's Day, 29 January, in 1394, the sea came in like armies and the whole village, streets and houses, found itself on the sea side of the dunes.

There was no money for the works needed to repair what the sea had done to the land. All around tenants were late with the rent, or unable to pay at all 'given the poverty of the people' as the accounts of the Abbey of St Peter say. The village had to be rebuilt on the safe side of the dunes, but the people were pushed to the sea to make a living. At least herring was still in demand, and a herring boat needed twenty men. The ships were partnerships, with each man bringing his own net as his investment, and taking a share of the profits at the end: shareholders in a company. When there were no fish, there was peat to dig on the shore, so saline that it could be burned and the ashes washed to produce a commercial quantity of salt. There were also fleets passing by, wide open to pirates striking out from the shore; the fishermen were enthusiastic raiders, a little too enthusiastic for the Duke of Burgundy when they stole from ships that were not, at the time, enemy ships. The aldermen of Bruges had to warn that 'nobody should set sail to sea to plunder or damage ships, unless if ordered by our redoubtable lord'.

All this time the water pulled back at each low tide to show the broken square foundations of the old village houses, the outlines of the old peat pits in the sand: a reminder of impermanence. On the margins, only the present mattered.

Fishermen were known for being violent, for being away from home too much and not always following the law, not being properly settled and landed like farmers and landsmen. They lived with terror out at sea, carried crosses and wore amulets against water demons and sea devils, built a chapel so holy bells could ring out to drive off storms, and went to shrines of the Virgin Mary to pray for protection or thank Her for it. The settled rhythms of the land were not where their minds played. They, or rather the women they left onshore, had no fields or gardens, no stables, none of the things that seemed essential inland. Instead they had pigs to gobble up the prodigious quantity of fish guts spilled in the business of cleaning and preserving plaice and herring. They had weapons – crossbow bolts, daggers and cannon shot – to steal other people's ships and keep their own from being stolen. More than anything, they had their work: the ground was scattered with cork floats for the nets, weights to make them hang in the water, wooden needles for mending them, which were often carved with the owner's sign or name.

They also had games when they came back to shore, not just dice but also an early form of golf; the butt ends of the clubs survive.

Sailors carried the game all around the North Sea, so that even now the old great courses are usually close to shore. They had spectacles with frames of bone, and styluses for writing and booklets made of wood: they could read and they could write.

Their village, by the thirteenth century, was already much more than a seasonal camp because it had distinct streets. By the fifteenth, thanks to herring, theft and peat, it was a proper settlement. The houses were made of brick, some of it glazed green from the peat and laid to make patterns in the floors and walls, plastered over inside and sometimes outside. There was glass in the windows; some of the houses even had brick latrines. At night the close-packed houses, a hundred of them with no great differences in size, must have looked like a town waiting for the sea, the candles and oil lamps glinting in the windows.

There were all the amenities of a town: a brewery, a chapel and a brothel. Inside the houses there were even luxuries. Everyone ate meat because they had the money to get it, and only a little fish; they could always fall back on fish if they had to. They had curtained beds and wooden chests. There were fishwives eating pomegranates and figs, one of them had gold velvet from Genoa, they used the fierce red melagueta peppers in their cooking and they had dishes, plates and cups of Spanish majolica, painted brightly and glazed to look like porcelain. Fishermen travelled, after all, and they could bring back tastes. Pirates found such things on ships coming up from Spain to ports at Bruges or Ghent; and it seems things fell off ships as easily as once they fell off lorries onto the stalls of some London markets.

The village knew the advantages of being marginal; it never tried to be official. There was a chapel with three aisles and family monuments and a solid, monumental tower, but Walraversijde was never a parish in its own right. It was not even an independent village because it was always subject, in theory anyway, to the farming hamlet of Middelkerke. It was a place for people who needed nothing more. Their real world was the water, in the open sea, off the coasts of England and Scotland where they went to fish. Water and the shore made them valuable; towns like Bruges needed them to pilot ships in and out of the rapidly silting estuary of the Zwin and for the salt they had to have to preserve their fish.

It was a balance more delicate than anyone could know. What storm had started a century earlier the market now finished.

When fishermen started heading far out into the North Sea, to the Dogger Bank that lies between Jutland and England, they needed more capital for stronger, larger ships. To get the money, they ran up debts with the fish merchants in town, and quite often they could not pay and they lost their ships; or else they had to take jobs on the ships owned by the fish merchants. In Walraversijde only those locals who dealt in salt and peat, the van Varssenare family, had the money to run ships of their own. Everyone else had to stop being the great man he once thought himself to be. Captains became contractors, crewmen were no longer partners in the business but working for a wage. Fishermen who had once been their own financiers now depended on financiers in the towns.

The sea was not safe from war, either. Throughout the sixteenth century the various wars and rebellions made the sea so dangerous that fishing boats went about in convoy with an armed escort. There was no refuge inland; the country was torn up by the revolt against the Spanish rulers that would eventually make the Netherlands to the north an independent country. When mercenaries came to the shoreline around Walraversijde they came to wreck and to steal, to take away all the comfort that the people of Walraversijde had made for themselves. Fishermen lost their sense of owning their trade, of being independent rather than borderline. The heart of the place died.

Some of the houses at Walraversijde, a whole quarter of the village, were abandoned suddenly and left to rot. The brewery closed. By the time peace returned, the wind had pushed the dunes over the sea-dike and changed the shoreline again. Nothing could come back except as memories, and when the people who remembered were gone, as ruins. Nature has, as always, the last word.[27]

# 8.

# Science and money

They were not just different: they were the opposite of everyone else. Flat noses, little eyes far apart, prominent chins, eyebrows from their foreheads to their noses and an absolute refusal to wash their clothes 'especially in time of thunder'; their thick, short thighs, their short feet and pigtails made them seem ominously different from people who imagined they had noses like Roman statues, big blue eyes and long legs to show off with short clothes. The faces of the Mongols were 'contorted and terrible', so the archbishop Ivo of Narbonne heard from an Englishman who had lived with them.[1]

They were nomads, always moving, just when Europe was netted with solid towns. They didn't use money as Europeans did for almost everything from buying a better afterlife to settling the account on a market stall; William of Rubruck said 'there was nothing to be sold among (them) for gold and silver, but only for cloth and garments', and if you offered them a gold coin from Byzantium 'they rubbed it with their fingers and put it to their noses to try by the smell whether it was copper or no'.[2] They hadn't got the point of money at all, the Westerners said; they still thought it was a kind of barter.

They were single-minded drunkards and 'when any of them hath taken more drink than his stomach can well bear, he casteth it up and falls to drinking again'. They ate their dead, and even the vultures would not touch the bones they left; they gave their old and ugly women to the cannibals,[3] and subjected the better-favoured ones to 'forced and unnatural ravishments'. They seemed to be doing their best to be appropriate for the world east of the Baltic and the

Caspian, which Europeans had populated thickly with their own fears and legends, with dog-headed, ox-hoofed men who hopped on one foot and lived on the steam from their soup.

They were a surprise, because nobody had known about the Mongols. They were appalling because they were winning.

Even the Assassins, the Ismaili Muslims of modern Syria who were famous for their courage, their ingenious killings and perhaps their smoking habits (although the name 'assassin' probably does not come from 'hashish'), sent ambassadors to France and England to ask for help in beating them back. By 1241, Mongol armies had taken Hungary, taken Poland; they had all of Russia except for Novgorod, which was their vassal. They had defeated the Teutonic Knights, they were harassing the borders of Bohemia and Saxony. Their spies were all around Vienna, but when the Duke of Austria asked for help from the West, there was silence. Indeed, for all the flurry of talk and arming and planning in various castles, there seemed to be nothing that could stop them moving west as far as the edge of the world. Christendom was cut up between factions, between the friends of the Pope in Rome and the friends of the Roman Emperor, and there was no time to spare from that struggle just to save Christendom itself. The Pope declared a crusade, but nobody came. The Emperor was suspected of making it impossible to help the Hungarian king unless the king became his vassal, and the chronicler Matthew Paris thought it possible the Emperor had somehow 'plotted this infliction . . . and that by his grasping ambition he was like Lucifer or Antichrist, conspiring against the monarchy of the whole world, to the utter ruin of the Christian faith'.

This is after the time of the great Genghis Khan, the 'mighty hunter' who 'learned to steal men and to take them for a prey'. His successor, his son Ögedei, also knew how to hunt and trap human beings, and when Franciscans on a papal mission reached Kiev they saw for themselves what it meant to be defeated by the Mongols: 'an innumerable multitude of dead men's skulls and bones lying upon the earth'. 'They have no human laws, know no mercy, and are more cruel than lions or bears,' Matthew Paris wrote.[4]

Also, they were quite brilliant fighters. They were better, suppler horsemen than the Europeans, which was hardly surprising since they almost lived on horseback; they were manoeuvring while the Westerners were still charging forwards in a fixed line.[5] They fought in lighter armour than the clanking mail of the West, and the backs of the armour, Ivo of Narbonne reported, 'are only slightly armed, that they may not flee'; anyone running away was shot. They had the distinct tactical advantage in an age of siege warfare that, as William of Rubruck reported after his mission there, 'they have in no place any settled city to abide in'; so they had no special place to defend, no sense of loss if they moved on. William regretted that his best metaphors were spoiled by their way of life; 'neither know they of the celestial city to come'.[6]

They had magic, or so it must have seemed. Their catapults were light and portable, and could hurl metal a full hundred metres from anywhere in the field; there is no proof they had cannon, but they did not need them. They had gunpowder to fire rockets and create smoke and confusion, to raise a true fog of war. They also knew how to pitch burning tar at the enemy, and how to firebomb towns and armies. In his encyclopaedia, Vincent of Beauvais reckoned they let loose a whole series of evil spirits. Their courier services kept every part of the army informed and they had signalling systems by flag and by torch; so they were always connected, and their tactics could be complicated. Dividing their army into separate sections actually gave them an advantage. They could swing around and harry and pretend to retreat so the enemy would fall into traps.[7] They were everywhere on the other side of the smoke, and they had spies all around, and they were ruthlessly disciplined. Where Europeans worked by weight and mass and force, armies like battering rams made of men and horses, 'the Tartar fights more by policy than by main force'.

Or so John of Plano Carpini reported in the 1240s, having seen them at first hand; he considered them 'like devils . . . always watching and devising how to practise mischief'. 'I deem not any one kingdom or province able to resist them,' he wrote. The more they advanced, the more absurd it seemed to imagine that Christendom could ever be united as the Mongols were, that Church or Emperor or both together could rule as effectively as the khans. Christendom was losing both authority and its identity. Confusingly, some of the Mongols also seemed to be Christian, even to have chapels in their camps with bells ringing and psalms chanted;[8] and the Mongols looked down on the Westerners not just as dogs but also as 'idolaters because they worship wood and stones when the sign of the Cross is carved on them'.[9]

It was hard to think straight about the Mongols, which gave a new use for some very old and abject certainties. There was an old legend that Alexander the Great had locked away a whole race of people in the mountains of the Caucasus behind a great wall sealed with bitumen; so maybe these Mongols were 'those Jews who were enclosed by the great king Alexander'. Mongols were nomads, which meant they were landless, and Jews 'had no proper land of their own'; that was almost evidence. The year 1240 was the year 5000 in the Jewish calendar, which was the due date for the coming of the Messiah according to some traditions, which led some Jews in Germany to think that perhaps the Mongols were indeed the 'enclosed people' come to save them at last. The name of King David was mentioned. The Jews of Prague sold all they had and quit the city in 1235, expecting the astonishments to come. It is possible the Mongols, who were excellent manipulators and always prepared the ground before their attacks, were encouraging the rumours; there were certainly a remarkable number of Mongol spies deployed along the Rhine and in Bohemia.[10]

Riot followed: Jewish houses burned and Jews died. There were the usual blood libels, the usual Christian fury at the very idea that the Jewish community might prevent a Jew converting,[11] but there was also a wider and terrifying idea: that all the outsiders in the world were conspiring together against Christendom.

The alarm had practical results: around the North Sea the rumours stopped the boats from Gotland and Friesland risking their brief, regular haul across the North Sea to Yarmouth, so that herring was left unsold and almost worthless in 1237–8, even when it was carted far inland, where people should have been grateful.

But more than anything, the terror made people think even more about the end of the world, which was already the usual and obsessional subject.

The world survived when a comet drew a line of light across the sky in 1066; all that happened was the Norman invasion of England. Nothing final happened in 1096 when the Irish expected to be punished for their part in cutting off the head of John the Baptist (they thought a druid called Mog Roth killed the saint); there was terrible plague, but not terrible enough to undo all St Patrick's good work of conversion.[12] But in the 1240s the end seemed truly and horrifyingly imminent, what with mankind coming close to the end of the sixth age of the world, so it was calculated, and the unstoppable threat from the East.

The khans made apocalyptic minds think of the Antichrist. The chronicler Roger of Howden painted him 'expert in all the false and wicked and criminal arts', able to upset the whole natural order and bring on 'all the might of his devil's power'. Men, especially Franciscan friars, were fascinated by the Calabrian abbot Joachim of Flore, who had worked out that the Antichrist was arriving in 1260 precisely; some of their associates reckoned the very fact of a new prophet like Joachim was proof the world was ending, that mankind was in the *dies formidandi*, the terrible days when evil runs wild in the world and judgement is close.[13]

The Franciscan friar Roger Bacon was much alarmed by the prospect of dark magicians in the East, people with appalling knowledge; he valued secret things, strange things alongside his respectable experiments, but he wanted the secrets in the right hands and minds. He was sure the West would need all the magic of the East to fight back. He wanted everything in the books of the East before it was turned against the Christian West. In writing to the Pope, he didn't just boast about the twenty years he had laboured on such things, the two thousand pounds he had spent on books, experiments, tables, but mostly on books; he also made promises. He listed wonders: a flying machine, boats that moved on their own without sails or rowers, an instrument three fingers long which could lift a man and his companions, even out of a prison; he was clearly preparing for hostages and war. He said that 'these things have been made in our days'.[14]

He proposed them all against the coming of the Antichrist, the darkest magician of them all. He was absolutely sure that science was now an urgent matter.

He could not know that the Mongols did not only have magic; they had politics. Their Ögedei Khan had long been a famous drinker, even by Mongol standards, with servants whose only job was to count up his diet of alcohol and a liver whose survival was almost miraculous. In 1242, just when he seemed to have decided on moving as hard into Europe as his father had gone into Asia, he died quite suddenly, so suddenly that there were rumours his wife had poisoned him. Once he was gone, the Mongol nation was obliged to choose a new khan, and to do that they had to assemble from the edges of Europe, from the edges of Asia, so the camps near Vienna were rapidly and surprisingly dismantled, and for the time being the threat moved back east. Pope and Emperor couldn't save Europe, but drink did.

When the Mongols withdrew, they left behind all the alarms and worries they had caused in the first place. Christendom was very vulnerable, the world was still coming to an end, the Last Judgement was close, there was magic about that the West did not share and it was an urgent matter to make sense of all the changes that had happened in people's minds over the past hundreds of years. Those changes were coming to a crisis.

The world had not been exactly itself for the longest time. We think we know the world with our senses, the stars we see, the cold of a snake or the warmth of a cat, the likelihood of rain from a certain kind of cloud, and when we think about such things we usually begin from what our senses tell us. We examine what we know. In the times of the Mongol invasions, people thought rather differently. They did not see and sense the world in its own terms; they saw it only through a different dimension, what others had already written about it, what God might be trying to say.

The world was more like a picture in a church that had to be read, studied, interpreted and learned, or some set text whose meanings had to be teased out. Any event might turn out to be a promise, or more likely a warning, and everything would be clear after the event.

When the Vikings raided Lindisfarne, the great Alcuin demanded what it had meant when, months before, a rain of blood 'fell threateningly on a clear day from the peak of the roof on the North side' of the church of St Peter in York, 'the principal church of the entire kingdom'. He was sure of the answer, of course; he could find it in his assumptions about how God would adjust the world to give rewards or warnings. He wrote to the King of Northumberland: 'How can it not be thought that a blood price was coming down to the people from the North?'[15]

The idea of thinking of weather as a phenomenon in itself, not the expression of some higher power, took another three hundred years, when William of Conches, grammarian and natural philosopher, discussed blood rain in his *Philosophia*.[16] He didn't deal in miracles or omens, but in a world that is mechanical and physical, in which the wind raises water in droplets from the ground, which then fall back as rain; he had noticed that downpours often follow intense heat, and he reckoned the sun's warmth turns the coldness of the earth to moisture just as fire melts ice. He saw that the same process could lift living things into the air – tadpoles, fish and frogs – so they could rain down later and look exactly like plagues. As for the colour of blood rain, he put that down to the bright-red colour of heat, so when rain was hot and condensed it was bound to look very much like blood.

A change has happened. Alcuin looked about for meanings that he expected; William looked and thought about his experience of the immediate world, and how it worked. Once men looked and observed, the next stage was measuring, calculating, subjecting the world to the rules of logic rather than relying on God's interventions, or those of angels, or even demons.

Adelard of Bath, in the twelfth century, wrote dialogues with an imaginary and inquisitive nephew who asked questions like: why do green things grow out of the earth? 'It is the will of the Creator,' Adelard tells him, 'that green things grow from the earth. But that doesn't mean there is no other explanation.' He says later: 'I do not want to take anything away from God, because everything that is exists for Him and because of Him; but things are not all random and muddled. When human knowledge advances, we should be listening to it.'[17]

Adelard was ready to find things out by experiments of sorts: to understand how veins and muscles work, he left a corpse in running water until the flesh was washed away. He got the idea, it seems, from a magic water jar belonging to some witch. He sometimes used observation rather brilliantly, as when he claimed to know which part of the brain handled reason and which part did the imagining; he had seen the changes in a man who had been injured in the front of his head.[18] He disapproved of simple wonder, simple terror at natural things; he dared to disagree with St Augustine's insistence on feeling awe at the mighty works of God instead of trying to see how the world worked. His nephew says thunder is 'an object of wonder to all nations', but Adelard insists on a simple explanation: the collision of frozen clouds. 'Look more closely,' he writes, 'consider the circumstances, propose causes and you will not wonder at the effects.'[19]

He did not find it easy to teach such things. His nephew asks why he prefers the 'opinions of the Saracens', the texts that were arriving in Arabic and Greek from Spain and the Middle East, to the Christian 'schools of God'. Adelard says the present generation is biased against 'modern' discoveries and unfamiliar things, he's afraid he would not get a hearing for his own ideas; 'therefore it is the cause of the Arabs that I plead, not my own'.[20] The Arabs had conserved Euclid's geometry and Aristotle's will to investigate, and added Arab astronomers' sophistication about the irregular movements of the heavens, all of which were unfamiliar and so 'modern' ideas; but their books were easy to accept because they were still authorities to be studied and interpreted in the old, familiar ways, as you might with the Church fathers and the Gospels. They were just a different kind of old.

The bishop, scientist and teacher Robert Grosseteste grew to believe in the thirteenth century that knowledge came from the mind facing outwards to the world and making sense of it, and not from some miraculous illumination from God. Knowledge of this world was worth while in itself. That sounds startling from a senior priest, but it is not at all what we might think. The process of investigating the world, Grosseteste thought, was also the glimpse of a trace of a glimmer of light, God's light, so that asking questions about the world might lead straight on to a sense of God and Godliness. Science could easily fit into the very heart of a religious view of this world, and even the next.[21]

The point of view has changed. What began with the kind of thinking we call superstitious or dark or plain medieval was beginning to allow the very start of the modern world.

Take observation, for example: the hunger to look hard and direct at things. That was needed for the quest to calculate the calendar of the world, to find out in which age men were living, to work out when the end and the Last Judgement were coming. The world had to be checked for signs to find out exactly how much history was left. There is a tenth-century list of the signs of the last days which went round Christian Europe: the sea flooding the land, earthquakes to make mountains and valleys disappear, stars falling to earth, mankind going mad, universal fire and, of course, a rain of blood. The world had to be watched for these things.[22]

Yet when the seas boiled around Iceland, fire belched from the earth and a mountain surged quite suddenly out of the water, the author of the *History of Norway*, writing around the start of the thirteenth century, refused to see omens of the last days. He preferred to go back to the Latin writer Solinus, who said there was a deep crack in the earth, and caves full of the winds created by the breathing of the water, which sucks the sea through hidden passages and starts surges and waterspouts and makes the earth roar and tremble. That breath muddles with the hot heart of the earth and pushes smoke and sulphurous flames out in the middle of the ocean. It is an elaborate explanation, which acknowledges the heat at the centre of the earth but otherwise is pure invention out of an old book; but it is a mechanical explanation, which is remarkable. 'Although we do not clearly understand these marvels in the world, or others greater still,' the author of the *History* says, 'they are not therefore to be taken as omens or reckoned portents foreboding the deluge.'[23]

Roger Bacon, even though he was a friar, went further. 'We do not see the wonderful actions of nature that are all day brought about in us and in things in front of our eyes,' he complained, 'but we judge them to be brought about either by a special divine operation, or by angels, or by demons, or by chance and fortune. But it is not so, except insofar as every operation of a creature is in some way from God.'[24]

Human beings set out to test the world, using their own eyes and minds, and mathematics; they were still tangled up with invisible, mysterious, metaphysical things but the relationship had changed. Science could be separated out. A man looking at the stars was no longer obliged to do metaphysics, not even to hunt out an astrological meaning for an eclipse; he could do astronomy. Mind you, a kind of astrology mattered to doctors well into the seventeenth century; it was always possible the stars still ruled men. But a man seeing some new volcanic island come up out of the sea was looking now at physical changes in the earth that he might be able to explain, not trying to decode some message from God about the end of time. That did not diminish the sense of wonder. The remarkable Dominican Albertus Magnus thought there could be no philosophy found in the details of specific things, like the species of plants. But he was still curious, and he went on writing down specifics. He showed by experiment that turtles won't drink sea water; he was told that ostriches eat metal, but they turned down the snacks of iron that he offered; he cut off the head of a cicada and heard it sing on and on. He also insisted that toads crack emeralds just by staring at them, which suggests he was a collector of everybody else's wonders, too.[25]

Even magic was becoming self-conscious. In a twelfth-century manuscript there is a kind of experiment: split a green hazel rod while saying the Lord's Prayer, then have two men make the sign of the cross and take an end of the rod, then say a spell: 'Ellum sat upon ella and held a green rod in his hand and said Rod of green unite again.' The rod should come back together to make a magic wand. By the start of the thirteenth century William of Auvergne said he had seen this happen, but he wrote that the rod put itself back together, naturally and of its own accord, and all the ceremony and all the words, even the holy ones, were of no significance at all. When it came to explaining things, magic and its paraphernalia were fading.[26]

God wasn't; and so a kind of scientific thinking could be comfortably bundled together with theology, sometimes metaphysics, mathematics and inspiration. It was easy for new thinkers to be smeared, accused and ruined for heresy, so it was also useful to invoke God. The mathematics was new, as was the rediscovery of texts in ancient languages that had nothing to do with the Bible, but they were tools to do an old job.

Robert Grosseteste launched the science of optics, which was known as *perspectiva*, and he drew out diagrams and used mathematics to try to show how we see things; but he saw light as the cause of everything, something from God that multiplies itself and produces matter that takes up space in the world. His geometry was a way to put the intangible on paper, to get a physical grip on mystery; physical fact and spiritual visions were both in his mind.[27] Roger Bacon thought optics was a useful science precisely because it gave men access to the miraculous in nature. 'There are,' he writes, 'an infinite number of truths in living things.'[28]

It was beginning to be agreed that observation was not enough, though. Logic and calculations were needed, too: a way to order what you sense so you can think more clearly about it. Mathematics was all-important, and especially the idea of finding proofs for rock-solid general ideas just like the ones Euclid found in geometry. There were new tools for examining the relationships and the ratios between things – quadratic equations, finding the roots of numbers, trigonometry. Lines and points and numbers became as important in philosophy or theology as they were, more obviously, when it came to measuring the rates at which objects fall, or trying to draw diagrams to show the lines by which the eye sees. 'The usefulness of considering lines, angles and figures is very great, since it is impossible to understand natural philosophy without them,' Robert Grosseteste wrote. Roger Bacon called mathematics 'the gate and key of these sciences'; he said the Devil found it most convenient when people ignored maths 'since that made theology and philosophy useless'.[29] All the effort of measuring the ages of the world in the expectation of the end of the world had the unexpected effect of getting mathematics off the page and into the real world, where its

1. (*Previous page*) The Vikings arc coming: the men who will make saints and martyrs. They also made our modern kind of town, and taught the North to sail into the unknown.

2a. The scribe at work in the *scriptorium*, with a knife for sharpening his goose feather quill pen and an ink of oak galls.

2b. The first calculator: using fingers and other body parts to show numbers. Put a number to each letter of the alphabet and a scribe could talk silently this way.

3. The book as gift and glory: Guillaume Fillastre presents his history of the Order of the Golden Fleece to the very fashionable Burgundian court of Charles the Bold.

4a. Huge shoals of herring off the Scandinavian coast made the fortunes of merchants who reckoned they had the right to bring down kings.

4b. Herring could be dried, smoked or packed into barrels with brine. The barrels crossed Europe with their packers' mark: the first multinational brand.

4c. On the dangerous seas off Norway, the fishermen took cod among other large fish. Dried and salted, it was the basis of early trade.

5. In the Hansa town of Hamburg merchants line up (*bottom*) to pay their harbour dues alongside the crane (*left*) whose great arm dominates the harbour and the barges moored at the quay. Trade is not always so peaceful; one ship bristles with arms against pirates and rivals (*mid-picture*).

6a. Forests are felled as towns grow and need the connection of good roads and good bridges; and the natural world mutates.

6b. In the Bourse at Antwerp, there are manufacturers, wholesalers, retailers of pictures, statues, drawings. Art is already a consumer good.

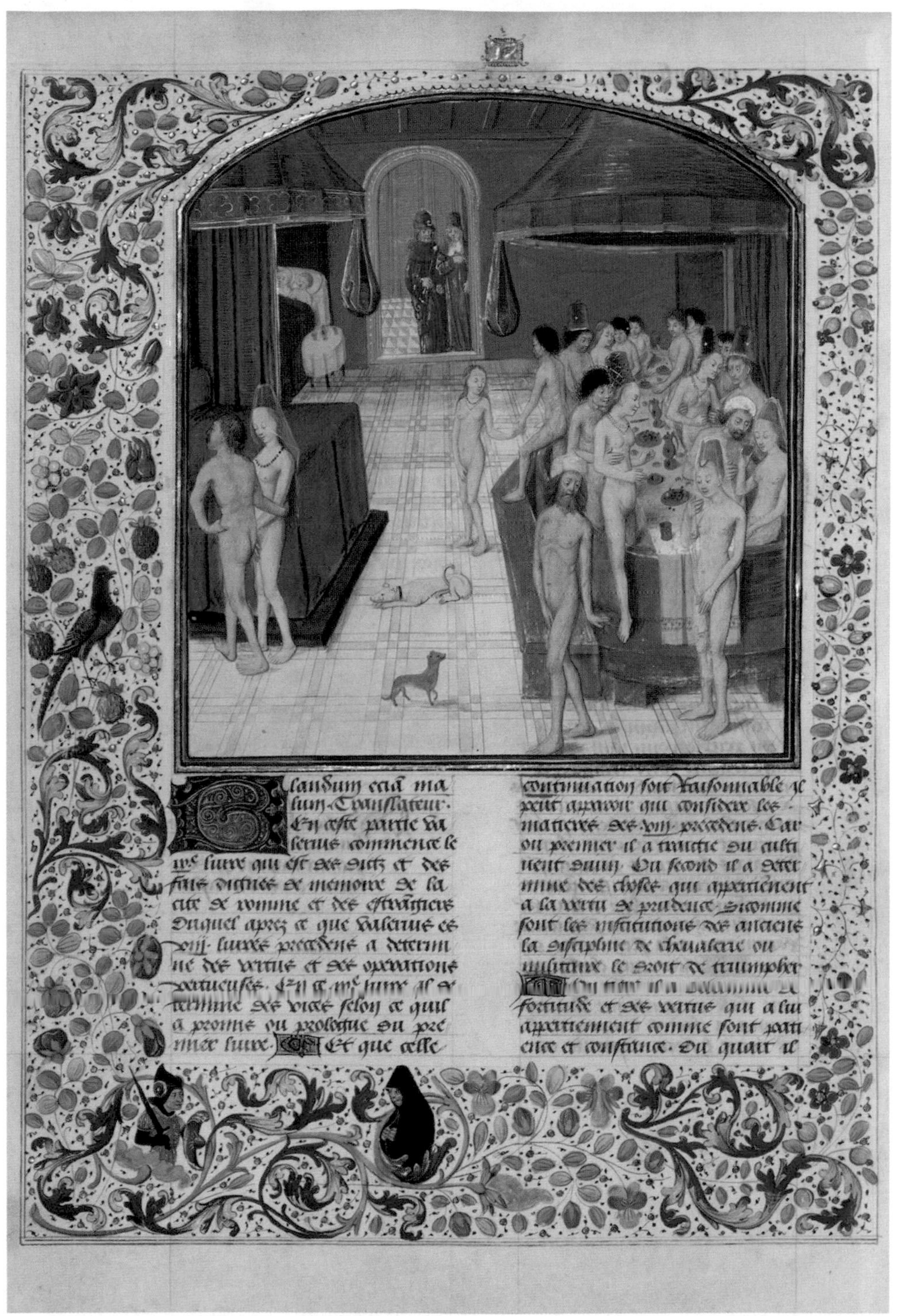

7. Sex, too, was a commodity in towns like Bruges: the bathhouse was a place to make love or find new friends. After dinner in a great wooden tub, the couples drift away purposefully to bed.

8a. The sea is terror: sailors beached on a hungry fish from a thirteenth-century manuscript.

8b. The sea is tamed: a great fish becomes a mechanical toy for an Antwerp parade of 1594.

effects were radical. Number became more complicated, more subtle and more useful. Thomas Bradwardine took Aristotle's formula for speed, force and resistance, the theory of how objects move, and respectfully showed that its plain arithmetic was far too simple, and needed a kind of geometric thinking (which in modern terms is logarithmic).[30] That was a whole new way to work figures, and to see unfamiliar shapes and structures in the well-known world.

This was classroom stuff, mostly reserved for those who could read and afford to buy books. It ought to have been hedged about by older ways of thinking, which by now had the power to call new thinking 'heresy'. Yet this change of mind proved so powerful that we're allowed to wonder: had it already begun outside the classroom, in the world? Was the scientific, the logical, the ability to see reality in an abstract ratio, simply the new form of something that was already built into everyone's everyday lives around the northern sea?

It was. The sheer scale of the change can't have depended on what we might expect: the traffic in secret books, communities with esoteric knowledge, ideas of divine inspiration or plain human terror at the prospect of the end of the world. All those mattered, but this change of mind goes much further back. Remember those Frisian traders working the coasts, and how they carried with them a way to put ideas of price and value on paper, along with coins to settle their deals whose meaning was something abstract, not the market value of the metal they contained. They dealt in ratios between shiploads, ratios between wood and wool, grain and pots, wine and iron, so that everyone could understand them and use them the next market day. They calculated the content of their ships, their goods at a fair; they turned the very physical world of barges and cargo into numbers. The sea which carried their business also brought ideas, books, thinkers back and forth; but, more than anything, it carried the idea, the fact, the use of money.

Consider this: from the 1330s, Paris theologians could talk in terms of calculating and measuring ratios for grace and love and charity, virtues written down almost as sums. Just before they began this, the Pope had published a kind of price list for indulgences, which laid down how much each year of pardon cost: one penny from Tours.

Salvation was priced. An *Ordonnance* of 1268 in France condemns 'those who blaspheme against God, the Virgin and the Saints' and lays down penalties that carefully match the poison in the blasphemy ('horrible' blasphemy cost between twenty and forty pounds) and also the ability to pay.[31] When both virtue and sin can be turned into numbers, and calculated and assessed, mathematics has entered the minds of theologians and philosophers and not just engineers and merchants; and it did so because it already permeated their whole world every time they bought something, sold something, paid the rent or taxes or fees. They knew just how complicated were questions of finding the right price. In the 1300s the philosopher Jean Buridan imagined being given ten pounds by a stranger and thanking him, '*Grates domine*', which sounds a quite unfair exchange; the money will buy things, but the words are lost on the wind. Buridan pointed out that maybe the stranger was grossly rich, but much in need of respect and honour; and maybe the man who said 'thank you' was known to be particularly honest and good. The rich man's needs and the virtue the poor man had to share became a matter of market forces, and the price turned out to be right.

The Frisians went trading and they brought money with them, which is a way to bring very different objects into one equation and do the sums. Now that same kind of equation took in music, blasphemy, pardon from Hell, love and charity: it took in the world.

This isn't a simple story, no revelations, no discoveries, and it may be easiest to begin with what science is not. It is not just experiment, otherwise we'd honour Eilmerus, that old and most learnèd monk at Malmesbury, a man who had great difficulty walking, and everyone knew the reason: when he was young, he thought he knew how to fly.

He 'used some skill to weave feathers into his hands and feet', William of Malmesbury records. 'Then he took to the air from the top of a tower, but he began to shake because the winds were so strong and turbulent, and also because he was all too aware of what a foolhardy thing he was doing. He fell, broke his legs and was crippled ever after.' He imagined man could fly like the birds, he made an experiment to test it, and afterwards he had his explanation for what went wrong with the experiment; but he had no general principles, no general theory, he was testing and he made no calculations and no diagrams. 'He used to say,' William writes, 'the cause of his catastrophe was that he forgot to put a tail at his rear end.'[32]

We might say: he didn't experiment, he just tried.

Robert Grosseteste, Robert 'with the big head', helped begin the move from writing about *experientia*, which means experience, to becoming an experimenter who staged tests and experiences to prove theories. He came to the bishop's household at Hereford, with a brilliant testimonial from a man who had known him in the bishop's household at Lincoln: 'will be a great support to you', the letter promised, 'in various kinds of business and legal decisions, and in providing cures to restore and preserve your health'. He had 'highest standards of conduct', he had 'wide reading' and if he was going to cost money then the bishop was reminded that he knew branches of learning, law and medicine, which 'in these days are most highly rewarded'.[33]

This Grosseteste was a remarkable man. He was the first to look closely into the role of experiment in science, to think that falsifying an idea could be quite as important as proving it. Other people were looking carefully at the stars, the world, the rainbow or comets, just as Grosseteste did, but he insisted that 'those who form their own opinion from their own experiences without any depth of reasoning will inevitably fall into wrong opinions'.[34] Add mathematics to what you see and sense, make big general ideas that are supposed to work in any circumstance, and you have the groundwork for science.

Matthew Paris thought Grosseteste was 'a man of too much learning', who must have been in the schools 'from his earliest years'; and by 'the schools' he meant the formal debates and seminars of the new universities, Paris or Oxford. Grosseteste certainly lectured at Oxford, taught with the Franciscans there and was so closely linked to the university that scholars used to assume he must have been its first chancellor. But his background was rather different, which may explain why he thought so fiercely for himself: he knew Paris, but he started in provincial England.

He was born in a small Suffolk village with Stow in its name, brought up for a while by a widowed mother, whose death left him begging on the streets. Some civic grandee in Lincoln paid for him to go to a local school, which may not have taught him all that much of what he needed to know; to the end of his life he needed help translating Greek, so Roger Bacon wrote, and although he had a passion for languages, he knew very well he had started them too late.[35] His learning was founded in Lincoln in the bishop's household, and in the school and library at the cathedral in Hereford, where he could learn from foreigners, outsiders, men who were trying things out.

It took money to study in Paris, which would have seemed the next likely move for him, but he had no money and he never formally enrolled to learn or teach there. A certain Robert Grosseteste did write a will in Paris in 1224, leaving to his children a lifetime interest in a house in the courtyard of the church of Sainte-Opportune, a holy island just off the Rue Saint-Denis and a bit south of Les Halles. When his children were gone, the house was to go to the church; and in 1249 his children were evidently gone because his grandchildren went to law to hold on to their property.[36] This is extremely curious on the face of it: Grosseteste was a serious cleric, who should not have been married, let alone involve a Paris church in providing for his children. But at the time of this bequest, which is just before Grosseteste turns up again in England, he was not yet a priest or even a deacon. In fact, he was not ordained until very late in life. Having been married could explain that delay, and not being ordained would help explain why he could not formally study or teach in Paris. But he was there; one witness of the bequest is William of Auvergne, Bishop of Paris, and when Grosseteste wrote to William in 1239, recommending a clerk who was coming to Paris, he calls him with unusual intimacy his 'dearest friend'.[37] If Grosseteste did live in Paris, did he take the learning of Hereford to the learnèd schools in the big city?

His origins, his ghostly presence on the outskirts of the university in Paris, all fit with the sense that Grosseteste was not quite 'one of us', where 'we' are all good and orthodox and mannerly schoolsmen with a bit of money behind us. He quarrelled with the canons of

Lincoln Cathedral, who at once remembered his origins, 'so very humble'. Matthew Paris, used to the quiet and even elegant life of a rich monastery, thought he was 'heartless and inhuman' for 'the violent acts which he did in his lifetime . . . his canons whom he excommunicated and harassed, his savage attacks on monks and even more savage against nuns . . .'; he acted, perhaps, 'not according to knowledge'. Matthew Paris also felt he should point out that Grosseteste was 'born from the very humblest stock'; the man was simply not couth. When cardinals insisted he give parishes to some Italian priests, he objected because they could handle the sins of the French-speaking gentry but not all the English-speaking others. When the cardinals persisted, Grosseteste made a scene. He went down on his knees before the priests, made his confession in English, and then, when they did not understand a word and sat looking puzzled, he began to hammer on his breast, he began to sob and to bellow. The priests went off in confusion.[38]

Now imagine this man staring at a rainbow, and thinking for himself.[39] He began by sorting out the various ways a full spectrum of colours can appear: in rainbows, in the spray made by millwheels or the oars of a boat, or just by squirting water from the mouth, when sunlight shines through a crystal, and lastly the colours that reflect off the shine of a starling's feathers. The reflections, he saw, were something different; but the rainbow, like light through a crystal, was a matter of refraction, colours produced, as he thought, 'by the weakening of white light' as it passed through something dense like water or stone. So he decided that rainbows were colour made by sunlight passing through water, the drops and spheres of water, and coming out brilliantly at an angle of 42° to the source of the light. He had described a rainbow and also put it on paper to think about it more clearly.

He had an idea of what a rainbow was; now he asked how a rainbow happens. Grosseteste had watched light passing through a spherical glass full of water and spraying an arc of colour onto a screen; so he reckoned that water was involved, and some kind of surface where the colours could show. He knew about lenses that 'make things very far off seem close at hand . . . so that it is possible for us to read the smallest letters at an incredible distance or to count sand or grain or grass or any other minute objects' – did he in his fifties wear the newly invented spectacles? – and he thought a lens broke the 'visual ray', refracting the light.[40] He brought all these thoughts together to imagine the moist layers of a cloud together forming a single lens, and he thought there must be a second cloud which worked as a screen. He had a theory, and he set out to test if it was true or false, complete or incomplete.

It was, of course, wrong; but it took time to prove that. In the meantime, some of Grosseteste's ideas on the rainbow were still influential when Isaac Newton was working: the idea that each colour in the rainbow was somehow a different kind of ray, created as white light was changed by refraction. It is remarkable that he realized it is not distance that puts things out of sight, but the increasing narrowness of the angle under which we see distant objects. His ideas of falsification worked so well that he managed to dispose of a good many bad theories about comets, even though he never found the truth of what they are.

He was inventing our idea of science. He drew on ancient writers, on Aristotle and on Galen, and he presented methods that allowed the very beginning of the methods we recognize as modern: testing theories, falsifying some, proving some things impossible, insisting on combining observation and ideas. He was still tentative. He said he wouldn't ask, for example, why the moon was a sphere, because he was sure the reasons lay outside nature and no astronomer could know them; much later, the astronomer Kepler would show how a sphere forms because of the various gravitational pulls of the moving planets.[41] Grosseteste started the move to the methods that would let Kepler find out such things.

Roger Bacon, in the thirteenth century, was Grosseteste's most obvious, even notorious follower. Francis Bacon, in the seventeenth century, looked back and patronized him: 'like a boy who picks up a boat peg on the shore and then yearns to build his own whole boat,' he wrote. But he was still impressed with Roger 'having not concerned himself just with theories, but with combining them with understanding the mechanical aspects, grasping how theory reaches into practical things'.[42] In his grudging way Francis Bacon acknowledged the great change that Grosseteste began, and Bacon continued.

Grosseteste taught Franciscans, Bacon was a Franciscan, and it is largely in Franciscan minds that we can track this tangle of ideas. They were the ones who went out to meet the Mongols and report on their ways (there was a Dominican, too, but his testimony is lost); so they knew about the immediate, practical prospect of disaster. They were fascinated by the end of the world, and how to calculate when it would come. Both men saw the world through mathematics as the Dominican Albertus Magnus, equally scientific in ambition, did not. Both men valued experience, even if it was a second best to Godly illumination.

Roger Bacon said experience was fundamental; it was the right way to test a mathematical result or even a revelation from God. Human agency and curiosity mattered. He much admired his contemporary Peter de Maricourt, who not only knew all kinds of science from his own experience but asked other people about theirs, going out of the study and the abbey to question soldiers and farmers and old ladies on the street and in the fields 'to complete his philosophy'.

So Bacon also tested things. He set out to break a diamond with goat's blood, which was an old tradition, and when that didn't work he tried cutting other gems with diamonds, and he found the diamonds broke; he falsified his first theory, thought again and tested again. He blew bubbles from his mouth to watch the colours on the sheen of the surface. He used crystals and hexagonal stones to watch how light is refracted. He practised a rather cheap kind of science which needed no raw materials, none of the precious metals or laboratory equipment that alchemists used, but which allowed him to think about the stars he had watched, the rainbows he had seen.

He took the world into his mind. He thought his kinds of knowledge should be a weapon against the invading enemy from the East; he thought in a grand, almost strategic way. He studied and tested, he found out and brought together other people's work, he was so obsessed with knowledge that he was annoyed at monastic duties and tried to take credit for bothering to teach at all, which was his job. He seems the perfect academic, in a closed world, a friar who did not have to count his pennies or even buy his food.

And yet the most furious argument that divided his own order, the Franciscans, all century long was about money: was it right to give up all riches and leave yourself with nothing to give away in charity? It defined them because they were so determined to be poor. It separated them from clergy making a living.

Money also shaped the new universities and how they worked. Money, in fact, shaped minds.

Gerard of Abbeville – at least we think it was him – scratched down his accounts as a theology student in Paris in the middle of the thirteenth century: sixty-four items, sixty-four payments. There were all the obvious costs – parchment, pumice, ink and candles and rent – and some that suggest he was moving or at least reorganizing his rooms: he bought chamber pots and grease lamps, a table, a lectern for reading and a solid chair (because no gentleman would keep a folding chair). The very basic things like food and drink cost him rather little, but he had to pay for 'wine with a master' and a tip to his landlady and fees to whoever took away all of his shit and rubbish; he was always paying people. There is also a payment to a 'Master John' which looks like settling a debt, and three *solidi* for 'usury'; this was a student comfortable enough to dine out with friends and stand his teacher drinks, but he also knew all about debt, moneylenders and business.[43]

Now, Paris was a university run by its masters, its teachers. A law school like Bologna was quite different in the beginning: students wrote the contract with teachers, paid them directly and so they also wrote the rules. Other Italian universities like Perugia, and some French ones like Montpellier, were run in much the same way. Paris, and Oxford, and Orleans and later Cambridge ran on different principles. They taught theology, philosophy and liberal arts as well as providing a professional grounding in the law, so there was not the same sense that most students mostly expected to be trained to make good money. The difference meant that the ambitions and standards of the professors ruled.

These professors were 'brutes', so said Daniel of Morley, who studied law in Paris at the end of the twelfth century; they read out loud from volumes too heavy to carry, they made lead pencil notes in the margin, but otherwise they hid their ignorance by saying nothing much.[44] They taught the basic texts by reading them out loud in the afternoon; students had to swear they had heard some three times over, some just once, in lecture rooms with hard benches, or sometimes straw bales for desks and chairs.[45] Even the fee for an exam was spent on straw for the floor, so people could sit and watch; and since this made no more sense in the thirteenth century than it does now, there had to be a rule to stop people assuming they ought to give money also to the chancellor or his examiners.[46]

To stay in this dusty world of learning, students paid for the salaries of the beadles, the seals on their diplomas, a fee for matriculating, a fee that first years paid to senior students for the right to be a student, fees for moving up in the academic hierarchy and fees to persuade the lecturers to keep talking. Students needed money for the rent you paid to borrow a book to copy it, and the fee you paid to have someone else copy it; law students needed a servant to carry all their books about. They had to pay to look like students: to buy or hire student gowns. Many of them were foreigners doing all this with unfamiliar coins whose value they had to calculate in terms of their own resources, back home or in Paris. Unsurprisingly, the books of model letters for students in England show how to write about the lack of food, heat, bedding, clothes, books or parchment, and above all the lack of cash.[47]

Somebody had to get and handle all this money. It was complicated work, almost a system of taxation: a fee depended on what you wanted but also on who you were, your social standing and your ability to pay. In Paris the students paid a progressive kind of tax: their fees were based on the *bursa*, how much money they had to live on for a week. Once the sum was set, somebody had to collect. The word *computus* was not always a matter of holy arithmetic; in the 1320s it meant the street-by-street, house-by-house account of which students lived where, what fees to collect and from whom, name by name by name. The university acknowledged that sometimes people were told to come and pay their fees, but somehow didn't bother, so it was very helpful to ask more directly on their doorsteps. It is likely that many philosophers and theologians spent as much time administering the money as they did writing and teaching.[48]

When masters rule, the running of the university becomes their business. Masters, bachelors, even stewards whose knowledge was mostly how to buy food and fuel: they could all rent a house in Oxford and set up halls or hostels, after which they had the desirable title of 'principal'. University masters at Cambridge, Paris and Oxford were involved in working out the true rentable value of any place a student might find to live; they had to think in terms of a just price, a true value, not to mention yields and assets. From 1250 the university in Cambridge insisted they had to find a guarantee for the rent on their houses, so they needed capital or credibility to get started; Oxford wrote down the same rule in 1313. Principals were keepers of the loan chests that took pledges and financed students, collectors of university rents and proctors who enforced the students' fines and dues. In return for the right to do all this business they had to keep their lodger students in line, which was serious work; the unattached scholars living in unlicensed rooms are denounced in an Oxford statute of 1410 as 'sleeping by day and haunting taverns and brothels by night, intent on robbery and homicide'.[49]

In Paris, students lived in 'nations', communities from the same territory assembled around a master who came from more or less the same place; small businesses again. Around the start of the thirteenth century the preacher Jacques de Vitry knew exactly how to tell them apart: 'The English are drunken cowards, the French proud, soft and effeminate; the Germans are quarrelsome and foul-mouthed, the Normans vain and haughty . . . the Romans vicious and violent, the Sicilians tyrannical and cruel, the men of Brabant are thieves and the Flemings are debauched.'[50] Their masters often had a sideline in lending students money, for students were always in need of cash. Paris students could call on official moneylenders, citizens under oath to the university, and there were more than 250 of them at any time. Pawnbrokers offered the university special rates.

Not all the Paris hostels were in the better parts of town. Jacques de Vitry was a student there in the last years of the twelfth century, in a house with a school upstairs and a brothel downstairs; which he seemed to see as trouble and not as an asset. He remembered that 'on one level, the whores fought among themselves and with their pimps; and in the rest of the house, there were clerics shouting and arguing'.[51]

All this had legal pitfalls, like any business. Consider Master Petrus de Arenciaco, who taught in Paris and leased an apartment by the Seine from a rather wealthy lawyer. He then let out rooms to three students, two brothers and one other. For whatever reason, the brothers were not happy; in the autumn of 1336 they moved out with all their goods to lodge with a woman called Johanna 'la Pucelle' – who with that nickname may just possibly have been pure, but was certainly young and a woman. The master was left with his lease, and he started to pay rent only for himself and the one student he had left, and naturally the lawyer went to law; he seized the brothers' goods to make them go on paying him. The brothers said the problem was the master's, and the rent was due only from the men still living in the apartment and not them; and they won their case. Students came and went, but the masters took the blame.[52]

There were also rivalries, trading blocs, cartels, unfair trade practices and trade wars. Franciscans and Dominicans came to Paris to teach and to learn, but they came late, in the 1210s; masters and students from outside the religious orders were already settled and established. The friars had an awkward relationship with the university from the start, because they were not allowed to study law or the arts, the schools which swore an actual oath to the university itself;[53] competition for students, and for chairs in theology, only made things worse. The friars were supported and subsidized by their orders, even though the Franciscans insisted they had nothing, not even property in common, while the secular masters had to piece together parishes and benefices, rents and student rolls to make a living. They were, in two words, unfair competition.

When celebrations went wrong in Lent 1229, and city guards arrested some students and casually killed some, the secular masters called for '*cessatio*', which means roughly a strike. They objected to the breach of academic privilege – students were clerics and should never have been hauled off the streets – rather than the death of students, and they walked out of Paris, some for Orleans down the road, some off to Toulouse, some to Oxford and even Cambridge; the strike was the making of Cambridge. The friars stayed put in Paris, took the chance to acquire some more chairs of theology, and started a very pointed campaign against the multiple benefices on which the absent masters depended. They persuaded the Bishop of Paris to rule that two benefices disqualified a man from salvation, at least if one was worth more than fifteen Parisian pounds, and then salted the wound by insisting on teaching the ruling in their classrooms.

Worse, John of St Giles, a secular master, took to teaching Dominican students and gave a great sermon on the beauty of voluntary poverty, which was something the seculars reckoned was quite close to heresy; after all, how can a man be charitable and virtuous if he has nothing to share or give away? Halfway through the sermon, John stepped down from the pulpit and made a quick change; he finished the sermon dressed in the Dominican habit. He was a heretic but he was also now a traitor.[54]

The language of this holy rivalry was all about money: about the right not to have property. But money and trade and dealing defined even the basic institutions of the universities. Each hostel owner was a source of dinner, but also of credit, and each hostel was run to make money. Suppose you had come south to Paris from some great merchant town like Bruges; the hostel at the University of Paris might seem familiar from the hostels at home where merchants stayed and did business and stored their goods.

Foreigners lodged together in those merchants' hostels, far from home,[55] and they also lodged goods and money to establish their credit, got involved in dealing and borrowing, met and talked and found things out and did business: the men who stayed in a hostel belonged to the hostel. The men in a professor's house were much the same; they were brotherhoods with a purpose. Traders had to go to Bruges to do business. Likewise students from Flanders or Frisia had to go to Paris because there was no university in all Flanders until

Louvain was founded in the 1420s. Those old traders the Frisians were still travelling – but now as students.

Money was not just the clutter and rush of traders, foreigners, people with goods and money to spend, all coming and going, to ports, to fairs, to markets, although a Paris student could see all that just by crossing the Seine to buy an apple or a loaf of bread. Money was everyone's everyday calculation, which coins were worth what, how much silver in a coin; everyone had to know how to work things out. True, great traders paid with ingots of silver, solid bars of the kind which were used to buy land or provide a daughter with a dowry, but even they were under pressure to pay some bills with the variable coins. In Cologne a trader could be arrested if he didn't change his ingots for coins. Flemish traders sometimes melted down coins to make new ingots, and in England the local business was done in coins but goods were sent abroad in the expectation of getting back ingots.[56] Since the Church kept forbidding usury, the way to make money out of money was not to lend it out but to watch the money markets.

So money became a great issue for theologians and philosophers, at the very heart of how to define a good civic life. Money was the spiritual riddle of the age: how to define the worth of things, make a profit on it and still avoid damnation.

William of Ockham was another Franciscan. He read the newly rediscovered and fashionable Aristotle, and then he wrote of mathematics as a language for talking about things, a tool you could use to think hard about subjects even where nothing at all was being measured – a very useful figment of the imagination. In Ockham's account, science didn't just have to be about describing things and explaining them; it could be about measuring and calculating. What's more, the things you can count and calculate could be quite abstract; you didn't trip over them in the world of real objects. Maths was about the kind of statement Euclid made when he said that even if two parallel lines were extended to infinity, they would never meet; nobody expected to draw those lines, or find them in the real world, and yet the statement was useful in the real world. Thanks to equations, it was now reasonable to make comparisons between unlike things and concentrate on just one quality: you could compare the brownness of a brown horse with the brownness of a brown cow.[57]

In Aristotle's thinking, money was the way you evened out the deal when you were bartering goods and services; imagine a shoemaker doing business with a housebuilder, and it's easy to see how a bit of cash sorts out the differences between the goods each man is offering. But money had become more than this useful expedient. According to Thomas Aquinas it was a way of expressing value: the value of all the work and materials that go into building a house compared with the time and work you need to make a pair of shoes. Such trading was tolerable, more or less, but dangerous, because it led to the possibility of profit. Greed was sin, and profit was excusable only if it was not the whole point of a deal. Prices had to be calculated with a moral equation: a 'just price'. Prices might change when things were plentiful or things were scarce, but out there was a fine, high notion: a 'true' economic value.[58]

Everything was in motion now. Money meant trade, and trade seemed to mean the end of the 'perfect city' that Aristotle imagined, strong and self-sufficient. Money was the engine of the new ways and it corrupted things: strangers came with different customs; there were never enough strong soldiers because trading requires no muscle in itself; business was thought to weaken the body and the heart. The unsettling of the world was very uncomfortable, so naturally it was generally agreed that Aristotle had the right idea about trade and merchants: doing things just for the sake of money was wrong. And yet profit, as the thirteenth-century Pietro di Giovanni Olivi learned at Paris, still happens. He wrote of 'various chances to buy and sell things with advantage; and this comes from God's Providence, just like all man's other good things'. It could be a gift of God, but 'only if it does not go beyond the proper amount'.[59]

A man who sells something for a profit, without carving or painting it like a craftsman, without making some material changes, is not within God's law; the writer known as Fake Chrysostom said anyone who bought goods and sold them on for a profit, unaltered, was 'the merchant who was thrown out of the temple'.[60] The theologian Henry of Ghent was especially bothered by the man who bought at a low price and sold for a profit at once, because an object can't change its value instantly; he implies that everything has a true value and a just price, something that should not be changed artificially.

All dealers constantly face the moral test of being as just as possible. He added: 'Few succeed.'

There was also the question of whether an object gains value just because it is shipped from one place to another, whether food can be cheaper or dearer depending on the weather and the harvest. Value was a complicated equation, and the merchant's job was to work out the value and set the price; that, too, was a service, and it was worth paying for.

Being modern, we want someone to say that the market sets the price, the comfort of something as impersonal as the market's 'invisible hand', but price and value depended, in the medieval mind, on the immediate moral decisions of many individuals: their will to be just and fair, the decision not to chase always and only after money. It was so much a matter of theology, and not economics, that not much thought was given to checking and regulating the market. When Henry of Ghent put a value on the merchant's useful work in considering different places and different seasons when setting a price, he didn't actually deal with the possibility that the merchant might get things wrong or be speculating to make money, or organizing a comfortable monopoly.[61]

There is no economics here, not as we know it, but there are fierce discussions and disputes and doubts about the economic world, and some convenient conclusions. From now on, profit is not always usury. Private property is fine. Theologians could agree that there was no private property before the fall of man and the end of the garden of Eden; but now that man was rotten with original sin, private property was the only way to stop the bullies and the strongarms taking over absolutely everything that in an ideal world would be held in common. This flatters those lucky or forceful enough to have property already; at least, it says, they might be much, much worse.

Nicholas Oresme went to Avignon, where he preached fiercely in front of Pope Urban V, so fiercely that some called him a heretic.

'Everything the prophets in the Bible said about Jewish priests, he turned against the priests of his time; he called them dogs without the strength to bark, shameless, not knowing how much is enough, and shepherds who cared for their own interests rather than their flocks.'[62] At the heart of his anger was money: the fact that the Church was selling pardons and positions, making money the reason for doing things and also for claiming that God did things in return for the money, like forgive sin. Men who should be holy were burning up with a passion for the grand and luxurious and rich; he talked furiously about the merchants selling doves in the temple, the men that Jesus expelled.[63] He was, after all, the author of a *Traité des monnaies*: an *Essay on Money*.

He was a bishop, and used his fine training in the abstract questions and answers of the scholastic method to write a work on the mathematics of the sphere, the basics of Euclid and Aristotle's account of the weather, the sky and how things are born and how they die. He did serious business with texts: for the king's benefit he turned Latin into French. He also wrote ideas that were his own. He examined the movements of the heavens and whether they could be measured; and with that last investigation, he started what was almost a campaign against astrology. He came to believe, through quite original mathematics, that the heavens turn in a way that can't be reduced to charts and exact oppositions and conjunctions; all those things are ratios and the more you try to relate all the pairs of numbers you can imagine, and the ratios between them, the more you end up with numbers that can't be reduced to ratios at all – irrational numbers. He had the young king Charles V as a friend, and he wanted to shuffle him out of the influence of the court astrologers, using mathematics with a clever twist here, a downright radical speculation there.

He was properly academic, properly intellectual. He was also the man who managed to block the spoiling of French money, the process of clipping and muddling the metals in coins. Money was an issue for him – and not just money when it went wrong, when the official rates differed from the rates in the marketplace, when silver was cut with copper to make more coins – but money as a mathematical idea and its meaning in the world. In Oresme's view, the world was unstable, always changing – because the amounts of food, drink, metals, pots, pans and necessities were always changing – and money was the essential way to test and calculate real value.

Money certainly was not just one more merchandise, to be sold and bought like cows or grain or stone; a man could not be rich only in money terms, like old King Midas who could turn everything to gold. It was a test of what things were worth in general, not just some cartload or bargeful. Metal could be melted down, bought and sold, but when it became money it was the measure of things. That is why Oresme reckoned it was fraud and crime, almost sin, to tamper with it; and only a tyrant like the Emperor Nero would dare. Fake the money, make it bad, and trade will fail because nobody wants bad money and everyone will be less truly rich.

This is money as the moral measure of all human needs, so Oresme said. He looked for the same kind of measure in making his scientific investigations, the same kind of abstract ideas about objects as solid as spheres or planets, about facts as fundamental as death and life. He wanted to examine and calculate those ideas, as a trader might work out a price. He wanted a way to express what was just, and to do it in numbers.

Science and theology were not far apart. What connected them was the great issue of the times all around the North Sea: price and value and above all money.

# 9.

# Dealers rule

Those threatening ships were not pirates after all; they were police. They were heavy vessels, trading 'cogs' built of thick oak planks, one tall spruce tree for a mast, caulked shut with tow and tar, their sides rubbed with resin and linseed oil: solid and boxy as safes. As the tide fell they could come to rest on their flat bottoms without rolling over, just like the Frisian boats before them; they had ungainly bows and sterns at sharp angles to their hulls, a big box for goods or soldiers.[1] They also had hinged rudders at the stern, which was new, and decks over their whole length, and down below there were gratings to hold the freight out of the sea water.[2] Whatever business they were doing, they were built to do it right.

Their business this day was to stop other ships doing business. They challenged and stopped ships in the narrow water of the Øresund between Sweden and Denmark, they were armed and insistent, and they were ready to confiscate anything the ships were carrying and demand a ransom or a fine; but they didn't empty every ship that passed. They were interested only in the ships that were sailing to stop Norway starving.

It was 1284, the weather was turning colder, the summers were not certain any more and there was pack ice drifting south around Iceland: the times felt tough. The Norwegian ports, Bergen in particular, were waiting for the last shipments of the things they needed for the winter: grain for bread and beer, peas, beans, malt and flour. They had come to depend on these shipments; their year was measured out by the ships from Lübeck that took away their butter and dried cod, their furs and their good axes, and brought back basics from around the Baltic – where there was land to grow things, not like their own narrow fields between mountains and fjords and forests. They had once done business with the English as well, but now they depended on the Lübeck merchants of the Hansa.

This Hansa had no flag, no seal and no king of its own: it was a loose arrangement between trader towns, a sort of economic community. It was nothing like a nation or a kingdom because it had no responsibilities and no territory to defend, and sometimes it seemed downright allergic to either. All it had was power.

A hundred years earlier King Sverre of Norway had complained that the Hansa towns brought in far too much wine, which could only do harm to his country. He had to put up with them. Another king in 1248 had to write to Lübeck to ask for grain, malt, flour, because Norway was miserably short of all those things. Merchants from Lübeck and the other Hansa towns now began to spend the whole year in Bergen, not just the sailing season in summer. They had their own office there, although it was so small at first that the heat of one man's body could keep it warm in winter.[3] They rented houses by the waterfront, settled down, enjoyed the right to do business on the streets, in the docks, on board boats, to be exempt from guard duty and from the arduous business of hauling ships up onto the beaches. This mattered because Bergen sits on a calm fjord where the water hardly moves, no tide and no river current, and ships had to be manhandled off the flat, muddy beach.[4]

It was too much for the Norwegians at times. Bergen was the king's town, a port kept open by the warmer Gulf Stream waters and sheltered behind islands, a rich town where 'a very great number of people live . . . ships and men arrive from every land; there are Icelanders, Greenlanders, Englishmen, Germans, Danes, Swedes, Gothlanders and other nations too numerous to mention'; at least that is what a band of crusaders found in 1191. A century later the English had gone, there had been a trade war with Iceland and the Germans were installed. German craftsmen, shoemakers and tailors, were setting up business and their own associations; they were joined by barbers, bakers, goldsmiths and fur dealers. The town spoke two languages, Norwegian but also German. The merchants seemed to do business just as they liked, and they liked to bring in beer and bits and pieces, not the grain that Norway needed. Their power was all too obvious.

Norway made a new rule: either bring in grain or get out during the winter. The Hansa merchants objected, and they complained furiously about the 'injustices' they were suffering. The Norwegians commissioned Alv Erlingsson, a local noble, diplomat and thug, to go out and do serious injustice to them in a small pirate war; at least one ship was wrecked.

So the Hansa decided to correct the Norwegians' attitude. It banned the sale of grain, flour, vegetables and beer to Norway, the winter essentials. They policed the Øresund, and of all their town allies on the Baltic and the North Sea only Bremen declined to help. It was as though the whole trading world was putting Bergen under siege. And they waited, knowing that their actions meant hunger for a whole nation of civilians, until the merchants got what they wanted.

Hansa members reckoned on support from other merchants in other countries: the business community of the time. The town of Rostock on the Baltic wrote to Edward I of England to ask him to ban the sale of grain and legumes from England to Norway; Wismar, just to the east of Rostock, wrote a few days later; Emperor Rudolf I and his imperial city of Lübeck asked for help 'against the ravages of the Norwegians', so Germans could once more freely visit English ports for business. England had only just renewed its treaty of friendship with Norway, so England helpfully did nothing at all.

As for what happened in Norway, the Lübeck chronicler Detmar wrote with some satisfaction: 'there broke out a famine so great that they were forced to make atonement'. Within a year, the Norwegians begged for Swedish help to reach a settlement. They paid a price – two thousand marks in silver, although probably they paid up in fish – and they gave the Hansa extraordinary privileges, even including the right to go out and salvage its own cargo from wrecked ships.

Everything the Norwegians did after that seemed only to make them more dependent on the Hansa. Bergen's great export was stockfish, the dried cod from the waters off the northern coast: hard boards, almost indestructible, cut with saws, and cheaper for very good reason than salted cod or smoked fish. Before it could be soaked, let alone cooked, it had to be thoroughly beaten with a hammer; the Earl of Derby's kitchen accounts for 1390–91 show a man paid eight pence for giving the fish at least two hundred blows.[5] Still, it was a universal protein with ten years or more of shelf life and the Hansa had the whole valuable trade locked. It had good things from Lübeck, and the fishermen wanted them and had them on credit; the fish was somehow never quite enough to settle the debt. The whole coast of Norway could hardly think of selling their fish anywhere else. Fifty years later King Magnus Eriksson meant to do something about the situation, but he could do nothing because he needed credit from the Hansa to keep his economy moving.[6]

The merchants followed the logic of their trade all the way. They flourished in a time when nations were struggling to find their shapes and frontiers, when kings were trying to create a rule which was only as absolute as a well-fed army and an insistent faith could make it. The Hansa stood outside all that. It was a cartel of towns in the north, mostly on the Baltic, all more or less German-speaking, which banded together to keep their ships safe, make sure they were well treated in foreign ports, and get as close as they could to the perfect state of traders: monopoly. They acquired power without the ceremony and pretence of kings, and without any of the occasional royal sense of responsibility, or moments of weakness. Kings and chancellors and politicians might have to concede things under pressure, liberties or land; they owned so much, ruled so much that they were always vulnerable. They might even change their minds about what was most important. The Hansa was townspeople with only two things in mind: trade and the profit to be made from it, and for most of the time everyone around them agreed; as long as ships were sailing on the Hansa's terms, there was no need for talk.

Kingdoms needed the philosophic kind of foundations: God or heredity or precedent or else God's favour as shown by battle victories. The power of a Hansa town like Lübeck rested on the fact of where it stood, at the head of the slow canal and river that cut across the neck of Denmark, where ships could be pulled across the inland route from the Baltic to the North Sea and avoid the challenging seas around Jutland. Controlling that route was enough to launch a group which made its first treaty with a foreign prince in the twelfth century and was still around almost five hundred years later to join the talks in 1648 that ended the wretchedly persistent war that had ruined Germany for thirty years.

Hansa towns lived from the water: sea ports like Bremen, Hamburg and especially Lübeck, and river ports like Cologne. Almost everywhere else power and title and position depended on land: estates or kingdoms, the income from rents, the service of serfs. In the water towns, on the edge of things, there was only one source of wealth: trading outwards. Their world was offshore. Even when they did choose to expand and set up new towns, they worked their way along the coasts: from Lübeck along to Gotland in Sweden and then all the way to Novgorod in Russia.[7] These new towns were also all about trading, hardly connected with the land powers around them. No feudal lord had the ships to interfere with business at sea.

Something is beginning on the edge of the world: the kind of multinational power that does not depend on where it is based, which flirts or fights in the modern world with the obvious kinds of political and state power, which usually gets its own way.

This is money at the start of its great war with nations.

The merchants who traded with Bergen were not the grandest men back home; they were known as country toughs, boys who went out to brutal initiations in Norway and came back self-made men, never quite as perfectly urbane as the stay-at-home merchants thought themselves. In Lübeck they bought houses alongside the grandest citizens, in the broad streets leading west down to the harbour, and for a while they joined the religious guilds, which combined the roles of intelligence service and gentlemen's clubs. They got respect just as long as their trading connections were intact, especially since they dominated the trade to and from England so much that the English hesitated to compete; when English ships went sailing again, their social standing collapsed. Then they had to be happy with the second-rate clubs, and they were no longer in the running for town office.[8]

Their boys served a tough apprenticeship, oddly like the kind that turned out the servants of the British Empire in the nineteenth century. Boys didn't learn languages at school, even though the Hansa merchants were famous for speaking English, Russian, French and even Estonian; they tried to stop outsiders, especially their Dutch rivals, learning the languages of the Baltic. Language was their advantage, but they did not teach it. Nor did they teach mathematics, which might account for the slowness with which the Hansa adopted sophisticated Mediterranean ideas like maritime insurance. Instead the teacher carried a cane, and the boys fooled around: authority that hurt, high spirits that meant trouble.

The boys went off on voyages which their fathers no longer needed to do – they had sons, or other men to do that for them – and they carried an almost imperial spirit: domineering, slightly anxious, away from the daily respectability of home.[9] They were meant to make good in Bergen, to make the money to buy their own business; and then to go home and hire someone else to run things for them.

The fleet came into Bergen each spring with the newcomers. Their first challenge was the 'games'. The boys had to be men, and they had to be initiated. They were keel-hauled, tied up with rope and pulled right under a ship; they were held over barrels of burning, stinking stuff; they were hoisted up smoking chimneys to be cross-examined on nothing in particular while they choked. They were thrown three times into deep water and had to get back into the boat to stay alive while a congregation of older merchants beat them. They were given drink until they were drunk, stripped naked and blindfolded, and then whipped until they bled, with drums more or less covering their screams; after which they had to sing a comic song. They had their mouths and noses stuffed with dogshit and catshit, they were subject to 'unclean shaves'; they went 'eel treading' and 'pig scalding'. They learned to say nothing, never to complain, never to cry.

These games must have mattered very much because they survived into the middle of the sixteenth century. Established merchants took turns to organize them; they served as the last chance to check a man's credentials, his town of origin and his single-mindedness, before admission to the club. It might seem as though the games were meant to discourage rich, soft, comfortable townee kids from coming to a trading post run by tough country people who knew about dung and muck; but things were not that simple. There were townspeople, and rich ones, going under the keel or up the chimney at Bergen, and it's not clear that anyone was ever put off by the games: once they were over, after all, a boy was a Hansa man for life.[10] In any case, the games fitted the Hansa style. When members from Dutch towns were accused of trading with outsider Dutchmen in 1468, they weren't just barred from business and told they could no longer eat at the Hansa's common table. They were taken out, stripped to their underwear and made to grovel for forgiveness before all the other assembled merchants.[11] Read *Tom Brown's Schooldays* and it all makes a queasy kind of sense.

Hansards settled in Bergen, but they were meant to keep their distance from the town. By the mid fourteenth century they lived cramped in their own district on the docks, in double rows of long wooden sheds with the narrower end towards the water: like loaf pans or train carriages made of planks. There were warehouses on the narrow ground floor; above were the living quarters where the building widened out, with balconies along the side to take the air. Between each pair of buildings ran a boardwalk with gates at the end, which could be shut tight and locked, so that it was a world that was open mostly to the water and the ships.[12]

This was known as the Kontor, which is now Bryggen, and there were three others: in Novgorod and London and Bruges. They were warehouses, dormitories, embassies for the Hansa, and defensible positions and a source of judgement and rulings; and they ran on secrets. Any man who revealed a rule or law of the Kontor to an outsider lost his merchant rights. No outsider servants were allowed, which is why the newcomer boys could expect to do the sweeping, washing, scrubbing, for a while. No outsider could join any of the brotherhoods inside the Kontor, the clubs which bound the members together with faith and beer.

No man could come to Bergen with a wife from a Hansa town but no man could marry a woman who was not from the Hansa. A hansa, a guild or a union, was a kind of family in which people had to know each other to do business; most agreements were verbal, not written, known only to men who had to trust each other. Since just doing business with a non-Hansa member could cost a man two fingers, it is not surprising that marrying out was rare.[13]

And yet there were children in those wet, narrow alleys in the Kontor, and not just the teenagers who cleaned and cooked and made the beds; we know because their toys survived. There are bones with holes for a string, noise-makers, made like the ones from Lübeck; so someone brought either toys or the idea for the toys with him. There are curious dolls, some of them like flat-headed priests, some just sticks with faces carved at both ends, and ceramic horses that may have been weights but might also be from the model tournaments that children liked in Lübeck. There are small skates and balls made of leather, some made from six or more pieces, and marbles that might have been for adults, and humming tops and what look remarkably like yo-yos. There are also toy weapons in the ground, but fewer and fewer once the Hansa arrives and the time of civil wars comes to an end in Norway. Those walkways heard children laughing, shouting, crying.[14]

The Hansa did make room for women. Some accounts talk of boatloads arriving from Hamburg and Bremen every spring.[15] The rules forbade bringing a prostitute into the Kontor on four holy evenings in the winter and any night there was free beer, but that left a fair number of nights wide open. The greatest cluster of various businesses, hostels, taverns, boarding houses with 'poor women' – which means women without family, husband or mentionable trade – was right at the North End of the Kontor, with 243 women in residence; there were only thirty-three others in all the rest of Bergen.[16] Pleasure was on the doorstep, and the Hansa had no great enthusiasm for moralizing when a merchant strayed. They promised to throw out any man having an affair with a woman in Bergen, married or unmarried; but around 1440 Hermann Luckow was accused of stealing the wife of a rival Norwegian trader and the Kontor invaded the courtroom and broke up his trial. Somehow, in the process, it was the Norwegian who disappeared without trace.[17]

Men had outdoor families, the ones away from home, which is an old imperial habit; and we know because they sometimes acknowledge them in their wills. Henricus de Staden in 1369 wanted to look after 'Elizabeth, my daughter in Bergen';[18] others left forty marks for 'my surviving sons in Bergen in Norway'[19] or the same amount, as Herman Pael did, for 'in Norway, a woman whose name is Tzolewich, and her daughter Gherdouden'.[20] Hans Boyseman's will, from 1441, suggests he had quite a family in the north: 'Item: to the three children I have in Norway, I donate altogether 100 marks and 80 marks Lübeck and to their mother I donate 20 marks Lübeck.' Fathering a child was an offence against the Kontor's rules, but since the only penalty was to provide a barrel of beer for everyone else, it also sounds like something to celebrate.

Their local rivals never amounted to much. Any Norwegian could do business for a while; doing business simply meant going out to sea for yourself, or walking the roads for yourself, with whatever money you could borrow or scrounge or save. It was individual and amateur, not organized. So many country people went sailing, leaving the fields untended, that in 1260 the law changed; you needed a fortune of at least three marks to go trading in the summer season. Even then, Norway's international traders included peasants and middling people. The only boss on any ship was the one elected by the crew of fellow merchants, and the guilds stood ready to cover the losses of traders and peasants equally when they were doing business – as long as they did not sail through war zones.

The Hansa was different – more serious. Hansa ships were much more rigidly disciplined, and the merchants ruled. In the general law of the sea, the merchant couldn't complain if the ship's captain thought it necessary to throw cargo overboard in a storm, and the crew had the right to vote on whether to leave harbour in bad weather. With the Hansa, it was the merchants, not the sailors, who would decide if and when to jettison. In Lübeck, and this was one law that went through all the Hansa towns, a sailor who didn't save the freight would have his ears cut and spend time in jail; anywhere else he just lost pay and had to find another ship.[21]

Over the years grander Norwegian persons, with money to invest, began to take over the trading, but they had many other interests and they always felt the need to draw a line between their 'distinguished' trading and plain, vulgar money-making, for fear of being confused with 'those who call themselves merchants but are nothing more than crooks and rag and bone men'. The instructions to young nobles who wanted to buy and sell, in a manual called the *Speculum regale*, include close observation of other distinguished merchants, working only until you lunch at mid-day, and having a white cloth for your dinner table. A gentleman was meant to stop sailing the moment he had enough money and when he knew as much about the world as any gentleman wanted to know.[22]

The Hansa merchants, on the other hand, made business their whole life. Some of them did have land but land was not enough to guarantee a man's living or his standing. There were some two hundred villages attached to Lübeck at one point, a third of the whole duchy of Saxony–Lauenburg, but that was territory bought along trade routes to protect them better; and the land was a burden. It made men take their eyes away from the sea.

By the 1400s, though, the Hansa had factions: those who approved of owning land, having territory like any duke or prince, against those who cared only for business on the sea. In Lübeck there were flares of trouble and then in 1408 a full-scale uprising. The councillors of Lübeck were mostly older, enthusiasts for the influence and standing of the Hansa, and they were landowners who cared about the countryside around the town and not just the business on the docks; but this old guard had already lost enough members in plague years to be unsure of their power. A council which had been solid for prestige and territory was now open to factions. A debate began about what kind of ambitions the Hansa should have. The new men demanded what they called their 'old rights', which meant the town should concentrate on trade and the sea, its special genius, and pay no attention to being a land power; the town should never go beyond the ambitions of its citizens, or at least not theirs. A Committee of Sixty formed against the town council, and at least thirty-four of them were merchants; some were *Bergenfahrer*, traders to Bergen, including their leader, Johan Grove. They risked insurrection to make sure that power came back to the sea traders, the merchants and shopkeepers whose world was inside their ledgers, and inside the city walls. They wanted only to be traders.

The town was electric with rumours that the council had turned all the weapons on the city's towers inwards on the citizens. Come January, and the annual procession of the town council, a mob broke up the ceremonies and ran the terrified council members indoors. The burgomaster begged their spokesman: 'Tell them what you want, and what you can answer for, but for God's sake quiet them down.' The protesters' man bellowed out of a window to the crowd: 'You will choose the council!' The prospect of change was enough to start a party so raucous that fifteen out of the twenty-three town councillors decided to take their chances, get out of town and go to live for ever in exile.[23]

This was not a people's revolt; it was a taxpayers' rising, with the brewers taking the lead alongside the merchants. The rebels were alarmed by the council's incompetence; they had somehow managed to let the town mint go bankrupt. They refused to pay higher taxes to get rid of the town's debts because they were against all the ambitions and ideas that caused the debts in the first place: an interest in acquiring territory, not protecting trade, with pursuing power like an ordinary nation, risking the costs of wars and feuds.

The uprising was political in an almost modern way: not so much about who has power but what they ought to do with it and what limits should be put on a state.

The Hansa almost always tried to preserve the old guard and their familiar old ways; it had thrown out the town of Brunswick for daring to eject its council and now it threw out Lübeck. The Emperor made Lübeck an outlaw town for daring to opt out of the great game of nations, but the revolt spread alarmingly, to the port of Hamburg, which like Lübeck commanded the river route to the North Sea, to Rostock and Wismar, which could make endless trouble in the Baltic. Since there was nobody to quell the uprising, the result was a kind of merchants' coup: no undue ambition, no international politics, nothing except the duty to keep the ships sailing.

There were advantages in these limits. Unlike landowners, the

Hansa men could sail away from trouble, sail somewhere else or go back home, and they did. Their emperor and overlords were sometimes their enemies, but never quite their masters. They had no overbearing clergy to remind them to agonize over how to set a just price and whether profit was a sin. They could concentrate.

The divisions in Lübeck help explain why Hansa men were oddly reluctant to say exactly what a Hansa was, or who belonged to it; a bit of doubt kept things together. It was a corporate kind of power which liked its privacy.

An irate letter to the English privy council in 1469 said the Hansa was definitely not a *societas*, a *collegium* nor yet a *universitas*. It didn't have property in common, each merchant traded for himself, it had no common seal and no common business manager and, besides, the member towns were 'widely separated ... as the royal letters acknowledge'. The merchants didn't control it, because various lords and magistrates controlled each member town, and when the Hansa wrote a letter it carried only the seal of the town where it was written. The Hansa said it was a 'mere grouping of towns', 'a kind of alliance', 'a firm *confederatio* of many cities, towns and communities' to make sure business went well and there was 'effective protection against pirates and highwaymen, so that their ambushes should not rob merchants of their goods and valuables'.[24]

They had good reason at the time to write that letter: they were trying to save all the Hansa towns, whichever ones happened to have ships in harbour at the time, from being made to pay for the politics or the misdeeds of a single member. Rostock and Hamburg wanted to be able to sail on even if Lübeck or Bruges was deep in some dispute over tax or sailing rights; they were happy to share privileges, but not responsibility. They relished the very obvious paradox: here was a seemingly vague, amorphous sort of group, barely able to organize a meeting every few years to make decisions, and yet able to make war efficiently on Flanders, France, England, Denmark, Norway, Sweden and Holland at various times, to raise the money for ships like a nation, sign treaties at the end and even manage kings, imposing them and deposing them.

It took effective control of trade over the Baltic and then the North Sea, without even a sniff of legal right. In the law that was general in Europe, but not so settled in the north, the sea belonged to nobody, and everybody had the right to sail on it. Justinian's version of the civil law of Rome lays down that 'The sea is for everyone's use, but nobody's property, just as air is for common use but has no owner . . . but the jurisdiction is Caesar's.' In other words, a proper power, a king or emperor, had the right to police the sea and beat back thieves and pirates. The more pirates bothered shipping, the stronger the idea of territorial waters grew, a right of self-protection on the water.[25] But nobody thought the Hansa was such a proper power, not even the Hansa, and no such power had the right to decide who could sail where and why and when. The Hansa made its own legal reality by wars and blockades and treaties, an alternative law which made its merchant members perversely legalistic with other people; the citizens of Bergen in 1560 were furious about the damage the Kontor was doing and asked the king for help because the Hanseatics 'always sent such learned men to any negotiations that the people of Bergen could not defend themselves'.[26]

The Hansa was a new kind of body when it emerged, but its name was familiar. In a fourth-century translation of the Bible in Gothic, *hansa* was the word used for the gang who come to take Christ prisoner in the garden at Gethsemane: a band of men, a club. This was not a promising start. Charlemagne worried in the eighth century about the guilds called *hanse* because they swore oaths of loyalty when they should have been loyal only to him; they were rivals. *Hansa* became the word for a union of merchants, usually from one town, sometimes from several; there was the Flemish Hanse of the Seventeen Towns and the Danish Guild of St Canute, campaigning to get and hold on to privileges in foreign ports. There were the fishermen who spread their risks by 'sharing a herring ship with someone else'.[27] They were little arrangements, minimal alliances until the twelfth and thirteenth centuries.

Then came the Emperor Frederick II, the wonder of the world, some said, and fiercely ambitious to rule Italy and keep down the Pope. He called his birthplace Bethlehem and his followers called him Messiah; the Pope called him Antichrist and felt obliged to excommunicate him four times. Such a man could not be expected to attend to the details of what was done in his name and, in the interests of his Italian campaigns, the Emperor thought it wise to allow the feudal lords all the powers they needed to raise all the money he needed for war. They each imposed different laws and different coins and different weights and measures. This had consequences they never intended. You could make a profit just by buying cloth by the ell in Lübeck and selling it in Riga, even if you didn't put up the price, because the Riga ell was shorter than the one in the west. The tolls for passing up and down the Rhine became such a confusion that English merchants called them 'the German madness'.

The Emperor didn't interfere with the towns, but he didn't help them or make alliances with them as the French kings did; he was too distracted. The towns felt entitled to act independently, with just enough co-operation to make sure they could act as they wanted. They already had their associations from before Frederick was born. They were used to meeting each year from the last weeks of August to the first weeks of October to buy herring at the beach fairs in Scania, in southern Sweden: a free-for-all market which became in the thirteenth century the start of new towns. The Gotland association of merchants who did business in Sweden combined to sail in convoys for greater safety, to act together overseas, to bury any merchant who died abroad. The association thrived without any undue interference, it became the Hansa and the Hansa took over the Scania fairs. In 1189, it signed its first treaty with a foreign prince: promising trade and profits, demanding privileges and especially low taxes.

The modern trade-off between politics and money had begun.

Town leagues replaced the more personal, almost family associations of merchants because the town was the one political power to which they might have to answer; so it was logical that the Hansa be organized town by town, with a man's standing defined by the town he came from. Town was family now. There were eventually some two hundred towns involved around the Baltic and the North Sea. Beside the member towns, who expected to be heard from time to time on matters of policy, there were other ports like Lynn in England whose livelihood was tied to the Hansa, and some like Boston in Lincolnshire that were downright dependent. And then there were the Kontors, Hansa towns inside other towns, often walled away. The Bergen Kontor put up a wall after a violent row with the town, but it lasted only three years in the 1520s before the town insisted it come down.[28] The Peterhof at Novgorod was something between a fort and a tenement with its own locked and private church for storing valuables, and the Steelyard in London was a walled enclosure that could be closed down. In Bruges, the Hansa had no walls, just a tendency to cluster around the Bourse. Its meeting place was the refectory of the Carmelite monastery and eventually it built a guildhouse of solid brick and painted beams, but hardly had a chance to use it before the harbour at Bruges silted over and it quit the town.[29]

The Hansa acknowledged no centre, although in practice it was often Lübeck that called meetings of its council, the Hansetag. The council did not meet every year, which was one more problem when the group wanted to take action. The one clear interest you'd think the whole Hansa shared was open seas, and as little trouble as possible from pirates. It did not work that way.

In the 1380s the Danes were at war with the German Duke of Mecklenburg, who was busily trying to use pirates to beat up his Danish enemies; but these pirates, the *Vitalienbrüder*, were not so easy to control. Rostock and Wismar were on the duke's land, and for once they felt obliged to do their duty by their overlord and shelter the pirates who were making the Baltic almost impassable. They went on protecting them when the campaign went far beyond Denmark and the pirates raided even Bergen, where the Hansa merchants were unimpressed by their offer to leave the Kontor alone and pillage just the rest of the town. Feeling some kind of local loyalty, they took up arms to defend the town and saw the Kontor plundered in revenge.[30]

Rostock and Wismar were unrepentant about sheltering the enemies of their allies in Bergen. They declined to hand back the goods the pirates had stolen and taken to their harbours. The disturbances went on long enough to force up the price of herring by ten times in

Cologne, by three times in the lands of the Teutonic Knights, but even the knights were not inclined to save the Danes trouble by suppressing the pirates because they were busy with their own territorial ambitions. Punishing the rogue towns would have to wait perhaps years for a council meeting where there might or might not be a majority to vote for sanctions.[31]

The pirates left Rostock to become a freebooting scourge. They occupied the islands of Bornholm and Gotland for bases, and took any vessels that passed, killing the crews or throwing them overboard to die; their motto, logical enough, was 'God's friends and the foe of all the world'. They had every reason to avoid capture ruthlessly; the merchants of Stralsund took one pirate crew and stuffed them into barrels on the deck, heads sticking through holes cut at one end, packed like herring, and shipped them back to the gallows. They were also cunning. Around Stockholm one winter the commander Master Hugo realized his ships were at the mercy of the enemy Danes. He cut trees, made a wooden wall around the ships and poured water over the wall; it soon froze. Just outside the wall, he cut the ice to make a moat for his ice fortress, and in the night the cold and a scatter of light snow hid what he had done. The Danes attacked, they did not notice the thin ice on the moat, men and machines tumbled down into the frigid waters. The pirates could wait in their stockade for warmer weather so they could sail on.

Like the Hansa itself, the *Vitalienbrüder* were single-minded; their name for themselves was *Likendeelers* meaning the ones who divide the loot equally, and loot was what mattered. Even when the first excuse for their campaign was gone, and Rostock and Wismar were on better terms with the Danes, they sailed on; according to the chronicler Detmar of Lübeck they hit at Russia, they spoiled the Hansa's trade, and they sailed on to the Caspian, to the Holy Land, to the world. That says something about Lübeck's hopes for controlling them.

Hansa towns often did go each a different way. Bremen was more different than most. It was the 1440s and the Dutch were beating their way into the Baltic, which had been a Hanseatic sea for a century or more; war happened, inevitably. France and Scotland were busily attacking English ships because the Hundred Years War had not yet finished, and Scots pirates sometimes took ships from Flanders. The seas were constantly unsafe. The citizens of Bremen had lost ships to the Dutch, and lost other ships on Hanseatic missions against the Dutch, and nobody was willing to pay them the compensation they were sure was due; so they decided on their own radical solution to the problem of piracy.

They became a pirate port.

They brought Grote Gherd, 'Big Jerry', from Wismar, and captains from nearby Hamburg and Lübeck itself, and they offered a deal: sail from Bremen and you got to keep two-thirds of all the goods you captured, and half the ransoms of anybody who had not been pitched overboard. Do well at this, follow the quite detailed rules and regulations for what could be stolen and from whom, and orderly, successful pirates could be citizens of Bremen for life.

Bremen now declared war on Flanders and Flanders declared war on Bremen and the pirates sailed out. They struck off the south English coast at Portland Bill, in the shelter of the Firth of Forth in Scotland as well as around the mouths of the Elbe and Weser rivers near their home port. Big Jerry ran up the flags of Hamburg, another Hanseatic town, to fool his prey, and worked the Øresund to such good effect that he took thirteen ships from Flanders in a single expedition. All this was extremely political in an incoherent sort of way: a Hansa town was often stealing from Hanseatic merchants in the interests of beating back the Hansa's rivals. Hanseatic towns had difficulty getting their property back from Bremen, but when Big Jerry's associates stole goods bound for Edinburgh, the Scots negotiated a deal: if there was proof of where the goods were headed, the pirates would hand them back. It was worth making deals to make friends; as long as the Baltic was sealed shut, Bremen had hopes of selling its own grain to Scotland.[32]

Now, piracy was crime, but it was also war being waged by towns that had no clear way to declare war. It was a practical business that sometimes seems almost respectable. In the National Museum at Gdansk there is the most glorious triptych painted by Hans Memling in Bruges in the 1460s, commissioned by a Medici agent who meant to ship it to Florence. It shows the Day of Judgement, Christ sitting on a rainbow waiting for the righteous, who are being helped by angels through a great marble gate, and on the other side the wicked endlessly falling into scarlet fire. In the centre, St Michael weighs man against man against woman in delicate scales. The picture was packed up with all kinds of spices and furs, and sent off from Bruges, but it never got beyond Dunkirk; the ship was taken by a Gdansk pirate, Paul Bencke. His ship sailed back through the North Sea and the Baltic and he presented the painting to the Basilica in Gdansk. It was pirate stuff and Medici agents threatened legal action to get it back, but the church still felt able to accept it. It would have seemed absurd to refuse such a Godly, lovely thing.[33]

The wonder is that the Hansa survived its ruinous divisions, that the merchants thought it so priceless that they paid a price to be in it.

Law divided it, for a start. Although Lübeck law was applied in some forty-three Hansa towns, the law of Frankfurt ruled in forty-nine, and there were outrider towns that took their law from Bremen or Hamburg. Until quite late, the Hansa had laws of its own only on issues like keeping a big crew under control, not shipping out during winter and not buying or selling goods that had been stolen or shipwrecked. Everything else was local. For anyone used to a state with a single source of authority, king, Parliament or constitution, it looks a quite impossible alliance, and it did sometimes come unglued: the Dutch Hanseatics wouldn't go to war with their neighbours in Holland and Zeeland, the Prussian towns wanted to sell grain directly to the English without giving Lübeck a profit and when the Hansa blockaded the English out of Bruges the Hanseatic merchants of Cologne were perfectly happy to do business with the English at Antwerp. Even the epic Hanseatic war against Denmark involved fewer than a dozen Hanseatic towns.

Something did hold the Hansa together, though, and it was common purpose: the need to act like a modern cartel, impossible for one seaside town, possible for an association of towns. The first rule was to make sure of making money, which was not a simple matter. The Hansa ports dealt mostly in bulk goods: grain from the east, herring from the Baltic and cod from the Norwegian coast; timber from the north as well as pitch and tar from burning it, and cloth from Flanders and from England. The profit margin on these things was low, so the only way to make money was to control the trade, to have a monopoly at sea: to fight for privileges in every port and then control the sea lanes between them.[34]

Language mattered very much; all the Hansa towns, from the Low Countries to Russia, understood the same Low German. Taste also travelled with the Hanseatic ships: the same clothes and crockery, the houses built of brick and stone with their step gable roofs and their granaries in the loft and their salt stores, just like any Saxon farm. The towns all have narrow alleyways that run from the harbour to the central market square, the churches are all built as meeting halls. It is as though Hansa households carried their hometowns with them, a shared defence against the foreignness of where they were: like the English drinking gin in the Himalaya. They all had stoneware for cups and plates, which carefully imitated fine glasses and platters, and tile-stoves that heated their houses and were dressed with painted and moulded tiles; in later years, a Hansa stove was almost holy, stuck all over with portraits of the heroes of the Reformation.[35] There was also the insistence that a merchant who travelled was as good as any fixed and static noble any day: the Hansa creed. Rostock town council put doubtful coats of arms on their signet rings to prove the point, and so did Rostock merchants based in Malmö in Sweden (which never was a Hanseatic town and belonged to the Hansa's Danish enemies); and so the habit went about the Baltic.[36]

Then there was violence, which may have been the strongest link of all: the immediate, instant response to any threat or rival, the powerful solidarity of the fight. Nations and courts can appeal to history and high-flown ideas of continuity and purpose, but two hundred Hanseatic towns had two hundred histories, often of fighting each other. Their mindset was traders defending the moment they make the trade, like soldiers in mid-battle dealing with each shot, each move, without needing a strategy for the whole war. They did not have to think about what seems ruinously obvious, the differences and even contradictions between the interests of the towns. If they ever did, if they thought like a single entity, they might all have to take the blame.

In the 1440s, the Bergen Hanseatics were angry with the king's representative, Olaf Nielsson; they accused him of supporting the English, trying to separate the German craftsmen in Bergen from the Kontor and encouraging pirates to steal their ships. Nielsson was deposed and sent packing but he traded his castle to the king for the chance to return for another six years in Bergen. On his way back in 1445 he happened to capture three Hanseatic ships, and he gave permission for English ships to sail north of Bergen to buy stockfish, something the Hansa had long ago agreed not to do. Lübeck was appalled. It sent out an old Bergen hand to remind the merchants of their privileges, but by the time of the meeting the men had already heard about the loss of three ships and they could guess what Nielsson's return might mean. They scrambled out of the meeting and down to the quays and they wrecked the ship which brought Nielsson back. The king's man did not stay around to see what the merchants meant to do next; he went across the water to the Munkliev monastery, with his followers and with the Bishop of Bergen, and he waited.

The merchants went up against the monastery as though it were an enemy town. They killed the bishop among many others, and after one night they found Olaf Nielsson hidden in the bell tower. He was allowed a few hours to confess and repent all his sins, and then they killed him, too. The Hansa men had to make their excuses later to the Norwegian authorities, which they did with a fifteen-point complaint about the dead man, his various sins including the illegal capture of the castle he had just given to the king and a suggestion that they had been encouraged to attack so they were not the only ones to blame. It was a classic defence: it wasn't just us, he deserved it, things aren't as bad as they look. The Hansa, like a modern corporation, didn't know about personal responsibility. But the Norwegian king was busily struggling for the Swedish crown and he wanted no trouble with them; his people had to be fed, the seas had to stay open, he didn't want pirates. For the life of Olaf Nielsson, the Bishop of Bergen and all the other men who were in the way, the

Kontor agreed to pay a penalty: a small fine. You can't hang a confederation, after all.[37]

Their violence began to seem old-fashioned after a while, but not because their rivals were peace-loving and considerate. Their rivals simply had other ways of waging trade wars by making them into hot wars, nation to nation, which national interests and alliances might bring to an end; their rivals fitted the new system of states.

In 1484 the Amsterdam town council complained to the Bergen Kontor about German trouble-making, and demanded that the violence stop. 'All good merchants should support each other,' Amsterdam wrote, 'and never hinder each other; they should not scare each other or resort to violence.'[38] That had never occurred to the Hansa men, who constantly tried to get rival merchants thrown out of ports or disadvantaged when they weren't organizing blockades or pirate raids or incidents in which inconvenient people ended up dead or disappeared. They knew their power depended on other people's needs, Norway's lack of grain for a start, and they had no intention of sharing their power by letting others satisfy the needy.

In Amsterdam they now faced a major trading power, soon to be the greatest of them all, which seemed to see business quite differently from the simple force on which the Hansa relied. The Dutch talked about credit, which the Hansa resisted, and kept sophisticated double-entry books, which the Hansa adopted late; they could make trade abstract. The Hansa was going out of style before it went out of business.

The legend of the Hansa is much more golden than the reality. It was taken once to be a time of German hegemony on the seas, a matter of national pride, but the Hansa had nothing to do with nations, least of all Germany: its flexibility, its success, depended on not being national, and often on staying far away from the Emperor who was the one central power in what now is Germany or else opposing him. It was taken as some kind of model for the European Union, even though it lacked any centre, any commissioners in Brussels, any common law and common regulations, any attempt to have one point of view on the world and where to fight it. It was too loose to be a model for a nation or a true federation.

What makes the Hansa seem modern is something quite different. It is the abstract idea of trade, business, money, as a profession and a force without roots in the world or responsibilities, ready to go anywhere in pursuit of profit and deals. Nothing mitigates. Nothing softens. Nothing forces or even allows compromise. Those ships in the Øresund were chasing profit by rigging a market, they were trying to enforce a legal arrangement that Norway did not want, and they expected to kill people on the way: to starve them, women, children and men.

Money rules.

# 10.

## Love and capital

She was shouting, and Katelijne Vedelaer had every reason to shout. There were three men and one woman who grabbed her and took her by force out of the quiet of her community, over the water and out of the town of Bruges. They were not just kidnapping her. They were telling her she had no right to choose her own life among the holy women, that she had to be married and she had to marry Lievin van Aerlebecke and she had to share all she had with him instead of the community of her friends.[1]

She shouted to prove she wanted her life back. She wasn't running off with a lover, she was being snatched for her property, taken off for the rape that would force her to marry. She made such a racket that the town aldermen were alerted, but they could do nothing; the holy women, the 'beguines', were under the special protection of the Count of Flanders. Aldermen went to the count's bailiff and it was the bailiff who sent out the sheriff with a band of law officers. They knew which way to ride because van Aerlebecke came from Harelbecke in the flatlands to the south of Bruges, but they lost so much time on the Harelbecke road that the posse caught up with the kidnappers a full half-day later, twenty-five miles away, in the town of Roeselaere.[2]

The man van Aerlebecke, his brother and his servant were all arrested, along with Lizebette van Dudzele, who rode with them: all respectable persons, even grand. Their families had position in the town, guaranteed the money lent to churches, supervised the tanners and shearers in the cloth business, went abroad to serve as jury in cases which involved citizens of Bruges. They still considered rape and kidnap as a tactic. The Church was preaching marriage between those who freely consented, even loved each other, and the law in Flanders agreed, but money was money and property was property and a woman like Katelijne was forced to keep shouting.

Back in Bruges, she was handed over to the official who took care of abducted women; he also kept watch when there was a duel being fought, for which he got a fat half-pound candle for Candelmas and a feast four times a year. The bailiff himself came to take Katelijne back to the beguines. Her kidnappers were brought to trial, and van Aerlebecke was given the harshest sentence possible: one hundred years and a day of banishment, and the promise that he would have his head cut off if he ever came back to Bruges. The accomplices were all banned for six years each, the men to be hanged if they came back early, the woman to be buried alive; they had to pay sizeable fines, fifty pounds a head.

The women in the beguinage were not quite sure the matter was settled, even so. They asked for an official record of the verdict, carrying the seals of the bailiff, the mayor and the two citizens who wrote the report; they wanted it quite clear that Katelijne did not want to leave them, that she had no part in her own kidnapping. That record survives in a private collection, which is how we know what happened.

The beguines had every reason to be careful. They had chosen a religious life, but outside the rules of convents and religious orders: they made a woman's world. They did not marry, although some had been married and were widows, and they made their own living, often by manual labour: working fields or making cloth, which is why every beguinage had to be built by a body of running water to wash the wool. Their independence worked, and that disrupted other people's plans to use them to make alliances by marriage, to get land or money.

The beguines were known for teaching girls manners, but also Latin, French and theology in a time when Philippe de Navarre, soldier, diplomat, lawman and a monster of official standing, could say flatly that 'a woman must not be taught letters or writing, unless she is to be a nun; for many evils come from women writing and reading . . . you don't give venom to a snake who has quite enough already.'[3] Sometimes they even preached, which was not proper: grudgingly Henry of Ghent conceded a woman could teach, but privately and in silence, and she could teach only women 'both because their address might incite the men to lust (as they say) and also would be shameful and dishonourable to the men'.[4] Worse, they talked about God as though they loved Him, body and soul, with all the madness and passion of love, and as though they could go to Him directly, without church or priest in the way; this was such an alarming heresy that Marguerite Porete died for it in 1310. And, to make matters even worse, they used everyday language and not Latin; everybody knew what they were saying.

The beguines flourished all across the lands of Northern Europe in the thirteenth and fourteenth centuries. In Strasbourg, for example, one woman in ten was a beguine. In Cologne, there were a hundred beguine houses. In the Northern countries as a whole, perhaps three women in every hundred were beguines. The poet and mystic Hadewijch of Brabant, who most likely fell out with her fellow beguines and then went wandering, mentions beguines in Flanders, Brabant, Paris, Zeeland, Holland, Frisia, England and 'beyond the Rhine', the territories of the edge of the world.[5]

Seventeen years before Katelijne was taken in 1345, church inspectors had visited the Bruges beguinage.[6] They reported that the house had been set up by two countesses 'by divine inspiration, as it is piously believed', to preserve the respectability of women who couldn't marry, couldn't afford the 'dowry' needed to enter a convent and who were about 'to go begging or shamefully support themselves'. The beguinage allowed them to 'support and clothe themselves by suitable work, without shaming themselves or their friends'. Each woman had her own routine of washing wool and cleaning cloth, each had her own garden to grow food, working in silence on a diet of 'coarse bread and pottage'. No beguine could spend a night in town without the permission of the mistress of the court, and nobody could leave even for an hour without beguine companions; and out in town they wore coarse, frumpish clothes to disguise any individuality; all the town would see was that they were a beguine.

This is the time when people flowed, steady as a river, out of the countryside and into the towns, pulled by the prospect of wages, independence, work in the new small factories that made cloth and needed hands. Life for those newcomers was not easy, especially not for women, and at the beguinages they knew they were among friends. Newcomers accounted for half the women in some city beguinages. In the beguine courts, a woman knew she would never need a bit of prostitution on the side, or face a time of going hungry when things were slow. She could survive a crisis in her trade, and if she was sick, when she was old, she had a home. Women rebuilt their families in the safety of the court, mothers with daughters, aunts with nieces, sisters together.

Sometimes they shared a single house, more usually they had courtyards like villages inside the cities, closed off from the outside life and big enough to have streets and their own church, hospital, school. They could come and go, they could change their minds. Usually, they did not have to buy their way into a community, unlike novice nuns, who needed sponsorship, cash or land to enter a nunnery. They might be widows under pressure to marry one more time, a woman like Katelijne who might be marketed any day as a wife; there was protection with the beguines.

Out of a pious duty, they took on the tasks other people did not want. They were the ones who handled the dead, laid them out and made them ready for the grave, and they nursed the living dead, the lepers in their colonies outside the towns. They also tended the sick in their hospitals, but since they were not meant to nurse men, they had to leave the beguinage if their fathers needed help.

They were teachers; when the priest Lievin vander Muelene wrote his last will in 1559, he acknowledged 'a good and devout little beguine' as his spiritual mother, 'often punishing my misdeeds in writing or speech, correcting me and leading me towards virtue'.[7] Some were housekeepers in the city; the Paris gentleman who laid down instructions for his wife in *Le Ménagier de Paris* around 1392 has a whole list of duties for 'Dame Agnes the beguine', who is there to teach the wife 'wise and ripe behaviour and to serve and train you'. Dame Agnes hires the maids, supervises them, counts the sheep in the country, takes out stains on dresses with warm wine, keeps the keys, puts out the fires at night and goes round 'with a lighted candle, to inspect your wines, verjuice and vinegar, to see that none has been taken away'.[8]

They went out from the edge of the city to herd animals, grow vegetables, raise chickens. More usually, they worked in the textile trade: they spun wool and finished cloth, were tailors and embroiderers, sometimes weavers even when that had become an officially, overwhelmingly male trade. The new and growing towns gave everyone a chance, and women most of all. Men, after all, had a habit of being distracted by war or civil strife.

Material possessions were not important; they owned nothing much, just the pots, knives and plates that each stored in her section of a special divided cupboard, known to this day as a beguine cupboard. The poorer women lived from wages, the richer women sank their money into houses they often shared with other beguines. That did not stop them being very successful in the new commercial world around them; the beguinage of Sint-Truiden was attacked and plundered in 1340 by townspeople furious at how well the women were doing, especially since they were free of some taxes.[9] Some of them were traders, not just artisans. Mergriete van Ecke in 1306 complained to the commissioners of the Count of Flanders that his bailiffs had destroyed some fine white wool cloth of hers because they mistakenly thought it was not made in Ghent. She said she had sent it to a friend in Antwerp but he thought it was too expensive, and so it had come back, but she insisted she had 'proved sufficiently by a weaver and a fuller that the cloth was made, woven and fulled in Ghent'. If she had to find witnesses then she wasn't the one making the cloth; she was the merchant.[10]

Beguines were chaste, but it was not out of terror of the flesh. At Mechelen, around 1290, the rules said a beguine who fell pregnant had to leave 'as soon as her condition becomes obvious' and stay away for a year, after which she could come back 'if she demonstrates good behaviour attested by good witnesses'; she had to stay inside the compound for six months afterwards, but she could raise her child there. The same applied in 1453 at Tongeren, unless the woman's partner had been a married man or a priest. In some places the rules were stricter – a pregnant beguine was banned for life at 's-Hertogenbosch – but it was quite usual to have children playing between the houses of the beguinage and usual for the women to tolerate other women's mistakes. The one great sin was questioning the authority of the grand mistress of the beguinage; that always meant a lifetime ban, everywhere.[11]

You couldn't be so very practical as this without annoying anyone who liked the comfort of strict rules that they were never likely to disobey. Go to the theatre and you'd hear catcalls and snickers the moment a beguine character came on stage; some of the oldest farces in Middle Dutch have beguines fucking so hard their beds come crashing through the floor. You couldn't be a learnèd woman, teaching Latin and even theology to girls, without being mocked for it.

Carnival parades at Huy in 1298 included men who 'had shaved their beards and dressed as ladies or beguines, marching through the streets two by two as if in a procession, some singing, others holding an open book in their hands as if they were reading'.

There was a quarrel even over the word 'beguine': whether it came from *benignitas*, which is 'goodness', or as one Benedictine said from *begun*, meaning 'dung'.[12] Its most likely origin is a word for a mumbler, someone whose speech you can't quite hear and can't check or control. That was especially worrying when the speech was prayer, which was meant to be spoken loud and clear in a church; the beguine's prayers were between her and God, not laid down or certified by authority. She could be telling God anything.

There was also the beguines' licence to moralize, even over the trading they did so well and the profits they made. Some were most unhappy that their parents made money by lending money, although richer beguines loaned out money themselves; quite aside from helping other women in the court, two beguines of Arras lent two hundred pounds to the town of Calais in 1300, a solid deal at 10 per cent, which was at least a lower rate than usual. Still, Ida of Louvain thought her merchant father's wealth was ill-gotten, was only mildly relieved to be told that usury was not involved and made her opinion so obvious to her father that 'losing all restraint, day after day he would beat with the harsh blows of his curses this girl so innocent, so commendable, so unused to answering back'. He bought casks of wine to sell at a profit, and she disapproved, offering to buy only what she could use, which made her father furious. When the wine went off, miraculously or not, lost colour and flavour and started to froth, her father was growling with fury. Ida saw her father grieving and said her prayers, and the wine was made good. 'She completely forgot about the wrongs her father had done her,' her biographer says.[13]

The beguines were in need of a history, any man could see that: something less spontaneous, more miraculous, involving the suffering that women were meant to endure as part of their spirituality. The beguines talked of the ecstasy of their love for God, but obviously they meant pain.

Various sympathetic priests began to tell their stories, to make them fit the Church.

In place of the scatter of communities, women choosing their own rules and their own way of life, there had to be a founder saint: St Begga, a seventh-century abbess who married the son of a saint, whose father had been a great local power under the Merovingian kings and who had nothing much to do with beguinages except living in roughly the same part of Flanders.[14] The spontaneity of the beguines' story was weighted down with royal connections, saintliness and the rigid governance of religious orders.

The written stories of early beguines, in texts that went back and forth across the North Sea in Middle English as well as Latin, allow nothing at all ordinary; they seem to doubt that work, calm, prayer and kindness could be enough. They take the women out of the world. One, Elizabeth of Spalbeek, becomes a phenomenon, a woman with the stigmata of Christ; 'in wounds and in pain she affirms the faith of the Passion', as her story says.[15] If women put their whole bodies and souls into their faith, if they were as vivid as the poet Hadewijch when she writes of 'a whirlpool turning so fearfully that heaven and earth might wonder at it and be afraid . . . the deep whirlpool that is so fearfully dark that is divine union in its hidden storms',[16] then obviously faith must hurt. Elizabeth became famous for knowing women who were suffering even more than she was.

Another, Christina Mirabilis, starts her life by dying; her terrified sister sees the body fly to the rafters of the church, where Christina is given a choice between Heaven and Earth and chooses Earth. She is raised from the dead, and goes about as a creature on the edge of madness. She has to be chained because she keeps going to high places, towers or trees, and she lives for nine weeks on nothing but her own breast milk. She goes into red fire and iced water and comes out unscathed, which must mean God's approval as it does in ordeals. She begs alms, so she has to live as a man because women were almost never given a papal licence to go out and beg; but she tactfully does not preach because that is a man's work. Her wildness is personal; she never joins any kind of community, although she does at one point go to Germany, as did some other holy women, to be with a famous anchorite called Jutta. There is nothing to say she was a beguine, but she is written into stories about beguines, and she brings with her all the sulphurous reputation of mystics, madwomen, women who won't be happy being women.[17]

Marie d'Oignies is a very different story. For a start, she was married at the age of fourteen to a man called John, which meant she no longer owned her own body, and as a kind of penance she 'wore discreetly under her smock a rough, sharp cord tied tight around her'; her biographer, the beguines' advocate Jacques de Vitry, insists he isn't 'praising the excess but telling her fervour'. She'd been a serious child, unhappy with bright clothes and the company of vain girls, and although now she knew the 'hard heat of burning youth' she decided that what she wanted in marriage was chastity.[18] Her husband agreed to treat her as though she were his ward, not his wife.

This was dangerous thinking, close to the heresy of the Cathars and their dislike of the flesh and their insistence that sex was fine for anything except making babies, which was the exact opposite of the Church's teaching that procreation was the only excuse. Marie was suspected of sharing their error. The problem was not so much that she chose chastity, because virginity at best and chastity if you couldn't manage virginity were virtues. Marriage was an expedient for weak persons, and the best kind of childbirth was virgin birth, bringing nothing but virtues into the world.[19] The problem with Marie's version was the fulminous atmosphere of her times, when an age was supposed to be coming to an end, and maybe the world with it.[20] In his first letter to Timothy, St Paul writes that 'in the latter times some shall depart from the faith' and one sign will be 'forbidding to marry'.[21] Preaching chastity within marriage came to much the same thing; it could bring on the end of everything.

Marie persisted. She and her husband went to serve in a leper colony. Their relatives 'respected them rich, but afterward despised and scorned them'. She moved on to Oignies, a place she didn't know and hadn't seen, and she again worked with lepers; it was there that she set up what must have been the first beguine house.[22]

She worked with her hands: sewing, weaving, nursing the sick, but sometimes healing sickness just by her touch. She went through the whole psalter on her knees, beating herself between psalms, so she could certainly read, and her deathbed words are written in Latin even in the Middle English version of the text, although earlier in her life she could not make sense of Latin words. She had a bed in her cell made of straw, but she went without sleep, 'she served our Lord in the night watches'. She dealt with demons by long fasts and direct confrontation; she saved one nun simply by running a demon through by the sheer force of her prayer so 'it seemed that he had cast out all his bowels and he was wretchedly carrying on his neck all that was within him'. Then she asked a 'familiar friend and master' what to do with the demon, and then she checked with a man who was an intimate friend; she deferred to men.

A man wrote her story, and it shows. We're told she had two men in her life, her husband and her brother-in-law Guy, who served as her spiritual adviser, but she does not belong to either of them; independence is the essence of being a beguine. She was also known as 'the mother of the brothers [meaning monks] of Oignies', which makes her someone of authority in the monastic system; but beguines were suspect precisely because they stayed outside that system. She works, and she fills every minute of the day and she is thoroughly devout; she labours and she also acts out of charity. That you might expect, but beguines were discreet persons, dressed like ordinary middle-class women and keeping mostly to their own walled courts; and Marie was dramatic, vomiting blood, running away into the woods from visitors, dressed rather meanly and not entirely clean for 'studiously sought cleanness pleased her never'. She even preached.[23]

She served her purpose admirably: a man's explanation of why any woman would choose to be a beguine.

There are reasons why women were able to make these choices in the north-west of Europe and nowhere else, and able to make them work. The first is the merchant business that crossed the seas, and the way it made families and marriages more flexible. It's not that women were liberated, or that men no longer ruled; but women who were not noble or royal were finding they had unexpected chances.

Consider Jewish women in the North, no longer required to keep to the rules of modesty that Judaism laid down and Islam imposed in Spain. If they had money to lend, they offered it to gentile women for their work and their homes, but they also lent to gentile men. When their husbands went travelling, the wives had to manage the business. They went out to bargain with men, some Jewish, some gentiles, and held talks with feudal lords; they could strike deals with merchant rivals of their husbands if they reckoned the merchants had better contacts. Where the great rabbi Maimonides thought no Jewish woman should ever be alone with a gentile, even if his wife was present, because 'they are shameless', the Tosafot commentaries on the Talmud simply say 'it is impossible that a woman not be left alone with a non-Jew at some time'. A woman went on business with a stranger, stopped to rest in a forest and was molested by two men. She was told she was committing adultery just to sit down with other men, that she should never be alone with a stranger; but the rabbis ruled otherwise. They said they turned a blind eye to women going about on business because it happened all the time.[24]

There was more: a subtle shift in how men were required to understand their marriages. Rabbis began to tell them to marry only one woman, not to stay away from home more than eight months at a time, and not to go at all if they were not getting on with their wives, because the journey was just an excuse to leave them.[25] Marriage was chosen, a companionship, not just a contract.

This edging towards a kind of equality, even among people who had no doubt that men should rule, had a very terrible side. Just as lives were opening up, crusaders were on their way to the Holy Land, and inspiring murderous pogroms against the Jews along the Rhine. Faced with forced conversion to Christianity, it was the women who had to decide whether and when to end their lives and their children's lives to save them from betraying their faith; and then they had to kill. They performed sacrifices as they never were allowed to do in the Jerusalem Temple; phrases used for high priests, even Abraham himself, now applied to women.

Mistress Rachel in Trier picked up the knife and beat herself, knowing what had to be done but 'with an embittered heart'. She killed three of her children and had to pull a fourth, her son Aaron, out by his feet from under a box where he was hiding and she sat lamenting over their bodies until the Christians came to demand 'the money you have in your sleeves' and then to kill her. We know the details of both her pain and her courage, but of her husband we know only that he 'yelled and cried upon seeing the death of his four beautiful sons . . . he went and fell on the sword that was in his hand . . . he rolled with the dead'.[26]

In the Flemish town of Douai in the thirteenth century, when the aldermen had to speak to a whole craft or a whole profession, they addressed 'boulengiers ne boulengiere' or 'drappiers ne drappiere' or 'taneres ne taneresse'. They always included both women and men who were bakers, drapers, tanners. In Bruges they went one step further: they addressed the bosses of the town as 'mester' and 'mestrigghe'.[27]

Out in the country women worked the land, helped plough and kill pigs, made ale and cheese, spun wool and wove cloth; but they did not inherit as their brothers might, and making a living had everything to do with having the use of property. If they were paid wages they earned much less than a man. A thirteenth-century bailiff in England, in a book that was copied again and again, says it is worth having a dairymaid to look after the small animals even if you don't have a dairy: 'it is always good to have a woman there, at a much less cost than a man'.[28]

The pull of towns, where a woman could earn more, change her job or her employer, maybe start a business of her own, was the prospect of having a household of her own in time.

Women worked in the cloth trades, of course, since Flanders was famous for cloth; but that was only the start. They were money-changers, not just informally pushing some useful cash across to friends and neighbours but acting as bank managers. They were ship-builders, too. They went out to run and clean houses, they formed their own hierarchy in the markets: from the ones who had their own businesses to the ones who had their own market stalls to the women who sold from a cloth spread on the ground and were relentlessly moved on.[29] In Bruges, they dominated the market for everything edible but meat; drink was another matter, but even so there was a Kateline van Denille who had a wine shop. They could be sureties for the debts of people who were not their relatives, and if they were married they did not have to follow their husbands' trades; a separating couple in Ghent in 1355 was reckoned able to live apart without being a burden on the town because they had been 'practising different trades and paying their own expenses'.[30] When married women were doing business, suing or being sued, the clerks keeping the records quite often did not find the marriage worth mentioning.

Women did not go travelling as merchants so they often had the city, the hostel, the shop, the warehouse or the money business to themselves while their husbands went away; they were the constant, stable heart of business. They represented the family, and in Flemish law that meant the present reality of the married couple much more than the children who would eventually inherit. Women shared. They had authority over children just like any father. A mother and her children, even if they were all born out of wedlock, formed a family with the mother at its head; there was a Flemish custom that a mother has no bastards, no need to make special provision for children who happened to be 'illegitimate'. So while families took the name of the father, should there be one available, the mother could perfectly well be head of the household: in the house, in the business, in the world.

That was the world around the beguinages: where women took responsibility for their families and for their own survival, where almost no trade or business was forbidden to them, where they could operate more or less freely and independently without their gender being an issue. The beguines learned. When they brought children into the beguinages, even ones born out of wedlock, they did what any mother would do. When they went out to work, they did what other women did: worked for wages. They could, like other women, protect themselves at law, by demanding back money they had loaned or claiming property that somebody else also claimed. The richer beguines brought their capital into the courts, built their own houses there and owned them; exactly as a woman could do out in the city. As for a woman's authority, and the power of the mistress of a beguinage, there were also women who controlled castles or abbeys and held public audiences, not to mention financial receivers who explained their accounts at public audit; citizens knew very well that women could have power. Only the countess was meant to have a male to speak for her, but then the countess belonged to a fading feudal system which never did have deep roots in Flanders.

The beguines begin to seem less exceptional.

William Aungier was eight when he lost his father, then his mother, then his stepfather to the plague. His new guardian, his uncle, sold the right to be his guardian to a local man who happened to have a niece called Johanna, aged ten. The pair went through a ceremony of marriage and were duly put into bed to spend the night. They then went their separate ways until they were old enough to consent to a real marriage, but just before William was fourteen and legally marriageable, Johanna turned out to be pregnant by one of her surprisingly various lovers. William was packed off to his notional wife in 1357, but he refused to consummate the marriage, not even after spending a night *solus cum sola, nudus cum nuda*, which means alone and naked in the same bed. He told friends: 'It displeases me that I knew her once for she does not care for any affection that is felt.' He wanted his marriage annulled because, he said, he wanted to base his marriage on 'an affection that is upheld'. He wanted love and constancy.[31]

He had learned well. After the Fourth Lateran Council of 1215, English priests worked from pastoral manuals that taught them what to teach believers, including the doctrine that marriage is a matter of consent.[32] The woman chooses, the man chooses, and the choice must be mutual: both partners almost equal for a moment, whether the motive is love or business. This teaching was meant to go all through Christendom, but when it came to the North Sea it was particularly powerful because it fitted perfectly with custom, and so with the law. In the law school at Bologna the scholars learned that what made a marriage real was the consummation, but in Paris and the North a marriage was already real when woman and man consented to it, although the next and essential stage was the consummation. When you see a picture of a wedding in an Anglo-French manuscript, there will be a priest because marriage is a matter of the spirit. In Italy, there will be a notary, because of the contract.[33]

The differences go much deeper, so deep they may well help explain what happened to the whole economic machine around the North Sea over centuries, and why it did not happen in quite the same way in the South. They explain, among many other things, windmills and pensions.

A woman marrying in the South brought a dowry with her, money or goods or land. Families negotiated the amount, which had everything to do with what the woman might contribute to the marriage: how young she was, how strong, how likely to bear children. The older the woman, the more expensive the dowry, so there was every reason to marry girls off as soon as possible. Even when the marriage involved rather little money or goods or land, the dowry mattered; it was the one time in her life when a woman could expect money from her parents. If she wanted money to get her life started, she had to marry to get it; but once she was married, the dowry was all she could control herself. If she and her husband built a fortune out of a business or their land, that was his fortune, not theirs.

The custom in the North was different. Women had the right to inherit, so they expected money from their parents, but only when their parents died. They could come into land, sell it off or give it away, all in their own names; it was theirs. They had no financial reason to marry early, and their parents had no reason to fret over when they married. Dowries were never as common as in the South and in a prosperous city like Ghent, in the late Middle Ages, they are hardly even mentioned.

When a woman did decide to marry, all that she had was put into a kind of marital fund: one pot of money for both wife and husband. The husband controlled the money for as long as he was alive, but the wife could inherit it, and she could do business with her share. She might have a deal, like one woman in Nivelles in 1471, that she took everything if her husband walked out, at least until he returned 'to talk and to remain in peace and love as suits the loyalty of married people'.[34] Her husband didn't always have to know what she was doing with their money; in York, Thomas Harman first knew his wife had bought a batch of candlewick so huge it took two servants to carry it when he was handed writs for debt and breach of commercial promise.[35]

Inheritance mattered because sickness and war so often cut lives short and left survivors. Second or even third marriages were common, and they were sometimes practical alliances made startlingly soon after a husband's death, marrying a rival, marrying the apprentice; look at marriage contracts for the town of Douai in the fifteenth century and a third of the brides were widows.[36] They brought with them the riches they had helped to build. In Douai the custom was that they kept half the assets of the marriage, and they seem to have been able to sidestep their husband's debts. A woman's economic life could be long in the North, where a husband's death was not the end of things and a woman could do well without being married.

The fact that marriage was tangled up with money did not make it less affectionate. True, in Douai the legal documents that allowed childless couples to leave each other their worldly goods only mention 'love and conjugal affection' from the 1550s; but those are legal documents, which do not need sentiment.[37] A better test is what happens after death, and whether couples choose to stay together. Most people until the thirteenth century ended up anonymous in mass and unmarked graves; but in 1374 one man wrote a will in Douai to ask that he be buried alongside his wife in the nave of a church. Graves were marked with marble slabs with carvings of the couple who lay there, sometimes their children as well, on one occasion a man lying between two wives. After plague came in 1400, one third of wills in Douai said exactly where the grave should be, and who should be near: spouse, father, mother. Again there is a frontier across Europe: in Italian towns, men wanted to be buried with their ancestors, with as much of a male line as they could find and if necessary some invented coats of arms. Around the North Sea, it was the marriage and the children that mattered.[38]

Out of that doctrine of 'marital affection', William Aungier's hope, came unexpected consequences. The custom of the North was reinforced: property was shared in a marriage, not separate, and women could expect their share. Women could do business, and it was worth their while. Women could take their time choosing a husband, wait at least until they were eighteen or twenty and more likely into their mid-twenties; they took responsibility for the marriage and they had a degree of equality within it. At the very least, they had a negotiating position. Women and men needed the time to get together the resources to start an independent life because being an adult in Flanders meant having a household of your own; just marrying, or reaching a certain age, was not enough. You were a minor if you ate your parents' bread, *en pain de père et mère*, and adult when you could keep yourself, *hors de son pain*. Real life took its time to begin.[39]

So there were years in their lives when young people could go into service as maids, or become apprentices, or work as journeymen hiring on by the day. Most of all, they could move. By the late thirteenth century, there are references to journeymen, to young and unmarried workers on short contracts who had special skills and travelled to find the demand for them. They had their own networks, often family connections, in building and shipping and mining; and quite soon they had more formal arrangements, the first masons' lodges in England and the franchises that Edward III of England offered John Kempe from Flanders in 1331 to come and show the English how to weave, full and dye cloth and so defy the guilds, who thought they already knew. The same privilege was on offer to 'all the clothworkers of strange lands of whatsoever country they be'.[40] German-speaking workers were tramping from Riga in the east to Bergen in the north, and the bakers went south to Rome because Romans, it turned out, loved German bread. Much later, some of these serious tramps would write down their own stories: like Emmanuel Gross in the seventeenth century, a shoemaker from Baden who went walking as a journeyman from Lithuania to France, from Sweden to England.[41]

These men were knowledge marching. They didn't like the idea of being used by officials, or made to hide from officialdom, so they shifted about in small groups in Flanders, and in Germany they kept crossing the boundaries between the various princedoms to stop any one authority coming down hard on them. By the fourteenth century they could get work by showing certificates of service, or proof of their indentures; they had hostels where they could stay, and special fraternal handshakes; and often they organized things so that if there was no work they could at least be given a bed for the night and enough money to travel on. Shoemakers in Troyes, just south of Paris, reported in 1420 that 'many compagnons and workmen . . . of a variety of tongues and nations, came and went from town to town to learn, discover, observe and see what others did'. Learning and tramping were so close that London became a kind of training centre for the whole of England.[42]

A man whose life was tied to land and early marriage and a single place and his father's authority could never have gone away, let alone stayed away so long; but these men were free to travel to make a living. They carried with them facts and techniques. Their predecessors took the windmill out of England into Flanders, or just possibly, if you reckon the date 1114 carved on a beam in a windmill just south of Dunkirk really does show when it was first built, out of Flanders into

England. Either way, the idea of the windmill crossed the sea with alacrity. The first one recorded in England goes back to 1155 when 'Hugo de Plaiz gave to the monks of Lewes the windmill in his manor Ilford, for the health of the soul of his father.' By 1200 there were at least twenty-three mills working from Sussex to Northumberland, with a sizeable number in East Anglia, just over the sea from Flanders. By then there were at least four windmills in Northern Europe, at the mouth of the Somme, just inland at Ypres, and at Silly and Wormhoudt: close enough to the coast to suggest the idea came by water.

We can't tell who first shipped the idea, but we do know why it was needed. In the lowlands, peat for burning was running short, and waterpower was not strong enough in the flatlands to be useful energy. Besides, the owners of the rights to use riverbanks wanted high fees from anyone who used the flow of the river water to power a mill. Windpower was not entirely reliable, and it required careful engineering to gear the vertical sails to the horizontal shaft that worked the grinding stones, but it was wonderfully available; and only in the Netherlands did a man have to pay a 'wind brief', a tax to the lord or king who thought he owned the weather. Elsewhere, a windmill let a man step outside the feudal order for a while. Dean Herbert built a mill for himself at Bury St Edmunds in 1191, which infuriated the abbot, who owned two local mills and the feudal rights to grind corn. The moment he heard, the abbot ordered carpenters to take the mill down 'and place the timber under safe custody'; he tongue-lashed Dean Herbert, told him: 'I thank you as I should thank you if you had cut off both my feet.' The dean said he wanted the mill only for himself, but the abbot could not tell the local farmers where to grind their corn, so the dean was competition. He was alarmed enough at the abbot's fury to tear down his mill even before the abbot's servants could arrive, so they found nothing to demolish; but he also had the technical knowledge to build the mill himself, and he must have learned from travellers.[43]

A century or so later, the first windmills for draining polder land started turning at Alkmaar, just north of Amsterdam; within twenty years the magistrates at Saint-Omer, close to Calais, needed to drain their marshes and they sent a delegation to Holland for the plan of a mill 'pour vider les eaux', to drain off the waters. The mill was running by 1438, but it was never effective, and it was abandoned twelve years later, but a process had begun: bringing in plans and workers with the expertise to build new technologies. Since mills were a source of power, that power could be applied in a hundred ways. Over the next centuries, it drained fens in the Polish part of Prussia, in Schleswig-Holstein in the late sixteenth century, in Friesland and around Norfolk in England. It made oil mills work across Northern Europe from Ireland to Sweden and Germany, crushing the seeds of rape; it milled paper in England and the Netherlands; it ran hulling mills in Germany and saw mills as far away as Portugal and Russia.[44] It created new land out of marsh and sea, it kept industries running, and all because the idea had journeymen to bring it where it could be most useful.

The pattern of marriage had one other side-effect: the very beginning of financial markets, of pension plans and annuities and trying to save your life by investing. When people marry late and set up their own households, they move away from their families and their obligations to them. They may leave town altogether, or even the country. They may decide not to marry at all. Even if a couple had children and grandchildren, they could still not be absolutely sure of their support in old age. Just as a couple had to save to set up their household in the first place, so they had to save to protect themselves when work and business no longer seemed possible; instead of protecting the future by keeping everything in the family, which was often the pattern in the South, they put their money out to work with strangers. So in Flanders, Brabant and Holland the main source of money to run the affairs of cities and towns was people worried about old age, who bought *renten* from the councils: annuities that paid out a heavy rate of interest on the amount invested for as long as the investor was alive. Sometimes, as in the cheese town of Edam and in East Anglia, these annuities were what parents got back when they handed over land and assets to their children, who then organized their pensions. Already by the end of the thirteenth century roughly four out of ten people in East Anglia, both women and men, had pensions to draw on.[45]

This idea of 'marital affection' changed the structure of families and the shape of people's lives in the North, which helped send ideas and technology across the continent and gave money quite surprisingly modern uses. The personal isn't just political; it is economic.

You will, of course, be wondering about sex. In marriage it was a legal duty to be available on demand to make love or something similar, so much so that the famous Héloïse wanted to be the girlfriend of the famous Abelard, even his whore, so she could express all the love she felt without compulsion; married love was an obligation, she said. The simultaneous orgasm was much touted by the influential medical books from Salerno, very widely read in the North, because it causes such delight that the married couple want sex again and again; it was also, for a while, a moral good, since man and woman were both supposed to come at the same time in order to have a baby, and babies were the whole point of sex. The return of Aristotle to libraries and to favour across Europe rather scuppered this happy moment, since he reckoned a woman could conceive without feeling pleasure. And there was always the question of how to get where you meant to go: Ovid suggested gentleness, caresses and murmurs, but his thirteenth-century French translator suggested biting like a dog.[46]

At least we know the rules and duties of marriage, and sometimes the troubles: the courts acknowledged cruelty as a reason to end a marriage while canon law was still limited to adultery, or spiritual fornication, which is heresy, or proven attempts to kill your spouse. But we don't know the reality of people's sex lives, and we don't know exactly what happened before all those late marriages in Northern Europe: what everyone did, and nobody talked about.

Our evidence comes from sermons and law courts, so what we know is a tabloid world.

Eleanor was not a lady, not if she was working Cheapside when the light had gone on a Sunday night in December in 1394. Mind you, Eleanor was not a woman, either.[47]

John Britby thought she was a woman, went to talk to her, asked her if she'd have sex with him; Eleanor wanted money, and Britby agreed. They went down Soper's Lane and found a stall there and got down to business. They had just got properly detestable, unmentionable and ignominious when city officials spotted them, and Eleanor, still in all his finery, came before the Mayor and the aldermen of London to explain himself.

Her name was John Rykener, he said, and he blamed a certain Anna, 'whore of a former servant' of a gentleman, who taught him to practise this vice 'in the manner of a woman'. He didn't mean dressing as a woman, though, because he said a woman called Elizabeth Brouderer had taught him that. This may be Elizabeth 'the embroiderer', in which case she may be Elizabeth Moring, who set up a school of embroidery with resident girls, who were then encouraged to stay out all night with friars and clerics. Elizabeth had some difficulty reminding the amateur girls they were supposed to bring home rewards for what they had done;[48] in Eleanor's case, she evidently did better.

Rykener had a talent for shakedowns. Elizabeth would put her daughter into bed with a customer in a darkened room, then get her to leave before dawn; in the morning, the punter woke up to face Eleanor. Eleanor was, to put it gently, self-assertive. One vicar had sex with him, after which Eleanor removed two of the vicar's robes; and when the victim wanted them back, Eleanor insisted his husband would be all too willing to take the vicar to court.

Sometimes, though, Eleanor was just a tart. He had three 'unsuspecting' scholars in the marshes at Oxford while working there as an embroiderer, and in Burford he notched up two Franciscans and a Carmelite friar. His best price was two shillings, his best gift a gold ring and he said 'he accommodated priests more readily than other people because they wished to give him more than others'. At Beaconsfield he seduced a certain Joan, 'as a man', and two foreign Franciscans 'as a woman'. He claimed a vivid heterosexual career with nuns and 'with many women both married and otherwise' and he couldn't count the priests who had had him.

There's something gloriously queenly in Eleanor's story: its insistence on what people gave him, his sheer exuberance totting up the numbers and ranks of his clients, his willingness to make love outdoors on a December night in London and the way all this must have mystified the aldermen. They were not a church court, so they couldn't bring charges of sodomy or even prostitution; and then his taste for being sodomized by priests and seducing nuns seemed to put him out of any obvious category. Since it was hard to know what names to call him, he went free.

We know the tarts on a Paris street, in the thirteenth century, shouted: 'Sodomite!' at any student who turned down their offers; Jacques de Vitry said so. We know that in an Iceland penitential in the 1180s there is a trace of some kind of sex toy; the priests considered a man making love to a woman rather less sinful than a man 'polluted by drilled wood'.[49]

What we know best is that there has always been a business in sex: not just selling sexual partners, but providing a chance to meet, a place to make love, and sometimes dinner, too.

Prostitution was a sizeable business in Bruges, which had the reputation of the whoriest city in Europe, which was saying something. The fifteenth-century Rabbenu Judah Mintz thought that 'it seems to the gentiles that it is a good thing to place prostitutes in the marketplace and town squares and in all the corners of their houses so as to save them from a graver sin, that is, from relations with married women'.[50]

In Bruges the bathhouse customers, women and men, sat down to their wine and their dinner at a common table in a vast wooden bath tub, women naked but with their faces slightly veiled, until it was time to step down to the floor between the dogs waiting there and then go to bed.[51] A Spaniard, Pero Tafur, was in Bruges in 1435, and he wrote that 'the bathing of men and women together they take to be as honest as churchgoing with us'. It sounds agreeable, but it was not quite as open as he thought. Leo of Rozmital, an ambassador from Bohemia, visited at around the same time and discovered that a woman could spend the night with any man she wanted at the Waterhalle, on condition the man never saw her face and did not know who she was. The penalty for being known, he wrote, was death.

The bathhouses were mostly by the port, since it was merchants and sailors who needed them. The brothels were women's business for the most part; which is perhaps not surprising since men who were merchants had to go travelling, and brothels need constant attention. So from the mid-1350s women ran the houses in the town, elbowing men out of the game, even old Weiter Balz, whose bath-houses had been fined every year without exception from 1305 to 1355 for one offence or another. Madames were left in control of the women called Frisian XX, Bette the Jewess, Marie the hatwasher, Katherine the candle seller and the occasional woman who claimed to be a beguine when she was appearing before the city authorities to get her licence to cruise.

All this regulation suggests a gentlemanly business, but gentlemen got other kinds of offers. Tafur arrived in a year of famine, and he was in the port when he was approached by a woman who offered him his choice of two very young girls. The woman explained 'she was almost dead with hunger, having had nothing to eat for many days except a few small fish, and that the two girls were like to die of starvation and that they were virgins'. Tafur gave her money; he says he did not take the girls.[52]

We know that the brothels of Southwark, the 'stews' just outside London, had whitewashed walls and signs like pubs; we know they offered baths because we know that their owners made their servants carry water in tubs; and they offered women, often from Flanders. From around 1400 the London authorities were especially wary of 'Flemish women, who profess and follow such shameful and dolorous life' and caused spectacular fights in which 'many men have been slain and murdered'.[53] Now this immigrant crew is a curiosity, because there were quite enough poor young women coming into London from the surrounding countryside. It almost seems that young women might go away from Flanders for a while to make money, just as their journeyman brothers did, and go on the game instead of going into service. They could then return home, leaving their reputations behind in London.

Prostitution was not the whole story: there was also the little war of guile that went before marriage. The Church considered any couple married if they had consented to marry and made promises to each other; the Church expected you to have the banns said, and to appear in daylight before a priest to make your vows, but in theory consent and a promise were enough. So the Bishop of Salisbury in the early 1200s had to tell men to stop weaving straw rings on the hands of young women 'in order to fornicate more freely with them'. Women who thought they had a man's consent often had to be resolute. Matilda from East Grinstead in 1276 had a particular grievance: that three of her friends had caught her making love and told her lover he could either marry her, die, or kiss her arse. He promised to marry her, but he never did.

Love required care, especially in England. A charge of fornication might lead to a public whipping, which was bad enough, but an unmarried mother would get no sympathy in the wide world, might be cut off by charitable bodies and even thrown out of town: four poor mothers and their six children were expelled from Horsham in the 1280s.[54] Something had to be done to hide pregnancy, to stop pregnancy, to avoid getting pregnant in the first place or to give the child away very quickly.

There were the usual expedients: anal sex, oral sex, the medieval speciality of separating out the male and the female orgasms so the male seed and the female seed could not mix, which everyone knew was required for pregnancy. Courting couples were allowed heavy petting and by the time anyone was printing books about such things, which in this case is 1637, there were sometimes healthy outdoor games: boys throwing the girls into the sea off a Dutch beach and then carefully drying them off, which was followed in very short order by walks in the nearby woods.[55] There was also coitus interruptus, but that required, as the sixteenth-century memoirist Pierre de Bourdeilles, Seigneur de Brantôme, put it, being careful and watching 'for the time of the tidal wave when it was coming'.

He also mentions a girl who was sleeping with an apothecary who gave her 'antidotes to guard from being pregnant' and knew about drugs which would make her fat flow away so gently if she did happen to conceive that she would 'feel nothing but wind'.[56] Long before that lecherous druggist, women knew very well how to avoid having babies, and so did rather holy persons. Abortion was wrong, contraception was wrong, the true purpose, and only excuse, for any sexual act was to get babies; and yet there are manuscripts written in ninth-century German monasteries which give detailed, even plausible, instructions for making the menses flow. One includes parsley, the coarse-leaved hartwart, rue, black pepper, lovage, thyme and celery seeds, a kitchen recipe. A bishop of Rennes in his twelfth-century herbal suggests spearmint applied to the womb – 'a woman will not conceive' – and artemisia, the wormwood of the Bible, to cause abortions. The saintly philosopher Albertus Magnus, the man who gave Aristotle back to the world, roared against contraception when he was writing theology; but in his work on minerals he writes helpfully that jasper, especially the green translucent kind, will marvellously check the flow of blood, prevent conception and help birth, and there is also oristes, a precious stone that stops a woman conceiving if she just wears it. Albertus, being an alchemist, knew such things.[57]

None of the rest was secret knowledge. An equally saintly woman, the twelfth-century Hildegard of Bingen in her closed convent, asked her neighbours about herbs which could make the menstrual fluids flow and some that deliberately provoked abortion. She wrote the details down, to share them: told her readers, in her book *Physica*, about feverfew to control menstruation, white hellebore to help a girl's first period, the wild ginger spikenard to bring on either abortion or else menstruation when it has not happened for a while. She was the first to mention the same use for the brilliant yellow tansy, a staple among Charlemagne's herbs and in monastic gardens. Even when Hildegard warns against a herb, as she does with the silver-leaved oleaster, the wild olive, she says 'it makes an abortion to a pregnant woman with a danger to her body', as though there were other ways that were not so dangerous.[58]

There is something even odder here. Contraception was wrong in marriage, more or less murder, but encouraged outside it. A man did more penance if he fathered a baby while misbehaving, perhaps because he caused more scandal; an Irish penitential, known from a ninth-century copy, lays down three years' penance for a layman who corrupts a virgin promised to God if he has a baby by her and ruins her reputation, but only one year for uncomplicated corruption. The means might be sexual practice – oral sex, anal sex, coitus interruptus – or they might be 'the poisons of sterility', which early on were associated with witchcraft, but the message was unambiguous: no babies. The sixteenth-century Thomas Sanchez, the greatest Jesuit expert on marriage, had all kinds of reservations about sex inside marriage – he was particularly against women on top in the sexual act – but he conceded that a fornicator could not be blamed for coitus interruptus because he was at least avoiding the greater evil of fathering a bastard.[59]

There's no way to know how this knowledge was used; what matters is that it was available. If a woman wanted to delay having children, or to prevent having children, she could find the means readily enough; and the information was as open in the most respectable convent in Bingen as it was in any brothel in Bruges. Her choice was real, for the time being.

11.

# The plague laws

The sick had fever, ulcers, vomiting and diarrhoea, choked lungs and great swellings in the groin or armpits or behind the ears. Those were not even the worst of it, because some people survived all those symptoms. More deadly were the small lumps that criss-crossed the body, 'brittle coal fragments', according to the Welsh poet Llywelyn Fychan mourning his four dead daughters, or 'shower of peas giving rise to affliction, messenger of swift death'.[1] The Black Death was an assault.

A sailor off a ship could infect a town. The opening of a cargo hold seemed enough to let loose the sickness, and just talking to someone could pass the disease; or so people thought because they thought they had seen it happen. Death was very quick. The menace was real, but not understood, and it seemed new so it must have been brought from somewhere else, somewhere over the seas; but because the information was so thin, plague unsettled everything and left a perverse residue of irrational fears about a very real danger. It was rather like a terrorist attack: something had to be done, but there was nothing to be done, so it was necessary to control everything, just in case. The death toll was unimaginable so people imagined the restoration of an order that never was.

This medieval horror had very long consequences. It is the start of the process we still know of anxious, insistent social controls, of policing lives; and what goes with it, an official suspicion of the poor and the workless, who are never just unfortunate. Our nightmares begin with their nightmares, in the 1340s.

The Black Death was perhaps the greatest natural catastrophe of the millennium. 'So great a death toll was never heard of before,' says the chronicle of England known as the *Brut*, in a version written around 1400. 'It wasted the people so that only the tenth person was left alive.' He is almost right; manorial records show villages around Worcester and in Cambridgeshire where four out of five people died. In two years, one person in three across Northern Europe would be dead.

There had been rain, every night, every day, and then around Michaelmas the plague came to London, and remained until the next August. 'He that fell ill one day was dead the third day after', according to the *Brut*. People ran from the sickness and carried it with them. 'There was death without sorrow, wedding without friendship, wilful penance, dearth without scarcity and fleeing without refuge or help.' It was an event so strange and radical that 'all that were born after that pestilence had two teeth less than they had before'.[2]

There had to be an answer to such a brute disease: something to do. You see it in the pictures between the prayers in the *Très Riches Heures du Duc de Berry* from the early fifteenth century: not just the processions of hooded men beating themselves with chains and cords, trying to make up for sin, but also the other processions, the dragon of plague being taken out to burn, the cross being carried back to show the devil dragon is dead. You could pray in all four directions, against all of the winds that carried clouds and mists of sickness. The Sorbonne doctors told Philippe VI, called the Lucky, to get out of town; they prescribed three words to chase the plague away, '*vite*', or quick, for 'leave quickly'; '*loin*', or far, for 'get a long way away'; and '*longtemps*', or a long time, for 'keep going'. If anyone stayed in Paris, the doctors suggested perfumes and spices to keep away the poisoned air, bleeding and purging, and a light diet. They had few ideas about what the community could do to save itself, but they were watching the horse slaughterers, the pigsties and the pig butchers, anywhere rotting flesh might stink above ground and corrupt the air. The butchers were too obstinately useful to move without a royal decree; only in 1415 were they finally pushed out of town to the Tuileries, which was close to the Louvre but just beyond the city limit. Trenches were dug there to collect the blood.

Nobody had moved a whole profession out of town before, or made such a drastic decision about the plan for the city; that was a consequence of plague. The moves were not even about basic hygiene, just about making the air seem breathable. The same decree that worried about the waters of the Seine in Paris told the people of Orleans to throw all their rotten meat into the Loire. Nobody knew about the fleas that rats carried, and the sickness the fleas carried; so plague persisted.[3] In time, quarantine and isolation may have helped control its spread in north-western Europe, fewer ships landing without being checked, but what made the disease disappear in the eighteenth century was largely accidental. People started to change their clothes when they went to bed at night, and to wash with a serious soap, the Marseilles soap made with olive oil, which kept down the fleas and lice. The price of arsenic tumbled, so there was a poison to dispose of mice and rats. But most important, and nothing at all to do with human beings, the bacterium that seems to cause plague, *yersinia pestis*, mutated into a close relative that was far less deadly; rats caught the mutant much as human beings would be immunized against diseases, and rats in Europe no longer carried plague. The rest of the world was not so fortunate.[4]

Until then there was no answer that worked, no solution, so the plague cut much deeper than other pandemics. Like terrorism, like AIDS in our time, it settled in memory and panic and stung a sense of guilt into life.

Plague had to be given a shape because you can fight something with a shape.

In plague legends from Sweden, Denmark and Norway plague can be a black mist, a blue vapour or smoke, as clearly ominous as clouds before a storm. It can be two children walking, or an old woman who carries a broom or a rake; she sweeps in front of houses where people will die, and if there are going to be survivors, she counts out the number of the dead by hitting the door with her broom. Young persons dancing in a barn all night meet a three-footed goat called Hel, and the next morning they are sick and plague gallops off across the land, now in the shape of a white horse. Sometimes plague is an animal that nobody has ever seen before. It takes away the young, the old, the sick and the women and it leaves whole districts barren. Since it took a hundred years for the population numbers of Scandinavia to recover, and four hundred in the case of Norway, you can understand why so often the stories try to end with a couple: the only living person on the north side of a fjord is a woman, the only one to the south is a man. 'They moved in together,' the story says, 'and were married.'

The sickness is sometimes a stranger, a foreigner, almost always a man: a merchant off the ships. There are stories of ships that ran aground with the crew all dead and their bodies blackened, occasionally a survivor, and when the bodies are buried and the cargo stolen, the people on the land start to die. The stories sometimes say 'the plague crept out of the cargo', just like rats. The image of the dead ship and black bodies is still with us; it is Dracula coming ashore from a silent ship at Whitby in the Stoker novel or the Murnau film. Sometimes the landing place seems unlikely – a death ship beached on the open Danish shore is very possible but a ship could hardly drift unmanned through the islands and channels that lead to the harbour at Bergen – but the stories agree that plague comes by sea.

The same images struck the writers of chronicles. Matthias van Neuenburg lived through the plague, and he wrote of 'pestilence – the greatest death rate, unheard of since the time of the Flood'. He libelled the Jews for poisoning wells. He ignored the sins of people like him, which would usually take the blame, but he mentions the sins of others: wandering holy persons flogging themselves for penitence, as though that were the natural consequence of any epidemic. He was mostly struck by a single image: 'ships out at sea, loaded with cargo, but with all the crew dead and no master'.[5]

Once ashore, plague goes about sometimes in a red shirt and sometimes a blue jacket: a woman carrying a book where she can read who will live and who will die. The written word had terrifying authority in a world where not everyone could both read and write; you could never escape the written record. Plague goes slowly and erratically overland, which makes its progress somehow more uncanny: it comes suddenly, kills suddenly, village by village. Children are left yelling alone in empty valleys. The bells ring out, fires are lit if there is anyone left to signal. Survivors go wandering, carrying with them the spirit of the plague; so they have to be burned alive, or else buried alive so the plague will stay with them and stop travelling. Children without parents, not known in the valley, begging for food: they were buried. So was a girl who watched a grave being dug, obediently got into the grave when the gravediggers asked her to see if it was deep enough yet; then 'they reached for the spade and buried the girl alive in the grave with the heaped up dirt'. A village is saved by killing an innocent young man who is then left in the road because everyone knows that plague cannot cross his body. Sometimes the solution is rather more rustic: in one story the woman who drives the dead to the cemetery does not get sick 'because she smoked a chalk pipe'.[6]

Nobody knew quite what plague was. We don't, either; there is room for debate about exactly what organisms, or what deadly marriage of organisms, caused the Black Death. We can agree, though, that rats matter, because they carry infected fleas and they move: slow, but persistent, always onwards.

Rats are missing from the archaeological record around the North Sea right into the early Middle Ages. To thrive in large numbers, rats need store cupboard places, tightly packed with people and food, and those were scarce. It is possible they came into Northern Europe on the Viking ships plying down the great Russian rivers from Byzantium; the first rat bones in York are from the time of Viking settlement, and there are no bones at the great trading centre of Birka in Sweden until around 810 CE, when the Viking routes were opened wide. Their timing was excellent. The growing cities and towns were full of opportunity. Rats do not like crossing wide streets, and the new towns were busy and cramped. Houses with several floors and wooden frames were just going up along London streets in the fourteenth century: boxes of people, and sewage and garbage,[7] 'heaped up together, and in a sort smothered with many families of children and servants in one house', as a royal proclamation in 1580 noticed, trying yet again to stop new building and families sharing, and failing yet again.[8]

The almost universal curfew at night suited rats because they have sensitive ears and like quiet; they stay away from any workshop where there is hammering. They have a human taste for warmth, and in the North, unlike the Mediterranean, they need houses and food stores, warm and solid structures, perhaps even the bathhouses; and in the busy North, shipping grain and wool and cloth about, there was constant transport for them, in and out of towns, between towns, out across the sea. Better still, their enemies were ruined by the same steady growth of towns. As human beings took the land that once had been forest for building streets or growing food, so there were fewer and fewer weasels and foxes, fewer owls out hunting silently in the night. Rats were warm, fed and safe from almost anything but the plague they carried.[9]

The plague was democratic: it killed anyone. Preachers blamed the sheer weight of human sin. Doctors blamed the pestilential air and suggested burning incense; they warned that bathing too much would open the pores to sickness; they tried to find some event in the skies and stars to explain everything. The astrologer Geoffrey de Meaux was in England when the plague came, and he was struck by the way sickness seemed to skip streets or even neighbouring houses, but he was sure he knew why: each house, street or side of a street had different stellar influences or rulers 'and therefore the impact of the heavens cannot affect them all equally'.[10] His confidence in the stars was not always shared. The Paris medical faculty was forced to concede that the conjunction of Saturn, Mars and Jupiter in 1345 'cannot explain everything we would wish'. Conrad of Megenberg decided that the conjunction had somehow made the earth tremble, putting out pestilential vapours, and the Flemish musician Louis Sanctus blamed 'the stinking breath of the wind' for sending the plague travelling. The fabric of prediction and analysis was beginning to look rather unsure.[11]

The plague did not undo all experts. The sovereign remedy for plague and its symptoms was a compound called theriac, a mix which in the beginning contained the flesh of vipers to build up immunity against snakebite.[12] The thirteenth-century version was thick and syrupy, made of wine and honey and sometimes containing eighty ingredients like saffron and rhubarb, cinnamon and ginger, ground coral, rose water and myrrh; theriac gives us the word 'treacle'. The standard text on cures, the *Antidotarium Nicolai*, used in Paris from around 1270, calls it 'the mistress of medicines', effective against asthma, epilepsy or dropsy, 'the most serious infirmities of the human body'. It could be sniffed, swallowed, sucked, spread as an ointment or used as a suppository. Naturally it was prescribed against plague, the older the better; evidently you laid down theriac like you lay down wine or whisky. Nobody knew quite how it worked, but that was true of many compound medicines, which were more effective than their ingredients taken one by one. Theriac was supposed both to strengthen the healthy body and save the sick from the worst of their suffering.

Theriac sounds as doubtful as the remedies that alchemists were pursuing, the fantastical dream of finding an 'elixir' that would heal just as well as miracles: the quintessence of wine or of gold. Theriac mixture can vary so much in its ingredients and its ageing that this one supreme cure only adds to the confusion about remedies that were handed out during plagues. The odd thing is this: theriac worked, and people knew it. What's more, it worked for a reason that modern pharmacists would recognize: it delivered a high dose of opium, which was basic to the recipe. It was probably given in its fastest acting form, which is laudanum. Opium blocked diarrhoea, calmed down coughing, relieved pain in the joints and pain from boils and ulcers, and most of all it settled anxiety for a while; it was a wonderful holiday from dying.

That was a huge relief for people who lived at close quarters with mortality, and did not expect to win. The Black Death of 1348–9 followed the failed harvest of 1346–7 and the prospect of famine. Hunger was familiar. In 1315 rain ruined the harvest and grain prices were six times normal; and the next two summers, in a Europe slowly getting colder, were just as bad. Twenty-three prisoners in Northampton jail died from lack of food. They were lucky in a way: there were rumours of cannibalism, prisoners eating prisoners, parents eating children.[13] Lice and the fleas on rats spread typhus among humans, and various murrains took the cows and the oxen. Rural life was disrupted because the workforce was weak and scarce and there were too few animals to dung the fields and keep them productive. The greatest burden lay on the poor.[14] They had no work to make money and not enough money to buy food if they could find any. Anyone with money could find supplies, of course; famine is not at all democratic since you can buy your way out.

Plague, on the other hand, takes anyone and everyone, a true shock to elites who fancied themselves protected by law, by strong walls, by money and other people's obligations.

The death toll made labour scarce, which should have pushed up its value or at least its cost; great persons who had been used to the constant labour of women and men who were glad to earn, or else the service of serfs, now had to contend with a whole new class of persons who thought they had choices. Labourers once ate bread made of beans, drank water, wore grey; 'then was the world of such folk well-ordered in its estate', as the poet John Gower wrote. Now there were fewer of them, they had drinks besides water, they wanted decent food and a good wage, they dressed well, they had money for beds and pillows; they went poaching and even hunting. Gower worried about who would grow the food on which city people depended since 'scarcely a rustic wishes to do such work; instead he wickedly loafs everywhere'. The thirteenth-century Bartholomaeus Anglicus, from the universities of Paris and Oxford, had warned about this. The peasantry, he said, usually kept down by various and clashing duties and charges, living with wretchedness and woe, would change if ever their circumstances changed: they would 'wax stout and proud'.

Workers now thought they could choose where to be, which master to serve, how much would be a fair wage. In his chronicle, Henry Knighton complained that workers were 'arrogant and obstinate' for wanting higher wages when the cost of food was soaring. A French labour law of 1354 expresses great crossness at those who worked 'whenever it pleased them, and spending the rest of their time in taverns playing games and enjoying themselves'. This was not just an irritant; it was a threat. A petition to the English Parliament in 1377 warned of peasants making 'confederation and alliance together to resist the lords and their officials by force'. When the peasants did march on Mile End in 1381 to present their own petition to the king, they demanded that 'no man should serve any man except at his own will'.

Everyone had to be fixed in place because the poor would never have chosen theirs. It was generally agreed that work was a punishment for Adam's fall from grace, and if nature refused to co-operate with man it was because sin had corrupted the weather, the soil and the natural world. Being poor brought no spiritual rewards unless you chose to be poor, and no great improvement, either; peasants seemed to have much the same anger, pride and greed as barons. Being poor was just wretched; an early-fourteenth-century poem, the *Song of the Husbandman*, suggests 'we might as well die now as struggle on like this'. The poor were not even attractive; Henry Grosmont, Duke of Lancaster, had to confess he did not like the way they smelled. He prayed for forgiveness for his reaction, but still he found them distasteful.

When in the thirteenth century peasants made a brief appearance in the new stained glass of cathedrals like Chartres and Le Mans, they were shown being busy where the donor of the glass would usually be, but only because they were shorthand for the gift of a vineyard or some land that had paid for the window, so their labour was support for the church. By the fourteenth century, even this sort of dependency was too much to acknowledge; peasants went back to the margins of lovely manuscripts for the delight of rich individuals. They were shown doing easy, orderly chores in perfect weather, rarely in groups of more than two and dedicated to the job.[15] The English market, having had quite enough of rebellious peasants, was particularly keen on this vision of order.

The language about workers began to sound curiously modern. In William Langland's great poem about Piers Plowman and his allegorical quest to save the world, there are 'shirkers' that Piers threatens with starvation, but their only response is to fake failing eyesight and twisted limbs, all the tricks that, he says, 'layabouts' know. The character Waster, the worst of the lot, is deeply unimpressed by anything that Piers can threaten to get the people to bring in his harvest; he says he doesn't give a damn for the law or any knight's authority, or Piers and his plough, and what's more he will beat up the lot if he ever sees them again. Workless is lawless; some of the poor are undeserving. You can't believe a cripple when he says he finds walking difficult. The world is full of idle people who must be goaded into action. Nobody respects old Romans like Cato any more, or his instructions to those born poor: 'Bear your poverty with patience.' This new kind of labourer wants hot food at mid-day and a 'lordly' wage, or else he feels exploited. In the end it is only the presence of Hunger, the memory of the terrible famines and the fact that food was always scarce at the end of summer when last year's grain was finished and this year's crop was not yet reaped which drives the men to the threshing floor.[16]

In the summer of 1349, the harvest was rotting in the English fields because of 'the many people, and especially workers and servants, now dead in this pestilence'. The answer was law: the Ordinance of Labourers and then the Statute of Labourers. Wages and prices were to be controlled and labour contracts were to be long, public and unbreakable; those were not new rules, and they were mostly directed at ploughmen and country workers and those who paid them. The law mentioned tailors, saddlers, goldsmiths, blacksmiths and shoemakers but they were not the ones who were prosecuted; it left out the professionals like notaries whose fees were controlled by law elsewhere, in particular by the laws that King John II proposed for the Île de France around the same time. But the next provision was quite extraordinary: anyone with nothing else to do could be 'bound to serve anyone who requires his or her services, as long as the service is appropriate to his or her estate'. Anyone under sixty, woman or man, bonded or free, had to obey, and to accept the wages being paid before the plague arrived when there was no shortage of labour. Anyone who failed to accept the work went to jail until they had a change of mind.[17]

This was something entirely new. There were still some slaves, mostly working for foreigners, but this is not slavery; nobody owns anybody else, but nobody controls his own labour any more, either. Peasants might hold land in return for doing work, which was not exactly an arrangement freely negotiated, but it was at least akin to some kind of payment on a lease. There were serfs, of course, who kept the great estates going with their unpaid labour and only sometimes held land in return; but this new law was not directed at serfs. Indeed, serfs had one of the few defences against compulsion; William Meere in 1352 told a court that he was already the serf of the prior of Boxgrove and so he could not possibly be required to work for anyone else.

There was a means test: anyone who did not have enough land or money or goods could be pushed into service. That does not mean paid work; in service, you got shelter and food and if you were lucky a bit of cash when the contract was finished. Otherwise, you were tied. People who themselves had servants could be caught by the rules, like Agnes, wife of a shepherd who had already been in court because he had the nerve to demand 'excessive' wages; she was ordered to come and hoe the corn of John Maltby, refused, and 'she also did not permit her two maidservants to do this work'. Neighbours in nearby houses could suddenly be labelled vagrants, and a person could be judged idle if she or he was happy to work for daily wages but did not want a long-term contract. The law was determined to settle a whole society down: no kindness to 'unworthy beggars', no travel for beggars or workers without letters of authorization.

All this was managed with one more new idea: summary punishment, no need to prove a case in court or even hold a trial. There had to be two witnesses to a refusal to serve, but once they had told their story anyone refusing work could be put in the stocks or taken off to jail, where they stayed until they agreed to labour. The new justices of labourers who made these laws work were kept quite furiously busy; those in Essex in 1352 handled thousands of cases, involving perhaps one in seven of the adults in the county. When the justices were eliminated in the 1360s, and cases came first to justices of the peace and then to the King's Bench, the records are sparse and sometimes missing altogether; but we know enough from the early years to see that the machinery of the law was mostly used against workers who wanted more money than employers wanted to pay. This is not surprising; if someone's offence was refusing work there was nothing to discuss. They were judged on the spot and punished until they agreed to do what was wanted. There was no need to go to the kind of court that keeps records.

Sometimes a boss wanted to avoid the prickly business of negotiating altogether, to sidestep the one time a worker could make some choices and lay down some conditions; the tailor Matthew Ruthin in Oxford demanded the services of Christine Hinksey, who had no job, and when she refused, she went to jail. But it wasn't just the wanderers, the persons without work, who had reason to be nervous. Roger Gedeney of Stainton in Lincolnshire was accused of refusing to 'serve in his trade' of thatcher in the village, and then going off 'through the countryside to get better and excessive wages'. A community was determined to hold on to its own, and not to pay him overmuch. John Bingham had a home and work as a ploughman and was doing fine as a day labourer; but his neighbours wanted to give him a contract and pay him less, accused him of refusing compulsory service for them and told the justices he was a vagrant.

The law could be twisted, abused but also defied, sometimes by the constables and justices. They did force labourers into contracts, but the contracts could be better than a man could otherwise expect. Not everyone went quietly: husbands brought back wives who had been assigned to labour for local grandees, and Richard Cross rescued Joan Busker with a show of force. On occasions, the constables themselves were hauled into court for letting people go or simply refusing to apply the law. There were signs of rebellion even from clerics; the vicar of Preston in Suffolk, in front of his startled congregation, excommunicated the constables who wanted to tell a day labourer called Digg that he had to serve various men in the village and he must not go travelling. Digg worked on, for himself. The constables got off lightly, whatever the harm to their souls; in the 1370s their colleagues in Wyberton put a vagabond in the stocks and were set upon by a small holy army, the rector, a chaplain and the rector's servant.

The greatest resistance came from the people paying the wages, who knew how hard it was to find workers and keep them. They paid the official wage, of course, for the sake of appearances, often put that amount in their accounts, but that was only the start. They also found extra payments for threshing, gifts of wheat, food and drink at mid-day, a bonus for working in the rain: all put down to general expenses but going to the workers. Employers were very aware that workers thought they had choices, the main one being to go and work elsewhere, or have a holiday when there was enough money for the year. At Knightsbridge in Lincolnshire even the carpenter who made the stocks, the punishment for anyone breaking the Statute, was paid an illegal rate: 5½d a day.

There were also new laws about spending money, especially on clothes. Preachers thought they had reason to condemn the way country people dressed: some 'wretched knave that goes to the plough and the cart, that has nothing but makes his living year by year . . . now he must have a fresh doublet of five shillings or more the price, and above a costly gown with bags hanging to his knee.' The law tried to stop the working classes buying their way out of their proper station. Likewise, in 1390, the law stopped 'any kind of artificer or labourer' from hunting 'beasts of the forest, hares or rabbits or other sport of gentlefolk'. The scaffolding of society, having rusted a bit and even fallen, was being put back; 'gentlefolk' were becoming a protected class. By English law in 1388, servants and labourers who had gone travelling were made to return to their home villages, 'to work at whatever occupation they had formerly undertaken'; an old, familiar world was being restored. A man who persisted in moving faced prison and, at least in theory, branding on his forehead: the letter 'F' for 'Falsity'.

All across Europe this kind of control followed the plague. In Sweden, after 1350, every able-bodied adult had to work unless he could show he had a fortune enough to keep him for a full year; in 1354 the Danes had the same law. They added a change that looks almost humanitarian at first sight: capital punishment was limited, as was any punishment that involved maiming. Workers were scarce and it was unhelpful to harm or kill them.

In Antwerp, the notion of deserving and undeserving poor took root, and by the sixteenth century virtue was being policed. Anyone pub crawling lost all right to help, and public sinners – like adulterers – were not eligible in the first place; to get outdoor relief, which means help without being shut up, you had to go to confession once a year and to Mass at Easter, and prove it. The nuns at St Elizabeth's Hospital refused to help anyone who was pregnant or who had a sexually transmitted disease, because helping the pregnant would just encourage sin. People with plague lay dying there alongside other patients and one magistrate reckoned 'a patient who has been in the hospital once would rather die than return there'.

In Hamburg the town physician, Johann Böckel, said plague broke out in poor areas and was spread by beggars in the street; so the vagabonds, the homeless and workless were bundled off to plague hospitals. In London, where the workhouse truly began, the poor were set to work in the 'house of labour and occupation' at Bridewell in 1552; within thirty years the house was 'a lock up for petty offenders', a 'nursery of rogues, thieves, idlers and drunken persons'. The wretched poor made tennis balls and felt and nails, and they spun wool, which inspired the Amsterdam house for inconvenient women called the Spinhuis. The poorhouse was meant to cure the poor of being poor, and make them useful; it was almost a medical idea.[18]

Plague, like the threat of terror nowadays, was the reason for supervising people's lives, examining, controlling and disciplining. The right to do so lay not with a Church that could preach against sin but with civil authorities who could act. They could adjust a society to their own tastes.

In this, the pioneer was Edinburgh, in 1498, with rules that trimmed back tavern hours, insisted that children be kept under supervision on pain of a forty-shilling fine and put a stop to fairs and markets; the point was to control movement of people and goods, so nobody could lodge an outsider without a licence, no English cloth could be imported and anybody visiting Glasgow without permission went to jail for forty days. Nobody could travel without explaining themselves, or arrive without being checked. A few years later citizens were told to report the presence of plague at once; one man was hanged for concealing a case of plague in his house. Nobody could deal in old clothes or even remove them for washing. The city was cleaned and cleaned again, the streets swept and scrubbed, all vagrants expelled on pain of branding if they ignored the order and death if they came back, because the fear of death easily justified a social cleansing. '*Timor mortis conturbat me*,' William Dunbar was writing, with reason: 'I am troubled by the fear of death.' One more gallows was built, like the one that already warned the lepers what would happen if they strayed, to show that the city was in earnest.[19]

The Scottish authorities also understood very well that plague came by sea and all the small east coast ports were at risk. Quarantine was long and careful. Ships from Gdansk in 1564 were told to land at 'quiet places', not the main ports, and they were kept there for two months. Some cargo could be kept on board, pitch and iron and timber and tar because nobody could see how they could carry infection, but flax had to be destroyed at once. The ships were half scuttled so that the tides could wash over the cargo; then it was fumigated with burning heather. In theory 'sick and foul people' who broke out of isolation were executed, although magistrates were usually lenient.[20]

In England, there were no general rules made for another century. There were only emergencies: particular ships to be searched and stopped from particular origins, ships from Lisbon in 1580, Bordeaux in 1585, sites of plague and places under suspicion. It was not enough. Plague was imported into England every time, striking first in a port, often London, sometimes Yarmouth, Hull or Plymouth: a sea-borne disease, a product of travel. From the ports, plague went town to town, market to market along the main routes inland on roads or rivers, wherever rats and fleas could hitch a ride. Fleas travelled on humans as well as on rats – people said they fell sick after sharing a bed with sick people – and perhaps sometimes mice and rats went on wild runs across the fields and infected new villages; but mostly it was the rats from the ships that settled in houses, infected other rats and infected humans.[21] So the best line of protection was a little out to sea at the mouth of rivers like the Thames, where a couple of warships and some customs officials could interrogate every ship, give out passes to any coming from clean ports and turn the others into the creek at Holehaven – 'a thing never done by us before', as Samuel Pepys writes in 1663 – to spend at least thirty days in quarantine. They were also to make sure that no passengers were 'permitted to be wafted over into England in the pacquet boats' from any Dutch port.[22]

The blockade did not stop plague returning to London. It did show seamen, forcibly, which side they were on.

Before there were solid, all-powerful nation states, choosing and changing sides was always an option; you went where you were known, where you could do the things you wanted to do and where someone would protect you from being jailed, hanged or broken on the wheel for doing them. Even bureaucrats could be flexible, if the situation allowed: Weland of Stiklaw was a canon at the cathedral of Dunkeld before he entered the service of the Scottish king in the 1280s; he was sent on a mission to bring the Maid of Norway back to her Scottish husband, the king, but then, after her sudden death in Orkney, he turned back round, crossed the sea properly and entered the service of the Norwegian king. Weland went back and forth across the sea on diplomatic missions as though his real nationality depended on the sea he sailed or the job he was doing. He certainly kept his distance from the situation in Scotland, which was under English administration, perhaps an exile on principle; and yet after the Norwegian king gave him control of the business of the earldom of Orkney, he turns up doing homage to the English king just to make sure of his rights over the other part of the earldom in Caithness. And then he may have offered safe refuge in Caithness to the family of Robert Bruce in his war against the English. And then, having started out as a foreign cleric, he turns up as a baron, ranking number five in the secular hierarchy of the Norwegian court.[23] Bureaucrats were technocrats, with skills that could travel.

So were pirates. The Flemish seaman John Crabbe is first recorded in 1305 for stealing 160 tuns of wine, burning a ship off La Rochelle and kidnapping the sailors: he was being a good Fleming since the ship came from enemy territory in Dordrecht. It proved difficult to arrest Crabbe in Flanders, mostly because he was now in Scotland;

again, as a good Fleming he was supporting the Scots against their English enemies, who were also enemies of Flanders, and making life hard for English vessels on the North Sea. In 1316 he turns up in Rouen, stealing two English ships full of victuals which were on their way to help out with the terrible famine in Flanders – the English and Flemish were making up their quarrel at the time. The same year, he intercepted a shipload of Bordeaux wine for the English market, and London demanded that Crabbe be punished. Flanders said he had already been banished as a murderer. London said he was well known in Flanders, where he lived 'whenever he wished'. They added that they knew the wine had been handed to the Count of Flanders himself.

In the war between the English and the Scots, Crabbe skippered a fleet which tried to wreck the English in the Firth of Tay, but failed. He escaped, but not for long; he was captured and handed over to the English forces, led as it happened by a soldier from Flanders. Everyone English wanted him punished; they remembered the sailors he hanged from the masts of their captured ships. He was guarded well and kept in chains. The English were marching on Berwick, where Crabbe had lived and his son still lived, so he was offered to the town on payment of a ransom. The town declined, so Crabbe the villain changed sides one more time. He knew Berwick well and he traded his information to the English: a full pardon for everything else he'd done in return for what the king called 'his good service in the siege of Berwick'. We can't know what exactly he revealed, but it was worth his life.

And now the English started to use Crabbe, the man they had meant to hang. He helped get their ships and weapons ready for action. He used his pirate's knowledge of the coasts around the North Sea to keep France out of the sea lanes between England and Flanders; for the French and English were now at war. At the battle of Sluys in 1340, he led forty ships on the English side in the hectic chase after another Flemish pirate on the French side, Spoudevisch: pirate against pirate under cover of war.[24]

Nobody thought such a man was a traitor; he was just available.

★

Ordinary sailors also had skills which could be useful to either side in a war between nations; so they could choose sides, sometimes freely, sometimes under pressure. It helped that there was a whole seaman's vocabulary that worked in Dutch or French or English. The Dutch United Provinces in 1672 issued a decree deploring the fact that 'inhabitants of these Provinces doe dayly in great numbers quitt their country to serve on foreign ships . . . to the great damage and prejudice of this state, most of them leaving their wives and children to the charge of the places where they lived'.[25] When in 1667 the Dutch captured the flagship of the British fleet, the *Royal Charles*, it was an English captain sailing for the United Provinces who accepted the surrender while an English trumpeter in his crew sounded out an English bawdy song called 'Jumping Joan' about a girl who also liked surrendering.[26]

After the Battle of Portland in 1653, the British took so many Scots and English prisoners of war off the Dutch ships that the numbers became a scandal. In 1667 when the Dutch were planning the Battle of the Medway, they had no difficulty recruiting pilots from the Thames and Medway to guide them; treason was a much better prospect than being shackled and cramped in the stinking holes where prisoners of war rotted away. What's more the British had a very casual attitude to paying actual wages to their men; they much preferred to hand out IOUs of doubtful value. After the great Dutch victory at the Medway Pepys wrote in his diary that 'in the open streets of Wapping, and up and down, the wives have cried publicly: "This comes of not paying our husbands, and now your work is undone."' His office at the Admiralty needed extra guards, 'for fear of firing of the office'; and the town felt, he said, like the time when London itself was on fire, 'nobody knowing which way to turn themselves'. 'The people that I speak with are in doubt how we shall do to secure our seamen from running over to the Dutch.'[27]

Lives were still so fluid that nationality could not keep a bureaucrat, a pirate, a sailor in his place; cross the sea, and you could change your loyalty, your paymaster or your role. Such times were coming rapidly to an end. There was a new enthusiasm for papers, and new difficulty getting them: certificates of health, exit permits, passports, visas and personal letters of recommendation in case all the other papers failed. Without papers, anyone could be anything, on any side; so without papers nobody moved. It took a certificate of health, in the plague years, to come within miles of the city of Geneva.

It could also be tricky to get away from Geneva, as Sir George Courthop found in the 1630s. He was 'searched . . . in relation to my bodily health before I was suffered to come into the town' and when he wanted to leave for Italy he found 'the city of Geneva being so visited with the Plague no other place or town will let us come into it, unless we lay in a Lazaretto forty days to air ourselves without the town'. To get away, he persuaded a secretary to the Duke of Savoy that he could add one or two Englishmen to his party and give them the cover of the duke's own papers. He slipped out of Geneva and met up with the duke's men three leagues away, and went on south. He had trouble again when landing on Malta, where the ship's captain had to go ashore 'to show his certificate that he came from a place that was not affected with the Plague'. Despite the certificate the Governor of Malta sent men to go on board the ship to check the health of the English passengers.[28]

Politics, too, made the paperwork for travel essential. The royalist Sir Richard Fanshawe was lucky: he got himself out of Commonwealth England just after Oliver Cromwell's death with a passage specially arranged to take an earl's son to school in Paris. He was free at last to contact the exiled Charles II and take up his cause, and he wanted his wife, Ann, and their three children to join him, to find a school for his oldest son alongside the son of the earl. Ann's problem was that she had money to travel at a moment's notice, but she did not have the pass for Paris, and without that she could not even board a ship at Dover. After Richard's escape, she counted as a 'malignant'.

She tried connections first, went to her cousin at the High Court of Justice, but he was not helpful; he said her husband had got out of England by a trick, and 'upon no conditions' should she try to join him. She sat down for a moment in the next room 'full sadly to consider what I should do' because she knew that 'if I were denied a passage then, they would ever after be more severe upon all occasions'. She decided she would go down to Whitehall to the office for passes and she would cheat. She went 'in as plain a way and speech as I could devise'; she left behind her maid 'who was much a finer gentlewoman than myself'. She went in to ask for her pass 'with many courtesies'.

The official asked: 'What is your husband and your name?' and she told him; she was Ann Harrison – her first son was called Harrison – and she was married to a young merchant. He raised no questions and he said the fee would be a crown; she said 'that is a great sum for me' but perhaps he could put a man, a maid and three children on the same pass. He did so, and he added that any 'malignant' would give him five pounds for such a paper.

In her lodgings, Ann took a pen to change the pass, to write over Harrison letter by letter and turn it into Fanshawe. She was sure 'none could find out the change' but she also knew she had to move at once: hire a barge to take her to Gravesend, take a coach to Dover. Even so the 'searchers' caught up with her at the port and took the pass for their records. 'I little thought,' one said, 'they would give a pass to so great a Malignant, especially in such a troublesome time as this.' At nine at night she was on board the packet boat, at eight the next morning she was ashore in Calais and the news that the English authorities were looking for her became a laughing matter.[29]

The English also worried, occasionally, about infiltration, especially by Jesuits. The traveller Fynes Moryson came back to England in Italian clothes in 1597 and was mistaken for a Roman priest, but the innkeeper was able to persuade the constable that he was, in fact, an overdressed Englishman. The French and Spanish were all too close on the other side of the Channel, which made papers essential. The diarist John Evelyn found in 1641 that crossing south from the United Provinces of Holland to the territory of Spaniards who considered the northerners still rebels could be very complicated. Evelyn had the right pass for leaving the north, issued at Rotterdam, but the commander of the border castle refused to recognize it; indeed, 'in a great fury, snatching the Paper out of my hand, he flung it scornfully under a table'. A little money sorted things out. Evelyn, meanwhile, had to hide his pass for entering Spanish territory, 'it being a matter of imprisonment, for that the States were therein treated by the names of Rebels'.[30]

Travel was always conditional; it could be blocked by war, opened by a bit of corruption. Plague helped change the conditions of movement around Europe, just as it policed laws about where anyone could live or travel inside England, what she or he was obliged to do for work and for how much pay. Such laws were not just the answer to an emergency, they persisted through the reign of Elizabeth I, into the first years of the nineteenth century. At frontiers, in the fields, plague changed the way a person's life was checked and trammelled, made it subject to official scrutiny from how you looked after your children in Edinburgh to what you were paid as a thatcher to whether you were worth helping when you were in trouble.

Plague justified the rules that kept a person in her place.

# 12.

# The city and the world

Leo of Rozmital was a Bohemian, and men from Bohemia were known for their long, long hair; so all across Europe as he travelled he was very obviously a foreigner, the one you watch, the one you try to impress. In England 'the length of our hair was a source of amazement to them,' he wrote. 'They persisted in saying that it was stuck on with tar.'

He set out in 1465 from Pilsen in what is now the Czech Republic with a mission: to persuade someone to persuade the Pope that his Catholic sister could marry a Hussite, a heretic who believed in taking wine as well as bread at communion. He travelled with some forty people, some of them grand, one jester, one lute-player and a cart for luggage and supplies, across German territory to Flanders and then by sea to England. It was a remarkable journey: one moment dancing with nuns, the next out swimming in a ship with horses.

The nuns belonged to 'a stately nunnery' at Neuss on the Rhine and they were 'the most beautiful nuns I have ever seen', Leo wrote. Nunneries often took the unmarried and sometimes the unmarriageable daughters of noble families and kept them safe but few had the rule of Neuss: that the women 'may leave the nunnery to get married'. To improve their social chances, 'they receive no-one . . . who is not of noble birth'. Leo's grand companions were made welcome and the mother superior gave a dance: 'the nuns were very finely dressed and knew all the best dances . . . each one had her own page who waited on and preceded her.'

Even so, Leo rode on to Brussels, to the great show that was the

Duchy of Burgundy. Everything was enormous there, everything was magnificent, at least as far as the eye could see; and the Burgundians were skilled at making sure how far you saw. At dinner, there were eight dishes at a time. The zoological garden was 'of vast proportions' with 'all manner of birds and animals which seemed strange to us'. He saw 'as fine pictures as can be found anywhere'. The keeper of the duke's jewels 'told us that his lord had so many jewels that he had not seen them all in many years and indeed did not know where they were'.

This spectacle had turned the flimsy duchy into the mentor, the coach of a continent: the true inventor of 'soft' power. The tactic was necessary. In 1369 the Count of Flanders had married his daughter Margaret to the Duke of Burgundy, first peer of France from the ruling house of Valois: the traditional kind of *Realpolitik* that dynasties like to work out in bed. The wedding feast was in Ghent in Flanders, the wine was a good Beaune from Burgundy. When everyone sobered up, the prospects were rather meagre since the economy of Flanders depended largely on trade with the wool merchants of England, and England happened to be at war with Valois France. The count had his family loyalties, but that did not stop him making a practical peace with England, and playing the two powers against each other. It was a game he knew very well, since his Flanders was a patchwork of quarrelsome towns and an ambitious count had to manage his subjects as much as rule them.

So Count Louis expanded his territory, marriage by marriage, deal by deal. His daughter Margaret was named heir apparent to Brabant, next door to Flanders in what is now Belgium and a short way north; a little later, in 1404, Flanders effectively annexed Brabant, which was in dire need of military help. In 1428 Philip the Good of Burgundy became lord of Holland and Zeeland to the north, in what is now the Netherlands. In 1430 he had wonderful luck when the Duke of Brabant died, so conveniently that many people thought Philip must have murdered him, and he inherited Brabant. He now had to worry about how to administer all this and make a state of it. The towns around him remained as obstinate as ever, Burgundy itself and its wines were becoming just a second thought on the other side of

France, and there was always the possibility of bloody revolt in the north; and yet Philippe de Commynes, diplomat and sometime historian, reckoned that the duchy was very like 'the promised land'.

To succeed the dukes of Burgundy had to be noticed across Europe, to be able to influence courts on both sides of long wars and to dazzle their own people. Politics had become what it remains: a show.

Burgundy made itself the fashion all around Europe. Go to Spain, and Queen Isabella's tournaments were organized by a Netherlander, as were her chapel music, her funeral chapel and most of her collection of pictures. The Sforzas of Milan needed good painters and decided to look beyond the Alps for them; they sent the painter Zanetto Bugatto to Brussels to study with the master Rogier van der Weyden because although he could paint, he could not paint in the Northern, Netherlandish manner. Zanetto was rapidly in trouble, probably for drink; the Milanese ambassador reported he had been made to promise 'not to drink wine during the year'.[1] Medicis and Sforzas bought Netherlandish pictures and tapestries for their Northern way of seeing the world. As for wooden altarpieces, those went out to Poland, Germany, all of Scandinavia, to Portugal, Spain, Italy, France and England; they were exports so important that guildsmen were allowed to break the general curfew and work at night if 'a sale or a contract has been made with a merchant whose ship is ready to sail'.

The world knew the skyline of Bruges because it was in the background of the paintings in their churches, halls and mansions. There is a Netherlandish townscape behind one Madonna by Botticelli. A Leonardo landscape echoes the famous rocks in Jan van Eyck's painting of St Francis receiving the stigmata. Assorted other Italian masters found it useful to adopt van Eyck's real, atmospheric landscapes, which stretched to the horizon behind his foreground figures.[2] Jan van Eyck, like Rubens after him, could be sent on diplomatic missions because he was a very famous man, and therefore a man that people would want to know.

Burgundy had the knack of showing people themselves as they wanted to be seen. The painter Hans Memling made a triptych for Sir

John Donne of Kidwelly and his wife, gentry in the service of the House of York in England, and he painted his patrons into the picture as usual. Elizabeth Donne is dressed in purple and ermine, which she probably never wore, and Memling painted her clothes before he ever saw her because her face had to be redrawn rather thinner than he first imagined; so status came before the individual face. She holds a lovely Book of Hours, a fine illuminated manuscript, to show she knows the fashionable form of piety; psalters were no longer the thing. Donne himself is shown in a black mantle with fur, hung about with gold chains in the sun-and-rose pattern of the House of York: we can see he is an intimate of the king. The Donnes are massed so close to the Virgin Mary at the heart of the picture you could imagine they were used to dining with her.[3]

These things were manufactured – painters imitating and borrowing and reworking other painters' work – by industries that produced the most lovely and vivid things. The gold and silver metalwork from Burgundy was famous, and so were the tapestries, some on classic themes like the Trojan War; as had been the music of the *ars nova*, a kind of polyphony which had a special clarity because it respected the rhythm of the words being sung. Netherlandish teachers were hired for Italian choir schools. Northern boys were in great demand to sing in Italian chapels because they were better trained and had more experience; north of the Alps, they sang much more music at many more services. The papal chapel at Avignon hired them, and paid them from the Pope's prebends, his cut of cathedral income in the North.[4]

All this was the official, splendid version, but the court itself could be rough. It was usual to get guests drunk, Leo found. There was a great bed kept for them in the palace at Breda, and 'if guests could not stand they were thrown onto it'. It was also usual for quite grand persons to wrestle in their tunic and hose, their 'underclothes'; 'it is no shame to wrestle thus clad, even though multitudes of matrons and maidens be present'.

When it was needed, when it was useful, this court understood theatre perfectly. Leo saw Charles the Bold, the duke's son, return from Paris. The guilds and the councillors greeted him in the streets of Brussels with lighted candles, 'an uninterrupted line of lights through the whole town', and with 'stately tableaux'.[5] Often there was a play, a masque, an opera, with the crowds cheering and also heckling. A century later, when Calvinists ruled Antwerp for a while after 1577, they went on staging civic processions as a substitute for the religious ones that they banned. By 1583, these performances of power were so usual they made nobody suspicious. The corporation of Antwerp footed the bill for the French Duke of Anjou to make a 'Joyous Entry' into the town, a civic and not a courtly occasion. They paid for a gold canopy to protect the duke, the white horse he rode, his cap and his robes, and wine for the patricians who carried the canopy; they built an arch of triumph with torches, flags, inscriptions and coats of arms.[6] They also slammed the gates shut and slaughtered Anjou's army, and the duke was lucky to escape with his life; it was all, after all, a show.

It was rather like Burgundy itself, whose land was largely man-made, dependent on constant work and artifice to keep it from going under water. Gilles le Bouvier, herald and chronicler, was in Bruges in 1417 with the new Dauphin of France and he reported that Flanders was 'a rich land with goods that come by sea from every Christian nation, heavily peopled and they make much woollen cloth and they have two very good towns, Ghent and Bruges'. He found the people honest, but rebellious. But he added: 'The country itself is a poor country . . . because it is all water and sand.' He saw the dikes along the coast of Holland and he reckoned 'if these dikes ever broke, all the land would be in the sea and drowned for ever and ever'.[7]

Within that show, the riches were dazzling; as the Spaniard Pero Tafur found when he visited in the 1430s. 'I saw there oranges and lemons from Castille which seemed only just to have been gathered from the trees,' he wrote, 'and wine from Greece as abundant as in that country. I saw also confections and spices from Alexandria and all the Levant, just as if one were there; furs from the Black Sea . . . all Italy with its brocades, silks and armour. There is no part of the world whose products are not found there of their best.' Bruges was 'one of the greatest markets of the world', ships were carried in and out by the tide 'to save the cost and bother of beasts' to pull them and 'they say that at times the number of ships sailing from the harbour at Bruges exceeds seven hundred a day'. At the great Antwerp fairs 'anyone desiring to see all Christendom or the greater part of it assembled in one place can do so here'.

And yet: 'there was a great famine in the year of my visit'.[8]

Outsiders noticed the huge difference between the dockside economy and the inland nation. The chronicler Froissart said Flanders had only cloth to offer in return for the products of seventeen nations (which rather missed the point of being merchants and living off the market). An English pamphlet sniffed that Flanders was 'just a market for other countries' and dependent on wool, naturally from England. The duchy had to buy in food and quite often could not feed itself, even though there was fine and profitable business passing through its ports: it lived by business.

In Bruges in the thirteenth century there was wool and cloth that came from England with lead, leather, coal and cheese; fish came from the north, including the dried salmon the Scots sold alongside their lard; there were furs from Russia, ermine and sable from Bulgaria, gold from Poland; there was Rhine wine; there were wood, grains, iron, almonds, goatskins, saffron, rice; there were wax and anis, copper and figs, cumin and mercury; dates and sugar from the North of Africa, cotton from Armenia, silk from Tartary.[9] Spring fleets brought wine and olive oil, figs and grapes from Portugal. Making jewels from amber and from jet, some from the North Sea coast and some from the Baltic, was a speciality. Later the Portuguese connection brought spices there from the East and the East Indies for buyers from the European heartlands.

Everything passed through Flanders and somebody took a cut. Italian bankers set up offices alongside the Hansa Kontor. When Philip the Good made his triumphal entrance into Bruges in 1440, there were 150 Italian merchants in the grand parade, 136 Hanseatics, 48 from Castille, men from Scotland, Catalonia, Portugal.[10] They rode in their parade clothes by torchlight: they saw the point of playing their part in the great show of power.

There were kings as well as merchants. Edward IV was there in exile from England for a year. So was Mulay Hassan, the deposed

Bey of Tunis, who came to ask the Emperor's protection. He was painted by the local painter Vermeyen, he went hunting the forest with the Duke of Taxis, both of them in splendid Arab robes; he disconcerted his hosts by eating very expensive peacock and pheasant, taking aubergines as a sauce for his meat and insisting on being blindfolded to listen to music. He was the start of an Antwerp tradition of painting exotic people in exotic clothes, making exiles useful; a hundred years later, the ex-bey was still the model for one of Rubens's Magi visiting Christ.[11]

The kings came for safety, for the relative ease of being on territory that was French but not in Paris, and later Hapsburg and imperial but not in Spain. Being in exile, however brief, they understood how a ruler's position could be weak, and they learned what show it took to stay in power. They watched the rulers of Burgundy bluff, as states were learning to bluff; the dukes played to an audience of citizens, subjects and the world. Tafur said: 'nothing could surpass in majesty the persons of the Duke and Duchess and the state in which they live, which is the most splendid I have ever seen'. The Duchess had two hundred maids of honour, all of them all the time, so he heard.

He arrived just as the duke put down a serious rebellion. He wrote: 'I myself saw many high gallows around Bruges.'[12]

The court lived with all kinds of glory, as the diplomat Prospero da Camogli told the Duke of Milan: he complained about the 'mad rush of dishes' at dinner every day, not to mention the habit of leaving the silver on the table at the end of each course just to show the duke owned more and had 'spare'. He was hugely impressed by the ceremonies of the Order of the Golden Fleece, the scarlet hoods when scarlet was costly, a piece of the True Cross, and a fleur-de-lys crusted in jewels, and 'of singers, heralds and such like there was an infinite number'. The banqueting hall was hung with cloth of gold and there were four unicorn horns 'like organ pipes' among the silver. Anyone would want to join, and the Burgundians knew it; the Order was a diplomatic instrument to seal their reputation as a knightly finishing school, the place to learn war, chivalry and how to behave at court. It was imitated in France and Denmark, Scotland and Germany, even among the Renaissance aristocrats of Italy.

Yet Prospero had to apologize a month later that 'I have not sent you the names of the lords and knights of the Order because the Duke of Burgundy's household is so lacking in organization that not a secretary in it has been able to give me the names.' Weeks later, he was judgemental: he wrote of the 'inept administration of the Duke of Burgundy, who is ruled by other men'.[13]

The show was brilliant and also insubstantial. There was a solid-looking throne of gold, hugely impressive unless you realized it was just gilt on a wooden frame. Diplomats, visitors, were constantly reminded of what was in the treasury; Gabriel Tetzel from Bohemia was told there was a 'hundred thousand pound weight of beaten gold and silver' but he never got to see or count it. Having gold meant you could afford to go to war; it was a kind of deterrent. It also meant you could act like a king. At dinner the duke was served by men riding a two-headed horse, drank aromatic wine from the breasts of a naked girl who was guarded by a live lion, was entertained by an elephant who begged: all illusions.

The Burgundian duke, Charles the Bold, rode into Dijon in January 1474 wearing armour covered with rubies, diamonds, huge pearls. Three years later he died in just such gaudy armour trying to take back the French town of Nancy in the Lorraine. His body was found in the snow, but all the armour was gone, he had been stripped naked and he was so badly mauled that his own doctor took days to identify him by the one remaining sign: a fistula in the groin. The show failed him.

Inside three years the Hapsburgs inherited Flanders by marriage and the Flemish were in full revolt against their new rulers: a rehearsal, in a way, for the final break a century later. The first revolt went on for fifteen years, the second started a relentless eighty-year war because it was scaffolded with the religious divide between Calvinist and Catholic and not just grievances over tax and local privileges; both revolts were against a state so weak that the show had to go on even in times of civil war. Giovanni Botero in the 1580s understood very well: 'There was not a country throughout all Europe neither more rich nor more indebted.'[14]

This was a mirror world, one we know: politics as theatre, power as a show. If the machinery became visible at times, that only made it clear that some people still wanted to believe.

Self-made men, senior bureaucrats, understood this very well. Peter Bladelin was the duke's moneyman and treasurer of the Order of the Golden Fleece and once he had become 'rich beyond measure' he was also master of the court, producer of its constant pageantry. He was allowed to use the money he guarded for his own personal investments, and he bought land, assembling a site parcel by parcel like any modern property developer. Nobody built whole towns any more because nobody was a feudal lord or an abbot who must be obeyed, and besides there were towns growing everywhere by themselves. But Bladelin did build a town, called Middelburg, to show that he was as good as any lord or abbot before him.

The town was as neatly organized as a model: a mill, a hospital, a church with a priest, two chaplains and six canons, areas for living, areas for working and naturally a town hall to administer everything because Bladelin was true to his trade. He brought in coppersmiths to work there, and tapestry weavers, the kind of artisans who suggested taste and sophistication; he built a canal to take their products out by water to Ghent and Bruges; he used his political position to make sure the copper could be sold in England and that the duke ordered tapestries when he happened to be staying.

He also built a castle: a stone fanfare, the loudest possible statement that Peter Bladelin was 'lord of Middelburg in Flanders', as his will said, not just a successful bureaucrat and certainly not some ambitious climber from Bruges. The spine of his town was the road from Bruges to Aardenburg, which went through the town and led directly to the castle walls; to go on to Bruges you had to turn sharp left. Everything inside the town led to the castle, and to the longest wall of the whole building, built out to impress. Anyone passing would see the moat which surrounded the wall of Middelburg and inside it the moat around the castle: the town separate from the ordinary countryside, the castle apart from the town in its own landscape of water. Ride in through the castle gates, if you were invited, if you were the right sort of person, and you went through a long high corridor to a bridge across the moat to Bladelin's own quarters, which had a drawbridge, a gatehouse, three massive round towers and two smaller ones for the stairs. They made a statement about Bladelin's knightly skills and warrior tendencies, but they faced the wrong way; an enemy would not see them, only friends.

The castle's next owner was another high civil servant, executed by the townspeople in 1477; he had looked after the interests of Duke Charles the Bold quite dangerously well. When the northern provinces rebelled and war moved back and forth, town by town, the castle stood in the way. It was knocked into ruins thirty years after it was built, because the towers were no kind of serious defence. By 1607 it was said to be 'a ruin . . . desolated and destroyed . . . ready to be totally dismantled'. It was no more durable than a trick on the stage.[15]

Leo left Burgundy and set sail from Calais for England, on a ship he shared with thirty-six horses. 'When we left harbour and reached the open sea the ship sprang a great leak and the water poured in so that the horses stood in water up to their bellies. Then our Lord God sent us good luck. The wind veered so that we had a good breeze. But if the wind had not changed, we should all have been drowned.' They found another ship, but this time it lay offshore and they had to take a small rowing boat to reach it; and again they almost drowned. 'My lord and his other attendants,' Leo said, 'were so distressed by the waves that they lay on the ship as if they had been dead.'

He found London 'a powerful and busy city, carrying on a great trade with all countries', and he was properly impressed by the English court. The king was announced with a choir, with trumpeters, pipers, players of string instruments. The queen sat alone at table 'on a costly golden chair' and her sister stayed on her knees until her majesty had drunk water; other noblewomen knelt silently all the time the queen was eating, which could be as much as three hours. Leo noticed the women's dress because they had 'long trains. In no other country have I seen such long ones.'[16]

It should have been familiar; it was one more imitation of Burgundy. Olivier de la Marche, who was master of ceremonies at the Burgundian court, was a kind of consultant to the English king Edward IV. He wrote him a detailed description of how things were done in Brussels, which served as the manual for the English court: how to eat, when to bow. The show of how to be king became even more important when the Tudor Henry VII took the throne of England in 1485. He had a weak hold on power and he had to act out being exceptionally powerful. He chose to build his palace at Richmond as much as possible like the Prinsenhof at Bruges with its covered walkways and its gardens with tennis courts, and he asked 'merchants of Flanders' to find the tapestries, jewels and stained glass that would make it officially regal.[17]

Show and debt and bluff: that, not Hobbes or Machiavelli, may be the true start of a modern politics.

Albrecht Dürer came to the Low Countries in 1520, and he kept a journal, which reads like an account book; so we know he spent two sous on 'the red colour you find at Antwerp in blocks newly cooked', that he bought varnish and colour in Bruges, where a single red crayon cost him a sou, that he spent three pounds on the grey-blue 'colour of lead' in Antwerp. He traded a batch of engravings that he said were worth ten ducats for a single ounce of ultramarine, the mineral compound out of Afghanistan that contains the blue of lapis lazuli,[18] and which probably came by way of Venice to the great Northern shop of Antwerp.

The town had artists because it had everything the painter needed: the docks bringing green verdigris from Montpellier, but also the dyes for cloth that made colours for paint as well, blue woad, red brazilwood or madder. Cochineal came from the New World on Spanish boats, landed at Antwerp and was sold on to Italy. There were local dealers prepared for the stink of making vermilion, the colour that 'makes all the flesh parts glow', as Karel van Mander wrote in his guidebook to the painters of the time; it was made from the sulphur and mercury mined in Germany, treated in Antwerp and then sold back by way of Cologne, on one occasion in 1543 in a load of four hundred pounds of colour on a single waggon. Like Venice, but nowhere else, Antwerp had at least four dealers in the 1560s who sold only colours; and the leaseholder of the galleries on top of the New Bourse, Bartholomeus de Momper, registered as an art dealer with the guild of St Luke but also found it worth while to enrol as a dealer in colours with the mercers' guild.[19]

Works from Flanders had a reputation for life, light, vividness, for a mastery of the new-fangled painting in oils, for clever attention to the real world. Florentines were rude about foreign artists – 'their brains are in their hands,' Anton Francesco Doni wrote – but they went on buying Netherlandish paintings from the North with enthusiasm.[20] They bought work on panels, the masterpieces we still know, but they also bought paintings on cloth, the kind that can be 'wrapped around a rod' for easy transport. Antwerp sent these out everywhere, dozens of them to England and once a 'barrelful'. They sold perhaps 2,500 in the course of fifty years.[21]

There were holy subjects, peacocks, carnival scenes, warnings against slander and just possibly some proto-porn: 'four women and three men who are giving each other pleasure'. These cloths could be very large, which suited Florentine tastes: Lorenzo Strossi sent down from Bruges three cloths for his dealer mother to sell in Florence, but she reckoned she could only get three florins each for the peacock and the three Magi because the pictures were small. She liked them, she even kept one, but the market wanted scale: something that looked rather like a fresco but was portable.

The rooms of the Medici were wrapped in Flemish taste. The family collected at least forty-two cloth paintings from the North, a third of their whole collection; some were in their city palace, and even more were spread around their country houses. Medici cousins hung a cloth Moses on the same chimney as Botticelli's *Primavera*.[22] The Florentine Raffaello Borghini sang the praises of Jan van der Straet from Bruges, who went to Italy 'hearing talk of the excellence of Italian painters', met in Venice one of the Flemish craftsmen making tapestry for the Grand Duke Cosimo and began a career making the cartoons for huge woven pictures: vivid hunts for a seethe of wild cats or a family of boar snouting out of a cornfield or a pack of sinisterly attentive wolves; some classical subjects, Jason and Medea waiting to sail away in a high-prowed ship that bucks in the water like a powerful horse, Time with a wicked sickle holding captive the goddess of wisdom and virtue because death will cut the brightest life short; a biblical theme, Samuel anointing King David as his heir but of course meaning to endorse Grand Duke Cosimo. The pictures are as ornate as some baroque carving, but they are criss-crossed with energy, human and lively, just as Borghini promised: 'with his many works he has much enriched the art of drawing men, animals, landscapes and views, with fresh and lovely invention'.[23]

The works were made by artisans in guilds, plain craftsmen, yet there were already famous persons whose styles could be discussed, whose genius was assumed. Jan van Eyck 'has been judged the prince of the painters of our time', the Naples humanist Bartholomeus Facius wrote; 'he is thought . . . to have discovered many things about the properties of colours recorded by the ancients.'[24] The legend as Vasari wrote it in his *Lives of the Artists* is even more striking: Van Eyck invented oil painting.

'Realizing the imperfection of tempera colours,' Raffaello Borghini said, 'after many experiments he discovered that mixing colours with the oil of walnuts or linseed gave a very strong tempera which, when it dried, not only had no fear of water but also gave life and lustre without varnish.'[25] Lodovico Guicciardini, who was a merchant from Florence living in Antwerp, called van Eyck 'the first inventor of the art of mixing colours in oil . . . a glorious and highly important invention, for it renders the colours eternal, nor is there any reason to suppose that it had ever been known before'.[26] His eighteenth-century translator, anonymous but wise, suspected that painting in oils was an old idea from Byzantium, but still Vasari's legend lives, alongside the idea that it was only by studying Italians, the ancient ones and Michelangelo and Raphael, that Northern painters could hope to 'escape the prison of their dry, archaic, even barbarous manner and become modern'.[27] Neither one is quite true.

For a start, there is a twelfth-century text all about using pressed oil to bind colours: Theophilus Presbyter's *Schedula diversarum artium*. Vasari says van Eyck was the one who taught Antonello da Messina how to paint in oils; Pietro Summonte, writing from Naples, says it was a Naples master called Colantonio who had wanted to move to

Flanders because he 'looked to the work of Flemish painters' but was kept at home by a king with the skill to 'show him . . . how to mix and use these colours'.[28] The point is that Italian painters looked at the life and brightness, the brilliance and the shadows, of the Flemish masters, and they were hugely impressed. They saw faces that could be alive, which suggested a new kind of portrait, and landscapes of a kind they had never yet tried, which could be used as details in their own paintings. *Mona Lisa* became imaginable, a woman whose name we still want to know in front of a landscape we still try to read. The Italians learned from the North in the way the Flemish went down to Rome to learn.

They also imitated particular painters, and recognized painting as something more than a craft which requires simply practice. They honoured the painter Hugo van der Goes by imitating the great altarpiece he painted for the Portinaris in Florence, commissioned by the head of the Medici bank in Bruges: the shepherds pressing in on each other to see the vulnerable baby on the ground, watched by a still, modest Virgin all in dark blue. Before the Virgin there are flowers: the usual lilies, but also black aquilegia, the flower of the Holy Ghost and the flower whose French name, *ancolie*, sounds like melancholy. Van der Goes had finished the painting just before he went into the monastery at Windesheim as a *conversus*, a plain craftsman and not a learnèd man. He was acknowledged as a great painter and he was very nearly mad.

Gaspar Ofhuys was Prior of Windesheim and also Master of the Sick, and he told the story thirty years later. 'He kept repeating that he was damned . . . and because of this, he even tried to do himself bodily harm and to kill himself – had he not been forcibly restrained with the help of bystanders.' Gaspar thought he was suffering like King David and might recover to the sound of music, but he did not improve; 'rather, he declared that he was a son of perdition, uttering strange things'. He became 'exceedingly anxious about how he would carry out the works he was supposed to paint'. He drank with his guests and got worse. The idea grew that somehow he must have hurt something in his brain, 'a very small slender vein that nourishes the power of imagination and fantasy'; his individual state, his individual fantasy, had somehow gone wrong.[29] In other words, he thought he had a talent, that it was personal and that it had been ruined; and the people around him agreed.

Most pictures sold in Antwerp did not need a genius as much as a steady hand, and a print or a drawing blacked on the back to trace out the outlines that the artist would then fill. There were 'patterns' for paintings, drawings that were pricked with tiny holes along the outlines; when they were put against wood or cloth, and blacked, a delicate outline showed through. Sometimes a painter took one of the many prints being published, traced it onto wood and invented colours for it; sometimes there was no painted original at all, just the pattern. The patterns were assets; Ambrosius Benson, a lacklustre Italian marooned in Flanders, went to court to get back the patterns in a chest he had left behind.

Copying was the business: to give people what they wanted, at a price they could pay. Art was no longer something that great persons commissioned for great churches in order to save their souls. Guicciardini listed among the excellent artists of Flanders 'Peter Brugel of Breda, a sedulous imitator of the fancies of Jerome Bosch whence he is commonly called the second Jerome Bosch.' This is Pieter Brueghel the Younger, who also turned out versions of the originals by his more famous father Pieter, copies for people who could never find or afford the originals. He was five when his father died, and he may never have seen his father's work, but he was taught to paint by his grandmother and he had access to the 'patterns' for his father's pictures, so he signed his pictures 'Bruegel/Brueghel/Brueghel'. He did copy Bosch but he did not do what forgers do: he did not smoke the canvas to make it look old. He was reproducing, not faking.

When the Valois Duke of Burgundy Charles the Bold was killed, and the Hapsburgs came riding into Flanders, the court commissioned far fewer paintings; genius had a hard time. Middle-class commissions were everything, and a line of product that could be made ready for each year's trade fair. The middle classes liked to pray at home and they bought 'contemplation pieces', holy pictures on a domestic scale, and they bought them on the open market from painters they never met. The *Madonna of Cambrai*, which was supposed to be painted by

St Luke himself although it looks suspiciously like a late copy of a Byzantine icon, was copied over and over again: three at a time for some great persons, and in dozens by the Cathedral of Cambrai, which sold them to pilgrims. Even Jan van Eyck turned out a couple of versions at a time; he did that for the merchant Anselmus Adornes, two virtually identical pictures of St Francis.[30]

Conspicuous consumption, with an unfamiliar holy accent, had already reached the middle classes, who in the North would make possible all the domestic glories of the Dutch golden age. So had the idea of genius, which they knew very well was something quite different.

Ten in the morning and the men are crowding into the Bourse: into a great Gothic quadrangle in the middle of Antwerp, arcades all around and shops upstairs, two great bell towers like a castle, shut in by streets of other people's houses but open to the business of the known world. It opened in the 1530s as a kind of engine for the town.

The men have letters that give the bearer a claim on money left at some fair in Spain or a warehouse in Cologne, credits or debts: the kind of money that crosses borders. They're here to trade them. Each trader needs to find a broker, maybe Spinola from Genoa or Fontoba from Spain, who knows the various exchange rates for the day; the big trading firms know them already, having fixed them. The movement of goods from as far away as Afghanistan or Africa depends on their deals.

Watch them and you watch the kind of market that will come to rule our lives: a market you play by handling paper rather than anything solid like spices, amber, cloth or fish. A man like Gaspar Ducci, who started with a firm from Lucca, could make money by arranging loans for the broke Emperor in return for the right to collect taxes. He could also make bets on the difference between prices and the cost of money in different markets, between Antwerp and Lyons, say, and take a profit. Theologians had once said that that kind of expertise could justify a profit when trading goods, a merchant doing real work, but Ducci dispensed with the goods altogether and took a profit just on the paper differences. He speculated.[31]

Merchants turned up at the Bourse every day because absence was taken as proof you were bankrupt. A trader who was still in business would have to have the day's information, to see what was changing and what might change next. Letters were unreliable; merchants always sent a copy of their last letter with a new letter, and sometimes sent three copies by different routes.[32] Information was talk and talk was raucous. In Amsterdam, before there was an Exchange, the traders met on a narrow street of shops called Warmoesstraat, or on the New Bridge, or in churches when the weather was foul. Neighbours complained about the racket coming from the churches.

The Bourse, the Exchange, was born in Bruges, in a town with merchants from everywhere, who needed a place to meet and do business, to deal information, paper, goods. They often met outside the hostel that belonged to the Van der Buerse family, and when the big trading powers, Venice, Florence and Genoa, built their headquarters around the Buerse square the talk began in earnest and the name Buerse and Bourse stuck to every exchange. The city added a bailiff to stand watch and keep order. The pattern was set: an open space with at least one portico for shelter against the weather, a narrow entrance with security, a semi-public square in the middle of the city.[33] There had to be room for goods to be shown. There had to be dry zones for all the paper.

The first exchange in Antwerp was a fine private house, a courtyard with arcades on three sides all sculptured and trefoiled like some Victorian railway station. More merchants came to town, there were more deals and more paper to be dealt, so the city planned a new and showy Bourse in 1531. They found an unbuilt parcel of land, and put the Bourse in the middle of it all, enclosed by streets and houses: 'an ornament for God and city' with a couple of towers to show where it was, but not a palace. It was a beautiful, shut-in courtyard, galleries all around, an upper floor with shops for art and luxuries. It was a public square, which the Florentine merchant Ludovico Guicciardini reckoned the 'most decorous' square in Antwerp. It would be the model for the Royal Exchange in London, and for the Beurs in Amsterdam, not to mention the exchanges in towns like Lille: the kind of space that every city wanted.[34]

In Antwerp if you wanted to trade goods – we'd say 'commodities' – you went to the English Bourse, which was the place on Wolstraat and Hofstraat where the English met customers to organize the sale of their wool. Their market was a futures market; they sold wool that had not yet been delivered for prices they had to predict. Anything even less solid was traded in the palatial new Bourse.

Climb the stairs there and you could buy a picture; Barbara Alleyns would sell you one of the paintings stacked around while her husband ran his workshop to paint more. There were already art dealers, and there are a good number of women among them, sometimes selling the work of women artists.[35] You could lend money, lots of money, to the Hapsburgs if you were so minded. You could insure your life, or someone else's; if you got paid, the insurer had seven years to try to prove the person wasn't dead after all. You could insure a ship to voyage as far as the Indies, East or West, almost anywhere, which had more to do with the flexibility of the Bourse than the traffic coming through the Antwerp docks. Antwerp brokers used insurance mostly as a speculation, a way to profit from trade without actually buying, selling or shipping. They liked the profit so well they blocked schemes to send fleets out with official naval protection, which would have spoiled the game.

To get prices right, traders had to know about the supply of solid, physical money, how much silver was flowing up from Spain, if the land route was open across France for couriers to pass with safe conducts, or if the metal would have to come by the rarer and riskier sea route. Money was a commodity, too, like grain or spices: the amount available changed its price. The good coins, solid silver, inevitably went abroad to do business, bad coins that were clipped or worn out stayed at home. Bad money was always driving out good.[36]

Besides what you knew, how you were known was all important. Even when the law allowed bad behaviour, like slow payment, a man lost all his standing if he made a fuss about paying a letter of credit. It 'looked bad'.[37] Everyone had to trust people he didn't know, from outside his family or even his nation; people of all nationalities were working together because trade required so many languages. Smaller firms were always going bust, so it was alarming if a bankrupt started to hide what he owned; the de la Peña brothers were notorious because Gaspar got his workers to pile the contents of his warehouse on a ship bound for Spain, so the Antwerp courts could not touch them, and his brother Diego sat down South to handle everything that was left to the firm.

It was harder and harder to know who could be trusted, and it would get worse.

Nobody went home after Vespers. The crowd stayed around the Cathedral of Our Lady. The city guard came to move them on, but more and more people kept arriving and standing and waiting. Most of them wanted to see something break the tension in the city like rain does in a thunderstorm. Some of them wanted to make something happen. They carried axes, heavy hammers, ropes and ladders, pulleys and levers.

20 August 1566, in Antwerp. Two days before, the statue of the Virgin Mary was booed in the streets and pelted with rubbish, but the statue got back safely to the cathedral. One day before, a crowd had come to jeer at the statue as it stood in its proper place. On 20 August things got worse, as everyone expected.[38]

A few street girls clambered onto the altars and brought down wax tapers, which they lit so everyone could see. The men went to work. They found all the painted images, wood or canvas, and tore them down from the walls and cut them up. They hooked down the statues and images, saints and martyrs slammed on the floor and cracked open. They broke the bright painted glass in the windows. First there was the dry sound of breaking glass, incident by incident, and then a sound like some great factory: axe-blows and hammering. Every image was brought as close to dust as the men could manage.

After the cathedral they moved on, chapel after chapel, thirty churches in all before dawn. The crowd ran howling alongside through the streets, torches flaring. They broke into sacristies and tried on the heavy silk robes of the priests, downed wine from gold chalices, burned missals and shined their shoes with holy oil. They burned monastery libraries and broached the barrels in the cellars; monks and nuns went scrambling in panic.

At the end of the night nobody was hurt. Nothing was stolen. A few works of art did survive. But everything else was broken, not just the magnificence of the cathedral but the possibility of any civic peace between factions. No harm was done to town halls, so the issue was not taxes, nor to any official or military building, so the point of the mob's fury was not the ruling Hapsburgs. A war was starting, and for the next eighty years the frontier ran between Calvinist and Catholic, Dutch and Spanish, in the Netherlands.

It was a campaign of sieges which made whole cities change sides one year and then change back the next, going hungry in the meantime: a war of attrition broken by moments of horror. Antwerp suffered in a dozen ways, its markets disrupted, its trust spoiled, its stock of silver exhausted by 1575 by taxes raised to pay for the war. The system in the Bourse was ruined. Exchange rates went wild. City creditors went bust. Everyone was paid late, if at all, and everyone borrowed what he could at higher and higher rates of interest. Nobody could assume the good credit or even the good intentions of the other men at the Bourse; everyone had to pay attention all the time to individual merchants and the amounts they wanted to trade. The market was just that bit more abstract, more dependent on a subtle kind of information: more minute by minute, more modern.

There was worse. The royal finances were frozen shut and the army went unpaid. The starving veterans of that army turned on their paymasters. They came into Antwerp for three long days of killing, stealing, raping, burning down some six hundred houses and the glorious new Town Hall with all its archives. They also demanded ransom from the merchants left in the city, unsettling the few English merchants left there by using 'naked swords and daggers' to get money from the head of the English House, the headquarters of the Merchant Adventurers; naturally, being an Antwerp veteran himself, he paid partly in promissory bills rather than cash.[39] The Bourse, that elegant palace for playing with money, insurance, shares, was invaded by soldiers dressed in velvet and satin stolen from merchant wardrobes who set out tables to play their own games with dice.

Merchants hate to be parodied almost more than they hate to be threatened or robbed; many left. They went north to get away from the warzone, and they were right to do so since it would be almost twenty years before Antwerp began to recover,[40] and in the meantime even the river worked against them, filling with silt. There were blockades by the Dutch, one more siege by the Spanish, a purge of all Calvinist citizens, who had to get out at once. Those refugees treasured their anger against the Spanish, against a regime that defined them by denomination, and they defined themselves by anti-Catholic feeling: Protestant and right.

They took with them a new and strong idea of what they needed to know to do business: information as the richest commodity of all. They carried ideas about deals, about taking shares in a ship or an insurance, about arbitrage between markets, about how paper could be almost more valuable than freight, and how the world could be written down, bought and sold. They knew how to deal in the future because the Antwerp wool trade had instant deals on future supplies even before the same kind of futures market opened in Amsterdam (where it balanced the value of fish going north with the likely value of grain being shipped south from the Baltic). They carried to the Protestant north most of the equipment needed for what we would come to know, after a while, as capitalism.

This great shaking of markets confused matters for centuries, made capitalism seem somehow Protestant by nature. Yet the Antwerp markets spoke Italian, were driven by the need to raise money for a Spanish overlord, did business constantly with the Portuguese and every other Catholic power. Capitalism came out of circumstances long before the divide over theology complicated the picture.

Catholics cannot try to look all moral and innocent. Protestants need not be unduly proud. As trade expanded and more money had to be found for bigger ships and bigger loads, as ambition crashed through frontiers, capitalism was happening anyway. It depended on, and it brought along, a world expressed in numbers, not images or legends or metaphors, in which mathematics had the power to change reality; and an industry of information long before our kind of newspapers, websites or broadcasts. It was making us modern.

There were a dozen reasons for going north. The war was very rarely fought as far north as Leiden, let alone Amsterdam: and a bit of order is always welcome when you have a living to make. Artists who could no longer make a living went north with all their ideas alongside Calvinists who could not tolerate being forcibly led astray by Spanish bullies, Catholics who had seen everything holy torn apart in a single night, merchants who might find everything changed day to day in their home port depending on the progress of the war. Those merchants had long memories; in 1621 they formed the West Indies Company with the special purpose of revenge on the Spanish in the Caribbean, a company with two sets of books, one for trade and one for war.

Simon Stevin went north and enrolled in Leiden University: a taxman from Bruges, one-time cashier in a merchant house, the kind of man who might usually have gone south to university at Louvain, where Erasmus once studied. Louvain was distinguished enough for him and practical enough; its mathematics had to do with surveying, and Jesuits took an interest in architecture and military science. And Stevin always thought of himself as a southerner; book after book, the title page calls him 'Simon Stevin of Bruges' even when he was in the service of the *stadhouder* of the north. Still, he did go north and he left behind his connections.[41]

He was the natural child of Cathelyne van der Poort, whose own connections were mostly in bed, and Anthonis Stevin, who was a bolter and leaves few traces on any records except when his sister pays up to protect his inheritance, 'her brother having been a long time out of the country without having any news from him'. Simon was raised with Cathelyne's other children, whose father was the grand burgomaster, alderman and magistrate Noel de Caron, a strict Calvinist in most other ways. He also had the protection of the one man Cathelyne did remember to marry, the merchant Joost Sayon, who made silk at the sign of 'the French Arms'.

Stevin was perhaps a teacher and then, as he wrote himself, 'well-versed in mercantile book-keeping and being a cashier; and later on in the matter of finance'. His business years were in Antwerp: if he didn't work for some partnership with offices in Venice, Augsburg, London, Cologne and Antwerp, he was certainly familiar with how such an office worked. He saw how one of the partners never did keep proper records, which meant he had to accept what the other partners decided.

At twenty-eight, which is not so very late for the time, he was officially declared an adult and not a dependent orphan any more; was staked some money by relatives; and went to work for the financial administration in Bruges, a settled job in an insecure world. That was 1577; the Calvinists were still in power four years later when he left for the new and deeply Protestant university at Leiden. He moved far too early to be a religious refugee. Most likely, he moved for ambition, away from the disorder and uncertainty of the south.

Even before he registered as a student at Leiden in 1583, he was putting out books: the southerner teaching business to the north. He produced a book on double-entry book-keeping, the system that balances out what you spend and what you have and get, which was not familiar but not unknown in the north. He also produced a little book on working out how much interest is to be paid on borrowed money. He knew how subversive he was being by publishing that information; 'such tables are to be found in writing with some people,' he wrote in the preface, 'but they remain hidden as great secrets with those who have got them and they cannot be obtained without great expense.'

He had started his revolution: making mathematics work in the everyday world.

Refugees went both ways: running out of Flanders for safety and advancement, but also running there for refuge and work. Richard Verstegan left England because he was in danger of being hanged, and in Antwerp he set up as a kind of dealer in a new kind of commodity: information. He wrote books, made brilliantly gruesome propaganda for his Catholic cause, wrote for the news sheets; he was one of the first newspaper humorists. He also worked on the hidden side of his business. In his coded letters and reports Richard Verstegan became '181': a spy.[42]

Information was already something to buy, sell and trade across the sea, like cloth or salt or wheat or silver; a necessity with a cash value. It could be hoarded like a treasure, or put about ostentatiously;

it could be secret knowledge of amazing alchemical transformations, smuggled very discreetly by couriers from court to court, or the boastful stories of battle and triumph in the new public news sheets. It could get you a living or get you hanged.

Printing put information in books, and sent it everywhere, but information also travelled in secret letters and open letters, in maps of newly explored countries, specimens of fruits and cuttings from unfamiliar plants, even the bones of strange animals. Letters were work in progress, long-distance discussions across the sea: the conversation of the times.

The idea of a 'fact' was beginning to move out from courts of law into the world. Judges were used to hearing witnesses who said what they did or what they saw or what they knew, and coming on that basis to an official kind of truth about what happened, and why. A 'fact' is a 'factum' – an event, something that has been done.[43] Outside the law, truth rested on authority: the great book, the great power, the Church's teaching. Now the idea of the 'fact' began to corrode that notion of truth. It would soon affect the natural sciences: Francis Bacon famously told his readers to put away ancient books, and then to make their words as simple as stones piled up for building, a clear, functional account of solid things. For a world used to studying the great theories of Aristotle, the nature of the spheres of heaven, Bacon prescribed something different: all things 'numbered, weighed, measured and determined'. Everything had to be tested. The instincts of Robert Grosseteste were becoming seventeenth-century practice.

Facts began to appear in news sheets, the pictures of battles so carefully drawn they turned the reader into a witness. When Verstegan wrote about his Catholic martyrs, he also showed pictures of them so the reader would be convinced. Facts had a money value which allowed Verstegan to work in various markets, including the black.

He had the right unsettled background for a spy: his family improvised their lives, running from wars in the Rhineland, remaking their lives across the sea in England, slipping social class and clambering back again. They knew how to play at belonging. Young Richard even seemed likely for a while to slip away from the Catholic Church.

He worked his way through Oxford as servant to Thomas Bernard, a hardline Protestant; he was around men who talked about things like 'predestination'. He must have known how convenient it would be to turn Protestant and be eligible to be a soldier, a lawyer, to hold a government job or even be a priest; but being Catholic had its own glamour for rebellious undergraduates. It was the risky, radical position. It showed deep doubts about the Church of England, and the whole reordering of the state under Queen Elizabeth; it was a chance to claim a certain purity of mind. So instead of bending, Verstegan left the university 'to avoid oaths' of loyalty.

His father pushed him to train as a goldsmith, a trade 'the most genteel of any in the mechanic way'. Goldsmiths were already rudimentary bankers, taking custody of other people's silver and gold plate, which could easily be sold, turning foreign coins into local cash sometimes by melting them down, so rich merchants were the very best kind of friend; Verstegan arranged to know grandees, to be associated with Sir Thomas Gresham, who founded the London Exchange. He then stepped up to being a gentleman himself: he wrote. He dedicated his first book to Gresham, a travel guide to Europe which he mostly stole from a German book; he added a guide to Catholic feast days, a list that was officially banned in England, but which he said was a wholesome and useful tool for travellers to work out dates for fairs and holidays.

That couldn't last, at least not in the Protestant England of Elizabeth. Even the friends of Sir Thomas Gresham himself were learning compulsory discretion; Martin de la Faille, son of one of the richest merchant houses in Antwerp, was told by his father that it was far too dangerous to handle political letters any more. Verstegan knew about arrests and executions, about the forbidden missions to convert or hold the English and the sudden escapes abroad of the devout, and he didn't seem to care. He was pulled in 'for religion' and imprisoned for a couple of days in the small, dank City prison that usually held debtors and the occasional martyr; the pretext was that the man who printed his travel guide had also printed a book of 'Spiritual Consolation'. Those days had no effect. Verstegan printed and published a pamphlet on the execution of the Jesuit Edmund Campion, which tactlessly quoted the Book of Revelations. In it the queen's justice was insulted, and the queen herself linked indirectly to the Whore of Babylon.

Men went to the gallows for printing such a text. When Verstegan was arrested one more time he knew he had to run. He broke out of England and got across to France; for a while he was in Rouen as a propagandist in the cause of the English Catholic martyrs. This won him friends and infuriated the English ambassador, Sir Edward Stafford, who wrote home to say: 'I would lose all my credit but I would bring the Englishman to the gallows, to teach all others by him to be honester men to their country.' The papal nuncio intervened, sprang Verstegan from jail and sent him on to Rome, where his cardinal contact rather tetchily said the Pope couldn't be expected to support every Englishman who managed to get to Rome.

Somehow he tacked back to northern France, but he knew he had to head for Antwerp even if the city was under siege. He had to be at the heart of the printing trade, which was the heart of the trade in information.

His prospects were good. The Spanish relied on their diplomats to report what was happening in enemy England, but their embassies were shut down in wartime. A private intelligence service could fill the gap, and spend a great deal of Spanish money. Even so, life was not easy for Verstegan. The money from Madrid did arrive, but not often and not when it was expected. He opened an account to buy books from the great publisher Plantin in March 1587, and handed over the first cash sixteen years later in April 1603. 'Good patient Job,' he wrote, 'lost only all that he had, but he was not molested for payment of that which he did not have.'

He published an extraordinary work – the *Theatre of Cruelties*, one more illustrated book of martyrs but this time all of them recent and most of them in England, a few in Ireland, some in France and the Netherlands, and Mary, Queen of Scots, about to be despatched by an axeman who is almost dancing with the joy of it all. He showed decent citizens, starched and ruffed, being escorted out of their ransacked homes. A horse is being persuaded to eat corn out of a priest's guts. Bishops have their feet held in the fire, saintly ladies are crushed under weight after weight, ears are cut off, the lights torn out of bodies, and figures in cassocks hang in mid-air from gallows: the book is truly sensational. It suited Catholic Antwerp, battered as it was, to know there was such cruelty somewhere else.[44]

That was only the start of Verstegan's work. The Jesuits were back in England, disguised because it was illegal to preach or convert in a country disturbed by Catholic resistance and Catholic enemies, and worrying out loud that priests might turn worldly since they could not wear the protection of their clerical dress. They needed books, information, money, propaganda and contacts. They needed agents, and the agents' business was 'brocage and spierie', as the Catholic poet Anthony Copley said – fixing and spying.

Verstegan dealt with the skippers who smuggled priests and books, found passports for anyone who needed them, published their works and missals where it was legal and made sure they reached England where they were illegal. He was lucky that he was moving books over the sea and not overland; it was far too easy to search carts and carriages at every frontier. Even barges on the inland waterways were not safe; one bargeload of Protestant books, seized between Geneva and Paris, took eight booksellers almost a week to inventory, and then suppress. It helped to have diplomatic backing, however indirect; the cook and valet of the French ambassador in London had a busy trade importing illegal books and sending back, in return, the better class of any church furnishings they could salvage.

Otherwise, printed pages were shuffled into heaps of white paper, or rolled and stuffed into barrels; whole books were buried in loads of raw cloth or raw fibres. They often had to be hidden as they were loaded on board because in some Netherlands ports the Scots merchants were particularly keen on stopping seditious books at source. They had to be landed in Scotland and England very discreetly. Sometimes customs officials could be bribed, but that drew attention to the cargo; it might be better to take a chance, since London customs officers were notorious for confiscating books and then selling them on at their high full price. That did at least mean the books were in England and in use. Anywhere else, it was better to beach the ship on sands, land the passengers first and then take the books off by dinghy – ideally at some small port or some empty beach where there was nobody who thought it worth asking questions. You landed troublesome books at Burntisland in Fife or in Queensburgh if they were meant for Edinburgh.

Along with the books went letters: the letters that made it possible to organize the English Catholics. Some went by the public post, mostly the Tassis service, which ran out of Italy by way of Frankfurt for Hamburg letters, via Brussels for Paris and via Antwerp for London; so there was plenty of traffic in which to hide important messages travelling from Antwerp to England. English intelligence liked to use mail drops, leaving letters with a London jeweller called Mulemaker or an Italian called Mynistrale; Verstegan may have done the same. Some letters even crossed the sea stuffed into the ornamental buttons on a man's coat. The public post was a fragile institution, so Verstegan used his own couriers when he could; the English kept an eye on 'one Laurence, a book-binder in Antwerp who is a little, slender man, with a yellowish little beard and lispeth in his speech and speaketh good French'.

The letters try to sound innocent. 'Concerning our marchandise,' Verstegan wrote, '... we are lyke to have heare a very plentifull yeare, so that we may make great commoditie of corne, yf we be secret in our course.' Nobody plants corn in secret, so it can't be a farmer's letter; there must be a second meaning, a harvest of souls. When the Zeeland authorities found letters like this, they wrote pamphlets about the shocking Catholic use of such mundane language to discuss sacred matters. 'The marchant that was arrested continued still in his distresse,' Verstegan wrote; the merchant was a priest. As for the sudden appearance in a farmer's letter of 'Mr Garlyke the fishmonger' who 'was oute of towne, but he saith he will very shortly be there and give orders for our affaires', you might wonder why a fishmonger is harvesting corn. Mr Garlyke was a Jesuit, most likely.

Verstegan kept a careful eye on his English enemies and London watched him back: the familiar, obsessional binary game of spying. He wrote to one Jesuit in England in 1592: '181 dothe thinck it best to stay for a few weekes to send any 239 to any 139 in 25, because Mr 9 m 12 . . . dothe here by 227 means very much seek to understand which way and how 181 dealeth.' That meant: Verstegan, who was 181, reckons it would be better for a few weeks not to send messages, which is 239, to any priest (139) in England (25); the reason is that some spy in Antwerp is trying to find out exactly how Verstegan operates. The spy, Mr 9 m 12, is probably a man called Robert Poley.

This breathless world could not go on for ever; the intrigue, the tradecraft, the moral purpose of it all. After Elizabeth's death in 1603, the English Mission was no longer a covert mission, there were no more moles and decoys to run, and the Spanish did not need Verstegan's tip-offs and rumours about what was happening in the English court. Verstegan changed business, which only made it clear how much information and intelligence had become a business.

He used his contacts; he was given a monopoly on importing English cloth into Flanders. He tried to sell the Spanish a cunning device that would stop water going stagnant and allow their ships to stay at sea longer; then he tried to persuade them of a scheme to cut the Dutch out of the carrying trade between the Baltic and the Mediterranean. He did rather well. He took up journalism and poetry; he was even a humorist. He wrote for the broadsheet usually known as the *Nieuwe Tijdinghen*, which came out three times a week, and continued when it became the *Wekelijcke Tijdinghen*, which came out only once a week because nobody wanted to read about the Spanish when they were being defeated. The commodity that he traded was fact and information and rumour, and he may well have gone on providing more private newsletters for money, but he was no longer quite a spy; he had graduated at last to being a proper hack.

He chose his time and his city well. The first English-language newspapers appeared in Amsterdam in the 1620s, translations of the very graphical Dutch news sheets, and came to London just as news in general did: across the North Sea, by way of Antwerp. If the North Sea were not open, England could not know what was happening abroad. John Pory of the *London Intelligencer* complained in 1632 that 'touching forraine news, we can have but very little because it is now a fortnight since we had any post from Antwerp'. The world around the sea was addicted already to fact, news, information, intelligence.

★

Twenty-eight people crowded on the machine with Prince Maurits at the helm: the sailing chariot devised by Simon Stevin, engineer, book-keeper, king of numbers. His famous toy went skimming the sands close to The Hague, two sails billowing, four great wheels turning, flags standing proud in the wind and a prince with a chance for mischief. 'At one moment, for fun and in order to play a trick on his gentlemen, his Excellency steered the chariot into the sea, which movement struck many with great fear; but as he moved the helm in good time the chariot struck the beach again and sped along its former course.'

The sailing chariot was something Dutch sailors had seen in the Orient, a Chinese invention; this one was devised as a pastime, a kind of compliment paid by a tutor to his student, a scholar to his prince and patron. Stevin had known Maurits since their days in the small community of students at Leiden; he was with him all through the war that followed, his tent pitched close to the prince during many sieges; he was physically so close to power he never seems to have written letters of advice or letters asking favours, so close we can't quite tell if the two men were friends or only colleagues.

He was the prince's tutor in mathematics, which also meant the sciences of navigation and fortification and how to aim a gun, and the prince was his patron and protector even when Stevin's ideas were officially outrageous. Stevin said the Earth went round the sun, and the very Calvinist geographer Ubbo Emmius let it be known that 'if these things are true, as I understand them, the writer vehemently declares that Moses is a liar and the entire Holy Scriptures are untrue. I regret that the name and the studies of the Prince are sullied by this filth.' The prince did not even blink.

Stevin thrived in his first years at Leiden. He registered for the university, a good move since students paid no tax on wine, beer or books, and only a year later he had his first patents: for ingenious machines to dredge the sand and mud out of the canals in Delft, including a large net that could be opened and closed from the surface above. That same year, 1584, a passing fanatic shot Maurits's father dead on the stairs of his quarters in Delft, and he died with impeccably tasteful last words: 'My God, my God, have pity on me and on this poor people.' The death could truly have been a pitiable moment for the rebels because William had been the great leader of the revolt against the Spanish; but his son took over his role, step by step, first the ruler of a couple of the United Provinces, then the general in charge of the army that had to fight for the survival of the whole United Provinces, then ruler of them all and a prince. His life was formed by war and its urgent needs, and so was Stevin's; his brilliant, practical and didactic mind was needed all the time. There were a hundred problems to solve, and without answers the war and the nation would be lost.

The urgency Roger Bacon once felt, faced with the stories of Mongol hordes, was now producing a stream of new devices and technology. Stevin became an army engineer and then a quartermaster for ten years. He devised sluices, pumps, dredgers, windmills, even a combined spade, axe and pick so soldiers needed only one tool when digging; he thought this important since digging 'is held to be one of the principal causes of Maurits' famous victories in the besieging of cities'. He wrote a treatise on fortifications without doing too much study of what happened in the field, but it turned out sound enough to change the tactics of real-life soldiers: polygon forts, five bastions or more, surrounded by double canals. When he wrote about longitude he devised a way to sail directly to any port without bothering about how to calculate longitude at sea, which was a conundrum not to be solved for decades. The constant tension between the practical and the sheer beauty of mathematical theory kept him fascinated.

The results were startling. He had been a student for two years when he published what seems a rather prosaic book: *De Thiende*, which means 'the dime'. It is, among other things, a plea for uniform measures and money in a country where the Amsterdam pound was not the same as the Nijmegen pound, and the Amsterdam foot was just an approximation of the Guelder foot. It would help trade, and it would help the United Provinces, which had a great muddle of moneys: each province was putting out a very various selection of coins, guilders, daalders and the rest. More important, it meant that people could be taught how to work out value and quantity from first principles, and all on the same basis, not just judging by eye or relying on their personal and disorderly experience.

In order to get to this nice bureaucratic solution, Stevin started as he always did, from mathematics. In the process, with the notion of making calculation easier and fractions more clear, he invented the first practical decimal system.

He knew of systems which divided by one hundred – in Antwerp the *aum* measured wine and it was divided into one hundred *pots* – but he wanted to set a standard for measuring that would work anywhere: for surveyors, for cashiers, for anyone who had to count and calculate.

He dedicated his book to 'Astronomers, Surveyors, Measurers of Tapestry, Gaugers . . . to Money-Masters and to all Merchants'. He showed how to write down numbers as decimals without awkward fractions, so it was easy to add or subtract or even find a square root simply by keeping the decimals lined up accurately; and he made the case for everyone using the same system, calculating on the basis of tens and not the sixties that were sometimes used. He did not waste time being modest about 'the great use of his invention'. On principle, he wrote in Dutch so everyone in Holland could understand, but the book was quickly translated into French, and almost as quickly into English and Danish; it was read everywhere.

He was also a physicist: he changed the science about the pressure water puts on anything under or in it. He wrote the first Dutch book on logic, and a book on man's civic duty. In mathematics he had a method to carry him almost anywhere. He reorganized the princely lands and money after the morning when the prince complained he 'had been handed certain accounts which he found obscure, and in his opinion unnecessarily long'. He ran experiments: he may even have beaten Galileo to the simple test of whether weight decides how fast solid bodies fall, taking the burgomaster of Delft up a church tower to drop two balls of lead thirty feet onto a sounding board and discovering 'they fall together onto the board so simultaneously that their two sounds seem to be one and the same rap'. He took on practical work dredging the canals of Delft and invented sluices where the force of water would scour away silt, and he was well-enough known to be called to Gdansk in Poland to deepen the harbour there; naturally, since he tested everything, he had to see the harbour for himself. He also devised new kinds of watermill, and built them to test his theories; the Delft magistrates wrote him a testimonial saying the mills 'rebuilt according to the art of the said Stevin have scoured at least three times as much water as the former mills usually did'. The people of IJsselstein were less complimentary when their mill failed and polder land disappeared back under the water. Stevin went to check, again and again, as though he couldn't quite believe that his ideas had gone wrong. He put the failure down to neglect and even sabotage.

Everything had to be engineered. That had been true when the first peat-diggers tried to defend the land against water, but now the scale of the work was hugely expanded. There were new trading companies going out to the East and West Indies, shareholder companies, not just shares in particular ships, and they depended on practical mathematics: ships had to be navigated, there had to be walls to keep enemies at bay, waterways to carry goods, surveys to parcel out the newly conquered lands. Someone had to aim the guns accurately. Someone had to keep the books and record the buying and selling of shares. *Stadhouder* Maurits saw the need to train engineers, surveyors, people who had enough maths 'but only as much of each as is necessary for a general practical knowledge of engineering'. He proposed a new school alongside the university at Leiden: the *Duytsche Mathematique*.

Stevin planned the school, organized it and taught there. The teaching was in Dutch because Stevin thought it better than Latin for practical subjects, a revolution in itself; a few years earlier he'd had to invent the Dutch words for a 'triangle' or something 'parallel' and it would be another eighty years before German universities started lectures in German. The change of language made the school open to anyone; the clerics, the ones who spoke Latin both as a *lingua franca* and as a code, had to make room for newcomers. The curriculum had nothing to do with the medieval plan that had shaped Stevin's own time at Leiden: he had studied philosophy or humanities, which included rhetoric and physics, maths, ethics, Greek and Hebrew. The new school meant to turn out people with specific skills, not a rather general culture: a modern school.

Stevin left one other monument, quite unexpected: the shape of cities round the world. He always meant to write a whole book on architecture and how to plan a town; he mentioned the subject often, and he left copious notes.[45] He started with drains and foundations, but he kept thinking about the human beings who would live inside his towns; the beauty of a facade, the rules of classical building did not matter half as much. When he wrote about the layout of a house, he worried about fire, he thought out loud about how to keep thieves out, where a man could exercise, how to save your wife or daughter from sitting in a window to be seen and 'being called at by people passing in the street'. Furnace rooms were a good idea for heating, but 'those who are not used to them become ill almost like people who are seasick'. He thought courtyards a good thing because lovers could not reach their sweethearts easily, but a bad thing because when you lean out of a window, you can't see what is happening on the street. You can tell he had children: two daughters, two sons.

He wanted streets to be regular and facades to be uniform, no great fuss of pillars and decoration when simple stone looked so good; he knew he had to plan traffic, and it seemed a good idea to make models before building. He proposed cities on a rectangular plan, cut up with canals, looking a little like the simple, squared-off layout of an army camp, but complicated with markets, with princely houses, with public squares for air and light.

And after he was dead, those cities were built at last: Recife in Brazil, where you can still pick out the framework of the streets of the Dutch city of Mauritsstad; Colombo in Sri Lanka, Cape Town in South Africa; the fort at Paramaribo in Surinam. His ideas went with empire all around the world.

The golden age of Amsterdam is just beginning: the art, the riches, the great fleets and the complex markets in anything from paper to grain for bread. Everything is ready.

Consider what had already happened in Antwerp and Flanders

and Burgundy. Power became a matter of show and glitz as well as armies and diplomacy, soft power perhaps but essential when a ruler is surrounded by disorderly, independent towns and dependent on the big merchant enterprises. Much the same will happen in Amsterdam. The city burghers insist on their own authority while down the road in The Hague a *stadhouder* prince has to act out the role of ruler as though he were on stage, all show and fashion and ostentatious rules. Meanwhile the whole nature of the United Provinces of the Netherlands will change with the great trading companies that work the East and West Indies: powers that are only partly political and mainly commercial, able to find, take and organize an empire. The ruler is one among many powers.

Markets like the Bourse in Catholic Antwerp have already emancipated themselves from actual, solid goods, so they can buy and sell the relationships between prices in different places, at different times, and dealers can speculate as well as calculate. On this, and the older traditions of sharing the cost of a ship or forming a company to defend the land against the encroaching sea, the machinery of capitalism can be built.

Information has become a commodity of great value, to be marketed, exchanged, sometimes hoarded. People want to know, and they expect to be told; they think knowledge means change. Finding things out is a priority even on merchant company ships sent to sink the enemy, take his silver and maybe do some peaceful business as well; the captains are told to bring back specimens and facts. The Amsterdam presses make the books and newsletters that carry the facts around Europe, that sometimes give away secrets and sometimes cause scandals.

Paintings have come off the altars and gone into houses, made for the market and not for the glory of God and the fame of some patron. The process started long before any Protestant iconoclasm took the pictures out of churches. Art has become domestic, a commodity; there were art dealers in Antwerp with crowded shops just as there will be in Amsterdam. Painting was still craftsman's work which often amounted to copying; but the idea of the importance of talent is being born, the value of the original and the personal. Amsterdam, too, will muddle these two ideas: the importance of genius, the importance of consumers.

Above all, the world is ready to be counted and engineered, to put mathematics at the heart of building a fort or a windmill, keeping the records of a business or laying out a town. Antwerp knew that change, but rebellion and a war of religious denominations took out the city's sense of order. Amsterdam inherited the idea. Both cities shared the same shining, seemingly reasonable faith which we still maintain.

That faith has roots very deep in time.

Empire fleets sailed out over the Atlantic and the Pacific and with their voyages our wider world began; a new world, so Francis Bacon thought, and as philosopher and politician and enthusiast for experiment he wanted to understand. 'In our time large parts of the New World and the farthest parts of the Old are becoming known everywhere, and the store of experiences has grown immeasurably,' he wrote in 1620. The Portuguese were all down the coast of Western Africa, then at the Cape of Good Hope in 1487, in India by 1498. They were on the shores of Brazil in 1500, to be followed by the French in the 1550s. They reached China in 1513 and Japan in 1543. Christopher Columbus beached at San Salvador in the Bahamas in 1492. The English were off the coast of North America in 1497. A century later Dutch merchants sent out their first trading mission to Indonesia, the English were about to try to settle parts of North America, and the French, Dutch, Swedes and others followed.

This is the usual story of 'discovery', how we came to know about the world and make it modern; but if 'discovery' means finding unknown places and peoples for the first time, it is not the right word. The Portuguese found a sea route to India, but the Romans were trading around Karachi and Gujarat more than a millennium earlier, selling coral and frankincense that went over the Himalaya to China, buying silk from China and animal hides and indigo, ivory and 'long peppers'. Once they knew about the monsoon winds the ships of Alexandria in Egypt began sailing out to India in the first century CE.[46] The Romans used cloves and nutmeg from the Moluccas in Indonesia in the fourth century CE.[47] Usually there were Arab middlemen involved, but the Romans knew about the world at least at second hand, and how it was connected. So did the Norsemen, as we have seen, all the way across Russia to Byzantium and beyond, and west to the shores of North America; the Buddha found in the fields in Sweden from the eighth century begins to seem less strange when you realize the strength of these long, long trading runs.

We knew the world. What changed with the empire fleets was our way of looking at it: of investigating it, not just collecting or trading it, and trying to use our guns and skills to dominate it. Our world and our way of thinking seem to start quite abruptly, but both have a long and complex story, the history of all the necessary conditions for being modern in our particular way. It could all have worked out very differently, but it could not have happened at all without the story I have tried to tell.

It starts with those Frisian traders in their flat-bottomed boats working the coasts of the North Sea and spreading the use of money: of an abstract way to think about the world and its value. Monks in their cold cells work out the mathematics of time, and they shape the way others think about the natural world: not just turning the page of an ancient text but looking, reasoning, calculating. They help along the process of exchanging ideas across the seas, a busy trade that keeps them in touch with the ideas of strangers and which gives great value to the written word. Trading cloth and iron in the shallows on the edge of the world begins to change the way we see the world; Francis Bacon himself is heir to a millennium of other people's work and history.

Norsemen come south and they become the enemies that the Christian missions need to be sure of their own righteousness. They also settle, and where they settle they create a new independent kind of town whose success will change the landscape. Some of them do far more: long before the empire ships went out, from the time of the Norseman Ohthere, we have evidence of men sailing on just because they did not know what lay ahead. They went into the unknown.

Bacon understood that: 'It is unthinkable,' he wrote, 'that there is some boundary or farthest point of the world; it always appears, almost by necessity, that there is something beyond.' He understood the power of all the new creatures, minerals, sights and information to be found; 'They are capable of shedding new light in philosophy,' he wrote. 'Indeed it would be a disgrace to mankind if wide areas of the physical globe, of land, sea and stars, have been opened up and explored in our time while the boundaries of the intellectual globe were confined to the discoveries and narrow limits of the ancients.'[48] The landings on Brazil and on Southern Africa, for example, flatly contradicted Aristotle's assumption that no living thing could survive in the burning world south of the Equator, that the north was all there could be on Earth. The process of opening up the Earth disrupted ideas of authority; man had to look for himself and think for himself. But authority was already challenged by the saintly Bede, a loyal churchman, and his notions of investigating the moon and the tides.

Travelling showed other ways of life, other lengths of robe, other colours and styles: it bred fashion, and fashion implies choices. Since it also involves change, it alarmed conservatives. A woman might choose to dress above her station. A man might insist that he could choose how he looked. Every kind of social confusion, even sexual confusion, could be read on the backs of the people in the street. It was dangerous, even monstrous proof that people could choose, and an anxious settled world could not ignore it.

At the edge of the world, the law written in Rome never quite worked; instead law had to contend with custom, with habit, with the Northern way of life. In doing so it became more flexible and perhaps more humane, more able to handle a business dispute, more able to consider the state of mind of some broken man who had done murder. Papers became all important with a special trust in the written word, which brought out the very best forgers to change history the way they wanted. On the edge of the world a profession of lawyers formed, to which we owe not just the high self-importance of the law but also the idea of a profession that was not priestly and its inevitable consequence: the idea of a middle class.

These changes were profound; they made possible the bureaucracy which made possible nation states. The changes to the natural world were arguably even more important. On the fragile shoreline, broken by tides, buried in sand drifts, where a single storm could change the whole shape of a community, man first came close to losing land in order to fuel the new and growing towns, and then came to believe he could engineer his world with dams, dikes, sluices. The forests, the clean waters gave way to a conditional world, which was our fault and also our duty.

Alongside this need to control went a new appetite for experiment: for finding things out and then testing and proving them. The process that Simon Stevin would develop had already begun out of terror of Mongol hordes and the end of the world. In the new universities mathematical thinking was tangled up still with the idea of money, of moral trading and just prices: the connection that began with the Frisians was still shaping minds.

Trading became a power in its own right. The towns of the German Hansa formed an alliance which could make its own treaties, see off kings, blockade a nation into starvation and force surrender. Money went to war with political powers.

The modern world is taking its shape: law, professions, the written word; towns, and what they do to the natural world; books and fashion, business and its relationship to power. We are not on the margins of history any more; we are dealing in the essential, the changes of mind that made our world possible.

We've seen how women made their choices, often surprisingly, and built worlds the way they wanted them. The possibility of love, of truly choosing a partner, turned out to mean later marriage, and with it the possibility of young people going about Europe and taking with them knowledge of all kinds of technology. The edge of the world found some of its economic advantages in bed.

We've seen how plague became the reason, just like terrorism today, for social regulation, for saying how children must behave, for taking away a worker's right to choose what work he wanted, for deciding which of the poor are worthy of help and which are just wastrels. Plague enforced frontiers that were otherwise wonderfully insecure, and made our movements and travels conditional. It helped make the state a physical reality, and give it ambitions.

In Antwerp all this produced a glittering civilization which spawned so many of our attitudes: to art, insurance, shares, genius, power as a great show; to the possibility of engineering the world as we want it. When war broke up Flanders, when the northern provinces broke away, those attitudes came to Amsterdam.

They came in glory. They look like something both new and brilliant, but the truth is that they grew out of the light in what we used to casually call the 'dark ages' and the central importance of what we used to call 'the edge of the world'. Around the cold, grey waters of the North Sea, the old, the marginal, the unfashionable made us possible: for much better, and for much, much worse.

It is time now to give them all their due.

# References

## *Introduction*

1 Warwickshire Record Office (WRO): CR1368/vol. I/66.

2 For Scarborough's visitors and their pastimes passim, see: *A list of the Nobility, Quality and Gentry at Scarborough* (1733); *The Scarborough Miscellany for the year 1733*; *A Journey from London to Scarborough* (1734). For the discovery of the spa: Robert Wittie, *Scarborough-Spaw: or a Description of the Nature and Virtues of the Spaw at Scarborough, Yorkshire* (1667). For the debate about the use and value of sea water: W. Simpson, *Hydrologia Chymica: or the Chymical Anatomy of the Scarborough and other Spaws in Yorkshire* (1669); Anon., *A dissertation on the Contents, Virtues and Uses of Cold and Hot Mineral Springs, particularly those of Scarborough* (1735); Robert White MD, *The Use and Abuse of Sea Water Impartially Considered* (1775).

3 WRO: CR1368/vol. I/67.

4 For a fuller sketch of this argument, see R. Dettingmeijer, 'The Emergence of the Bathing Culture Marks the End of the North Sea as a Common Cultural Ground', in Juliet Roding and Lex Heerma van Voss (eds.), *The North Sea and Culture 1550–1800* (Hilversum, 1996), pp. 482ff.

5 Peter Shaw's analysis of the waters was read as a lecture in Scarborough in 1733, then sent in a letter to the recorder of the corporation, then published in its own right in 1735. See Peter Shaw, *An enquiry into the contents, virtues and uses of the Scarborough Spaw-waters: with the method of examining any other mineral water* (London, 1735).

6 David Kirby and Merja-Lisa Hinkkanen, *The Baltic and the North Seas* (London, 2000), p. 53.

7 *Baedeker's Belgium and Holland* (Leipzig and London, 1894), p. 255.

8 See Ada Hondius-Crone, *The Temple of Nehalennia at Domburg* (Amsterdam, 1955), p. 7, and for a facsimile of the newsletter.

9 Marie de Man, 'Que sait-on de la plage de Dombourg?', in *van het Nederlandisch Genootschap voor Munt- en Penningkunde* (Amsterdam, 1899); Marie de Man, a most remarkable numismatist and local historian, describes all the revelations on the beach over two centuries and catalogues the coins found. She also reports the sporadic pilfering from the gravesites.

10 Stéphane Lebecq, *Marchands et navigateurs frisons du haut Moyen Âge*, vol. 1: *Essai* (Lille, 1983), pp. 142–4 for an account of Frisian Domburg; p. 144 for the specific discoveries.

11 B. Krusch and W. Levison (eds.), *Monumenta Germaniae Historica, Scriptores rerum Merovingicarum*, vol. 7: *Passiones vitaeque sanctorum aevi Merovingici* (Hannover/Leipzig, 1920), p. 128, ch. 14, lines 4–13.

12 Ephraim Emerton, *The Letters of Saint Boniface* (New York, 2000), letter XV, pp. 27–8.

13 Cf. John E. Pattison, 'Is It Necessary to Assume an Apartheid-Like Social Structure in Early Anglo-Saxon England?', *Proceedings of the Royal Society: Biological Sciences* 275, 1650 (7 November 2008), pp. 2423 ff.

14 Quoted in Sebastian I. Sobecki, *The Sea and Medieval English Literature* (Cambridge, 2008), p. 30.

15 John Trevisa's translation of Bartholomaeus Anglicus, *De Proprietatibus Rerum*, in my modern version: Trevisa quoted in Sobecki, *Sea and Medieval English Literature*, p. 39.

16 Martin W. Lewis: 'Dividing the Ocean Sea', *Geographical Review* 89, 2 (April 1999), pp. 192–5.

17 Cf. Rosemary Muir Wright, 'The Rider on the Sea-Monster', in Thomas R. Liszka and Lorna E. M. Walker (eds.), *The North Sea World in the Middle Ages* (Dublin, 2001), pp. 70ff.

18 Bernard McGinn, 'Ocean and Desert as Symbols of Mystical Absorption in the Christian Tradition', *Journal of Religion* 74, 2 (1994), pp. 156, 157.

19 For a full discussion, see Barbara Hillers, 'Voyages between Heaven and Hell: Navigating the Early Irish Immram Tales', *Proceedings of the Harvard Celtic Colloquium* 13 (1993), pp. 66ff.

20 'The Voyage of St Brendan', in J. F. Webb, *The Age of Bede* (London, 1965), p. 236.
21 Ibid., p. 261.
22 Dicuil (ed. J. J. Tierney), *Liber de mensura orbis terrae*, 7, 15 (Dublin, 1967), pp. 72–3.
23 Ibid., p. 115n.11; and cf. Gunnar Karlsson, *Iceland's 1100 Years: History of a Marginal Society* (London, 2000), pp. 9–12.
24 Francis J. Tschan (ed. and tr.), *Adam of Bremen: History of the Archbishops of Hamburg–Bremen* (New York, 2002), 4, 34, p. 215 for Orkney seas (in scholia) and ocean; 4, 35, p. 217 for the burning ice; 4, 38, p. 220 for Harold Hardrada's voyage.
25 Devra Kunin (tr.) and Carl Phelpstead (ed.), *A History of Norway and The Passion and Miracles of the Blessed Óláfr* (London, 2001), p. 4, lines 1–16, for icebergs and monsters; pp. 11–12 for volcanos.
26 Tschan, *Adam of Bremen*, 4, 25, p. 206, for hoppers, cannibals, cyclops; 4, 17, p. 198, for dragons; 4, 18, p. 199, for blue men and Prussians; 4, 19, p. 200, for Amazons and their offspring.
27 Cf. McGinn, 'Ocean and Desert', pp. 74–5.
28 Aleksander Pluskowski, 'What is Exotic? Sources of Animals and Animal Products from the Edges of the Medieval World', in Gerhard Jaritz and Juhan Kreem (eds.), *The Edges of the Medieval World* (Budapest, 2009), p. 114.
29 William Ian Miller, *Audun and the Polar Bear: Luck, Law and Largesse in a Medieval Tale of Risky Business* (Leiden, 2008), pp. 7ff.; p. 18 for the bishop and the Emperor and Icelandic law.
30 J. R. S. Phillips, *The Medieval Expansion of Europe* (Oxford, 1998), p. 197.
31 Kevin J. Wanner, *Snorri Sturluson and the Edda: The Conversion of Cultural Capital in Medieval Scandinavia* (Toronto, 2008), p. 82.
32 Eric Hobsbawm, *Fractured Times* (London, 2013), pp. 150–51.
33 See Bernadette Cunningham, 'Transmission and Translation of Medieval Irish Sources in the Nineteenth and Twentieth Centuries', Jan Eivind Myhre, 'The "Decline of Norway": Grief and Fascination in Norwegian Historiography on the Middle Ages', and Peter Raedts, 'A Serious Case of Amnesia: The Dutch and Their Middle Ages', in R. J. W. Evans and Guy P. Marchal (eds.), *The Uses of the Middle Ages in Modern European States* (Basingstoke, 2011).

34 Patrick McGilligan, *Fritz Lang: The Nature of the Beast* (London, 1997), pp. 104, 172.
35 G. Ronald Murphy SJ, *The Saxon Savior: The Germanic Transformation of the Gospel in the Ninth Century Heliand* (New York, 1989), p. 6.
36 See E. G. Stanley, *Imagining the Anglo-Saxon Past* (Cambridge, 1975), pp. 20–22, and Valentine Anthony Pakis, *Studies in Early Germanic Biblical Literature: Medieval Rewritings, Medieval Receptions and Modern Interpretations* (Ph.D. thesis, Minneapolis, 2008), pp. 30–32 and 246ff.
37 For example, Fritz Rörig, 'Les Raisons intellectuelles d'une suprématie commerciale: la hanse', *Annales d'histoire économique et sociale* 2, 8 (15 Oct. 1930), pp. 481–98. 'Derrière cette ensemble sont de puissantes forces spirituelles et intellectuelles . . .', p. 486.
38 David M. Wilson and Else Roesdahl, 'Vikingarnas Betydelse för Europa', in Svenlof Karlsson (ed.), *Frihetens Källa: Nordens Betydelse för Europa* (Stockholm, 1992).
39 I've used the Loeb Edition of *Historia ecclesiastica gentis Anglorum* (tr. J. E. King; Cambridge, Mass., 1930), which is a revision of Moberly's 1881 Oxford edition. King's translation is so eccentric at times – 'batful' for 'fertile' – that I have made my own.
40 Bede (tr. J. E. King), 'Praefatio', in *Historia ecclesiastica*, pp. 4, 6.
41 Quoted in Stephen Yeates, *Myth and History: Ethnicity and Politics in the First Millennium British Isles* (Oxford, 2012), p. 150.
42 Bede (tr. J. E. King), *Historia ecclesiastica* , pp. 68–74, chs. XIV, XV.
43 Ibid., pp. 66, 74–6, 76 for heresy; p. 80 for the speed of the conversions ('raptim'); p. 98 for civil wars; chs. XIV, XVI, XVII, XXII for civil wars.
44 Pattison, 'Is It Necessary to Assume', pp. 2425–6.
45 See Yeates, *Myth and History*, for a survey of how Bede's history is challenged by archaeological techniques. His bibliography may be stronger than his arguments.
46 Bodley MS Canon Misc 378, from *Cosmographia Scoti . . .* (Basel, 1436) for a map of the forts and an account of the forces the Comes (or Count) commanded.
47 Cf. Régis Boyer, *Les Vikings, premiers Européens, VII–XI siècle: les nouvelles découvertes de l'archéologie* (Paris, 2005). In the preface Jean-Robert Pitte, president of the Sorbonne, announces that 'La construction

européenne a permis enfin à toutes les ethnies et à toutes les nations d'Europe de s'unir dans la partage féconde de la diversité. Grâces soient rendues à nos ancêtres vikings . . .' (p. 5).

## *1. The invention of money*

1 Plinius Secundus, *Naturalis historia*, book 16, sections 2, 3, online at www.penelope.uchicago.edu/Thayer/L/Roman/Texts/Pliny the Elder.

2 Wilhelm Levinson, *Vitae Sancti Bonifatii* (Hannover/Leipzig, 1905), p. 68 for the text of *Vita Altera Bonfiatii, Auctore Radbodo qui dicitur Episcopo Traiectensi* (or, as we say, Utrecht).

3 See Gustav Milne, 'Maritime Traffic between the Rhine and Roman Britain: A Preliminary Note', in Seán McGrail (ed.), *Maritime Celts, Frisians and Saxons* (London, 1990), p. 83; and H. Wagenvoort, 'Nehalennia and the Souls of the Dead', *Mnemosyne*, 4th series, 24, 3 (1971), pp. 278–9.

4 H. Wagenvoort, 'The Journey of the Souls of the Dead to the Isles of the Blessed', *Mnemosyne,* 4th series, 24, 2 (1971), p. 153.

5 On pirates, see Stéphane Lebecq, 'L'emporium protomédiéval de Walcheren-Domburg: une mise en perspective', reprinted in Lebecq, *Hommes, mers et terres du Nord au début du Moyen Âge*, vol. 2: *Centres, communications, échanges* (Lille, 2011), p. 134.

6 L. Th. Lehmann, 'The Romano-Celtic boats from Druten and Kapel-Avezaath', in McGrail, *Maritime Celts*, pp. 77–81; and Milne, 'Maritime Traffic', in McGrail, *Maritime Celts*, p. 83.

7 Bede (tr. J. E. King), *Historia ecclesiastica gentis Anglorum* (Cambridge, Mass., 1930), pp. 122–4, 'vendidit eum Lundoniam Freso cuidam'; 'indubitanter' is how Bede qualifies the story. For commentary on this, see Stéphane Lebecq, *Marchands et navigateurs frisons du haut Moyen Âge*, vol. 2: *Corpus des sources écrites* (Lille, 1983), p. 232.

8 Lebecq, *Marchands et navigateurs frisons*, vol. 2, p. 109, for text: 'Fresones festinaverunt egredi de regione Anglorum, timentes iram propinquorum interfecti juvenis.'

9 Michael Swanton (tr. and ed.), *Anglo-Saxon Chronicle* (London, 1996), p. 90.

10 'Tam Saxones quam Frisiones vel alias naciones promiscuas', in Lebecq, *Marchands et navigateurs frisons*, vol. 2, p. 402.

11 Paraphrased from Wandalbert, *Miracula S. Goaris*, in Lebecq, *Marchands et navigateurs frisons*, vol. 2, pp. 153–5.

12 Willibald, *Vita Bonifatii*, ch. 8, in Lebecq, *Marchands et navigateurs frisons*, vol. 2, p. 85; and at p. 81 in George Washington Robinson's translation (Cambridge, Mass., 1916), but this is my translation.

13 For dunes, the unusual pattern of tides and the death toll, see G. Waitz (ed.), *Annales Bertiniani* (Hannover, 1883), p. 18. Waitz leaves the account at the end of 839 but I have followed Lebecq in combining it with other reports for the end of 838.

14 B. De Simson (ed.), *Annales Xantenses et Annales Vedastini* (Hannover/Leipzig, 1909), pp. 9, 10, 26.

15 Detlev Ellmers, 'The Frisian Monopoly of Coastal Transport in the 6th–8th Centuries', in McGrail, *Maritime Celts*, p. 91.

16 See Joachim Henning, 'Early European Towns', in Joachim Henning (ed.), *Post-Roman Towns, Trade and Settlement in Europe and Byzantium*, vol. 1: *The Heirs of the Roman West* (Berlin, 2007), pp. 19–21.

17 D. A. Gerrets and J. de Koning, 'Settlement Development on the Wijnaldum-Tjitsma Terp', in J. C. Besteman, J. M. Bos, D. A. Gerrets, H. A. Heidinga, J. De Koning (eds.), *The Excavation at Wijnaldum*, vol. I (Rotterdam, 1999), p. 111.

18 Lebecq, *Marchands et navigateurs frisons*, vol. 2, p. 137.

19 See William H. TeBrake, 'Ecology, Economy in Early Medieval Frisia', *Viator* 9 (1978), p. 16; and also H. A. Heidinga, 'The Wijnaldum Excavation: Searching for a Central Place in Dark Age Frisia', in Besteman et al., *Excavation at Wijnaldum*, p. 10.

20 G. Waitz (ed.), *Vitae Anskarii et Rimberti* (Hannover, 1884), p. 72.

21 J. P. Pals, 'Preliminary Notes on Crop Plants and the Natural and Anthropogeneous Vegetation', in Besteman et al., *Excavation at Wijnaldum*, pp. 145, 147, 149.

22 Ellmers, 'Frisian Monopoly of Coastal Transport', p. 91.

23 John Boswell, *The Kindness of Strangers* (London, 1989), pp. 211–12.

24 Lebecq, *Marchands et navigateurs frisons*, vol. 2, pp. 37–9; the translation is mine, but see L. Whitbread, 'The "Frisian Sailor" Passage in the Old English Gnomic Verses', *Review of English Studies* 22, 87 (July

1946), pp. 215–19 for a more stylish English version and a discussion of Frisian morals.

25 William Levison (ed.), *Vita Willibrordi ...*, in B. Krusch and W. Levison (eds.), *Scriptorum Rerum Merovingicarum* VII (Hannover, 1920), pp. 123–5.

26 Georg Weitz (ed.), *Ex Miraculis S. Wandregisili*, in *Scriptorum . . . Supplementa Tomorum I–XII* (Hannover, 1857), pp. 406–9.

27 Job 41:34, 33, 31, 14, 21, 32, quoting the Authorized Version.

28 Stéphane Lebecq, 'Scènes de chasse aux mammifères marins (mers du Nord VI–XIIème siècles)' (1997), in Lebecq, *Hommes, mers et terres du Nord au début du Moyen Âge*, vol. 1: *Peuples, cultures, territoires* (Lille, 2011), pp. 244ff.

29 Joe Flatman, *Ships and Shipping in Medieval Manuscripts* (London, 2009), pp. 50ff.

30 Lebecq, *Marchands et navigateurs frisons*, vol. 2, pp. 185–8.

31 Levison, *Vitae Sancti Bonifatii*, p. 20. I've read 'trepidantibus' for 'trepudantibus' as Levison's note allows because I can't quite imagine sailors rowing and dancing all at once as some translators (e.g. George Washington Robinson, 1916) can.

32 Ibid., p. 52.

33 See Keith Wade, 'Ipswich', in David Hill and Robert Cowie (eds.), *Wics: The Early Medieval Trading Centres of Northern Europe* (Sheffield, 2001), appendix 1, pp. 86–7.

34 M. O. H. Carver, 'Pre-Viking Traffic in the North Sea', in McGrail, *Maritime Celts*, pp. 119, 121.

35 See Heidinga, 'Wijnaldum Excavation', in Besteman et al., *Excavation at Wijnaldum*, pp. 9, 10.

36 Egge Knol, 'Frisia in Carolingian Times', in Iben Skibsted Klæsøe (ed.), *Viking Trade and Settlement in Continental Western Europe* (Copenhagen, 2010), p. 47.

37 Peter Spufford, *Money and Its Use in Medieval Europe* (Cambridge, 1988), pp. 9, 41.

38 Ibid., pp. 9, 15.

39 See Florin Curta, 'Merovingian and Carolingian Gift Giving', *Speculum* 81, 3 (2006), p. 683.

40 Spufford, *Money and Its Use*, p. 25.

41 Lebecq, *Marchands et navigateurs frisons*, vol. 1, pp. 54–6.
42 Spufford, *Money and Its Use*, p. 28.
43 Pieterjan Deckers, personal communication.
44 Hans F. Haefele (ed.), 'Notker the Stammerer', in *Gesta Karoli Magni Imperatoris*, vol. II (Berlin, 1959), ch. 9, p. 63.
45 Curta, 'Merovingian and Carolingian Gift Giving', p. 688.
46 Lebecq, *Marchands et navigateurs frisons*, vol. 1, p. 264.
47 Ibid., p. 76.
48 Peter Sawyer, *The Wealth of Anglo-Saxon England* (Oxford, 2013), pp. 98–9.
49 Spufford, *Money and Its Use*, p. 35.
50 Dirk Jan Henstra: *The Evolution of the Money Standard in Medieval Frisia* (Groningen, 2000), p. 263.
51 Ernst Dümmler, *Epistolae Karolini aevi*, vol. II (Berlin, 1895), letters 18ff., p. 145.
52 W. J. H. Verwers, 'Dorestad: A Carolingian Town?', in Richard Hodges and Brian Hobley (eds.), *The Rebirth of Towns in the West* AD *700–1050* (London, 1988), pp. 52ff.
53 Lebecq, *Marchands et navigateurs frisons*, vol. 1, pp. 149ff.
54 Lebecq, ibid., vol. 2, p. 21, for text of poem.
55 Verwers, 'Dorestad', in Hodges and Hobley, *Rebirth of Towns*, pp. 54–5.
56 Charles H. Robinson (tr.), *Vita Anskarii* (London, 1921), p. 104.
57 Lebecq, *Marchands et navigateurs frisons*, vol. 1, p. 259.
58 Ibid., p. 30.
59 Ibid., p. 28.
60 Based on Dagfinn Skre, 'Town and Inhabitants', in Skre (ed.), *Things from the Town: Artefacts and Inhabitants in Viking-Age Kaupang* (Norske Oldfunn XXIV; Aarhus/Oslo, 2011), esp. pp. 411ff. for the plan of the house and 431ff. for the use and inhabitants of the house.
61 Lebecq, *Marchands et navigateurs frisons*, vol. 1, p. 30, for Schleswig; p. 28 for Worms; p. 90 for Yorkshire; pp. 112–13 for Radbod.
62 Ibid., vol. 2, p. 258, quoting the *Chronicles of Pseudo-Fredegaire*.
63 'Normani in Walcras interfecerunt Francos', in *Annales S. Martini Tornacensis* for 839, quoted in Lebecq, *Marchands et navigateurs frisons*, vol. 2, p. 341.

64 'Interfecta est de paganis non minima multitudo', in *Annales Xantenses* for 835, quoted in Lebecq, *Marchands et navigateurs frisons*, vol. 2, p. 335.

65 Lebecq, *Marchands et navigateurs frisons*, vol. 2, pp. 285–7.

## 2. *The book trade*

1 Bede, *Lives of the Abbots of Wearmouth and Jarrow*, ch. 8, in J. F. Webb and D. H. Farmer (trs.), *The Age of Bede* (London, 1988), p. 195.

2 Bede, *Lives of the Abbots*, ch. 6, in Webb and Farmer, *Age of Bede*, p. 192.

3 *The Anonymous History of Abbot Ceolfrith*, in Webb and Farmer, *Age of Bede*, p. 218.

4 Bede, *Lives of the Abbots*, ch. 17, in Webb and Farmer, *Age of Bede*, p. 205.

5 Bede writes of visiting Bishop Egbert for study, and meaning to do so again; see the *Epistola ad Ecgbertum*, in Bede (tr. J. E. King), *Historia ecclesiastica gentis Anglorum* (Cambridge, Mass., 1930), p. 446.

6 See Fiona Edmonds, 'The Practicalities of Communication between Northumbrian and Irish Churches c.635–735', in James Graham-Campbell and Michael Ryan (eds.), *Anglo-Saxon/Irish Relations before the Vikings* (Oxford, 2009), pp. 129ff.

7 Bede, *Lives of the Abbots*, ch. 13, in Webb and Farmer, *Age of Bede*, p. 200.

8 George Hardin Brown, *A Companion to Bede* (Woodbridge, 2009), pp. 7–8.

9 Bede, *Lives of the Abbots*, ch. 4, in Webb and Farmer, *Age of Bede*, p. 190.

10 Bernard Bischoff, *Manuscripts and Libraries in the Age of Charlemagne* (Cambridge, 2007), p. 15.

11 Bede, *Lives of the Abbots*, in Webb and Farmer, *Age of Bede*, pp. 192, 193.

12 Bede (tr. J. E. King), *Historia ecclesiastica*, book II, pp. xxiv, 382, 384.

13 Bede to Acca, Bishop of Hexham, quoted in Rosalind Love, 'The Library of the Venerable Bede', in Richard Gameson (ed.), *The Cambridge History of the Book in Britain*, vol. I: *400–1100* (Cambridge, 2012), p. 606.

14 Richard Gameson, 'Anglo-Saxon Scribes and Scriptoria', in Gameson, *Cambridge History of the Book in Britain*, p. 103.

15 For a brief account, see John J. Contreni, review of Martin Hellmann,

'Tironische Noten in der Karolingerzeit am Beispiel eines Persius-Kommentars aus der Schule von Tours', *Speculum* 77, 4 (2002), pp. 1305–7.

16 In the introduction to his Commentary on the Gospel of St Luke, Bede says that, tied down by monastic chores, he worked as 'dictator, notarius, librarius'. See J. A. Giles, *The Complete Works of the Venerable Bede* (London, 1844), vol. X, p. 268.

17 Bischoff, *Manuscripts and Libraries*, p. 7; Jennifer O'Reilly, '"All that Peter stands for": The *Romanitas* of the *Codex Amiatinus* Reconsidered', in Graham-Campbell and Ryan, *Anglo-Saxon/Irish Relations*, pp. 367ff.

18 Michelle P. Brown: *The Lindisfarne Gospels and the Early Medieval World* (London, 2011), pp. 143–8.

19 Michelle P. Brown: *The Book and the Transformation of Britain c.550–1050* (London, 2011), p. 54.

20 Sr Winifred Mary OP, 'The Medieval Scribe', *Classical Journal* 48, 6 (1953), pp. 207ff.

21 Bede, *Life of Cuthbert*, ch. 33, in Webb and Farmer, *Age of Bede*, p. 86.

22 O'Reilly, '"All that Peter stands for"', in Graham-Campbell and Ryan, *Anglo-Saxon/Irish Relations*, p. 379.

23 Brown, *The Book and the Transformation*, p. 19 for marks; p. 95 for binding; p. 55 for lightbox.

24 Diarmuid Scully, 'Bede's *Chronica Maiora*: Early Insular History', in Graham-Campbell and Ryan, *Anglo-Saxon/Irish Relations*, p. 48.

25 Bede (tr. J. E. King), *Historia ecclesiastica*, book IV, ch. II, pp. 10ff.

26 Faith Wallis (ed. and tr.), *Bede: The Reckoning of Time* (Liverpool, 2012), p. 202.

27 See John Maddicott, 'Plague in Seventh Century England', in Lester K. Little (ed.), *Plague and the End of Antiquity: The Pandemic of 541–750* (Cambridge, 2007), pp. 171ff. (p. 184 for Bede).

28 Wallis, *Bede*, p. 78.

29 Wesley M. Stevens, 'Sidereal Time in Anglo-Saxon England', in C. B. Kendall and P. S. Wells (eds.), *Voyage to the Other World: The Legacy of Sutton Hoo* (Minneapolis, 1992), p. 130.

30 Wallis, *Bede*, p. 260 for fifty-nine-times table; pp. 255ff. for finger calculations.

31 Cf. Pope Gregory's letter making Boniface a bishop, 1 December 722, in Ephrain Emerton, *The Letters of St. Boniface* (New York, 2000), p. 22.

32 Wallis, *Bede*, pp. lxxiff.

33 Paul Hughes, 'Implicit Carolingian Tidal Data', *Early Science and Medicine* 8, 1 (2003), p. 20 for the round Earth; p. 18 for Bede's Irish predecessors.

34 Wesley M. Stevens, *Bede's Scientific Achievement*, Jarrow Lecture 1985, rev. 1995; in Stevens, *Cycles of Time and Scientific Learning in Medieval Europe* (Aldershot, 1995), II, pp. 27ff.

35 Hughes, 'Implicit Carolingian Tidal Data', p. 12.

36 Bede's letter to Plegwin is in Wallis, *Bede*, pp. 405ff.

37 For the whole issue, see Jane Stevenson, 'The Beginnings of Literacy in Ireland', *Proceedings of the Royal Irish Academy* 89C (1989), pp. 127ff.

38 Ludwig Bieler (ed.), *The Patrician Texts in the Book of Armagh* (Dublin, 1979), p. 122 for Patrick's books; p. 94 for the contest with the druid; p. 126 for the alphabet in Tírechán's *Life*.

39 Boniface to Eadburga, 735, in Emerton, *Letters of St. Boniface*, pp. 42–3.

40 Boniface to Bishop Daniel of Winchester, 742–6, in ibid., p. 94.

41 M. B. Parkes, *Pause and Effect: An Introduction to the History of Punctuation in the West* (Aldershot, 1992), p. 23.

42 Brown, *The Book and the Transformation*, p. 30.

43 Bischoff, *Manuscripts and Libraries*, p. 17.

44 Brown, *The Book and the Transformation*, p. 45.

45 Parkes, *Pause and Effect*, p. 30.

46 Bischoff, *Manuscripts and Libraries*, p. 13.

47 Ibid., pp. 18, 20.

48 Brown, *The Book and the Transformation*, p. 40.

49 Gameson, 'Anglo-Saxon Scribes and Scriptoria', in Gameson, *Cambridge History of the Book in Britain*, pp. 103–4.

50 Emerton, *Letters of St. Boniface*, p. 145 for towels; pp. 101–4 for Mercia; p. 42 for 'solace of books'.

51 Richard Gameson, 'The Circulation of Books between England and the Continent c.871–c.1100', in Gameson, *Cambridge History of the Book in Britain*, p. 344.

52 Emerton, *Letters of St. Boniface*, p. 42.

53 Bede (tr. J. E. King), *Historia ecclesiastica*, book V, pp. xxiv, 384–8.
54 Rosamond McKitterick, *The Carolingians and the Written Word* (Cambridge, 1989), p. 194.
55 Bischoff, *Manuscripts and Libraries*, p. 148.
56 Ibid., pp. 67–8.
57 Emerton, *Letters of St. Boniface*, pp. 34–5.
58 Ibid., p. 167.
59 Ernst Dümmler (ed.), *Epistolae Karolini aevi*, vol. IV (Berlin, 1925), p. 17.
60 Gameson, 'Circulation of Books', p. 366.
61 Bischoff, *Manuscripts and Libraries*, p. 12.
62 See Patrick Sims-Williams, 'An Anglo-Latin Letter in Boulogne-sur-Mer', *Medium Ævum* 48 (1979), pp. 1ff. and especially 11ff. for commentary; pp. 15ff. for other women's letters.
63 Philippe Depreux, 'Ambitions et limites des réformes culturelles à l'époque carolingienne', *Revue Historique* 304, 3 (2002), p. 729.
64 Bischoff, *Manuscripts and Libraries*, p. 104.
65 McKitterick, *Carolingians and the Written Word*, pp. 261–3.
66 Bede, *Lives of the Abbots*, in Webb and Farmer, *Age of Bede*, p. 203; for the value of the land, see Michelle P. Brown, 'Bede's Life in Context', in Scott de Gregorio (ed.), *The Cambridge Companion to Bede* (Cambridge, 2010), p. 19.
67 Bischoff, *Manuscripts and Libraries*, p. 76.
68 G. Waitz (ed.), *Vitae Anskarii et Rimberti* (Hannover, 1884), p. 32.
69 McKitterick, *Carolingians and the Written Word*, p. 135.
70 Quoted in Peter Sawyer, *The Wealth of Anglo-Saxon England* (Oxford, 2013), pp. 103–4.
71 McKitterick, *Carolingians and the Written Word*, p. 217 for Gerald; pp. 247, 258; pp. 223–5 for Dhuoda (I have adjusted the translation).
72 Rosamond McKitterick, *History and Memory in the Carolingian World* (Cambridge, 2004), pp. 218–19.

### 3. *Making enemies*

1 Anne-Marie Flambard Héricher, Introduction to Héricher (ed.), *La Progression des Vikings des raids à la colonisation* (Rouen, 2003), pp. 9–10.

2 Abū Abd Allah Muhammad ibn Bakir al-Zuhrī in his *Book of Geography*; from Paul Lunde and Caroline Stone, *Ibn Fadlān and the Land of Darkness* (London, 2012), p. 110.

3 Cf. *Helgakvida Hundingsbana in Fyrri* 26 in Carolyne Larrington's translation of *The Poetic Edda* (Oxford, 1996): 'the nobles hoisted up / the well-sewn sail in Vasrinsfjord'. Other translators prefer simply 'woven' but the notion of sewing is present. (Carolyne Larrington, personal communication.) The army leaving port is based on the same poem, verses 26–9, pp. 117–18.

4 See Jan Bill, 'Viking Age Ships and Seafaring in the West', in Iben Skibsted Klæsøe (ed.), *Viking Trade and Settlement in Continental Western Europe* (Oslo, 2010), pp. 34, 38 for sails; p. 27 for oars and status; pp. 22, 23 for sailing season and times.

5 Cf. John Haywood, *Dark Age Naval Power* (London, 1991), pp. 71ff. for the limited evidence that Saxons used sails.

6 In *Óláfs Saga Helga*, ch. 175; at p. 464 in Snorri Sturluson (tr. Lee M. Hollander), *Heimskringla* (Austin, 2009).

7 Else Mundal, 'The Picture of the World in Old Norse Sources', in Gerhard Jaritz and Juhan Kreem (eds.), *The Edges of the Medieval World* (Budapest, 2009), pp. 40, 43–5.

8 Cf. Søren Thirslund, *Viking Navigation* (Roskilde, 2007), passim.

9 Cf. Kristel Zilmer, 'The Representation of Waterborne Traffic in Old Norse Narratives', *Viking and Medieval Scandinavia* 2 (2006), p. 242.

10 On the construction, see H. Hellmuth Andersen, 'Danevirke', in Pam J. Crabtree, *Medieval Archaeology: An Encyclopedia* (New York, 2001), p. 71; on politics, see Stéphane Lebecq, 'Aux origines du phénomène Viking', in Héricher, *Progression des Vikings*, pp. 17ff.

11 Cf. Knut Helle, 'The History of the Early Viking Age in Norway', in Howard B. Clarke, Máire Ní Mhaonaigh and Raghnall Ó Floinn (eds.), *Ireland and Scandinavia in the Early Viking Age* (Dublin, 1998), p. 244.

12 Wilhelm Holmqvist, 'Helgö, an Early Trading Settlement in Central Sweden', in Rupert Bruce-Mitford (ed.), *Recent Archaeological Excavations in Europe* (London, 1975), pp. 121–3; pp. 119–20 for the crozier; cf. Jutta Waller, 'Swedish Contacts with the Eastern Baltic in the pre-Viking and Early Viking Ages: The Evidence from Helgö', *Journal of Baltic Studies* 13, 3 (1982), p. 259.

13 Thomas S. Noonan, 'Why the Vikings First Came to Russia', *Jahrbücher für Geschichte Osteuropas* 34, 3 (1986), pp. 321ff.; for the cataracts, see Sigfús Blöndal and Benedikt S. Benedikz, *The Varangians of Byzantium* (Cambridge, 1978), pp. 8–12.

14 Dagfinn Skre, 'Town and Inhabitants', in Skre (ed.), *Things from the Town: Artefacts and Inhabitants in Viking-Age Kaupang* (Norske Oldfunn XXIV; Aarhus/Oslo, 2011), pp. 443ff.

15 Inger Storli, 'Ohthere and His World – a Contemporary Perspective', in Janet Bately and Anton Englert (eds.), *Ohthere's Voyages: A Late 9th-Century Account of Voyages along the Coasts of Norway and Denmark and Its Cultural Context* (Roskilde, 2007), pp. 89 for fishing; pp. 91, 93 for oil production; p. 94 for reindeer.

16 Janet Bately's edition and translation of Ohthere's testimony, slipped into the text of the Anglo-Saxon version of Orosius' *Historiarum adversum Paganos Libri Septem*, is in Bately and Englert, *Ohthere's Voyages*, p. 46 for riches; p. 44 for ambition in his voyages.

17 Anton Englert, 'Ohthere's Voyages Seen from a Nautical Angle', in Bately and Englert, *Ohthere's Voyages*, p. 119 for winds.

18 Rudolf Simek, 'Elusive Elysia, or Which Way to Glasisvellir?', in Rudolf Simek, Jónas Kristjánsson and Hans Bekker-Nielsen (eds.), *Sagnaskemmtun* (Graz, 1986).

19 Francis J. Tschan (ed. and tr.), *Adam of Bremen: History of the Archbishops of Hamburg–Bremen* (New York, 2002), p. 206.

20 Ibid., p. 211.

21 Stefan Brink with Neil Price (eds.), *The Viking World* (Abingdon, 2012), pp. 564, 571 for Iceland; p. 606 for Tyrkir.

22 See Michael McCormick, 'New Light on the "Dark Ages": How the Slave Trade Fuelled the Carolingian Economy', *Past and Present* 177 (November 2002), pp. 42–3 for Muslim economy and slave prices; p. 46 for quotation from Paul the Deacon.

23 Wilfried Hartmann (ed.), *Die Konzilien der Karolingischen Teilreiche 843–859* (Hannover, 1984), p. 124.

24 Brink with Price, *Viking World*, p. 545.

25 Howard B. Clarke, 'Proto-Towns and Towns in Ireland and Britain in the Ninth and Tenth Centuries', in Clarke et al., *Ireland and Scandinavia*, p. 336.

26 Ibrāhīm ibn Ya'qūb reported so in 965; in Lunde and Stone, *Ibn Fadlān*, p. 163.

27 *Hávamál*, verse 13, in Andy Orchard (tr. and ed.), *The Elder Edda* (London, 2011), p. 16.

28 Stéphane Lebecq, *Marchands et navigateurs frisons du haut Moyen Âge*, vol. 1: *Essai* (Lille, 1983), vol. 1, p. 129.

29 Black skin in a dead body might mean nitre in the soil where it was kept, or even some crude kind of mummification; nitre would account for the preservation.

30 In Orchard, *Elder Edda*: *Thrymskvida* 17, p. 99, for Thor; *Helgakvida Hjörvardssonar* 20, p. 130, for Atli.

31 Ibn Fadlān's account is in Lunde and Stone, *Ibn Fadlān*, pp. 45ff.

32 David Wyatt, *Slaves and Warriors in Medieval Britain and Ireland 800–1200* (Leiden, 2009), p. 142.

33 Pierre Baudin, 'L'Insertion des Normands dans le monde franc fin IX–Xème siècles: l'exemple des pratiques matrimoniales', in Héricher, *Progression des Vikings*, pp. 114–15.

34 Lunde and Stone, *Ibn Fadlān*, p. 163.

35 Carolyne Larrington (tr. and ed.), *The Poetic Edda* (Oxford, 1996), in *Atlamal*, the Greenland poem of Atli, verse 98, p. 232.

36 Judith Jesch, *Women in the Viking Age* (Woodbridge, 1991), pp. 91, 95, 176–8.

37 Oliver Elton (tr.), *The First Nine Books of the Danish History of Saxo Grammaticus* (London, 1894), p. 277 for the generalization and pp. 229–30 for the story of Alvid.

38 Wyatt, *Slaves and Warriors*, p. 177; the interpretation is mine.

39 *Ethelwerd's Chronicle*, in J. A. Giles (ed. and tr.), *Old English Chronicles* (London, 1906), p. 19.

40 Michael Swanton (ed. and tr.), *The Anglo-Saxon Chronicle* (London, 1996), pp. 54–5.

41 Ibid., pp. 54–7.

42 Angelo Forte, Richard Oram and Frederik Pedersen, *Viking Empires* (Cambridge, 2005), p. 55 for the speculations on which this is based.

43 Swanton, *Anglo-Saxon Chronicle*, pp. 56–7.

44 Ernst Dümmler (ed.), *Epistolae Karolini aevi*, vol. II (Berlin, 1895), letter 16, p. 42.

45 Ibid., letter 20, p. 57.
46 Ibid., letter 6, p. 31.
47 Ibid., letter 20, p. 57.
48 Ibid., letter 21, p. 59.
49 Ibid., letter 22, p. 59.
50 Kevin Crossley-Holland, *The Anglo-Saxon World: An Anthology* (Oxford, 1999), p. 26, cites Wihtred's laws from Dorothy Whitelock, *English Historical Documents*, vol. I (London, 1979).
51 Peter Sawyer, *Anglo-Saxon Charters: An Annotated List and Bibliography*, accessible at www.esawyer.org.uk, item 134: 'nisi expeditione intra Cantiam contra paganos marinos cum classis migrantibus'.
52 Sawyer, *Anglo-Saxon Charters*, items 160, dated 804, and 186, dated 822.
53 Timothy Reuter, 'Plunder and Tribute in the Carolingian Empire', *Transactions of the Royal Historical Society*, 5th series, vol. 35 (1985), pp. 75–94. He quotes the *Annales Fuldenses* for 885 and notes a similar Frisian victory over the Northmen in 876 where the winners 'took away the treasure and divided it among themselves ...'
54 Henry Mayr-Harting, 'Charlemagne, the Saxons and the Imperial Coronation of 800', *English Historical Review* 111, 444 (November 1996), pp. 1113ff.
55 Charles H. Robinson (tr.), *Anskar: The Apostle of the North 801–865, Translated from the Vita Anskarii by Bishop Rimbert, His Fellow Missionary and Successor* (London, 1922), pp. 54, 56, 116, 105.
56 Florin Curta, 'Merovingian and Carolingian Gift Giving', *Speculum* 81, 3 (2006), p. 690.
57 Robinson, *Anskar*, p. 38.
58 Eric Vanneufville, *Heliand: L'Évangile de la Mer du Nord* (Turnhout, 2008), pp. 27–8.
59 I have used Vanneufville, *Heliand*, but also G. Ronald Murphy SJ, *The Heliand, the Saxon Gospel* (Oxford, 1992), especially for his notes and commentary. For a critique of Murphy, his interpretation and the possible errors in his translation, see the review by Joseph Wilson in the *Journal of English and Germanic Philology* 94, 3 (July 1995), pp. 454–6; I have moderated my account accordingly. With those caveats, G. Ronald Murphy, *The Saxon Savior: The Germanic Transformation of the Gospel in the Ninth-Century Heliand* (New York, 1989), is invaluable.

60 Murphy, *Heliand*, song 48, p. 130.

61 Ibid., song 2, p. 8.

62 Ibid., song 26, p. 72.

63 Ibid., song 14, p. 41, for nailed ships; song 27, p. 75, and song 35, p. 95. for 'high-horned'.

64 Ibid., song 16, p. 48 for salt.

65 Ibid., song 18, p. 52 for oaths; pp. 57, 157 for the cup and the toast; pp. 45, 122–3 for the moneychangers; pp. 50, 135 for 'arrogant men'; pp. 64, 177 for 'evil clan'.

66 Ibid., song 16, pp. 45–7, for these military Beatitudes.

67 Haywood, *Dark Age Naval Power*, pp. 118–19.

68 *Annales regni Francorum* for 804, 808 and 810, cited in Lebecq, *Marchands et navigateurs frisons*, vol. 2: *Corpus des sources écrites*, pp. 303–4.

69 Haywood, *Dark Age Naval Power*, p. 119.

70 Stéphane Lebecq, 'Les Vikings en Frise: chronique d'un échec relatif', in Pierre Baudin (ed.), *Les Fondations scandinaves en Occident et les débuts du Duché de Normandie* (Caen, 2005), p. 102.

71 Quoted from Ermentar, *De translationibus et miraculis Sancti Philiberti Libri II*, in Janet L. Nelson, 'England and the Continent in the Ninth Century: II, the Vikings and Others', *Transactions of the Royal Historical Society*, 6th series, vol. 13 (2003), p. 9.

72 Nelson, 'England and the Continent'. I have slightly adjusted Julia Barrow's translation from the *Liber Eliensis*, I, ch. 41.

73 Mechthild Pörnbacher, *Walahfrid Strabo, Zwei Legenden* (Sigmaringen, 1997), pp. 36ff. for Latin text of *Versus de Beati Blaithmaic Vita et Fine*, esp. lines 17, 95–8, 132–64. The English version is mine.

74 Christopher D. Morris, 'Raiders, Traders and Settlers: The Early Viking Age in Scotland', in Clarke et al., *Ireland and Scandinavia*, p. 77.

75 Dicuil (ed. J. J. Tierney), *Liber de mensura orbis terrae*, 7, 15 (Dublin, 1967), pp. 76, 77. Dicuil writes 'nimis marinarum avium'; 'nimis' suggests too many, not just very many.

## *4. Settling*

1 Quoted in Luigi de Anna, *Conoscenza e Immagine della Finlandia e del Settentrione nella Cultura Classico-Medievale* (Turku, 1988), p. 111.

2 Charles Doherty, 'The Viking Impact upon Ireland', in Anne-Christine Larsen (ed.), *The Vikings in Ireland* (Roskilde, 2001), p. 33.
3 Quoted in Judith Jesch, *Women in the Viking Age* (Woodbridge, 1991), p. 106.
4 See Donnchadh Ó Corráin, 'The Vikings and Ireland', in Stefan Brink and Neil Price (eds.), *The Viking World* (Abingdon, 2012), pp. 428ff.; and 'The Vikings in Ireland', in Larsen, *The Vikings in Ireland*, pp. 17ff.
5 *Annals of Ulster* for 840, quoted in Thomas McErlean, 'The History of Nendrum', in Thomas McErlean and Norman Crothers, *Harnessing the Tides: The Early Medieval Tide Mills at Nendrum Monastery, Strangford Lough* (Belfast, 2007), p. 313.
6 Ó Corráin, 'Vikings in Ireland', in Brink and Price, *Viking World*, pp. 17ff.
7 Egon Wamers, 'Insular Finds in Viking Age Scandinavia', in Howard B. Clarke, Máire Ní Mhaonaigh and Raghnall Ó Floinn (eds.), *Ireland and Scandinavia in the Early Viking Age* (Dublin, 1998), p. 60.
8 Donnchadh Ó Corráin, 'Bilingualism in Viking Age Dublin', in John Bradley, Alan J. Fletcher and Anngret Simms (eds.), *Dublin in the Medieval World* (Dublin, 2009), pp. 71–2.
9 David Wyatt, *Slaves and Warriors in Medieval Britain and Ireland 800–1200* (Leiden, 2009), pp. 96–7.
10 Ibid., pp. 70–82.
11 Doherty, 'Viking Impact upon Ireland', in Larsen, *Vikings in Ireland*, p. 34.
12 Jan Petersen, 'British Antiquities of the Viking Period, Found in Norway', in Haakon Shetelig, *Viking Antiquities in Great Britain and Ireland*, vol. V (Oslo, 1940), p. 7.
13 A. T. Lucas, 'The Plundering and Burning of Churches in Ireland, 7th to 16th century', in Etienne Rynne (ed.), *North Munster Studies* (Limerick, 1967), p. 176. Lucas examined and counted up the evidence for who raided which church and when, which is the basis for the arguments that follow.
14 Thomas McErlean, 'The Mills in Their Monastic Context: The Archaeology of Nendrum Reassessed', in McErlean and Crothers, *Harnessing the Tides*, pp. 324ff.
15 Doherty, 'Viking Impact upon Ireland', in Larsen, *Vikings in Ireland*, p. 32.

16 See McErlean and Crothers, *Harnessing the Tides*; and also Thomas McErlean, Caroline Earwood, Dermot Moore and Eileen Murphy, 'The Sequence of Early Christian Period Horizontal Tide Mills at Nendrum Monastery: An Interim Statement', *Historical Archaeology* 41, 3 (2007), pp. 63–75.

17 See Lucas, 'Plundering and Burning', in Rynne, *North Munster Studies*, for a forensic account of the evidence.

18 Patrick F. Wallace, 'Ireland's Viking Towns', in Larsen, *Vikings in Ireland*, pp. 39ff.

19 Howard B. Clarke, 'Proto-Towns and Towns in Ireland and Britain in the Ninth and Tenth Centuries', in Clarke et al., *Ireland and Scandinavia*, p. 342.

20 James Graham-Campbell, 'The Early Viking Age in the Irish Sea Area', in Clarke et al., *Ireland and Scandinavia*, p. 106.

21 Cf. Harold Mytum, 'The Vikings and Ireland', in James H. Barrett (ed.), *Contact, Continuity and Collapse: The Norse Colonization of the North Atlantic* (Turnhout, 2003), p. 128.

22 Jean Renaud, *Les Vikings et les Celtes* (Rennes, 1992), p. 167.

23 Christopher D. Morris, 'Raiders, Traders and Settlers: The Early Viking Age in Scotland', in Clarke et al., *Ireland and Scandinavia*, p. 90.

24 Máire Ní Mhaonaigh, 'The Vikings in Medieval Irish Literature', in Larsen, *Vikings in Ireland*, pp. 99, 100, 101, 102.

25 See Richard Hall, 'York', in Brink and Price, *Viking World*, pp. 379ff.; and R. A. Hall et al., *Aspects of Anglo-Scandinavian York* (York, 2004), in the series *The Archaeology of York*, 8/4, especially David Rollason, 'Anglo-Scandinavian York: The Evidence of Historical Sources', and Allan Hall and Harry Kenward, 'Setting People in Their Environment: Plant and Animal Remains from Anglo-Scandinavian York'.

26 Michael Swanton (ed. and tr.), *The Anglo-Saxon Chronicle* (London, 1996), p. 111, from Worcester ms. (D) for 943.

27 Lesley Abrams, 'The Early Danelaw: Conquest, Transition and Assimilation', in Anne-Marie Flambard Héricher (ed.), *La Progression des Vikings des raids à la colonisation* (Rouen, 2003), pp. 59, 61, 62, 65.

28 Swanton, *Anglo-Saxon Chronicle*, pp. 74–5.

29 See Hall and Kenward, 'Setting People in Their Environment'.

30 Quoted in Rollason, 'Anglo-Scandinavian York', p. 322.
31 Swanton, *Anglo-Saxon Chronicle*, p. 109, from Winchester ms. (A) for 937.
32 Wyatt, *Slaves and Warriors*, p. 125, quoting the twelfth-century Cogadh Gaedhel re Gallaibh.
33 Quoted in Wyatt, *Slaves and Warriors*, p. 339.
34 Egge Knol, 'Frisia in Carolingian Times', in Iben Skibsted Klæsøe (ed.), *Viking Trade and Settlement in Continental Western Europe* (Copenhagen, 2010), pp. 47, 55, 57.
35 Jens Christian Moesgaard, 'Vikings on the Continent: The Numismatic Evidence', in Klæsøe, *Viking Trade and Settlement*, pp. 135, 140.
36 Quoted in Wyatt, *Slaves and Warriors*, pp. 99, 169.
37 See Sigfús Blöndal and Benedikt S. Benedikz, *The Varangians of Byzantium* (Cambridge, 1978), p. 8 for the Chinese; p. 180 for Palm Sunday; p. 190 for satires; p. 200 for death; pp. 62–3 for rape; p. 223 for Swedish law; pp. 54ff. for Harald Hardrada; p. 61 for poem; p. 64 for Jerusalem.
38 Þorsteinn Vilhjálmsson, 'Navigation and Vínland', in Andrew Wawn and Þórunn Sigurðardóttir, *Approaches to Vínland* (Reykjavik, 2001), pp. 108ff.
39 Árni Björnsson, 'Prerequisites for Saga Writing', in Wawn and Sigurðardóttir, *Approaches to Vínland*, pp. 53–5.
40 P. Schledermann and K. M. McCullough, 'Inuit-Norse Contact in the Smith Sound Region', in Barrett, *Contact, Continuity and Collapse*, pp. 184–5.
41 Keneva Kunz (tr.), *The Saga of the Greenlanders*, in Gísli Sigurdsson (ed.) and Keneva Kunz (tr.), *The Vinland Sagas* (London, 2008), p. 3.
42 Birgitta Linderoth Wallace, 'L'Anse aux Meadows and Vinland', in Barrett, *Contact, Continuity and Collapse*, pp. 207ff.
43 *Erik the Red's Saga*, in Sigurdsson and Kunz, *Vinland Sagas*, p. 46.
44 Jenny Jochens uses the word 'molest' in this context. See 'The Western Voyages: Women and Vikings', in Wawn and Sigurðardóttir, *Approaches to Vínland*, p. 84.
45 *The Saga of the Greenlanders*, in Sigurdsson and Kunz, *Vinland Sagas*, p. 4 for characters; pp. 17–20 for deals and murders.
46 *Erik the Red's Saga*, in Sigurdsson and Kunz, *Vinland Sagas*, p. 48.

47 For commentary on the saga stories, see William P. L. Thomson, *The New History of Orkney* (Edinburgh, 2008), pp. 109–12.

48 Based on Herman Pálsson and Paul Edwards (tr.), *Orkneyinga Saga* (London, 1978), pp. 214–18; 'greatest man' at section 108; spring and autumn trips at section 105; last trip and death at sections 107, 108.

## 5. *Fashion*

1 *The Saga of Hacon* and a fragment of the *Saga of Magnus* in G. W. Dasent (tr.), *Icelandic Sagas*, vol. IV (London, 1894), p. 266.

2 Richard Vaughan (tr. and ed.), *The Illustrated Chronicles of Matthew Paris* (Stroud, 1993), p. 75.

3 Dasent, *Icelandic Sagas*, p. 266.

4 Vaughan, *Illustrated Chronicles*, pp. 75–6.

5 Ibid., p. 76; Dasent, *Icelandic Sagas*, p. 267.

6 Herman Palsson and Paul Edwards (tr.). *Orkneyinga Saga*, ch. 60, p. 109 for the Grimsby trip; p. 110 for the clothes.

7 Snorri Sturluson (tr. Lee M. Hollander), *Heimskringla* (Austin, 1964), chs. 2–3, pp. 664–5.

8 Ibid., ch. 31, p. 816.

9 Gitte Hansen, 'Luxury for Everyone? – Embroideries on Leather Shoes and the Consumption of Silk Yarn in 11th–13th Century Northern Europe', in Angela Ling Huang and Carsten Janhnke (eds.), *Textiles and the Medieval Economy* (Oxford, forthcoming 2014).

10 Henri Joseph L. Baudrillart, *Histoire du luxe privé et public,* vol. III (Paris, 1881), pp. 250–51.

11 See Else Østergård, *Woven into the Earth: Textiles from Norse Greenland* (Aarhus, 2009), p. 39 for use of sheep; p. 62 for *vaðmál*; pp. 95–7 for garment construction; p. 146 for imported cloth.

12 Quoted in Østergård, *Woven into the Earth*, p. 144.

13 Margaret Scott, *Medieval Dress and Fashion* (London, 2007), p. 169; p. 145 for necklines.

14 Gisela and Eberhard, Count of Friuli, cited in ibid., p. 16.

15 Laura F. Hodges, 'A Reconsideration of the Monk's Costume', in *Chaucer Review* 26, 2 (1991), p. 143n.9, citing C. G. Coulton, *Five Centuries of Religion* (Cambridge, 1923).

16 Bede, *Life of Cuthbert*, in J. F. Webb and D. H. Farmer (trs.), *The Age of Bede* (London, 1988), p. 67.
17 Ernst Dümmler (ed.), *Epistolae Karolini aevi*, vol. II (Berlin, 1895), letter 21, p. 59.
18 Hodges, 'Reconsideration of the Monk's Costume', pp. 134–5.
19 Janet M. Cowen and Jennifer C. Ward, 'Al myn array is bliew, what nedith more?', in Cordelia Beattie et al. (eds.), *The Medieval Household in Christian Europe c.850–c.1550* (Turnhout, 2003), p. 117.
20 See Michèle Beaulieu and Jeanne Baylé, *Le Costume de Bourgogne de Philippe le Hardi à Charles le Téméraire* (Paris, 1956).
21 Francisque-Michel (ed.), *Le Roman de la Rose* (Paris, 1864), vol. II, p. 10.
22 Martha C. Howell, *Commerce before Capitalism in Europe, 1300–1600* (Cambridge, 2010), pp. 210–11.
23 See Kay Stanisland, 'Getting There, Got It: Archaeological Textiles and Tailoring in London 1330–1580', in David Gaimster and Paul Stamper (eds.), *The Age of Transition: The Archaeology of English Culture 1400–1600* (Oxford, 1997), pp. 239–40.
24 Michael Rocke, *Forbidden Friendships* (New York, 1996), p. 30.
25 For a discussion of the wider motives for sumptuary laws, see Howell, *Commerce before Capitalism*, pp. 208ff.
26 Scott, *Medieval Dress and Fashion*, pp. 80, 131, 166, 126.
27 Ibid., pp. 44–5.
28 Beaulieu and Baylé, *Costume de Bourgogne*, say Poland; Scott, *Medieval Dress and Fashion*, names Fulk, Count of Anjou.
29 *Le Testament Maistre Jehan de Meun*, lines 1195–1201; see Silvia Buzzetti Gallarati, *Le Testament Maistre Jehan de Meun, un caso literario* (Alessandria, 1989), p. 171 for text; p. 85 for commentary.
30 E. Nicaise et al. (eds.), *Chirugerie de maître Henri de Mondeville . . .* (Paris, 1893), pp. 591–3.
31 James M. Dean (ed.), *Richard the Redeless and Mom and the Sothsegger* (Kalamazoo, 2000), III, lines 221–34.
32 See Camilla Luise Dahl, 'Mengiað klæthe and tweskifte klædher', in Kathrine Vestergård Pedersen and Marie-Louise B. Nosch, *The Medieval Broadcloth* (Oxford, 2009), pp. 129ff.
33 *Testament*, lines 1277–80, 1313–14, in Gallarati, *Testament Maistre Jehan de Meun*, pp. 174, 176.

34 Christine de Pizan (tr. Sarah Lawson), *The Treasure of the City of Ladies* (London, 2003), pp. 116, 132.
35 William Harrison (ed. Georges Edelen), *The Description of England* (Ithaca, 1968), p. 145.
36 Scott, *Medieval Dress and Fashion*, pp. 84–5.
37 Quoted in Christopher Breward, *The Culture of Fashion* (Manchester, 1995), p. 56.
38 Philip Stubbes (ed. Margaret Jane Kidnie), *The Anatomie of Abuses* (Tempe, 2002), p. 99.
39 John Warrington (ed.), *The Paston Letters* (London, 1956), vol. II, p. 50.
40 Ibid., II, 195.
41 Ibid., I, 161; I, 223; II, 23; II, 63; II, 32; II, 206; II, 178. The Howards' list is on pp. 37–9 of vol. II.
42 Cited from the reissue of Eileen Power's translation *The Goodman of Paris* (1928) (Woodbridge, 2008), p. 37; cf. Daniel Roche, *La Culture des apparences* (Paris, 1989).
43 Scott, *Medieval Dress and Fashion*, p. 89.
44 Ann Rosalind Jones, 'Habits, Holdings, Heterologies: Populations in Print in a 1562 Costume Book', *Yale French Studies* 110 (2006).
45 François Deserps (ed. Sara Shannon), *A collection of the various styles of clothing which are presently worn in countries of Europe, Asia, Africa and the savage islands: all realistically depicted* (Minneapolis, 2001), p. 28 for diversity; pp. 120–21 for Lübeck; p. 68 for Scots; p. 60 for Dutch; p. 56 for Brabant; p. 82 for Zeeland.
46 Cesare Vecellio, *Habiti Antichi et Modeni di tutto il Mundo* (Venice, 1589), p. 276 for Englishwomen; p. 239 for women of Antwerp; pp. 293–4 for Northern women's habits; unpaginated front matter for 'capriccio'.
47 Stubbes, *Anatomie of Abuses*, on these pages: 236 for music; 199 for actors; 251 for football; 156 for 'cankers'; 134 for 'fashions'; 123 for flowers; 67 for 'sin'; 122 for 'Arithmetician'; 92 for 'Ruffs'; 90 for hats; 100 for slippers; 96 for doublets; 10 for 'apparel lying rotting'; 107 for make-up; 111 for hair; 117 for Devil starching; 112 for fair hair; 120 for daughters; 66 for Pride; 71 for 'who is a Gentleman'. Kidnie's immaculate edition reproduces Stubbes's spellings, which I have adjusted without changing his vocabulary.

48 See Stanisland, 'Getting There, Got It', in Gaimster and Stamper, *Age of Transition*, p. 244.

49 Stubbes, *Anatomie of Abuses*, p. 29 for 'according to degree'; p. 95 for soft shirts; pp. 30–31 for effeminacy; p. 32 for women in doublets.

## 6. *Writing the law*

1 The rules for ordeals varied. Anglo-Saxon rules (the diet for the fast, for example) are discussed in M. H. Kerr, R. D. Forsyth and M. J. Plyley, 'Cold Water and Hot Iron: Trial by Ordeal in England', *Journal of Interdisciplinary History* 22, 4 (Spring 1992), pp. 582–3. Those rules are set out in the twelfth-century *Textus Roffensis*, excerpted and translated in Michael Swanton, *Anglo-Saxon Prose* (London, 1975), pp. 5–6. Rules in the Frankish kingdoms included the kissing of the Gospel, the specific forms of prayer; see Karl Zeumer (ed.), *Formulae Merowingici et Karolini aevi* (Hannover, 1886), pp. 638ff. For shaving and the three days of fasting, see Peter Brown, 'Society and the Supernatural: A Medieval Change', *Daedalus* 104, 2 (1975), p. 134.

2 Zeumer, *Formulae Merowingici et Karolini aevi*, pp. 639, 654.

3 Ibid., p. 640.

4 James A. Brundage, '*E Pluribus Unum*: Custom, the Professionalisation of Medieval Law and Regional Variations in Marriage Formation', in Mia Korpiola (ed.), *Regional Variations in Matrimonial Law and Custom in Europe 1150–1600* (Leiden, 2011), p. 37.

5 Zeumer, *Formulae Merowingici et Karolini aevi*, p. 639.

6 *Atlamál in Grœnlenzku* 11, in Andy Orchard (tr. and ed.), *The Elder Edda* (London, 2011), p. 217.

7 Hermann Pálsson and Paul Edwards (tr.), *Orkneyinga Saga* (London, 1978), p. 108.

8 Quoted in Alain Marez, 'Une Europe des Vikings? La leçon des inscriptions runiques', in Regis Boyer, *Les Vikings, premiers Européens, VIIIème–XIème siècle* (Paris, 2005), p. 143.

9 *Sigrdrífumál* 6, in Orchard, *Elder Edda*, p. 170.

10 *Sigrdrífumál* 10, in ibid., p. 171.

11 *Hávamál* 142, in ibid., p. 36.

12 *För Skírnis* 31, 36, in ibid., p. 65.

13 *Gudrúnarkvida in fyrsta* 23, in ibid., p. 182.

14 *Atlamál in Grœnlenzku* 3, 4, 12, in ibid., p. 216–17.

15 *Gudrúnarkvida in Forna* 22–4, in ibid., p. 199.

16 Jenny Jochens, 'La Femme Viking en avance sur son temps', in Boyer, *Vikings*, p. 224.

17 Catharina Randvere, 'The Power of the Spoken Word', *Viking and Medieval Scandinavia* I (2005), pp. 182–3.

18 Judith Jesch, *Women in the Viking Age* (Woodbridge, 1991), p. 56.

19 Birgit Sawyer, *The Viking Age Rune-Stones: Custom and Commemoration in Early Medieval Scandinavia* (Oxford, 2000), p. 119.

20 Magnus Olsen, 'Runic Inscriptions in Great Britain, Ireland and the Isle of Man', in Haakon Shetelig (ed.), *Viking Antiquities in Great Britain and Ireland* (Oslo, 1954), p. 191.

21 Jesch, *Women in the Viking Age*, p. 51.

22 Ibid., p. 64.

23 Olsen, 'Runic Inscriptions', in Shetelig, *Viking Antiquities*, p. 215, and Marez, 'Une Europe des Vikings?', in Boyer, *Vikings*, p. 140.

24 Marez, 'Une Europe des Vikings?', in Boyer, *Vikings*, p. 155.

25 Ibid., p. 156.

26 Ibid., p. 160.

27 Ibid., p. 170.

28 Ibid., pp. 172, 174.

29 Gitte Hansen, 'Kontekst, avsetningshistorie og frekke runeristere i Bergen', in Årbok for Bergen Museum 2005, pp. 44–7.

30 A. Liestøl, *Runer fra Bryggen* (Oslo, 1964); I am grateful to Gitte Hansen (personal communication) for the citation, the translation and the dating. The stick is BRM 0/18959 in the Bryggen Museum, Bergen.

31 Swanton, *Anglo-Saxon Prose*, p. 6.

32 Zeumer, *Formulae Merowingici et Karolini aevi*, p. 649.

33 Swanton, *Anglo-Saxon Prose*, p. 5.

34 Finbarr McAuley, 'Canon Law and the End of the Ordeal', *Oxford Journal of Legal Studies* 26, 3 (2006), p. 481.

35 Kerr, Forsyth and Plyley, 'Cold Water and Hot Iron', p. 579.

36 Ernest C. York, 'Isolt's Ordeal: English Legal Customs in the Medieval Tristan Legend', *Studies in Philology* 68, 1, p. 7, for the list.

37 Kerr, Forsyth and Plyley, 'Cold Water and Hot Iron', pp. 579–80.

38 *Gudrúnarkvida in Thridja* 6–11, in Orchard, *Elder Edda*, pp. 203–4.

39 Michael H. Gelting, 'Poppo's Ordeal: Courtier Bishops and the Success of Christianization at the Turn of the First Millennium', *Viking and Medieval Scandinavia* 6 (2010), p. 104, quoting Widukind, *Rerum gestarum Saxonicarum libri tres*.

40 Alfred Levison (ed.), *Capitularia Regum Francorum* (Hannover, 1883), p. 129, under *Divisio Regnorum*, dated 6 February 806, par. 14.

41 Zeumer, *Formulae Merowingici et Karolini aevi*, p. 641.

42 Ibid., p. 651.

43 Ibid., p. 641.

44 Swanton, *Anglo-Saxon Prose*, p. 6.

45 John W. Baldwin, 'The Intellectual Preparation for the Canon of 1215 against Ordeals', *Speculum* 36, 4 (October 1961), pp. 613ff.

46 Wolfgang P. Müller, 'The Recovery of Justinian's Digest in the Middle Ages', *Bulletin of Medieval Canon Law* 20 (1990), pp. 1–6, 25–7.

47 Brundage, '*E Pluribus Unum*', p. 97.

48 Ibid., pp. 21, 31, 34–5.

49 Quoted in McAuley, 'Canon Law', p. 473.

50 Baldwin, *Intellectual Preparation*, p. 620.

51 For objections to ordeals and the arguments of Peter the Chanter, see ibid., esp. pp. 627ff.

52 James A. Brundage, *The Medieval Origins of the Legal Profession* (Chicago, 2008), pp. 1–8 for start of profession; pp. 70–72 for Ireland; p. 37 for Martial and Juvenal.

53 A. G. van Hamel (ed.), *Lamentations de Matheolus . . . de Jehan le Fèvre, de Resson* (Paris, 1892), vol. I, p. 283: in French, lines 519–30; in Latin, 4579–83.

54 William Langland (tr. A. V. C. Schmidt), *Piers Plowman* (Oxford, 1992), p. 7.

55 Michael Haren (ed. and tr.), 'The Interrogatories for Official, Large and Secular Estates of the *Memoriale Presbiterorum*', in Peter Billen and A. J. Minnis (eds.), *Handling Sin: Confession in the Middle Ages* (Woodbridge, 1998), pp. 132–3.

56 See Adriaan Verhulst, *The Rise of Cities in North-West Europe* (Cambridge and Paris, 1999), esp. pp. 153ff.

57 Howell, *Commerce before Capitalism*, pp. 61–3 for trees; pp. 38–41 for property and law.

58 Sister James Eugene Madden, 'Business Monks, Banker Monks, Bankrupt Monks: The English Cistercians in the Thirteenth Century', *Catholic Historical Review* 49, 3 (1963), pp. 341ff.

59 William M. McGovern Jr, 'The Enforcement of Informal Contracts in the Later Middle Ages', *California Law Review* 59, 5 (1971), pp. 1145ff.

60 F. R. (Fritz Redlich), 'A Fourteenth Century Business History', *Business History Review* 39, 2 (1965), pp. 261ff.

61 Pamela Nightingale, 'Monetary Contraction and Mercantile Credit in Later Medieval England', *Economic History Review* 43, 4 (1990), pp. 573–4.

62 Anton Englert, 'Large Cargo Vessels in Danish Waters 1000–1250: Archaeological Evidence for Professional Merchant Seafaring before the Hanseatic Period', in C. Beltrame (ed.), *Boats, Ships and Shipyards* (Oxford, 2003), pp. 273ff.

63 Jacques Heers, *La Naissance du capitalisme au Moyen Âge* (Paris, 2012), pp. 229–30.

64 For a full account of these new complexities, see Peter Spufford, *Power and Profit: The Merchant in Medieval Europe* (London, 2002), esp. pp. 12–42.

65 Eric Knibbs, *Ansgar, Rimbert and the Forged Foundations of Hamburg–Bremen* (Farnham, 2011), p. 135 for Charlemagne; p. 153 for archbishop; p. 207 for Rimbert's role.

66 Alfred Hiatt, *The Making of Medieval Forgeries: False Documents in Fifteenth-Century England* (London, 2004), p. 22 for scale of forgeries; p. 25 for John of Salisbury; pp. 36–7 for Crowland; pp. 156ff. for Austria; pp. 70ff. for Cambridge.

67 McAuley, 'Canon Law', pp. 490–97.

68 James Bruce Ross (tr. and ed.), *Galbert of Bruges: The Murder of Charles the Good* (New York, 2005), p. 160 for the 'murderers'; p. 192 for the body; p. 204 for the law.

69 R. C. Van Caenegem, 'Customary Law in Twelfth-Century Flanders', in Ludo Milis et al. (eds.), *Law, History, the Low Countries and Europe* (London, 1994), pp. 97ff.

70 R. C. Van Caenegem, 'Roman Law in the Southern Netherlands', in Milis et al., *Law, History, the Low Countries and Europe*, pp. 123ff.

71 Marc Bouchat, 'Procedures *Juris Ordine Observato* et *Juris Ordine Non Observato* dans les arbitrages du diocèse de Liège au XIIIe siècle', *Tijdschrift voor Rechtsgeschiendenis* 60 (1992), pp. 377ff.

72 Oscar Gelderblom, 'The Resolution of Commercial Conflicts in Bruges, Antwerp and Amsterdam (1250–1650)', in Debin Ma and Jan Luiten van Zanden (eds.), *Law and Long-Term Economic Change* (Stanford, 2011), pp. 246–7 for Veckinchusen case.

73 Wendy J. Turner, 'Silent Testimony: Emotional Displays and Lapses of Memory as Indicators of Mental Instability in Medieval English Investigations', in Wendy J. Turner (ed.), *Madness in Medieval Law and Custom* (Leiden, 2010), p. 81.

74 James R. King, 'The Mysterious Case of the "Mad" Rector', in Turner, *Madness in Medieval Law and Custom*, pp. 70ff.

## *7. Overseeing nature*

1 Richard Vaughan (tr.), *The Illustrated Chronicles of Matthew Paris* (Stroud, 1993), p. 187.

2 J. M. Bos, B. van Geel and J. P. Pals, 'Waterland 1000–2000 AD', in Hilary H. Birks et al. (eds.), *The Cultural Landscape Past, Present and Future* (Cambridge, 1988), pp. 321ff.

3 J. C. Besteman, 'The pre-Urban Development of Medemblik: From an Early Medieval Trading Centre to a Medieval Town', in H. A. Heidinga and H. H. van Regteren Altena (eds.), *Medemblik and Monnickendam: Aspects of Medieval Urbanization in Northern Holland* (Amsterdam, 1989), esp. pp. 21–8.

4 William H. TeBrake, 'Taming the Waterwolf: Hydraulic Engineering and Water Management in the Netherlands during the Middle Ages', *Technology and Culture* 43, 3 (2002), pp. 475ff.

5 Jill Eddison, 'The Purpose, Construction and Operation of a 13th Century Watercourse: The Rhee, Romney Marsh, Kent', in Anthony Long, Stephen Hipkin and Helen Clarke (eds.), *Romney Marsh: Coastal and Landscape Change through the Ages* (Oxford, 2002).

6 Alan Mayhew, *Rural Settlement and Farming in Germany* (London, 1973), pp. 47–9, 148; G. P. van de Ven (ed.), *Man-Made Lowlands: History of Water Management and Land Reclamation in the Netherlands* (Utrecht, 2004), pp. 98–100, 139–40.

7 C. T. Smith, 'Dutch Peat Digging and the Origin of the Norfolk Broads', *Geographical Journal* 132, 1 (1966), pp. 71–2.

8 On this and the 'lake phase', see Petra J. E. M. van Dam, 'Sinking Peat Bogs: Environmental Change in Holland 1350–1550', *Environmental History* 6, 1 (2001), pp. 32ff.

9 Tim Soens, 'Floods and Money: Funding Drainage and Flood Control in Coastal Flanders from the Thirteenth to the Sixteenth Centuries', *Continuity and Change* 26, 3 (2011), pp. 333ff.

10 J. M. Bos, 'A Fourteenth Century Industrial Complex at Monnickendam', in Heidinga and Altena, *Medemblik and Monnickendam*, p. 59.

11 Bas van Bavel and Oscar Gelderbloom, 'Cleanliness in the Dutch Golden Age', *Past and Present* 205 (2009), pp. 41ff.

12 James H. Barrett, Alison M. Locker and Callum M. Roberts, '"Dark Age Economics" Revisited: The English Fish Bone Evidence AD 600–1600', *Antiquity* 78 (2004), pp. 618 ff.

13 James H. Barrett, Roelf P. Beukens and Rebecca A. Nicholson, 'Diet and Ethnicity during the Viking Colonization of Northern Scotland: Evidence from Fish Bones and Table Carbon Isotopes', *Antiquity* 75 (2000), pp. 145ff. Compare James H. Barrett et al., 'Archaeo-ichthyological Evidence for Long-Term Socio-economic Trends in Northern Scotland: 3500 BC to AD 1500', *Journal of Archaeological Science* 26, pp. 353ff.

14 Kevin Crossley-Holland (tr.), *The Anglo-Saxon World: An Anthology* (Oxford, 1984), p. 223.

15 Astri Riddervold, 'The Importance of Herring in the Daily Life of the Coastal Population of Norway', in Harlan Walker (ed.), *Staple Foods* (London, 1990), pp. 189–90.

16 Sophia Perdikaris, 'From Chiefly Provisioning to Commercial Fishery: Long-Term Economic Change in Arctic Norway', *World Archaeology* 30, 3 (1999), pp. 397–9.

17 Carsten Jahnke, 'The Medieval Herring Fishery in the Western Baltic', in Louis Sicking and Darlene Abreu-Ferreira (eds.), *Beyond the*

*Catch: Fisheries of the North Atlantic, the North Sea and the Baltic 900–1850* (Leiden, 2009), pp. 172–6.

18 Richard C. Hoffmann, 'Economic Development and Aquatic Ecosystems in Medieval Europe', *American Historical Review* 101, 3 (1996), pp. 631ff.

19 Jean Desse and Nathalie Desse-Berset, 'Pêches locales, côtières ou lointaines: le poisson au menu des parisiens du Grand Louvre du 14ème au 18ème siècles', *Anthropozoologica* 16 (1992), pp. 119–26.

20 Oliver H. Creighton, *Designs upon the Land: Élite landscapes of the Middle Ages* (Woodbridge, 2009), pp. 114–19.

21 Odile Redon, Françoise Sabban and Silvano Serventi, *The Medieval Kitchen: Recipes from France and Italy* (Chicago, 1998), pp. 123–4.

22 Naomi Sykes, 'Animal Bones and Animal Parks', in Robert Liddiard (ed.), *The Medieval Park: New Perspectives* (Macclesfield, 2007), pp. 50–51.

23 Aleksander Pluskowski, 'The Social Construction of Medieval Park Ecosystems: An Interdisciplinary Perspective', in Liddiard, *Medieval Park*, pp. 63ff.

24 Richard C. Hoffmann, 'Fishing for Sport in Medieval Europe: New Evidence', *Speculum* 60, 4 (1985), pp. 884–5 for Perceval; pp. 887–8 for Wallace.

25 Christopher K. Currie, 'The Early History of the Carp and Its Economic Significance in England', *Agricultural History Review* 39, 2 (1991), pp. 97–107.

26 Thomas Hale, *A compleat body of husbandry*, II (London, 1758), p. 116.

27 See Dries Tys, 'Walraversijde, Another Kettle of Fish? Dynamics and Identity of a Late Medieval Coastal Settlement in a proto-Capitalistic Landscape', and on material culture Marnix Pieters, 'The Archaeology of Fishery, Trade and Piracy: The Material Environment of Walraversijde and Other Late Medieval and Early Modern Fishing Communities along the Southern North Sea', in Marnix Pieters, Frans Verhaege and Glenn Geveart (eds.), *Fishery, Trade and Piracy* (Brussels, 2006).

## *8. Science and money*

1 Ivo of Narbonne's letter is in C. Raymond Beazley, *The Texts and Versions of John de Plano Carpini and William of Rubruquis as printed for the first time by Hakluyt in 1598* (London 1903), p. 41. Hygiene and pigtails are in the *Journal of John of Plano Carpini*, in Beazley, *Texts and Versions*, p. 109; Hakluyt's translations and his idea of editing may be troublesome, but his verve is irresistible.

2 Beazley, *Texts and Versions*, p. 203, lines 25–8.

3 Ibid., p. 40 for eating women.

4 Quoted in Sophia Menache, 'Tartars, Jews, Saracens and the Jewish-Mongol "Plot" of 1241', in *History* 81, 263 (July 1996), p. 324 for 'infliction'; p. 321 for 'lions or bears'.

5 Robert Marshall, *Storm from the East: From Genghis Khan to Khublai Khan* (Berkeley, 1993), pp. 91–6.

6 Beazley, *Texts and Versions*, p. 114, line 13, for hunters; p. 122, line 17, for skulls; p. 188, line 8, for lack of cities.

7 Marshall, *Storm from the East*, p. 132 for fishermen; p. 133 for evil spirits.

8 Beazley, *Texts and Versions*, p. 126, line 11, for spies; p. 126, line 28, for 'policy'; p. 126, line 38, for 'devils'; p. 125, line 26, for 'not any one kingdom'; p. 138, line 3, for chapels.

9 Menache, 'Tartars, Jews, Saracens', p. 325.

10 Ibid., p. 334 for Messiah; p. 332 for 'enclosed people'; p. 336 for David; p. 337 for rumours.

11 For a discussion of this, see Simha Goldin, *The Ways of Jewish Martyrdom* (Turnhout, 2008), pp. 213ff.

12 Benjamin Hudson, *North Sea Studies* (Dublin, 2006), pp. 188ff.

13 Davide Bigalli, *I Tartari e l'Apocalisse* (Firenze, 1971), pp. 110–14.

14 Stewart C. Easton, *Roger Bacon and His Search for a Universal Science* (Oxford, 1952), p. 176 for revelation; p. 32 for diamonds; pp. 114–15 for cheapness; pp. 87–8 for letter to Pope; p. 112 for list of inventions.

15 Ernst Dümmler (ed.), *Epistolae Karolini aevi*, vol. II (Berlin, 1895), letters 16–21, p. 43.

16 J. P. Migne (ed.), *Patrologiae cursus completus: sive biblioteca universalis*, vol. 172 (Paris, 1854), cap. IV, col. 76, for rain and cap. VII, col. 77, for blood rain and why it is red. For a fuller discussion, see Paul Edward Dutton, 'Observations on Early Medieval Weather in General, Bloody Rain in Particular', in Jennifer R. Davis and Michael McCormick (eds.), *The Long Morning of Medieval Europe* (Aldershot, 2008), pp. 177ff.

17 Charles Burnett (ed.), *Quaestiones Naturales*, in *Adelard of Bath: Conversations with His Nephew* (Cambridge, 1998), C1 at p. 92 and C4 at p. 96. The translations are mine.

18 Lynn Thorndike, *A History of Magic and Experimental Science* (New York, 1923), vol. II, p. 39.

19 See Lorraine Daston and Katherine Park, *Wonders and the Order of Nature* (New York, 1998), pp. 109ff.

20 Thorndike, *History of Magic*, vol. II, p. 24 for 'modern' attitudes.

21 See Steven P. Marrone, *The Light of Thy Countenance: Science and the Knowledge of God in the Thirteenth Century* (Leiden, 2001), vol. I, pp. 11, 78–9, 105.

22 Johannes Fried (tr. Denise Modigliani), *Les Fruits de l'Apocalyspe: Origines de la pensée scientifique au Moyen Âge* (Paris, 2004), pp. 54–5.

23 Devra Kunin (tr.) and Carl Phelpstead (ed.), *A History of Norway and the Passion and Miracles of the Blessed Óláfr* (London, 2001), p. 11.

24 Quoted in A. George Molland, 'Colonizing the World for Mathematics: The Diversity of Medieval Strategies', in Edward Grant and John E. Murdoch (eds.), *Mathematics and Its Applications to Science and Natural Philosophy in the Middle Ages* (Cambridge, 1987), p. 50.

25 Thorndike, *History of Magic*, vol. II, p. 541.

26 Ibid., vol. I, p. 726, and vol. II, p. 361.

27 Molland, 'Colonizing the World', in Grant and Murdoch, *Mathematics and Its Applications*, p. 47.

28 Roger Bacon, *Opus Tertium*, in J. S. Brewer (ed.), *Opera Quaedam Hactenus Inedita*, vol. I (London, 1859), pp. 51–2.

29 David C. Lindberg, 'Roger Bacon and the Origins of *Perspectiva* in the West', in Grant and Murdoch, *Mathematics and Its Applications*, pp. 254, 258–9.

30 Angelo Crescini, *Il Problema Metodologico alle Origini della Scienza Moderna* (Rome, 1972), pp. 308–9.

31 Joel Kaye, *Economy and Nature in the Fourteenth Century: Money, Market Exchange and the Emergence of Scientific Thought* (Cambridge, 1998), p. 143; pp. 166–73 for Buridan.

32 J. A. Giles (ed.), *William of Malmesbury's Chronicle* (London, 1847), pp. 251ff.; cf. Maria Elena Ruggerini, 'Tales of Flight in Old Norse and Medieval English Texts', *Viking and Medieval Scandinavia* 2 (2006), pp. 222ff.

33 Quoted in R. W. Southern, *Robert Grosseteste: The Growth of an English Mind in Medieval Europe* (Oxford, 1992), p. 65 (for the importance of this book, see infra).

34 Ibid., p. 147; I have slightly adjusted the translation.

35 Southern, *Robert Grosseteste*, is the basis for this account: p. 64 for humble origins; p. 17 for his Greek. Grosseteste's life before he became a bishop has been hotly disputed – if he was chancellor at Oxford, it is unlikely to have been in the years when such an honour might be taken as evidence of an earlier career in Paris and Oxford, for example – but Southern's account seems more convincing than that in D. A. Callus (ed.), *Robert Grosseteste: Scholar and Bishop* (Oxford, 1955). For a summary of the arguments, see James McEvoy, *Robert Grosseteste* (Oxford, 2000), pp. 19ff.

36 N. M. Schulman, 'Husband, Father, Bishop? Grosseteste in Paris', *Speculum* 72, 2, pp. 340ff.

37 'amico carissimo': Grosseteste to Willelmus Avernus 1239, letter LXXVIII, p. 250, in Henry Richards Luard (ed.), *Roberti Grosseteste . . . Epistolae* (London, 1861).

38 McEvoy, *Robert Grosseteste*, pp. 20–21.

39 A. C. Crombie, 'Grosseteste's Position in the History of Science', in D. A. Callus (ed.), *Robert Grosseteste: Scholar and Bishop* (Oxford, 1955), pp. 104ff.; and for a fuller account, A. C. Crombie, *Robert Grosseteste and the Origins of Experimental Science 1100–1700* (Oxford, 1953), which is, as the author acknowledges in later editions, 'a moment of enthusiasm'.

40 Quoted in Thorndike, *History of Magic*, vol. II, p. 441.

41 Crescini, *Problema Metodologico*, p. 266n.

42 James Spedding, Robert Leslie Ellis and Douglas Denon Heath (eds.), *Temporis Partus Masculus*, in *Works of Francis Bacon: Philosophical Works* (London, 1858), p. 118.

43 R. H. and M. A. Rouse, 'Expenses of a Mid Thirteenth-Century Paris

Scholar: Gerard of Abbeville', in Lesley Smith and Benedicta Ward (eds.), *Intellectual Life in the Middle Ages* (London, 1992), pp. 207ff.

44 Thorndike, *History of Magic*, vol. II, pp. 172–3.

45 P. Glorieux, *La Faculté des Arts et ses maîtres au XIIIème siècle* (Paris, 1971), p. 56.

46 Elizabeth Mornet, 'Pauperes scolares: Essai sur la condition matérielle des étudiants scandinaves dans les Universités aux XIVème et XVème siècles', *Le Moyen Âge* 84 (1978), pp. 54ff.; p. 75 for straw rules; p. 55 for records and bursae.

47 Alan B. Cobban, *The Medieval English Universities: Oxford and Cambridge to c1500* (Berkeley, 1988), p. 301.

48 Rainer Christopher Schwinges, 'Student Education, Student Life', in Hilde de Ridder-Symoens (ed.), *A History of the University in Europe*, vol. I: *Universities in the Middle Ages* (Cambridge, 1992), pp. 236–8; William J. Courtenay, *Parisian Scholars in the Early Fourteenth Century: A Social Portrait* (Cambridge, 1999), pp. 9, 36 for the *computus* of 1329–30, and Kaye, *Economy and Nature*, p. 7 for the estimate of time spent.

49 Cobban, *Medieval English Universities*, pp. 146, 159, 149.

50 Quoted in Hilde de Ridder-Symoens, 'Mobility', in Ridder-Symoens, *History of the University*, p. 282.

51 James A. Brundage, *The Medieval Origins of the Legal Profession* (Chicago, 2008), pp. 122–3. I have adjusted the translation slightly.

52 Courtenay, *Parisian Scholars*, pp. 82–3.

53 Virpi Mäkinen, *Property Rights in the Late Medieval Discussion on Franciscan Poverty* (Leuven, 2001), p. 22.

54 A. G. Traver, 'Rewriting History? The Parisian Secular Masters' Apologia of 1254', in Peter Denley (ed.), *History of Universities*, vol. XV: *1997–1999*, pp. 9–45.

55 James M. Murray, *Bruges, Cradle of Capitalism 1280–1390* (Cambridge, 2005), pp. 178ff.

56 Peter Spufford, *Money and Its Use in Medieval Europe* (Cambridge, 1988), pp. 209, 215, 216.

57 André Goddu, 'The Impact of Ockham's Reading of the "Physics" on the Mertonians and Parisian Terminists', *Early Science and Medicine* 6, 3 (2001), esp. pp. 214–18.

58 For a discussion of Aquinas, Henry of Ghent, Duns Scotus and others,

see Amleto Spicciani, *La mercatura e la formazione del prezzo nella iflessione teologica medioevale* (Rome, 1977).

59 '. . . solum mensuram debitam non excedat', in ibid., p. 267, text of Olivi, *Tractatus de emptione et venditione*, lines 85–6.

60 Spicciani, *Mercatura e la formazione*, p. 158.

61 Ibid., p. 179.

62 Matthias Flacius, *Catalogus testium veritatis* (Basle, 1556), p. 876.

63 Lucien Gillard, *Nicole Oresme, économiste, Revue Historique* 279, 1/565 (1988), pp. 3ff., and Marshall Clagett, 'Nicole Oresme and Medieval Scientific Thought', *Proceedings of the American Philosophical Society* 108, 4 (1964), pp. 298ff.

## *9. Dealers rule*

1 Joe Flatman, *Ships and Shipping in Medieval Manuscripts* (London, 2009), pp. 81ff.

2 Kasimirs Slaski, in Albert d'Haenens, *Europe of the North Sea and the Baltic: The World of the Hanse* (Brussels, 1984), p. 160.

3 D'Haenens, *Europe of the North Sea*, p. 201.

4 For the topography of early Bergen, see Edward C. Harris, 'Bergen, Bryggen 1972: The Evolution of a Harbour Front', *World Archaeology* 5, 1 (1973), pp. 69–70, and Asbjørn E. Herteig, 'The Excavation of Bryggen, Bergen, Norway', in Rupert Bruce-Mitford (ed.), *Recent Archaeological Excavations in Europe* (London, 1975), pp. 65–89.

5 Moira Buxton, 'Fish-Eating in Medieval England', in Harlan Walker (ed.), *Fish: Food from the Waters* (Totnes, 1998), p. 54.

6 Oscar Albert Johnsen, 'Le Commerce et la navigation en Norvège au Moyen Âge', *Revue Historique* 178, 3 (1936), pp. 385ff.; Justyna Wubs-Mrozewicz, *Traders, Ties and Tensions* (Hilversum, 2008), pp. 38–41; Philippe Dollinger, *The German Hansa* (London, 1970), pp. 49–50; Knut Helle, 'Norwegian Foreign Policy and the Maid of Norway', *Scottish Historical Review* 69/188, 2 (1990), pp. 147–8; Nils Hybel, 'The Grain Trade in Northern Europe before 1350', *Economic History Review* 55, 2 (2002), pp. 226–7.

7 Fritz Rörig, *The Medieval Town* (Berkeley, 1967), pp. 32–6.

8 Mike Burkhardt, 'Testing a Traditional Certainty: The Social Standing

of the *Bergenfahrer* in Late Medieval Lübeck', in Geir Atle Ersland and Marco Trebbi (eds.), *Neue Studien zum Archiv und zur Sprache der Hanseaten* (Bergen, 2008), pp. 84ff.

9 Johannes Schildhauer, *The Hansa: History and Culture* (Leipzig, 1985), p. 104.

10 Dollinger, *German Hansa*, p. 183; Schildhauer, *Hansa*, p. 104, and Justyna Wubs-Mrozewicz, 'Hansards and the "Other"', in Justyna Wubs-Mrozewicz and Stuart Jenks (eds.), *The Hanse in Medieval and Early Modern Europe* (Leiden, 2013), pp. 158–9.

11 Wubs-Mrozewicz, *Traders, Ties and Tensions*, p. 11.

12 Herteig, *Excavation of Bryggen, Bergen*, pp. 74–9.

13 Hendrik Spruyt, *The Sovereign State and Its Competitors* (Princeton, 1994), p. 126.

14 Sigrid Samset Mygland, *Children in Medieval Bergen: An Archaeological Analysis of Child-Related Artefacts* (Bergen, 2007).

15 Haenens, *Europe of the North Sea*, p. 197.

16 Mike Burkhardt, 'Policy, Business, Privacy: Contacts Made by the Merchants of the Hanse Kontor in Bergen in the Late Middle Ages', in Hanno Brand (ed.), *Trade, Diplomacy and Cultural Exchange: Continuity and Change in the North Sea Area and the Baltic c.1350–1750* (Hilversum, 2005), p. 148.

17 Ibid., pp. 140, 148.

18 Frederich Bruns, *Die Lübecker Bergenfarhrer und ihre Chronistik: Quellen zur Geschichte der Lübecker Bergenfarhrer*, vol. 1: *Urkundliche Quellen* (Berlin, 1900), p. 15, will 14.

19 Ibid., p. 16, will 16.

20 Ibid., p. 64, will 94.

21 Klaus Friedland, 'Maritime Law and Piracy: Advantages and Inconveniences of Shipping in the Baltic', in A. I. McInnes, T. Riis and F. G. Pedersen (eds.), *Ships, Guns and Bibles in the North Sea and the Baltic States c1350–c1700* (East Linton, 2000), pp. 32–5.

22 Johnsen, 'Commerce et la navigation', pp. 394–7.

23 Rhiman A. Rotz, 'The Lübeck Uprising of 1408 and the Decline of the Hanseatic League', *Proceedings of the American Philosophical Society* 121, 1 (1977), pp. 1–45.

24 Text in Dollinger, *German Hansa*, document 26, pp. 411–13.

25 Sebastian I. Sobecki, *The Sea and Medieval English Literature* (Cambridge, 2008), pp. 32, 140–42.
26 Justyna Wubs-Mrozewicz, '"Alle goede coepluyden": Strategies in the Scandinavian Trade Politics of Amsterdam and Lübeck c1440–1560', in Hanno Brand and Leos Müller (eds.), *The Dynamics of Economic Culture in the North Sea and Baltic Region* (Hilversum, 2007), p. 96.
27 Dick E. H. de Boer, 'Looking for Security: Merchant Networks and Risk Reduction Strategies', in Hanno Brand (ed.), *The German Hanse in Past and Present Europe* (Groningen, 2007), pp. 52–5.
28 Wubs-Mrozewicz, *Traders, Ties and Tensions*, p. 111n.45.
29 James M. Murray, 'Bruges as *Hansestadt*', in Wubs-Mrozewicz and Jenks, *Hanse in Medieval and Early Modern Europe*, pp. 183–5.
30 Burkhardt, 'Policy, Business, Privacy', in Brand, *Trade, Diplomacy and Cultural Exchange*, p. 145.
31 Dollinger, *German Hansa*, pp. 78–81.
32 David Ditchburn, 'Bremen Piracy and Scottish Periphery: The North Sea World in the 1440s', in McInnes et al., *Ships, Guns and Bibles*, pp. 3–8.
33 D'Haenens, *Europe of the North Sea*, p. 143.
34 Hendrik Spruyt, *The Sovereign State and Its Competitors* (Princeton, 1994), pp. 109–29 for a detailed development of this argument.
35 David Gaimster, 'A Parallel History: The Archaeology of Hanseatic Urban Culture in the Baltic c.1200–1600', *World Archaeology* 37, 3 (2005), pp. 412–19.
36 Anders Reisnert, in Andris Caune and Ieva Ose (eds.), *The Hansa Town Riga as Mediator between East and West* (Riga, 2009), pp. 210–11, 219.
37 Mike Burkhardt, 'One Hundred Years of Thriving Commerce at a Major English Seaport', in Brand and Müller, *Dynamics of Economic Culture*, pp. 81–2.
38 Wubs-Mrozewicz, '"Alle goede coepluyden"', in Brand and Müller, *Dynamics of Economic Culture*, p. 86.

## 10. *Love and capital*

1 Jos de Smet, 'Een Aanslag tegen het Brugse Begijnhof', *Biekorf* 27 (1971), pp. 33–7 for the text of the court judgment on which this is

based; I am very grateful to Willem Kuiper and Lidewijde Paris for their help with the translation. Cf. Walter Simons, *Cities of Ladies: Beguine Communities in the Medieval Low Countries 1200–1565* (Philadelphia, 2001), pp. 71–2.

2 For travel speeds on horseback, see Norbert Ohler, *The Medieval Traveller* (Woodbridge, 2010), pp. 97ff.

3 Marcel de Fréville, *Les Quatres Âges d'homme de Philippe de Navarre* (Paris, 1888), vol. I, 25, pp. 16–17.

4 Quoted in Bernard McGinn, 'Meister Eckhart and the Beguines in the Context of Vernacular Theology', in Bernard McGinn (ed.), *Meister Eckhart and the Beguine Mystics* (New York, 1994), p. 1.

5 Anne Winston-Allen, *Convent Chronicles: Women Writing about Women and Reform in the Late Middle Ages* (University Park, 2004), pp. 66–8.

6 Jean Bethune de Villers (ed. and tr. Emilie Amt), *Cartulaire du Beguinage de Sainte-Elisabeth à Gand* (Bruges, 1883), in *Women's Lives in Medieval Europe* (New York, 1993), pp. 263–7.

7 Simons, *Cities of Ladies*, p. 139.

8 Eileen Power (tr. and ed.), *The Goodman of Paris* (Woodbridge, 2006), pp. 138ff.

9 Hans Geybels, *Vulgariter Beghinae* (Turnhout, 2004), p. 151.

10 Shennan Hutton, *Women and Economic Activities in Late Medieval Ghent* (New York, 2011), p. 125.

11 Simons, *Cities of Ladies*, pp. 73–4, 188nn.71–3.

12 Ibid., p. 123 for satire; p. 80 for carnival; p. 124 for etymology.

13 Ibid., pp. 63–4.

14 See David Farmer, *Oxford Dictionary of Saints*, pp. 207–8, under Gertrude of Nivelles.

15 *Life of Elizabeth of Spalbeek*, line 527, in Jennifer N. Brown (ed.), *Three Women of Liège* (Turnhout, 2008), p. 50.

16 Saskia Murk-Jansen (tr.), in *Hadewijch and Eckhart*, in McGinn, *Meister Eckhart*, p. 23; cf. Amy Hollywood, 'Suffering Transformed', in McGinn, *Meister Eckhart*, pp. 87ff.

17 *Life of Christina Mirabilis*, in Brown, *Three Women*, pp. 223, 227, 230; p. 65, lines 276, 284, for living as a man; p. 74, lines 472ff., for Jutta.

18 *Marie d'Oignies*, in Brown, *Three Women*, p. 57 for married; pp. 36, 47

for childhood; pp. 64–6 for cord; p. 81 for husband; p. 98 for 'hard heat'.

19 For virgin birth and virtues, see Osbert of Clare's letters to Adelidis and to his nieces in Vera Morton and Jocelyn Wogan-Browne, *Guidance for Women in Twelfth-Century Convents* (Cambridge, 2003), pp. 23, 116.

20 *Life of Christina Mirabilis*, in Brown, *Three Women*, p. 256 for end of world.

21 I Timothy 4: 1–3.

22 *Marie d'Oignies*, in Brown, *Three Women*, p. 104 for lepers; p. 106 for relatives.

23 Ibid., p. 107, I, 454, for deference; p. 112, I, 563, for cleanness.

24 Avraham Grossman, *Pious and Rebellious: Jewish Women in Medieval Europe* (Waltham, 2004), pp. 117–19.

25 Ibid., p. 74.

26 Simha Goldin, *The Ways of Jewish Martyrdom* (Turnhout, 2008), pp. 112–17.

27 Ellen E. Kittell, 'Guardianship over Women in Medieval Flanders: A Reappraisal', *Journal of Social History* 31, 4 (1998), pp. 897–930, and James M. Murray, *Bruges, Cradle of Capitalism 1280–1390* (Cambridge, 2005), pp. 306–26.

28 Elizabeth Lamond (tr.), *Walter de Henley: Husbandry . . .* (London, 1890), p. 75.

29 Hutton, *Women and Economic Activities*, pp. 119–20.

30 Kittell, 'Guardianship over Women', p. 912.

31 Frederick Pedersen, *Marriage Disputes in Medieval England* (London, 2000), pp. 153–6.

32 Tine de Moor and Jan Luiten van Zanden, 'Girl Power: The European Marriage Pattern and Labour Markets in the North Sea Region in the Late Medieval and Early Modern Period', *Economic History Review* 63, 1 (2010), pp. 5–6. This and Kittell, 'Guardianship over Women', are the backbone of my argument here.

33 Anthony Musson, 'Images of Marriage, a Comparison of Law, Custom and Practice in Medieval Europe', in Mia Korpiola (ed.), *Regional Variations in Matrimonial Law and Custom in Europe 1150–1600* (Leiden, 2011), p. 140.

34 Philippe Godding, 'La Famille dans le droit urbain', in Myriam

Carlier and Tim Soens (eds.), *The Household in Late Medieval Cities: Italy & Northwestern Europe Compared* (Leuven, 2001), p. 34.

35 P. J. P. Goldberg, 'Household and the Organization of Labour in Late Medieval Towns: Some English Evidence', in Carlier and Soens, *Household in Late Medieval Cities*, p. 65.

36 For discussion, see Martha C. Howell, *Commerce before Capitalism in Europe, 1300–1600* (Cambridge, 2010), pp. 104–7.

37 Ibid., p. 94.

38 Samuel K. Cohn Jr, 'Two Pictures of Family Ideology Taken from the Dead in post-Plague Flanders and Tuscany', in Carlier and Soens, *Household in Late Medieval Cities*, pp. 170–73.

39 Kittell, 'Guardianship over Women', p. 911.

40 Ramon A. Klitzike, 'Historical Background of the English Patent Law', *Journal of the Patent Office* 41, 9 (1959), pp. 622–3.

41 James S. Amelang, *The Flight of Icarus: Artisan Autobiography in Early Modern Europe* (Stanford, 1998), p. 294 for Gross.

42 Stephan R. Epstein, 'Labour Mobility, Journeymen Organisations and Markets in Skilled Labour in Europe 14th–18th Centuries', in Mathieu Arnoux and Pierre Monnet (eds.), *Le Technicien dans la cité en Europe Occidentale 1250–1650* (Rome, 2004), pp. 251–67.

43 Richard L. Hills, *Power From Wind: A History of Windmill Technology* (Cambridge, 1996), pp. 36–9.

44 Karel Davids, 'Innovations in Windmill Technology in Europe c1500–1800', *NEHA Jaarboek* 66 (2003), pp. 47–51.

45 De Moor and Van Zanden, 'Girl Power', pp. 23–4.

46 John W. Baldwin, 'Consent and the Marital Debt', in Angeliki E. Laiou (ed.), *Consent and Coercion to Sex and Marriage in Ancient and Medieval Societies* (Washington, 1993), p. 266 for Héloïse; p. 262 for orgasm; p. 269 for Aristotle; p. 263 for Ovid.

47 The text of 'Eleanor's' examination is in Ruth Mazo Karras and David Lorenzo Boyd, '"Ut cum muliere"*:* A Male Transvestite Prostitute in Fourteenth-Century London', in Louise O. Fradenburg and Celia Freccero (eds.), *Premodern Sexualities* (New York, 1996), pp. 111–12.

48 Amt, *Women's Lives*, pp. 211–22.

49 James A. Brundage, 'Prostitution in the Medieval Canon Law', *Signs* 1, 4 (1976), esp. p. 841; Amt, *Women's Lives*, pp. 210–13; Bjorn Bandlien,

'Sexuality and Early Church Laws', in Per Andersen, Mia Münster-Swendsen and Helle Vogt (eds.), *Law and Private Life in the Middle Ages* (Copenhagen, 2011), p. 200.

50 Grossman, *Pious and Rebellious*, p. 134.

51 See the miniature in Valère Maxime, *Faits et dits mémorables* (1475), reproduced in André Vandewalle (ed.), *Les Marchands de la Hanse et la banque des Médicis* (Oostkamp, 2002), p. 88.

52 Malcolm Letts, *Pero Tafur: Travels and Adventures 1435–1439* (London, 1926) p. 199 for bathing; p. 200 for girls; Malcolm Letts, *The Travels of Leo of Rozmital through Germany, Flanders, England, France, Spain, Portugal and Italy 1465–1467* (Cambridge, 1957), p. 31; Murray, *Bruges*, pp. 340–43.

53 Henry Ansgar Kelly, 'Bishop, Prioress, and Bawd in the Stews of Southwark', *Speculum* 75, 2 (2000), passim.

54 Judith M. Bennett, 'Writing Fornication: Medieval Leywrite and Its Historians', *Transactions of the Royal Historical Society* 6, 13 (2003), pp. 146, 147, 155.

55 Benjamin B. Roberts and Leendert F. Groenendijk, '"Wearing out a pair of fool's shoes": Sexual Advice for Youth in Holland's Golden Age', *Journal of the History of Sexuality* 13, 2 (2004), p. 145.

56 Etienne van de Walle, '"Marvellous secrets": Birth Control in European Short Fiction 1150–1650', *Population Studies* 54, 3 (2000), pp. 325, 323.

57 Augustus Borgnet (ed.), *B Alberti Magni Opera Omnia*, vol 5: *De mineralibus*, book II, tract II (Paris, 1890), p. 39b for jasper; pp. 42b–43a for oristes.

58 John M. Riddle, *Contraception and Abortion from the Ancient World to the Renaissance* (Cambridge, Mass., 1992), p. 104 for monastic recipes; p. 111 for pseudo-Bede; pp. 114–15 for Bishop of Rennes; pp. 116–17 for Hildegard.

59 Jean-Louis Flandrin, 'Contraception, mariage et relations amoureuses dans l'Occident chrétien', *Annales, Histoire, Sciences Sociales* 24, 6 (1969), esp. pp. 1374–5; pp. 1386–7 for Sanchez.

## 11. *The plague laws*

1 Samuel K. Cohn Jr, 'Epidemiology of the Black Death and Successive Waves of Plague', in Vivian Nutton (ed.), *Medical History Supplement*

27 (London, 2008), *Pestilential Complexities: Understanding Medieval Plague*, pp. 79, 81, 83, 89.

2 Friedrich W. Brie (ed.), *The Brut or the Chronicles of England* (London, 1906), ch. 228, pp. 301–3.

3 Georges Vigarello, *Histoire des pratiques de santé* (Paris, 1999), pp. 51–4.

4 Henri H. Mollaret, 'Les Grands Fléaux', in Mirko D. Grmek (ed.), *Histoire de la pensée medicale en Occident*, vol. 2: *De la Renaissance aux lumières* (Paris, 1997), p. 256.

5 Adolf Hofmeister (ed.), *Die Chronik des Mathias von Neuenburg* (Berlin 1924–40), chs. 114–17; p. 263 for ships; p. 265 for blaming the Jews; p. 270 for flagellants.

6 See Timothy R. Tangherlini, 'Ships, Fogs and Travelling Pairs: Plague Legend Migration in Scandinavia', *Journal of American Folklore* 101, 400 (1988), pp. 176ff.

7 Daniel Antoine, 'The Archaeology of "Plague"', in Nutton, *Pestilential Complexities*, pp. 101ff.

8 Quoted in Andrew Wear, *Knowledge and Practice in English Medicine 1550–1680* (Cambridge, 2000), p. 196.

9 Michael McCormick, 'Rats, Communications and Plague: Toward an Ecological History', *Journal of Interdisciplinary History* 34, 1 (2003), p. 23 for repopulation; p. 22 for predators.

10 Rosemary Horrox (tr. and ed.), *The Black Death* (Manchester, 1994), p. 170, from Bodleian MS Digby 176, folios 26–9.

11 Ann G. Carmichael, 'Universal and Particular: The Language of Plague 1348–1500', in Nutton, *Pestilential Complexities*, pp. 17–52.

12 Christiane Nockels Fabbri, 'Treating Medieval Plague: The Wonderful Virtues of Theriac', *Early Science and Medicine* 12, 3 (2007), pp. 247ff.

13 William Chester Jordan, *The Great Famine* (Princeton, 1996), pp. 148–51.

14 Bruce M. S. Campbell, 'Ecology v. Economics in Late Thirteenth- and Early Fourteenth-Century English Agriculture', in Del Sweeney (ed.), *Agriculture in the Middle Ages: Technology, Practice and Representation* (Philadelphia, 1995), pp. 76–7.

15 Jane Welch Williams, 'The New Image of Peasants in Thirteenth-Century French Stained Glass', and Bridget Ann Henisch, 'Farm

Work in the Medieval Calendar Tradition', in Sweeney, *Agriculture in the Middle Ages*, p. 299 for glass; pp. 310–16 for attitudes to work.

16 A. V. C. Schmidt (ed. and tr.), *William Langland: Piers Plowman* (Oxford, 1992), pp. 67–74.

17 Judith M. Bennett, 'Compulsory Service in Late Medieval England', *Past and Present* 209 (2010), pp. 7ff., is the basis of my story here; cf. Samuel Cohn, 'After the Black Death: Labour Legislation and Attitudes towards Labour in Late Medieval Western Europe', *Economic History Review* 60, 3 (2007), pp. 457ff., and John Hatcher, 'England in the Aftermath of the Black Death', *Past and Present* 144 (1994), pp. 3ff.

18 In Ole Peter Grell and Andrew Cunningham (eds.), *Health Care and Poor Relief in Protestant Europe 1500–1700* (London, 1997), see Thomas Riis on 'Poor Relief and Health Care Provision in Sixteenth Century Denmark'; Hugo Soly on 'Continuity and Change: Attitudes towards Poor Relief and Health Care in Early Modern Antwerp'; Robert Jütte on 'Health Care Provision and Poor Relief in Early Modern Hanseatic Towns: Hamburg, Bremen and Lübeck'; and Paul Slack on 'Hospitals, Workhouses and the Relief of the Poor in Early Modern London'.

19 Charles F. Mullett, 'Plague Policy in Scotland 16th–17th Centuries', *Osiris* 9 (1950), pp. 436–44.

20 John Booker, *Maritime Quarantine – the British Experience c1650–1900* (Aldershot, 2007), pp. 17–18.

21 Paul Slack, 'The Response to Plague in Early Modern England: Public Policies and Their Consequences', in John Walter and Roger Schofield (eds.), *Famine, Disease and the Social Order in Early Modern Society* (Cambridge, 1989), pp. 168–77.

22 Booker, *Maritime Quarantine*, pp. 1–4; John Warrington (ed.), *Diary of Samuel Pepys* (London, 1953), vol. I, entry for 26 November 1663, p. 461.

23 Barbara E. Crawford, 'North Sea Kingdoms, North Sea Bureaucrat: A Royal Official Who Transcended National Boundaries', *Scottish Historical Review* 69, 188 (1990), pp. 175ff.

24 Henry S. Lucas, 'John Crabbe: Flemish Pirate, Merchant and Adventurer', *Speculum* 20, 3 (1945), pp. 334ff.

25 Andrew R. Little, 'British Seamen in the United Provinces during the Seventeenth Century Anglo-Dutch Wars: The Dutch Navy, a Preliminary Survey', in Hanno Brand (ed.), *Trade, Diplomacy and Cultural Exchange: Continuity and Change in the North Sea Area and the Baltic c1350–1750* (Hilversum, 2005), pp. 78, 79, 81, 85.

26 Ibid., p. 88.

27 Warrington, *Diary of Samuel Pepys*, vol. I, entry for 14 June 1667, pp. 485–6.

28 S. C. Lomas (ed.), *Memoirs of Sir George Courthop* (London, 1907), pp. 109–10 for Geneva; p. 132 for Malta.

29 H. C. Fanshawe (ed.), *The Memoirs of Ann Lady Fanshawe* (London, 1907), pp. 87–90; p. 31 for son's name.

30 Antoni Mączak, *Travel in Early Modern Europe* (Cambridge, 1995), pp. 112–15.

## 12. *The city and the world*

1 Paul Murray Kendall and Vincent Ilardi, *Dispatches with Related Documents of Milanese Ambassadors in France and Burgundy 1450–1483* (Athens, 1971), vol. 2, pp. 200–201.

2 Bernard Aikema, 'Netherlandish Painting and Early Renaissance Italy: Artistic Rapports in a Historiographical Perspective', in Herman Roodenburg (ed.), *Forging European Identities 1400–1700* (Cambridge, 2007), pp. 110–20.

3 *The Virgin and Child with Saints and Donors* (*The Donne Triptych*) in the National Gallery, London.

4 Marina Belozerskaya, *Rethinking the Renaissance: Burgundian Arts across Europe* (Cambridge, 2002), passim, but p. 132 for music.

5 Malcolm Letts (ed. and tr.), *The Travels of Leo of Rozmital through Germany, Flanders, England, France, Spain, Portugal and Italy 1465–1467* (Cambridge, 1957), p. 54 for hair; pp. 1–2 for biography; p. 23 for nuns; p. 27 for dishes; p. 28 for zoo and treasury; p. 37 for drunk; p. 36 for wrestling; pp. 29, 35 for candlelight.

6 Margit Thøfner, *A Common Art: Urban Ceremonial in Antwerp and Brussels during and after the Dutch Revolt* (Zwolle, 2007), pp. 13–17.

7 Gilles de Bouvier dit Berry (ed. E. T. Hamy), *Le Livre de la description des pays* (Paris, 1908), p. 47 for Flanders; p. 106 for Holland.

8 Malcolm Letts, *Pero Tafur: Travels and Adventures 1435–1439* (London, 1926), p. 200 for 'oranges', 'famine'; p. 198 for Bruges; p. 203 for Antwerp.

9 Raymond van Uytven, 'Les Autres Marchandises à Bruges', in André Vandewalle (ed.), *Les Marchands de la Hanse et la banque des Médicis* (Oostkamp, 2002), p. 73.

10 Giovanna Petti Balbi, 'Bruges, port des Italiens', in Vandewalle, *Marchands de la Hanse*, pp. 58ff.

11 Alastair Hamilton, *Arab Culture and Ottoman Magnificence in Antwerp's Golden Age* (London and Oxford, 2001), pp. 9, 26.

12 Letts, *Pero Tafur*, p. 194 for 'majesty'; p. 199 for 'gallows'.

13 Kendall and Ilardi, *Dispatches with Related Documents*, vol. 2, pp. 228–9 for 'dishes'; pp. 348ff. for ceremonies; p. 394 for organization.

14 Robert Peterson (tr.), *Giovanni Botero: A Treatise Concerning the Causes of the Magnificence and Greatness of Cities* (London, 1606), p. 51; *Delle cause della grandezza e magnificenza delle città* appeared in Italian in 1588.

15 Wim de Clercq, Jan Dumolyn and Jelle Haemers, '"Vivre noblement": Material Culture and Élite Identity in Late Medieval Flanders', *Journal of Interdisciplinary History* 38, 1 (2007), pp. 1ff.

16 Letts, *Travels of Leo of Rozmital*, pp. 45–7.

17 Belozerskaya, *Rethinking the Renaissance*, pp. 151–4.

18 Charles Narrey (tr.), *Albrecht Dürer à Venise et dans les Pays Bas* (Paris, 1866), p. 104 for 'red'; p. 107 for price; p. 111 for Bruges; p. 117 for 'colour of lead'; on the ultramarine see Stan Hugue, *Albrecht Dürer: journal de voyage aux Pays-Bas* (Paris, 2009), p. 79, for a fuller text. Dürer did not pay cash, so the price is a bit subjective.

19 Filip Vermeylen, 'The Colour of Money: Dealing in Pigments in Sixteenth-Century Antwerp', in J. O. Kirby Atkinson (ed.), *European Trade in Painters' Materials to 1700* (Leiden, 2010), pp. 356ff.

20 Margaret L. Koster, 'Italy and the North: A Florentine Perspective', in Till-Holger Borchert, *The Age of Van Eyck* (Bruges, 2002), p. 79.

21 Catherine Reynolds, 'The Function and Display of Netherlandish

Cloth Paintings', in Caroline Villers (ed.), *The Fabric of Images: European Paintings on Textile Supports in the Fourteenth and Fifteenth Centuries* (London, 2000), p. 91.

22 Paula Nuttall, 'Panni dipinti di Fiandra: Netherlandish Painted Cloths in Fifteenth-Century Florence', in Villers, *Fabric of Images*, p. 109.

23 *Il Riposo di Raffaello Borghini . . .* (Florence, 1584), pp. 579–84; Lucia Meoni, *La nascita dell'arazzeria medicea* (Florence, 2008), pp. 34, 78 for hunts; p. 27 for Medea; p. 82 for Time; p. 66 for Samuel.

24 Michael Baxandall, 'Bartholomaeus Facius on Painting: A Fifteenth-Century MS. of *De Viris Illustribus*', *Journal of the Warburg and Courtauld Institutes* 27 (1964), p. 102.

25 Borghini, *Riposo di Raffaello Borghini*, pp. 326–7.

26 *Guicciardini's Account of the Ancient Flemish School of Painting* (London, 1795), pp. 3–4.

27 Giovanna Sapori, *Fiamminghi nel cantiere Italia 1560–1600* (Milan, 2007), p. 10 (author's translation).

28 Till-Holger Borchert and Paul Huvenne, 'Van Eyck and the Invention of Oil Painting: Artistic Merits in Their Literary Mirror', in Till-Holger Borchert, *The Age of Van Eyck: The Mediterranean World and Early Netherlandish Painting 1430–1530* (Bruges, 2002), pp. 221, 225.

29 Faith Wallis, *Medieval Medicine: A Reader* (Toronto, 2010), pp. 351–4.

30 Peter van den Brink, 'The Art of Copying', in Peter van den Brink (ed.), *Brueghel Enterprises* (Maastricht, 2001), pp. 13ff.; p. 44 for grandmother.

31 Valentin Vazquez de Prada, *Lettres marchandes d'Anvers* (Paris, 1960), vol. I, p. 112, for opened; pp. 124, 133 for credit; p. 132 for Ducci.

32 De Prada, *Lettres marchandes*, vol. I, p. 19.

33 Sheilagh Ogilvie, *Institutions and European Trade: Merchant Guilds 1000–1800* (Cambridge, 2011), pp. 368–9.

34 On the influence of the Bourse, see Krista de Jonge, 'Bâtiments publics à fonction économique à Anvers au XVIème siècle: l'invention d'un type', in Konrad Ottenheym, Monique Chatenet and Krista de Jonge (eds.), *Public Buildings in Early Modern Europe* (Turnhout, 2010), pp. 183ff.; on the siting of the Bourse, see Jochen de Vylder, 'The Grid and the Existing City', in Piet Lombaerde and Charles van den Heuvel (eds.), *Early Modern Urbanism and the Grid* (Turnhout, 2011); on

the Bourse and the city, see Konrad Ottenheym and Krista de Jonge, 'Civic Prestige: Building the City 1580–1700', in Konrad Ottenheym and Krista de Jonge (eds.), *Unity and Discontinuity: Architectural Relationships between the Southern and Northern Low Countries (1530–1700)* (Turnhout, 2007), pp. 232–4.

35 For the Alleynses and the structure of art dealing, see Filip Vermeylen, *Painting for the Market* (Turnhout, 2003), esp. pp. 70–77.

36 De Prada, *Lettres Marchandes*, vol. I, pp. 122–3.

37 Hernando de Frias Cevallos to Simon Ruiz, 16 March 1564, in de Prada, *Lettres marchandes*, vol. II, pp. 11–12.

38 Frederic Schiller (tr. A. J. W. Morrison), *History of the Revolt of the Netherlands* (New York, 1860), pp. 189–94.

39 G. D. Ramsay, *The Queen's Merchants and the Revolt of the Netherlands* (Manchester, 1986), pp. 183–90.

40 See Jonathan I. Israel, *The Dutch Republic: Its Rise, Greatness and Fall 1477–1806* (Oxford, 1995), for excellent summaries of Antwerp's fate, esp. pp. 185, 413–14.

41 The best source on Stevin is J. T. Devresse and G. Vanden Berghe, *'Magic is no magic': The Wonderful World of Simon Stevin* (Southampton, 2008).

42 Paul Arblaster, *Antwerp and the World: Richard Verstegan and the International Culture of the Catholic Reformation* (Leuven 2004).

43 For a discussion of the development of the 'fact', see Barbara J. Shapiro, *A Culture of Fact: England 1550–1720* (Ithaca, 2000).

44 Frank Lestringant (ed.), *Le Théâtre des Cruautés de Richard Verstegan* (Paris, 1995).

45 On Stevin's international influence, see Ron van Oers, *Dutch Town Planning Overseas during VOC and WIC Rule 1600–1800* (Zutphen, 2000); for the notes on buildings, see Charles van den Heuvel, *De huysbou*, a reconstruction of an unfinished treatise on architecture, town planning and civil engineering by Simon Stevin (Amsterdam, 2005).

46 Xinru Liu, *Ancient India and Ancient China: Trade and Religious Exchanges AD 1–600* (New Delhi, 1988), pp. 8–11.

47 Jon Solomon, 'The Apician Sauce', in John Wilkins, David Harvey and Mike Dobson (eds.), *Food in Antiquity* (Exeter, 1995), p. 128n.9.

48 Lisa Jardine and Michael Silverthorne (eds.), *Francis Bacon: The New Organon* (Cambridge, 2000), p. 44, XLVIII, for 'unthinkable …'; p. 69, LXXXIV, for 'disgrace to mankind'.

# Acknowledgements

A thousand years and a hundred kingdoms is far beyond the competence of just one writer; which is why this book owes everything to the help of others – to texts which set me thinking, to the people who suggested, corrected, interpreted and encouraged, and to the institutions that made the work possible. The problem now is: how to share any credit due without sharing the blame, because the latter belongs to me alone.

I would never ask them to admit paternity, but my ideas owe much to Stéphane Lebecq's work on Frisia; to Rosamond McKitterick's studies of history, memory, writing and reading; to James A. Brundage's magisterial account of the start of the legal profession; to Joel Kaye's *Economy and Nature in the Fourteenth Century*; to Judith M. Bennett's work on plague and labour laws; to Tine de Moor and Jan Luiten van Zanden on 'girl power'; and Marina Belozerskaya's brilliantly revisionist view of Flanders in the Renaissance. They started me thinking, but that is where their responsibility ends. From there on, I owe this book also to the hundreds of specialists who make it possible to generalize, from the editors of the *Monumenta Germaniae Historica* in the nineteenth century to twenty-first-century archaeologists whose papers, monographs and reports gave me raw material. Endnotes are nothing like enough to settle debts like these.

I am especially grateful to the people without whose help I would have known less, made more mistakes and gone down many more dead ends. I thank: Simon Bailey; Esther Banki; Rachel Boertjens; Gerhard Cadee; John Carey; Alan Coates; Bernadette Cunningham; Pieterjan Deckers; Geir Atle Ersland; Linn Kjos Falkenberg; Piet Gilissen; Rob van Ginkel; Matthew Goldish; Irene Groeneweg; Gitte Hansen; Harald Hansen; Peter Henderikx; Joe Hillaby; Brian Hillyard; Susan Hitch; Neil Jones; Ephraim Kanarfogel; Espen Karlsen; Willem Kuiper; Rune Kyrkjebø; Carolyne Larrington; Moira Mackenzie; Martin Maw; Roy Meijer; Thomas McErlean;

Bernard Meijlink; Liesebeth Missel; Tore Nyberg; Aslaug Ommundsen; Hilde van Parys; Anna Petre; Marnix Pieters; Michael Prestwich; Julian Reid; Anna Sander; Caroline van Santen; Dagfinn Skre; Målfrid Krohn Sletten; Peter Doimi de Frankopan Subic; Filip Vermeylen; Ed van der Vlist; Yvonne de Vroede; and Anne Winston-Allen.

The librarians of the University of Amsterdam have treated me with such unfussy generosity for years that I cannot imagine working without their help any more. I thank the Bodleian Library in Oxford, the library of St John's College, Oxford, the Warburg Institute of the University of London and the Wellcome Library in London, the Openbare Bibliotheek in Bruges, the Koninklijke Bibliotheek in The Hague and the Bibliothèque Nationale de France in Paris (not least for the inconvenient charm of working at the Richelieu site). I owe much to the library of the University of Bergen, to the Special Collections of St Andrew's University, to the Royal Irish Academy in Dublin, and to the Staatsbibliothek in Munich for the online version of the *Monumenta Germaniae Historical*, which has made wonderfully accessible what used to be dusty and time-consuming. David Rymill at the Hampshire Record Office and Malcolm Boyns at the Warwickshire Record Office were very helpful. I thank the Alumni Office of the University of Oxford for access to JSTOR. And the best of bookshops helped enormously; I'm grateful to the wonderful Athenaeum and the knowledgeable men at Architectura et Natura in Amsterdam, and the indispensable Oxbow Books in Oxford.

I also needed more immediate help and I could depend on the prodigious skill of Mary Boyle, who mined brilliantly for the more obscure materials. Verity Allen helped greatly at the start.

The pictures in this book, in the order they appear, are: **Vikings** from a 1130 ms. of the *Life of St Edmund*, The Pierrepoint Morgan Library, copyright © Photo SCALA, Florence, 2014; **scribe** from the 1121 *Liber Floridus* in Ghent University Library; **finger counting** from a French collection on *computus* around 1100, copyright © The British Library Board; **court scene** from the 1480 *Histoire de la Toison d'Or* in the Bibliothèque Nationale de France; **images of fishing** from Olaus Magnus: *Historia de gentibus septentrionalibus*

(Rome, 1555), the Bridgeman Art Library; **Hansa harbour** from the Hamburg Staatsarchiv, the 1497 *Van Schiprechte*; **road building** from Jean de Guise, *Chroniques de Hainault*, in the Bibliothèque Royale de Belgique; **art-dealing** from a painting around 1590 by François Bunel II, in the Royal Picture Gallery Mauritshuis, The Hague; **bathhouse** from a 1470 edition of Valère Maxime, *Faits et dits mémorables* in the Bibliothèque Nationale de France; **the sea monster** from a thirteenth-century manuscript, MS Ashmole 1511, in the Bodleian Library, Oxford; the **toy sea monster** was made for an Antwerp parade and drawn for Joannes Bochius, *Descriptio Publicae Gratulationis* (1594, also in the Bodleian). I am very grateful to everyone – librarians and photographers alike – for their help in making these images available; and to Huw Armstrong for his help in the research.

Along the way my old Oxford college, St John's, gave me a room while I was digging in the Bodleian, and David and Joyce Robinson were the kindest of hosts in Edinburgh. In Amsterdam, the people at Résidence Le Coin must sometimes have wondered if I was ever going to leave, and still they smiled; I thank Corina, Rik, Dimitri, Jesse and the others for their kindness, and their coffee. My good friends Emma, Peter and Alfred Letley, Lynda Myles, Sharon Churcher, Wesley van den Bos, Mickle O'Reilly and Penny Morley, and Lidewijde Paris cheered me on, especially in the last stages when the circumstances turned dark.

You might never have read this book without the zest and attention of Venetia Butterfield at Viking in London, alongside Jillian Taylor, who steered and nursed the book to publication, and Ellie Smith, Mark Handsley and Emma Brown, whose care improved everything. The maps are the work of the brilliant Phillip Green. I owe the cover to John Hamilton's eye. The index was made by Douglas Matthews. And the book might not have been begun, let alone finished, without three men. David Godwin, my most humane and ruthless agent, staged a resurrection for me; I am very grateful, but then David is becoming famous for miracles. Will Hammond, who commissioned the book at Viking and guided it along was clever, exact, supportive and properly sceptical about any date I typed; I owe the book to all his enthusiasm and his care. And my partner, John Holm, made the book possible because he makes my life possible. I would mention the dogs, but I'm told it is now considered bad form to thank dogs and professors on the same page . . .

London, 17 March 2014

# Index

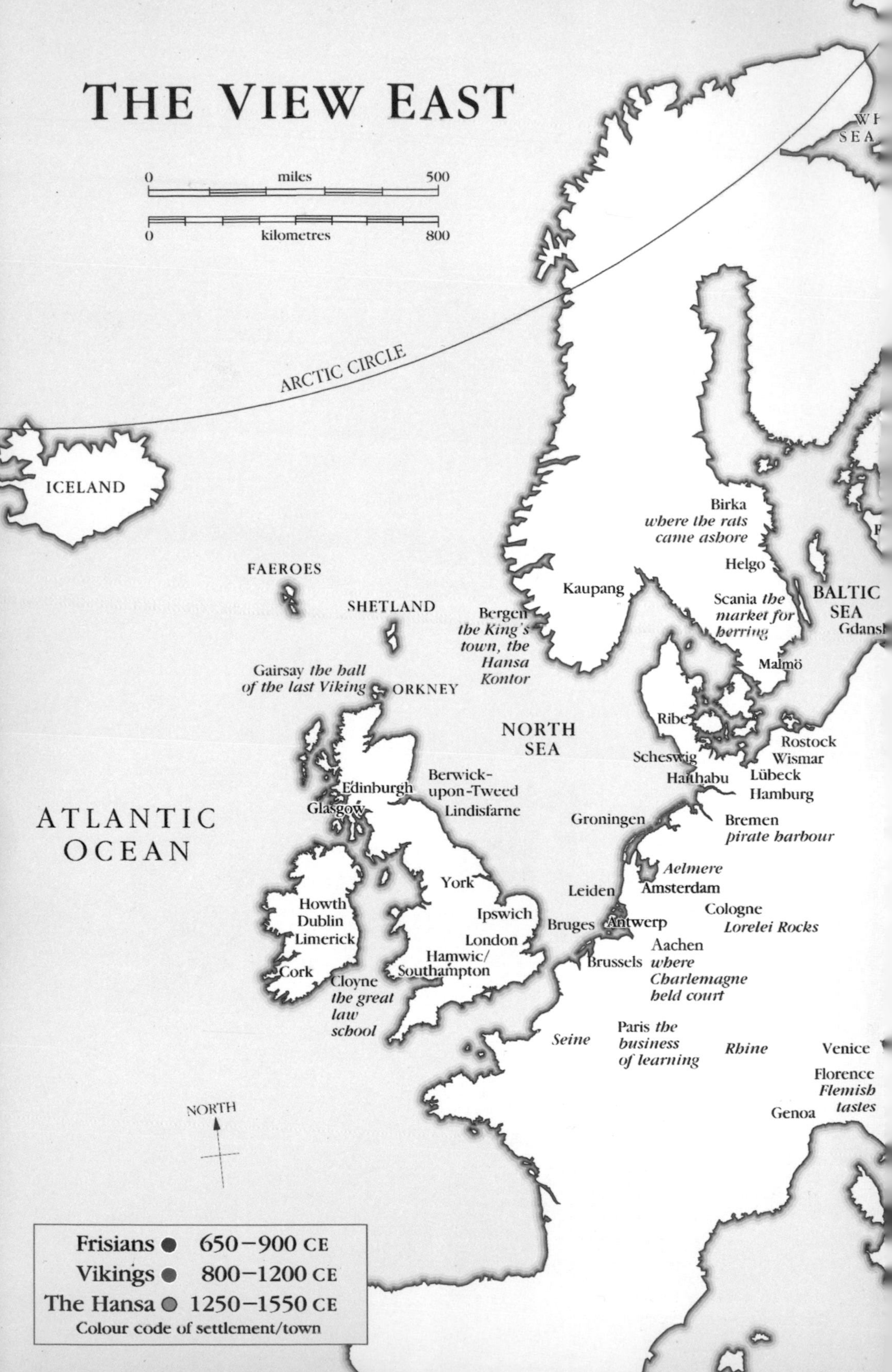
THE VIEW EAST
0 miles 500
0 kilometres 800
ARCTIC CIRCLE
ICELAND
FAEROES
SHETLAND
Gairsay the hall of the last Viking
ORKNEY
Bergen the King's town, the Hansa Kontor
Kaupang
Birka where the rats came ashore
Helgo
Scania the market for herring
BALTIC SEA
Malmö
NORTH SEA
Ribe
Scheswig
Haithabu
Rostock
Wismar
Lübeck
Hamburg
Berwick-upon-Tweed
Lindisfarne
Edinburgh
Glasgow
ATLANTIC OCEAN
Groningen
Bremen pirate harbour
Aelmere
Amsterdam
Leiden
York
Howth
Dublin
Limerick
Cork
Cloyne the great law school
Ipswich
London
Hamwic/Southampton
Bruges
Antwerp
Cologne
Lorelei Rocks
Aachen where Charlemagne held court
Brussels
Seine
Paris the business of learning
Rhine
Venice
Florence Flemish tastes
Genoa
NORTH
Frisians ● 650–900 CE
Vikings ● 800–1200 CE
The Hansa ● 1250–1550 CE
Colour code of settlement/town